BJ

2014

JACQUELINE
BOUVIER
KENNEDY
ONASSIS

ALSO BY BARBARA LEAMING

Churchill Defiant: Fighting On, 1945–1955

Jack Kennedy: The Education of a Statesman

Mrs. Kennedy: The Missing History of the Kennedy Years

Marilyn Monroe

Katharine Hepburn

Bette Davis: A Biography

If This Was Happiness: A Biography of Rita Hayworth

Orson Welles: A Biography

Polanski: A Biography, the Filmmaker as Voyeur

JACQUELINE BOUVIER KENNEDY ONASSIS

THE UNTOLD STORY

Barbara Leaming

THOMAS DUNNE BOOKS
ST. MARTIN'S PRESS 🐿 NEW YORK

THOMAS DUNNE BOOKS.

An imprint of St. Martin's Press.

JACQUELINE BOUVIER KENNEDY ONASSIS. Copyright © 2014 by Barbara Leaming. All rights reserved. Printed in the United States of America. For information, address St. Martin's Press, 175 Fifth Avenue, New York, NY 10010.

www.thomasdunnebooks.com

www.stmartins.com

Photo research and editing by Laura Wyss, Wyssphoto, Inc., with the assistance of Elizabeth Seramur, Amy Hikida, and Emily Vinson

Library of Congress Cataloging-in-Publication Data

Leaming, Barbara.

    Jacqueline Bouvier Kennedy Onassis / by Barbara Leaming.

      pages cm.

    Includes bibliographical references and index.

    ISBN 978-1-250-01764-2 (hardcover)

    ISBN 978-1-250-01763-5 (e-book)

  1. Onassis, Jacqueline Kennedy, 1929–1994. 2. Celebrities—United States—Biography. 3. Presidents' Spouses—United States—Biography. 4 Post-traumatic stress disorder—Patients—Biography. I. Title.

    CT275.0552L43   2014

    973.922092—dc23

    [B]   2014026768

St. Martin's Press books may be purchased for educational, business, or promotional use. For information on bulk purchases, please contact Macmillan Corporate and Premium Sales Department at 1-800-221-7945, extension 5442, or write specialmarkets@macmillan.com.

First Edition: November 2014

10 9 8 7 6 5 4 3 2 1

JACQUELINE
BOUVIER
KENNEDY
ONASSIS

One

A t a cocktail party in Newport, Rhode Island, in the waning summer of 1945, a loquacious college boy was delivering a chest-thumping monologue to a frizzy-haired, snub-nosed sixteen-year-old named Jacqueline Bouvier. As the young man talked on, her wide-set hazel eyes settled on his face. Jackie, as she was known, allowed him to speak without interruption, but at intervals she nodded to signal that she understood him and the many important things he had to tell her. An observer of the scene would have had no reason to surmise that the quiet, worshipful beneficiary of the collegian's wisdom had information and strong opinions of her own about his theme. Jackie was only just discovering boys that year, but she already understood that it was her duty to ensure that he enjoyed himself immensely and had no inkling of what she actually knew or thought.

The boy's subject was Marshal Philippe Pétain, the former head of the collaborationist Vichy government. When, in the last days of World

War II, a French court sentenced Pétain to face a firing squad, the provisional government's president, General Charles de Gaulle, had moved swiftly and controversially to commute the sentence to life imprisonment, in the interest of relegating the war to the past as soon and as much as possible.

A similar determination to get on with life animated the reopening of Newport society's marriage market eleven days after Japan surrendered unconditionally following the destruction of Hiroshima and Nagasaki. At the time, young men in military uniform were everywhere to be seen throughout the moneyed American resort, presaging a whole series of Newport debutantes' marriages to returning soldiers. Immediately, the expansive spirit of the first grand-scale debut party since before Pearl Harbor carried over to other gatherings of the Newport tribe in the final days of August and early September, before the rich summer residents— along with those less fortunate souls who, having no money of their own, lived and maneuvered among them—dispersed for the winter.

It was at one such gathering that Jackie Bouvier was treated to the lecture on the Pétain affair. As it happened, the college boy had had the misfortune to speak of matters she probably knew a good deal more about than he. When Jackie was eleven, her paternal grandfather had dedicated to his ten grandchildren a privately printed family history asserting that the American Bouviers were descended from French nobility. The claim would later prove to have been fraudulent, but it had a tremendous impact on her nonetheless. She was a child who loved to escape into her books, and now French history had become not just reading to her, but a source of personal identity, a guarantee of her own specialness and superiority, consolation for the indignities of a daily life where money was not always as plentiful and one's parents' behavior not always as spotless as one might wish. When the Vichy regime signed an armistice with Hitler in 1940, de Gaulle, speaking on BBC Radio from the sanctuary of London, had urged his countrymen to resist. The broadcast provoked Pétain, the idol of de Gaulle's youth, to charge de Gaulle with treason and threaten him with death. Impressed by de Gaulle's staunch refusal to accept defeat, little Jackie Bouvier seized on him as her hero. For five years, she avidly followed him in newspaper accounts. She named her poodle "Gaullie" in his honor.

Yet when the young man at the cocktail party held forth, she did what most sensible, well-brought-up girls who hoped to win the Newport matrimonial sweepstakes circa 1945 would have done. The point was to seem bright enough to interest a man but not so bright as to imperil his ego. So Jackie played her part and said nothing. Afterward, her only outlet was to vent her frustration in the form of mockery when she recounted the episode to a female friend: "He sounded like a little boy who's just read a big book and is having a lovely time expounding it all to a little country urchin without really knowing what it was all about. I wanted to give him a big maternal kiss on the cheek and tell him he was really a big boy now!"

The author of those spiky sentences delighted in being very different from the shy, timid girl, in her own phrase petrified of everything, who had first appeared in Newport two years before, after her mother, Janet Lee Bouvier, married investment banker and Standard Oil heir Hugh D. Auchincloss Jr. Previously, the dissolution of Janet's marriage to Jackie's father, John "Black Jack" Bouvier, a stockbroker with a Social Register background, had been prominently chronicled in the tabloid press under the headline "Society Broker Sued for Divorce." Accompanying the article, which documented a pattern of infidelity on Mr. Bouvier's part, had been a photograph of small-boned Janet and her daughters, Jackie and little Lee. It was not the first time Jackie and her mother had made news. Both were ribbon-winning equestriennes, and prior accounts had spotlighted their accomplishments in the riding ring. Now this new coverage seemed to chip away at the idealized public image to expose the ugly family reality beneath. Taunted by classmates at the private day school she attended in New York at the time and teased by certain of her Bouvier cousins, Jackie reacted to the publicity as if she had been flayed alive. In the aftermath of the ordeal, she became secretive, withdrawn, willfully impossible to read or know. The summer of 1945 was important to her for a number of reasons, not least her newfound popularity among the boys of Newport. It was certainly not that Jackie, who had oddly broad features, a splash of freckles across her nose and under both eyes, and disproportionately large hands and feet, was prettier than her female contemporaries, only that in a world where most of the young people had known one another all their lives, she suggested a flavor the boys had not tasted before.

On her return to boarding school, Miss Porter's in Farmington, Connecticut, two of those boys wrote repeatedly to her from Harvard. Jackie judged that her replies had better be "devastatingly witty." She also calculated that since her correspondents knew each other well and belonged to the same college social club, the Owl, it was necessary to compose entirely different letters to each. This required a good deal of labor on her part. Half in earnest and half in jest, she was soon bemoaning the agony she had to endure drafting separate missives to nineteen-year-old John Sterling and twenty-year-old R. Beverley Corbin Jr. Despite her laments, both boys struck her as tremendously appealing. John Sterling was the son of a distinguished career diplomat and former U.S. ambassador to Sweden, Bev Corbin of an attorney who was also the president of Bailey's Beach in Newport. When she was with him, she loved talking to John, who was smart and interesting and had actually seen a bit of the world. The problem, by her own account, was that she was not physically attracted to him. With Bev, by contrast, it was "all physical."

Jackie found Bev shallow and was ashamed of liking him as much as she did, but there it was. She acknowledged that some of her friends, mystified by what she saw in Bev, had begun to look at her as though she were insane or had "queer glands." "I'm beginning to think so myself!" she declared. Neither fellow had kissed her yet. Jackie said she would love it if Bev tried, but would "upchuck" if it were John. Still, on paper John enjoyed a distinct advantage. While Bev's letters tended to be ordinary, John's were clever and funny. In Jackie's own letters, instead of the backbiting about mutual friends and acquaintances she might have indulged in had her correspondent been a girl, it seemed wiser to reserve her venom for prison, as she referred to her boarding school and the quiet, conservative New England town where its porticoed white-clapboard dormitories were set. "If schooldays are the happiest days of your life," she deadpanned to Bev, "I'm hanging myself with my skip-rope tonight."

Sarah Porter, who established the school in 1843, never married, yet she had persisted in regarding marriage as a woman's fitting and proper state. A century after its founding, Miss Porter's endeavored to prepare young women, most of them Wasp and rich, for essentially the same lives their mothers had led. In 1945, as in Sarah Porter's time, it was the purpose of a woman's education to make her a more pleasing companion to her husband. In important ways, Jackie Bouvier (though Catholic and relatively poor) was the model Farmington girl. She rode, she wrote, she sketched. She read widely and acted in school plays. She was by turns hardy and graceful, pragmatic and romantic, serious and fey. She did not question the assumption that it should be her goal in life to marry becomingly. She did not doubt that one lived through a man and that without him there could be nothing. At the same time, her caustic remarks about Farmington suggest that she was beginning to sense she might want something more than was on offer.

Meanwhile, she looked forward to a reprieve from routine when she had a chance to attend the Harvard-Yale game in the company of both the Interesting Boy and the Sexy Boy. This year's Harvard-Yale matchup was to be the first in three years, one of football's oldest and best-loved rivalries having been suspended in wartime. Because a number of players were veterans who would be returning to the field for the first time since the war, in both New Haven and Cambridge there was a huge amount of emotion invested in the event, which could not be scheduled to take place until Saturday, December 1, after the traditional Thanksgiving weekend windup. John Sterling was set to escort Jackie, but as Bev Corbin had no date of his own, it had been agreed that he would sit with them and some others at the Yale Bowl. Two days before the football game of games, however, it looked as if she might not get to go after all. A combination of snow, sleet, and rain pounded Connecticut. The next day, when it seemed as if the game might have to be played in knee-deep snow, university officials had the field cleared, then covered over with a tarpaulin. That evening, Jackie took the train to New York to spend the night at her father's apartment. Black Jack Bouvier, whose nickname derived from his exceptionally (some might say weirdly) intense year-round tan, was scheduled to drive her to New Haven in the morning.

Jackie kept a photograph of her father—slim, suave, impeccably attired in plus fours, calf-hugging licorice-striped stockings, and immaculate two-toned shoes—on her desk at Farmington. In the picture, said to have been taken in Cuba or Florida in the 1920s, Black Jack was indeed, as his elder daughter judged him to have been, a beautiful specimen of a man. A slender mustache above sensuous lips looked as if it might have been finely penciled in. The crease darting from the center button of his slim-tailored, wide-lapeled suit jacket highlighted the flat, hard stomach beneath. By 1945, however, despite a punishing exercise regimen religiously pursued, that frame had thickened. And though at fifty-four he dressed and comported himself as though he were still the pretty boy Cole Porter was reputed to have fallen in love with decades before, his sunlamp tan could not conceal that he had begun to go jowly and pouchy-eyed. Instead of letting the air out of Jackie's father, a lifetime's disappointments and dissipation seemed to have inflated him to a parody of his former self.

After numerous martinis, he would sprawl on his living room sofa dressed in baby-blue boxer shorts and black patent-leather shoes, inveighing against all the people he blamed for the shipwreck of his life. High on the list were Janet and Hughdie, as Janet's second husband was known. Black Jack was sure that Janet had married again principally to spite him. He was certain the Auchincloss clan intended to steal away his daughters. Of the two girls, Jackie, who resembled him facially, was his favorite. He called her "the most beautiful daughter a man ever had." At his two-bedroom, fourth-floor apartment on East Seventy-fourth Street in Manhattan, her ubiquitous image stared out from walls, tables, bookshelves. But all the photographs on earth could not alter the fact that, as he believed, he was slowly losing her. How could he compete with all that Auchincloss money? Though Black Jack continued to work on Wall Street, his personal finances had never recovered from the Great Crash of 1929, after which he had burned through capital and borrowed from relatives in order to maintain a frail veneer of wealth. In the narrative he constructed of his life, he traced his inability to right himself to the tough new trading rules introduced by the fledgling Securities and Exchange Commission in 1934.

Before Janet remarried, he had insisted that her cash demands were suffocating him. Now that she had attached herself to riches, he resented any implication that he was incapable of providing for his own children. In the perpetual scramble for funds, he did business with several bookies, notably a Lexington Avenue butcher who took bets in a room-sized freezer thick with hanging carcasses. Black Jack always seemed to have money on various sporting events and followed the scores on four radios that blasted simultaneously in his apartment. He was ever at daggers drawn with his father about the latter's will, never grasping until it was too late that the old man had spent much of what he had on annuities that assured substantial returns during his lifetime but would stop paying when he died. Tellingly, while the forty-six-acre Auchincloss family estate in McLean, Virginia, where Jackie lived during the year when she was not at boarding school, gave long views of the Potomac, and while the seventy-five-acre Auchincloss estate where she spent her summers was perched high above Narragansett Bay, Black Jack's apartment faced a sunless ventilating shaft.

He was right to perceive that her stepfather's world had begun to envelop her. Yet she loved Black Jack no less for her attraction to that world. Years later, Jackie's first husband would laugh that she still suffered from a major father-crush. Since girlhood, she had worshipped Black Jack for the very things that her disciplined, driven, mercenary mother was not. Janet was a survivor who had done whatever was necessary for her and her girls to get on in life. By contrast, louche, self-pitying Black Jack was one of the beautiful losers. Jackie savored the worst in him, especially the compulsive womanizing that had doomed her parents' marriage from the outset. Through the years, she would speak with cringe-inducing glee of his having bedded another woman during his and Janet's honeymoon. She loved that, on a subsequent occasion, he had been photographed affectionately holding a pretty girl's hand while, a few inches away, poor oblivious Janet smiled idiotically and stared in the other direction. When, as often as possible, he visited Farmington, Jackie delighted in quizzing him about which of her classmates' mothers he had already slept with and which he had in his sights. Many years afterward, when she was herself a wife and mother, she liked to reminisce about how all her boarding school friends had adored Black Jack. They regarded him, in Jackie's telling, as "a most devastating figure." Had she been aware that a number of the girls thought him a cartoonish dirty old man? When certain of her classmates laughingly shook their backsides at him, did she register that they were making cruel fun of the parent they regarded as a repulsive lecher? Had she really been oblivious to the insult? Or had she just pretended not to notice? Such perhaps was Jackie's craft that, then and in retrospect, her father's tormentors could never be sure.

A Yale man himself, Black Jack delivered Jackie in his black Mercury convertible in time for her to meet her date before the 1:30 P.M. kickoff. Previously, she had confessed to being rather nervous in anticipation of the big day, which was to conclude with dinner and dancing in New York. Though she had yet to choose between John and Bev, she would be attached to one of her suitors for the course of the day while the other

8

tagged along. The choreography threatened to prove awkward. At the Yale Bowl, which had attracted a smaller crowd than anticipated due to icy temperatures, she and her Harvard friends watched the Elis trounce their team by a score of 28–0. When it was over, Jackie's group took a yellow trolley to the train station. En route to Manhattan, Jackie, a smoker since she was fifteen, made a game of lighting up whenever the conductor was not looking. In New York, John dropped her off at her father's apartment so she could change. That night, the couple's first stop was the Maisonette, an East Fifty-fifth Street supper club where the singer Dorothy Shay, known as the Park Avenue hillbilly and a particular favorite of New York debutantes and post-debutantes, was performing. Jackie to this point seems to have had little trouble navigating between the Interesting Boy and the Sexy Boy. But everything changed when she and John joined Bev at his table and she discovered that Bev had acquired a date in the interim. Worse, she spotted his prep school ring, as she later said, blazing away on the young woman's left hand. Seated between the two boys at dinner, Jackie reveled in the amount of attention she received from Bev, though technically he was with someone else. Still, she needed only to glance at that ring for her pleasure to be spoiled.

By the summer of 1946, when Jackie turned seventeen, glands had trumped mind. The physical attractions of Bev Corbin won out over John Sterling's intellectual appeal. Tall, lean, and muscular, with a long neck, high cheekbones, and a handsome face whose only flaw was a weak mouth, Bev seemed nothing if not cocky and confident. It struck her that gossipy banter about New York, its nightspots, and the people he knew there was about as serious as he was capable of getting. But then, she had not anointed him for the quality of his conversation. Besides, he made her laugh, and "sweet" was a word she used about him repeatedly. Late one night after a dance in Newport, Jackie brought Bev back to the Auchincloss estate. In the kitchen of the twenty-eight-room gabled Victorian house, she scrambled some eggs for him. Jackie seemed so at home at Hammersmith Farm, yet there was an element of illusion in that picture of ease and entitlement. From the first, she and her sister, Lee, four years her junior, had not been on the same footing in Hughdie's establishments as his three children from two previous marriages. As Jackie was not blood, the riches that surrounded her were not and never would be hers. Her monthly fifty-dollar pittance came from Black Jack, who also paid her tuition at Farmington, as well as medical and dental expenses. Appearances to the contrary, Jackie was a poor relation. The rambling house on the hill, with its faded crimson carpets, comfortable old furniture, and walls covered with looming moose, bear, and reindeer heads, was but a vast stage set for her.

When Jackie and Bev began their senior years at Miss Porter's and Harvard, respectively, they regarded themselves as a couple. For some girls, Miss Porter's functioned, as it long had, as a finishing school. Upon graduation they considered themselves finished—that is, ready for a proper husband. Other seniors preferred to continue their schooling, whether at a junior college, an art school, or a full-fledged four-year college. In Jackie's day, Miss Porter's placed new emphasis on college preparation. Still, for those who chose college, as for those who did not, the nearly universal objective was marriage. Few girls saw college as the prelude to a serious career of one's own. Seniors like Jackie who, though they had yet to be introduced to society, had already had established boyfriends appeared to be on a fast track to married life. For them, college could be a good place to wait until the boys were ready to become husbands. As Jackie solemnly advised a friend, the reason so many boys resisted marrying immediately was that they needed time to establish themselves in business. Besides, she stressed, marriages were so much more likely to last when the boys had had a chance to "sow their wild oats first." For her part, Jackie was keen to attend Sarah Lawrence, mainly, it appears, because of the school's proximity to Manhattan and its nightlife. Black Jack insisted that she select the rather more isolated and inconvenient Vassar. Though after a preliminary visit Jackie despair-ingly described Vassar as a huge lonely place, in the end Black Jack gave her no choice but to capitulate.

Meanwhile, addressing Bev as "darling" and "dearest," she recorded her ever-shifting feelings for him in blue ink on pale blue monogrammed stationery. Since she rarely saw Bev now that they were both at school, there was a sense in which the relationship existed more on paper than in reality, more in her head than in the flesh. She spent many hours alone, reading about romantic love, contemplating what it means to be in love. Keenly, she dwelled on the pleasures to come when she and Bev could be together. Yet when she was actually with him, more often than not he was a disappointment to her and she pulled back. In the beginning, Jackie had admitted to being ashamed of liking him as much as she did. Now it was Bev's turn to be embarrassed.

Jackie had not seen him for a good many weeks when, on a Saturday afternoon in October, he materialized at Farmington in the role of a caller. In accord with tradition, Bev arrived at two P.M. and departed after tea at the headmaster's residence. At some point in between, the twenty-two-year-old made a blundering attempt to kiss Jackie, who refused him. Writing afterward, she sought to assuage his hurt. "I do love you—and can love you without kissing you every time I see you and I hope you understand that." As Christmas drew near, her fantasy of Bev seemed to recover from the ambivalence that a dash of reality, in the form of actually seeing him, had provoked. Suddenly, she could hardly wait to be with Bev in New York during the holiday break. Yet when at length she did meet him there, the experience proved as awkward and unhappy as before. At Rockefeller Center, Bev again tried to kiss her, and again she pulled away. He charged Jackie with not loving him.

"I do think I'm in love with you when I'm with you," she wrote initially. "But it's awfully hard for me to stay in love with someone when I only see them every three months and when the only contact I have with them is through letters." Unfortunately for Bev, there was worse in store. The more opportunity she had to reflect, the less willing she was to try to talk herself into believing that she loved him. At the outset of their correspondence, she had aimed to fashion a voice that was "devastatingly witty." A year and a half later, her words of January 20, 1946, were simply devastating. "I've always thought of being in love as being willing to do anything for the other person—starve to buy them bread and not mind living in Siberia with them—and I've always thought that every minute away from them would be hell—so looking at it that [way] I guess I'm not in love with you."

Behind his back, Jackie was even harsher. Bemoaning to another girl that Bev would never be much in the world, she predicted he would be content to be a party boy for the rest of his life. Despite Jackie's complete disillusionment, she and her first real boyfriend continued to correspond. He still visited her at Farmington, and in anticipation she merrily urged him to smuggle in cigarettes, chocolate, and even a hip flask, the latter expressly to shock the housemother charged with keeping order in the dormitory. Bev's passion for Jackie showed no sign of abating. On her side, however, fire had turned to ice. For Jackie, as for other Farmington girls, everything ultimately was about marriage and the future. Bev seemed incapable of a future she might actually want to share. Pointedly, Jackie had once asked him if he could think of anything worse than living in a small town like Farmington all one's life and competing to see which housewife could bake the best cake. She made it clear that she had higher ideas for herself than such a hidebound existence, yet she remained fuzzy about specifics. At seventeen, she was able to conceive of the future largely in negatives. Called on for the purposes of her class yearbook entry to state her life's ambition, Jackie flung back: "Not to be a housewife."

In Newport that summer, Jackie officially entered the marriage market. Positioned alongside Janet and Hughdie, who were also celebrating the christening of their second child together, Jackie "met" three hundred of the couple's friends at a tea dance at Hammersmith Farm. No matter that Janet's newborn son, as well as a daughter born two years before, bore a completely different relationship to the household than Jackie did. The optics of Jackie's debut seemed to confer upon her the Auchincloss imprimatur. Daughters of divorced parents often had two separate debut parties. For example, Jackie's friend Helen Bowdoin, known as "Bow," was formally presented by her very rich father at his home in Oyster Bay, Long Island, before being feted in Newport by her mother and stepfather. Both events were listed in the same notice in *The New York Times*. By contrast, on the occasion of Jackie's debut, it was as if her real father did not exist. He was not even mentioned in the *Times* announcement.

Black Jack's exclusion from anything to do with his daughter's social emergence was a triumph for Janet. Despite her status as the chatelaine of two estates, she remained imaginatively invested in the futile, unending war with her failed, frenzied ex-husband. As far as Janet was concerned, in the financially desperate pre-Auchincloss years when the girls lived with her and spent weekends with their father it had been easy for him to arrange to be the parent they always had fun with. In those days, Jackie had spoken of wanting to run away and move in with her father, and she had often gone so far as to tell Janet that she hated her. Long afterward, Janet, forgetting apparently that she had been a drinker, a yeller, a carper, a spanker, and a slapper, persisted in brooding about the injustice of Black Jack's favored status. At the time of Jackie's debut, when he reproached Janet for having presented their daughter under the Auchincloss banner in Newport, Janet retorted that he was free to give his own party for Jackie in New York. With an additional twist of the knife, she asked whether that was not the custom among divorced parents. What could Black Jack say? Obviously, financing such an event was beyond him.

In the fall semester of 1947, the photograph of Black Jack Bouvier taken in the 1920s went up in a college dormitory room, which was soon deluged with engraved invitations addressed to his eighteen-year-old daughter. Rarely spending seven consecutive days at "that goddamn Vassar," as Jackie referred to her school, she was observed at nearly every major event of New York's debutante season. She appeared among weeping willow branches and strings of clematis at the Tuxedo Autumn Ball. She posed at a table decorated with pink carnations and pompon chrysanthemums at the Grosvenor Ball. She danced before a background of artfully arranged tropical tree ferns at the first Junior Assembly. Genteel New York, as she experienced it that year, was a whirligig of large, lavish parties, intimate dinners beforehand, midnight champagne suppers, and special breakfasts for those revelers who stayed out all night. Despite the appearance of sybaritism, the purpose of these rituals was something other than pleasure. Tacitly understood by all, the objective of a debutante year was twofold: first, to show the suitable marriageable girls to the suitable marriageable boys, and vice versa (when Jackie was not in Manhattan for the weekend, there was further opportunity to consult the menu of possible husbands during football outings at Harvard and Yale), and second, to provide the debs with a preview of their future lives as wealthy, leisured married women who would be expected to pour their energies into volunteer work. Most of the classic cotillions therefore were fund-raisers. Exchanging the strapless gowns she wore at night for boxy sober suits that made her look like the young society matron she was expected soon to become, Jackie served on a number of junior committees. In November she was appointed to lead a committee tasked with organizing a night at the opera to benefit a free milk fund for ill and indigent children.

Every year, Igor Cassini, who wrote a gossip column for the Hearst newspapers under the pen name Cholly Knickerbocker, designated a leading debutante. Typically, Cassini focused on one of the showier, better-looking society girls who had made their debuts in New York that season. This time, however, the arbiter did something different. He named Jackie Queen Deb because he had perceived what certain of her rivals also had seen. She was shy and reserved, at times to the point of standoffishness, yet she had a knack of compelling attention, of getting herself noticed.

For rich American girls, as well as for those merely pretending to be rich, a European grand tour had long been part of the momentum toward marriage. They went to view the art and antiquity, to see and appreciate everything, and thereby, in theory at least, to become more entertaining companions for their future husbands. Bow, Jackie's Newport friend, was set to travel to Europe that summer of 1948, accompanied by a younger sister and another girl. At length, it was arranged that Queen Deb would go with them. A chaperone was hired; hotels, cars, and local tour guides were reserved; and nearly every hour of the seven-week trip to England, France, Italy, and Switzerland was blocked out and accounted for in advance. The goal was for the quartet to be able to explore the continent without ever having to emerge from a protective bubble. Still, so soon after 1945 there could be no shielding the young travelers from sights and sensations well outside their accustomed sphere of life. England, where the wreckage of war remained everywhere evident, made the strongest impression on them. The American girls, with their wide-brimmed straw hats and elbow-length white gloves, happened to be traveling at a moment of acute international tension, when the Soviet decision to sever Western road and rail access to Berlin threatened to spark a third world war.

At a garden party at Buckingham Palace (to which Bow's stepfather, Edward H. Foley Jr., undersecretary of the Treasury in the Truman administration, had secured an invitation for them), Jackie and the others went down the receiving line twice in order to shake the hand of Winston Churchill, like de Gaulle one of Jackie's particular heroes. Though widely regarded as the savior of his country, Churchill had been hurled from power in 1945. At the time Jackie saw him, in 1948, Churchill, ignoring demands that he retire as head of the Conservative Party, was maneuvering to become prime minister again. He hoped to "round out" his career by settling the unfinished business left at the end of the war when the last of the Big Three meetings, the Potsdam Conference, had broken off without resolving the matter of the ongoing Soviet presence in Eastern and Central Europe.

Jackie came home at the end of August and spent the last days of summer at Hammersmith Farm. She was nineteen and her year was over. Ostensibly, as Number One Deb she had been more successful than most of her peers. Yet in the one way that really mattered, the deb experience had backfired for her. At length, having seen all the suitable bachelors, Jackie balked. "Not because of them," she later said, "but because of their life." The distinction was crucial. Previously, she had cast off Bev Corbin because of his individual limitations, as she perceived them. Now she was inclined to rule out the entire group of young men that had just been confidently presented to her as the cream of the haut bourgeois crop. Most were in business, finance, or law. It was by no means the idea of marriage she had rebelled against, just marriage to any of them. It certainly was not their money she objected to, just how they and their families chose to live with all that wealth. Having previewed what it would be like to be the committee-minded wife of one of these vanilla fellows, all with the right pedigrees and jobs, she realized it was not for her. There was a bland predictability to what they offered, and she was eager for an alternative. As to what that other option might be, she had yet to form a definite conclusion. "I didn't know what I wanted," Jackie said years afterward of the quandary that beset her when she was nineteen. "I was still floundering." In conventional terms, her grand tour also had failed to work out quite as it was supposed to. Abroad, she had had her first hurried but tantalizing glimpses of some unfamiliar vistas. What she sought now was the chance for a more leisurely look.

She found it in the form of a notice on a bulletin board at Vassar, where she had begun her sophomore year. Smith, another of the elite Seven Sisters schools, offered a junior year of study in Europe. In the absence of such a program at Vassar, Jackie sought permission to join the Smith group. Her partner in the endeavor was another Miss Porter's graduate who had gone on to Vassar, Ellen Gates. Puffin, as everyone called her, had been one of the Farmington girls who had thought Black Jack Bouvier a cartoonish dirty old man. At college, Puffin had sustained a friendship with Jackie based in part on the fact that both were exceedingly restless in Poughkeepsie, the Hudson River town where the campus was set. The friends also shared an interest in art. Unlike Jackie, however, Puffin had a steady boyfriend. Russell D'Oench Jr., who had attended the same prep school as Jackie's old Newport beaux, was then working in Pittsfield, Massachusetts. When he learned that Puffin intended to go to Paris for a year, he proposed that she marry him instead. In keeping with the perception of college as a convenient place to park oneself for a few years, it was routine for girls of their caste to drop out before completing a degree. Faced with the choice of Paris or a husband, Puffin chose the latter. Previously in letters to Bev, Jackie had flashed disdain for the insular, unadventurous life. Now again, she voiced her contempt in a poem addressed to Puffin. In the past, she had targeted cake-baking Farmington housewives. This time, she aimed her shafts at Puffin's future mode of life. The mocking text read in part: "Instead of boating on the Seine, alas, Puffin's floating down the drain in Pittsfield, Mass."

And it was not just Puffin. Other girls Jackie knew were beginning to marry precisely the sort of young men she was so eager to elude. Clearly, the rites and rituals had not failed to work for everyone. It was only natural that this year a good number of the invitations accumulating in Jackie's dormitory room were to engagement parties and weddings. Notable among the impending marriages was that of her friend Bow, with whom she had traveled to Europe the year before. In June 1949, Jackie served as Bow's bridesmaid. As it turned out, she would not be available to do the same for Puffin. In August, Puffin was awaiting her September nuptials when Jackie sailed for France.

The Smith group went first to Grenoble for an intensive six-week language course. In October they moved on to Paris to study French civilization and history at the Sorbonne. Rather than live in a dormitory, Jackie preferred to board in a household where only French would be spoken. During the war, she had followed press accounts of the French Resistance. Now she landed in the apartment of a woman who, along with her late husband, had participated in the struggle against the Nazi occupation and the Vichy regime. Eventually, both the Count and Countess de Renty had been arrested and sent to a concentration camp, where he perished. Four years after the war, the countess survived financially by taking in boarders. Fuel was so expensive that her rooms were often almost unbearably cold. Swathed in sweaters, scarves, earmuffs, and woolen stockings, Jackie, writing in graph-paper notebooks with mittened hands, did much of her schoolwork in bed. At sixteen, she had monitored the trial of Marshal Pétain and its aftermath. At twenty, she found herself in an environment where some of the very questions the Pétain affair had raised, about France's anguished recent past, but also about its postwar future, were being played out daily. She loved experiencing Paris as she could never have done when she visited under more guarded and gilded circumstances. She enjoyed spending part of the day as a university student and then, as she wrote home, "like the maid on her day out, putting on a fur coat . . . and being swanky at the Ritz." She prized the sense she had in France that in her dealings with others, men included, she need not conceal that she had a mind. Prior to her year in Europe, Jackie had lamented the stultifying sameness of the young men she knew and of the futures they seemed to offer. Paris suggested a bouillabaisse of other options. She dated authors, titled aristocrats, junior diplomats, political aspirants. The significance of these men in Jackie's story is not that she actually considered marrying any of them. It is that by their very existence, they confirmed that there were positive alternatives to the life she had seen looming ahead of her in Newport and New York, a life she remained determined to avoid.

Still, that life continued to beckon when she returned to Newport late in the summer of 1950. There were new engagement announcements, new wedding invitations, and requests that she serve as a bridesmaid. Puffin, who had chosen not to accompany Jackie to Paris, had just had her first child. By the standards of her group, Jackie was simply not where she ought to have been at the age of twenty-one. By this point, many of the most sought-after men of her year had already been taken. To make matters worse, another massive wave of debutantes—younger, fresher, less familiar to the eye—was about to break in New York. Highlighting the pressure of fleeting time in Jackie's case was that her sister Lee had already begun her deb year. The Bouvier girls had long been rivals, with Lee almost always cast as the lesser light. Nineteen fifty, however, was very much Lee's period overall. Presented by her mother and stepfather at Merrywood, the family's ivied Georgian-style winter home in Virginia, Lee made a second formal bow to society at the Junior Assembly in New York. Like her sister before her, she was crowned Queen Deb, but Lee differed from Jackie in being smaller, more fine-boned, and more exquisitely featured. At the time, she also tended to be the more stylishly dressed. Regarded as the prettier, sexier, and more accessible of the Bouvier girls, Lee was hugely popular with the young society men of whom Jackie claimed to want no part.

Loath to return to Vassar, Jackie transferred to George Washington University, where she majored in French while living at Merrywood. She had been in no hurry to come back from Europe, and now she yearned for the more flavorful life she had had there. In October she entered *Vogue* magazine's annual Prix de Paris contest for female college seniors. The top prize was a yearlong junior editorship: six months at the New York office and, crucially from her point of view, six in Paris. Her submission materials included an arch account of herself ("As to physical appearance, I am tall, 5'7", with brown hair, a square face and eyes so unfortunately far apart that it takes three weeks to have a pair of glasses made with a bridge wide enough to fit over my nose") and an essay on the three figures of history she would like to have known: Charles Baudelaire, Oscar Wilde, and Sergei Diaghilev. Jackie beat out more than a thousand girls from more than two hundred colleges, and was asked to report for her first day of work in the fall. In the meantime,

Hughdie, under pressure from Jackie and Lee, had agreed to send the sisters to Europe for the summer, in honor of their graduation from George Washington and Miss Porter's, respectively.

Before Jackie sailed in June, she accepted an invitation to dine at the home of friends in Georgetown. Charles Bartlett, a thirty-year-old correspondent for *The Chattanooga Times*, had first met Jackie some years before in East Hampton, Long Island, where the Bouviers summered, and he had dated her briefly in the interim. Now he and his wife, Martha, who had married the previous December and were expecting their first child, sought to play matchmaker. The purpose of the dinner party was to introduce Jackie to a thirty-four-year-old congressman from Massachusetts named John F. Kennedy. As it happened, she had previously met her voluble, boyishly attractive, dryly humorous dinner partner, who had long, skinny arms and legs, long, pale lashes over ice-blue eyes, and a mop of reddish hair, and looked substantially younger than his age: When she was still at Vassar, Jack Kennedy, as he was known, had flirted with Queen Deb on a train between Washington and New York. At the time his efforts had come to naught, and so it was again in 1951 when at evening's end he followed Jackie outside. "Shall we go someplace and have a drink?" Kennedy's murmured invitation fell flat. While Jackie was at dinner, a male friend of hers had spotted her battered convertible parked in front of the Bartlett residence and had concealed himself in the backseat to surprise her. Having found him there, Jackie declined the drinks offer and drove off with her friend. Kennedy, an incorrigible skirt chaser, had made the effort expected of him by his hosts, but he was not so smitten that he attempted to call Jackie afterward. In any case, for all of Charles and Martha's enthusiasm for the match, it hardly seemed to matter that Kennedy did not follow up. Jackie was soon off to Europe, and on her return was due to be away from Washington for at least a year.

At length, only the first part of her plan came to fruition, however. On the day Jackie started at *Vogue* headquarters in New York, the magazine's managing editor, Carol Phillips, sensed the twenty-two-year-old's ambivalence. After twelve months, Jackie would be perilously near an age beyond which young women of her background became increasingly less marriageable. Was Jackie really willing to take that risk? The *Vogue* editor perceived something in her that suggested she was not. Skidding between kindness and condescension, Phillips advised the younger woman to go back to Washington immediately, saying, "That's where all the boys are." The encounter seemed to unnerve Jackie. Instead of spending the anticipated year at *Vogue,* she did not last beyond that first day.

Living again with her mother and stepfather at Merrywood, Jackie began to attend Washington parties and dances frequented by the sort of young men she had previously ruled out. She was also soon looking for a job in the capital. A position at the CIA was in play for a time, but before long another possibility materialized. On her behalf, Hughdie approached a journalist friend, Arthur Krock of *The New York Times,* who had a history of placing "little girls," as he called them, at the *Times-Herald,* a conservative, colorful, and often controversial Washington paper that had been among the national publications to tout Jackie as Queen Deb. Its editor, Frank Waldrop, had made journalistic history when his paper was first in the nation to report the attack on Pearl Harbor. The *Times-Herald* looked to inexperienced girls like Jackie, many of them finishing-school graduates, as a source of fresh, unconventional points of view, not to mention cheap labor. Initially, Waldrop used certain of these girls as gofers in his office, both to assess what they were capable of and to give them a chance to see if the rowdy atmosphere at the *Times-Herald* suited them. If the new hires survived, he sent them on to other jobs at the paper. When Jackie came to see him shortly before Christmas, he demanded to know whether she intended merely to "hang around" until she got married. In this respect, he exhibited the same skepticism about her that the *Vogue* editor had shown. Eager to be hired, Jackie assured him she wanted a career in journalism. Waldrop told her to go home for the holidays and report to work after the first of the year. In parting, he warned her not to come to him in six months with the news that she was engaged.

Hardly had Jackie had that conversation when she met John G. W. Husted Jr. at a seasonal party for which he had driven down from New York. The twenty-four-year-old stockbroker, who had powerful shoulders, a high, slightly protruding forehead, and bright, clear, expectant eyes, was unmistakably of the milieu she had been in flight from since she was nineteen. He had been to prep school and to Yale, he worked at a prominent Wall Street firm, he belonged to exclusive clubs, his family was listed in the Social Register and had homes in Bedford Hills and Nantucket. Nevertheless, at this point John Husted appealed to the romantic element in Jackie. For him, their initial encounter was a coup de foudre. When he first saw her, Jackie had recently cut off her shoulder-length hair in favor of a feather cut that gave her a distinctly gamine look. Taken by what he perceived to be her sensitivity and vulnerability, he compared her to a deer that has just come out of the woods and beheld its first human being. The suddenness of Husted's feelings for her, and the swiftness with which he acted on them, harmonized with her bookish notions of romantic love. In the days that followed, he called her often, and soon she was traveling to New York to see him. On a snowy December day on Madison Avenue, she who tended to be so cautious and so fastidious acted impulsively, agreeing to marry this young man she had not even known the month before. Later, she wrote Bev Corbin suggesting that, given the speed with which she had become engaged, this time it really must be love.

"What I hope for you," she grandly told her spurned former boyfriend, "is for the same thing to happen as quickly and as surely as it did with me. It will when you least expect it." No sooner had Jackie assured Bev of all this than she was overcome by doubt. A meeting with her intended's mother proved to be a debacle. A former Farmington girl herself, Helen Armstrong Husted had had a debutante's pattern career. She had been presented to society twenty-eight years previously, had married a banker shortly after that, and had long been active in volunteer work. Everything about her background was intensely familiar, but for Jackie that was very much the problem. The sweet, shy, elfin child John Husted had fallen in love with seems to have been scarcely in evidence the day he brought her home to David's Brook in Bedford Hills. Alarmingly, Jackie became snippy when Mrs. Husted produced some family picture albums documenting a life the young woman was expected soon to become part of—indeed, to carry on in a new generation. Rudely, she refused her hostess's offer of a childhood image of John, commenting that if she wanted a photograph of him, she was capable of taking one herself. As if tone-deaf to the implications of that dispiriting exchange, John went on to make a huge mistake: He presented Jackie with a sapphire-and-diamond engagement ring that had previously belonged to his mother. Jackie wore that ornament for several weeks thereafter, and it is tempting to imagine it blazing away on her finger as she read a new novel that, to her amazement, seemed to clarify her situation uncannily.

The book was *Sybil,* and its author was thirty-four-year-old Louis Auchincloss, whose father was Hughdie's first cousin and whose grandfather had built Hammersmith Farm. The novel's heroine is a young New York woman who becomes a most reluctant participant in the marital sweepstakes that are of such compelling interest to others in her opulent milieu. For all of Sybil Rodman's gestures toward escape, in the end she is drawn ineluctably into precisely the kind of hemmed-in existence she had hoped to avoid. For all of her apparent "spunk" and individuality, at last she proves deficient in the qualities of courage and determination that would make it possible to break free. This protagonist does not triumph so much as resign herself to the inevitable. The book's icily ironic final vignette portrays poor Sybil, her capitulation to her husband's family complete, being toasted by her exultant mother-in-law and other members of "the assembled tribe."

"Oh, you've written my life," Jackie told beak-nosed "cousin" Louis when she encountered him at an Auchincloss family dinner in Washington not long after she had read his novel. He knew what it felt like to want to free oneself from a certain society, to create a new and different kind of life. Tracked to become a lawyer like his father, he had long aspired to be a writer. It was not that he wished altogether to remove himself from the luxe Wasp world of his New York upbringing, but rather to paint that world with ironic detachment in novels and short stories. His loving but overbearing parents had pressured him to publish previous fiction under a nom de plume for fear that his books might damage his legal career. *Sybil* was the first work to appear under his own name. When he and Jackie talked that evening, he was still in crisis over how he intended to live the rest of his life.

But it was Jackie's future they spoke of when, after a meal that had included a champagne toast on the joyous occasion of her engagement, they sat together in a corner apart from the others. Officially set to marry in June, Jackie pictured her life as the wife of such a man as she had finally chosen. Louis's new book had helped her see it all so clearly, and like the character in the novel, she seemed grimly resigned to the inevitable. "That's it. That's my future," Jackie declared. "I'll be a Sybil Husted."

Two

Everything had changed in the weeks since Jackie had had her interview with Frank Waldrop. As she had assured him of her commitment to the work, it was a matter of no small embarrassment now to have to disclose her wedding plans. Still, the only polite thing was to have that awkward conversation in person. So in January 1952, she visited his office for what she assumed would be the last time. After she told him her story, Waldrop, a West Point graduate who retained a certain military demeanor all his life, asked how long she had known John Husted. To Jackie's astonishment, her answer, that she had only just met him during Christmas, seemed to settle the matter. Waldrop actually appeared relieved. "Hell, there's nothing to that," he said. "Get to work." Falling into the frenetic pace of an institution known for putting out ten editions a day, she started immediately as Waldrop's secretary-receptionist. The editor jestingly described the position as consisting largely of saying over and over again, "Thank you very much for calling," and of drafting a polite letter whenever he thundered, "Tell him to go to hell!"

Now that Jackie was working, she wrote affectionately to John Husted during the week and visited him in Manhattan on weekends. Before long, however, she began to spend whole weeks in Washington, requiring her fiancé to travel to her. Clearly, it was not the job that was suddenly monopolizing Jackie's time. Nor was it Waldrop himself who appeared to be the agent of her newfound fascination with the newspaper business. Rather it was a wild-eyed, luridly tattooed forty-year-old ex-Marine and former crack features reporter at the *Times-Herald*, with a well-earned reputation in Washington as a lady-killer. In his prime, John White had been an outspoken freethinker, left-winger, and labor-booster at an ultraconservative paper; an almost fantastically prolific journalist, who simultaneously authored five different columns under as many pseudonyms, among them a regular feature on men's attire supposedly written by a fashion-obsessed Frenchmen utterly unlike his sartorially challenged, perpetually unkempt creator. White was also a self-described book and movie nut, whose combative conversational style echoed the staccato rhythms of the screwball film comedies he adored. In the manner of certain real-life gangsters who modeled their clothes and gestures on Hollywood films, White was more than a little in love with an image of himself, and of his newspaper friends, cast in the mold of the Ben Hecht–Charles MacArthur stage and cinema classic *The Front Page*. As is the case with many eccentrics who pride themselves on their naturalness, there was much about him that was studied and self-conscious, at times cloyingly so.

These days White worked at the State Department, but it was no secret that he still sighed for the *Times-Herald*, where he had had some of the best fun of his life. His heyday had been 1941–1942, when he fell in love with Waldrop's new secretary-receptionist, the sunny, relentlessly exuberant and extroverted Kathleen Kennedy, favorite daughter of Ambassador Joseph P. Kennedy and favorite sister of Jack Kennedy. She was known as Kick to everyone except John White. Nothing if not contrary, White dismissed her nickname, a reference to her irrepressible nature, as demeaning and inappropriate. Like her colleague and close friend, the lusciously beautiful Inga Arvad, Kathleen owed her job at the paper to Arthur Krock, who had recommended both women to Waldrop. White viewed her as exceptionally promising material that cried out to be shaped and sculpted only by the most expert hands, and early on he set himself up as her mentor. Whether or not he really had anything to do with it, she quickly catapulted to a reportorial post. In the course of their sweet and sour romance, Kathleen, a devout Catholic, steadfastly re-fused to sleep with him. Eventually, he concluded that to seduce her would be truly to violate her, so deeply ingrained were her religious principles, and he loved her too much to risk that. So he gave up trying, and the pair settled into a tensely chaste relationship, while he trawled for sexual satisfaction elsewhere.

Kathleen went on to marry the Marquess of Hartington, heir to a duke-dom, whom she had met when her father was U.S. ambassador to the Court of St. James's before the war. After Billy, as her young husband was known, was killed in action in Belgium, she embarked on a romance with the dissolute and exceedingly rich 8th Earl Fitzwilliam. Through it all, John White never wavered in regarding Kathleen as the love of his life. When, accompanied by Fitzwilliam, she died in a plane crash in 1948, a part of White seemed to die as well. Assigned to prepare an obituary, he experienced writer's block, apparently for the first time in his career. At length, he bled the necessary words, which read in part: "It is a strange, hard thing to sit at this desk, to tap at this typewriter (your old desk, your old typewriter), to tap out the cold and final word—good-by. Good-by, little Kathleen." Though his copy was typeset, it was scratched prior to the evening edition on the grounds that it was overly intimate and emotional.

In 1952, John White was unabashedly trying to recapture something of an earlier, better time when, in his own phrase, he "came at" the twenty-two-year-old Jackie Bouvier, upon learning of her arrival at the

Times-Herald from a mutual friend in Newport. He had left the paper after Kathleen's death, but he remained close to Frank Waldrop. So there was nothing unusual about his visiting the editor's office, though on this occasion it was really the new secretary-receptionist, the girl sitting in Kathleen's old seat, he wanted to see. The meeting was a critical event in Jackie's life. In the weeks that followed, she became a regular at "the cave," as White called his grungy living quarters in the basement of his sister Patsy Field's house in Georgetown. He often brought girls there, but his relationship with Jackie was uncharacteristically platonic. His interest lay more in the areas of guiding her professionally and influencing her intellectually, as he perceived himself to have done with another exceptionally promising protégée a decade before. He saw Jackie as a study in contrasts: the "winsome" face and "fadeaway" voice, but also the big, boyish hands that she self-consciously concealed beneath wrist-length white gloves. Casting her in the conventional role of "kooky" girl reporter, he encouraged her to have fun and take chances. He taught her that it was all right to make mistakes and laugh at herself. He nurtured her as a writer; he peddled her projects; he nudged her to tell Waldrop she was ready for a better assignment. When she took over the one column that no one else at the paper seemed to want, White puffed her work as Inquiring Photographer as the best escapist fare in town.

Jackie inhaled all that enthusiasm and encouragement as if it were opium. By contrast with White, John Husted, who was known to cheerfully make the rounds with her on weekends as she asked people lighthearted questions and took their photographs, viewed her new position as "insipid." Which it was, of course, but in the scheme of things that was far from the point. The threat White posed to Husted therefore was not so much sexual as aspirational. Jackie drew substance from White's talk as she simply did not from that of her fiancé. Curiosity was among her salient characteristics. For Jackie, evenings at the cave were, in the words of William Walton, a forty-two-year-old artist and former *Time* magazine correspondent who sometimes encountered her there, "just a glimpse into another world." Surrounded by the books that cluttered the cave, Jackie reveled in the dizzying rush and range of the older men's conversation. If her new role required her to play against type, to be sunnier and more outgoing than was natural to her, it was also much more fun and rewarding than the part she had recently been cast to play in Bedford Hills.

Walton, who, among other oft-recounted adventures, had liberated the bar at Jackie's beloved Ritz Hotel in Paris after the war with his friend Ernest Hemingway, was not the only ex-newsman she saw at John White's. One evening, she again found herself in the presence of Jack Kennedy, who, in 1945, had called the British general election in favor of the Labour Party at a moment when Churchill still seemed invincible. Hired to report the news from a serviceman's perspective, Kennedy, in a series of eye-opening dispatches from London, had warned American readers to prepare for the unthinkable. He laid out the reasons why Churchill might soon be hurled from power, chief among them the British electorate's dismay at social and economic conditions under Conservative rule. Though Kennedy had since abandoned journalism for politics (where he again emphasized his status as a returning serviceman), White and his journalist friends persisted in viewing him as one of their own.

White's personal relationship with Kennedy was fraught. In the course of Kathleen's short life, no one had been closer to her than Jack. So when John White grew besotted with Kathleen, he initially saw Jack's twin-like intimacy with her as an obstacle to his own designs. He claimed never to have liked Kathleen's brother in any case, and he felt Jack recoil from him as well. Nevertheless, these two men whose hearts had been cut to pieces by Kathleen's death had since been irresistibly drawn to and fascinated by each other. In postwar Washington, White chased some of the same women as Jack Kennedy, and he had made a point of quizzing these bedmates about him. Previously, White also had gleaned a good deal from Kathleen and Inga, the latter a married Danish woman in her late twenties who had set herself up as the then-twenty-four-year-old Kennedy's sexual instructress. Inga also had taken an interest in Jack's struggle to become a writer; she read and commented on the pages of his that Kathleen also sometimes passed on to her mentor, John White, to critique. In wartime Washington, Jack and Inga on one side, and John and Kathleen on the other, would go out as a foursome in an effort to conceal Jack's liaison with another man's wife, who, in a further complication, was falsely rumored to be a German agent.

Jack's father, who never flinched from interfering in his children's love lives, had initially approved of Inga in her capacity as sex tutor, but when the Nazi rumors materialized, he moved to snuff out the relationship before it damaged his son's political future. Thus, the two couples would begin and end the evening together in public, allowing Jack and Inga to slip off at some point in between. Given his frustrations with Kathleen, none of this had been easy for John White. And Kathleen, for her part, later admitted to having been jealous of Inga's relationship with her brother. Though John White and Inga Arvad had never been lovers, they were, in his phrase, "comfortably close," and she spoke to him extensively of Jack Kennedy. Inga absolutely adored Jack, thought him beautiful and brilliant, with, as she described it, "the charm that makes the birds come out of the trees." Still, Inga declared: "I wouldn't trust him as a long-term companion, obviously."

When Jackie Bouvier saw Jack Kennedy again in 1952, Patsy Field assumed they were meeting for the first time. It is easy to see why White's sister would have made that mistake, for the episode did contain overtones of a first encounter. The recent infusion of a certain amount of tragic-romantic backstory had encouraged Jackie to perceive Jack Kennedy with new eyes. And he, in turn, was having his first glimpse of her in the role John White had undertaken to direct her in. Evidently, Kennedy liked what he saw. In the days that followed, he pursued her avidly— "without much success," White was not sorry to observe. But for a man known to love the chase, difficulties would only have been an incentive.

In the present instance, Kennedy was sufficiently successful that he and Jackie were seen out together in Washington enough to cause her to worry about her fiancé's reaction. By this time, the engagement had been announced in the press and she had conferred with a priest about her wedding day. She wrote John Husted, urging him to ignore any "drivel" he might hear about her and Kennedy. "It doesn't mean a thing." But that was only to postpone the cataclysm. With each passing day, Mother Husted's ring seemed to weigh a bit more heavily on Jackie's left hand. In another letter, Jackie suggested to John Husted that they wait a little longer to get married, because they would be so much happier if they knew each other better. Crazily in love, Husted had no doubt that he knew her well enough already.

Finally, her fiancé was preparing to leave Washington after a weekend visit in March 1952, when, without warning, she discreetly dropped the ring into his pocket at the airport. That small, silent gesture was probably imperceptible to anyone but the two people involved, yet on Jackie's part it required all of the resolve that the girl in Louis Auchincloss's new novel lacked. Kinder than she had been to Bev Corbin, she offered the excuse, to which John Husted clung for the rest of his years, that Janet Auchincloss believed his family did not have enough money and that he did not earn enough on Wall Street. The explanation had the advantage of being true, as far as it went. Better that than to be informed that, in addition to her mother's objections, Jackie saw the life he offered as a trap.

So long as Jackie had been tethered to that ring, she had resisted Jack Kennedy's overtures. Their relationship entered a new phase when, at the suggestion of Martha Bartlett, Jackie invited him to accompany her to a dinner party at the Bartlett residence in May. As it happened, a great deal had changed in Kennedy's life in recent weeks. At the beginning of April he had announced his intention to seek the Democratic nomination to oppose Henry Cabot Lodge, the popular incumbent Republican senator from Massachusetts. By the evening of the Bartlett dinner, there was no question but that the campaign, first for the nomination and then for the seat itself, would often keep Kennedy away from Washington in the coming months. In that sense, it was hardly an optimal moment to begin dating him.

Looked at in another light, however, the timing could hardly have been better. If Kennedy went on to win a Senate seat, at some point in the very near future he was going to be in need of a wife. Like it or not, and Kennedy most certainly did not like it, that was a fact of political life. Upon leaving John White's basement apartment of an evening, one needed only to glance across Dumbarton Avenue for confirmation of that uncomfortable but un-avoidable reality. Another newspaperman lived across the street. He too was passionate about the business, revered books and ideas, and constantly entertained guests whose talk was some of the best in town. Strange to say, he too had been a great admirer of Kick Kennedy's. But there the similari-ties between the neighbors, John White and Joseph Alsop, ceased. The in-fluential forty-one-year-old *New York Herald Tribune* political columnist armored himself in Savile Row suits and an ersatz upper-class British ac-cent. His modern house was stuffed with fine art and antiques. His guests included some of the most powerful active political figures in Washington.

After the war, Joe Alsop had first encountered the former Kathleen Kennedy in London, when she was the recently widowed Lady Harting-ton. He subsequently described her as "one of the most enchanting women" he had ever known, mighty praise from a man who prided him-self on his intimate, affectionate, gossiping friendships with such grandes dames as Lady Diana Cooper, Odette Pol Roger, Pauline de Roths-child, and Lady Pamela Berry. Touted to Alsop by Kick, Jack Kennedy became a regular at the journalist's carefully choreographed Washing-ton dinner parties until he committed the sin of grousing that there never seemed to be enough pretty girls at his host's table. The remark conveyed to Alsop—who, it must be said, was very easily angered—that the young congressman, however "ornamental" and intelligent he might be, was not serious, and from then on Jack Kennedy's invitations to these evenings halted.

Alsop's decision to cut him off reflected a wider view that prevailed in many quarters of Washington that Jack Kennedy was a playboy and a lightweight, unambitious and uninterested in politics, who held office solely because his rich father, in an obnoxious act of political puppeteering, had put him there. Indeed, when this endlessly self-deprecating young man, who often dressed and acted like a lackadaisical frat boy, first sought a congressional seat, in 1946, his reluctance to run had been at the heart of his own campaign narrative. Jack Kennedy painted himself as having been drafted to take up the family flag that ought to have been carried by his older brother, Joseph P. Kennedy Jr., who had died in Europe as a flier in August 1944. In any case, it is suggestive that Alsop did not reinstate Jack Kennedy to his guest list until the latter gave proof of his new seriousness and maturity when he married Jackie Bouvier in 1953.

But in the spring of 1952, that day was still a ways off. Jack Kennedy liked Jackie well enough, but it could not be said that he was in love with her. He regarded her as just one of many, whereas for her he was already the one. In the past, she had conceived of the future more or less in negatives. She did not want to end up as a cake-baking housewife or a society wife. Yet she had lacked any clear picture of what she *did* want. Now, she believed, she knew. She had seen her future in the tousle-haired, insouciant person of Jack Kennedy. He was the Interesting Boy and the Sexy Boy in one compelling package. His darting conversation was of the sort she had learned to savor at the cave. His family possessed fabulous wealth, no small consideration for a young woman who had grown up in privileged circumstances but without money of her own. Through friendships cultivated with various young noblemen in London on the eve of the Second World War, as well as through his sister's marriage to the heir to the Devonshire dukedom, he had the aristocratic associations Jackie prized. The particular gifts he gave Jackie—books, principally English, that had helped him to define himself—were catnip for her imagination. Chief among those writings was the glittering literary portrait of

Raymond Asquith in the memoir *Pilgrim's Way* by John Buchan, which Jack had spoken of on one memorable occasion at John White's. Reading of the unflappable young World War I hero who had been prepared to sacrifice everything for his ideals, even his own life, she began to understand the kind of man Jack Kennedy wanted to be; to see him, as he no doubt wished to be seen, in a heroic light.

Even those personal qualities that some women might regard as deal breakers only made Jack the more attractive to Jackie. She thought him excitingly unconventional and unpredictable, full of angles and surprises, in the way that her father had been. And if, like Black Jack Bouvier, Jack Kennedy was also a little dangerous, so much the better; at least he was not bland and boring like the fellow she had almost married. At the same time, it struck certain of Kennedy's friends that Jackie thought she could succeed with him where her mother had failed with Black Jack; that drawn as she was to the bad boy in Kennedy, she believed she was the one to change him.

Whether he would ever allow her to get close enough to try was another matter. He had chased after her while she was engaged to another man, but hardly was she free again when he became elusive. Was it simply that he was preoccupied with the Senate race, or was there some other explanation? In his absence, he left her to commune with Raymond Asquith. Jack would call her if he was to be in Washington, but only if he did not intend to see someone else. Amid a crash of coins deposited in what she imagined to be a pay phone at some oyster shack on Cape Cod, Jack, whose voice sounded as if he were pressing his finger against his nose, would invite her to a movie or to dinner with friends.

Finally, he asked her, as he had asked other girls in summers past, to visit his parents' shingled waterfront home in Hyannis Port on Cape Cod for the weekend. Since Jackie was a child, Joseph P. Kennedy had been spoken of often and passionately in the Bouvier family circle. The name "Kennedy" fanned Black Jack's fury no less than the name "Auchincloss" would later do. In 1934, President Roosevelt had made Joe Kennedy

Wall Street's policeman when, on the principle that it takes a thief to catch a thief, he designated the former stock market operator as chair of the newly established Securities and Exchange Commission. Black Jack would long attribute his financial fall to Kennedy's decision to ban the very trading practices by which Kennedy, "the Judas of Wall Street," had himself previously made a fortune. It is all the more curious, then, that when Jackie Bouvier met Joe Kennedy in 1952, this same figure who had supposedly ruined Black Jack in the 1930s would at length prove to be the making of Black Jack's daughter. Jackie saw marriage to a man like Jack Kennedy as a way out of becoming just another society wife. Joe Kennedy saw Jackie as precisely the society wife Jack needed for his career. Jackie wanted to escape Newport. Joe Kennedy sought a Trojan horse into Newport. This son of a Boston-Irish saloon-keeper was fueled by no small amount of savage indignation of his own. The wound in Joe's case consisted of the innumerable social snubs and slights endured in life from the time when he was an undergraduate at Harvard. For Joe Kennedy, Jackie's double-barreled appeal was that she was a Catholic who, through her mother's strategic second marriage, also had the aura of the Wasp patriarchate he was determined to upend. "It's not important what you really are," old Joe was known to tell his sons. "The only important thing is what people think you are." Appearances being everything to him, it mattered not at all that Jackie was not really an Auchincloss, not really rich.

Never perhaps was it clearer that Jack would be wise to find a wife than it was during the poisonous 1952 presidential campaign, which overlapped with the Senate race. Adlai Stevenson, the Democratic nominee, was a bachelor, recently divorced. Republicans pumped out rumors that he was homosexual; that he had been arrested in two states on sex charges; and that he was known to friends by the female name "Adelaide." At one point during the election contest, Senator Joseph McCarthy planned to allude to some of this material in public, but he backed off after Democrats threatened to retaliate by releasing hard evidence of the extramarital affair that the Republican candidate, Dwight Eisenhower, had conducted during the war when he was Allied Supreme Commander in Europe. While the Stevenson rumors were unfounded, Eisenhower had indeed once contemplated leaving his wife for his mistress. In any case, even Jack Kennedy, allergic to the very idea of marriage as he was, eventually acknowledged that his bachelor status was a liability; given his age and presidential ambitions, he had better marry lest his political opponents suggest that he too was homosexual.

Meanwhile, acute pain due to an unstable back caused Jack to be on crutches a good deal during the campaign. When Jackie traveled to Massachusetts to hear him speak, she marveled at the contrast between the "pathetic" sight of him struggling to ascend the steps to the speaker's platform and the exhilarating sight of a man in full possession of his powers when he addressed the crowd. Such episodes made him seem so "vulnerable" to her, and so gallant. In 1952 just about anybody running as a Democrat seemed as if he might be politically vulnerable as well. After twenty years in power, the party of Franklin Roosevelt and Harry Truman was widely thought to be paralyzed. A visit by Dwight Eisenhower to Massachusetts was meant to confer the savor of power and historical inevitability to the Lodge campaign. Undaunted, Joe Kennedy invested so much money in his son's candidacy that it was jestingly said that a man could retire comfortably for the rest of his life on old Joe's billboard budget alone. Robert Kennedy, Jack's younger brother, oversaw a statewide campaign machine. The women of the family pounded on doors, presided over luncheon parties and teas, and harangued television viewers on Jack's behalf. Members of the aristocratic cousinhood that had adopted Jack in prewar London came to lend support and watch him campaign, as he had observed certain of them during the British general election of 1945. Targeting right-wing displeasure with the politically moderate Eisenhower and Lodge, an ardent Republicans-for-Kennedy organization painted the Democrat in the Massachusetts race as a more militant and more reliable anti-Communist than Lodge. Jackie undeniably had a huge personal stake in the state contest. Quite simply, should Jack Kennedy fall victim to what threatened to be a nationwide Democratic rout, there would no longer be any immediate need for him to marry. If Lodge triumphed in Massachusetts, her hopes of becoming Mrs. John F. Kennedy were probably at an end. On election day, Eisenhower won 442 electoral votes to Stevenson's 89. Republicans would be in charge in the Senate and House of Representatives as well. Massachusetts, however, marched to the beat of its own drum. "The first Irish Brahmin," as Kennedy was called, defeated Lodge, "the Yankee blue blood," by 70,000 votes. The senator-elect invited Jackie Bouvier to accompany him to Dwight Eisenhower's inaugural ball in January 1953.

Nevertheless, in the months that followed, Kennedy persisted in dating various other women—including the actress Audrey Hepburn—and the hoped-for marriage proposal failed to materialize. Jackie could hardly any longer suggest to others, let alone tell herself, that her inattentive lover was too busy campaigning to undertake anything like a conventional courtship. Yet, at least in his presence, she continued to smile and chatter as if all were exactly as she wished it to be. She surprised him at lunchtime in his new Senate office with meals for two. She featured him in her "Inquiring Camera Girl" column, as it was now called, and on other occasions she peppered interviewees with weightier-than-usual questions ("Malenkov said all issues between the United States and Russia are solvable by peaceful means. Do you agree?") that promised to draw Jack's interest and impress him with her range. She pounced on every opportunity to sustain and strengthen her bond with his father. She stayed up late many nights at Merrywood reading and summarizing various French-language books that touched on the Indochina question in an effort to assist Jack in his work. "He has got to ask me to marry him after all I have done for him," she later remembered assuring herself apropos of these translations. The danger, however, was that her actions threatened to put him on his guard. When it came to the women in his life, he did not like to feel that he was being pushed into anything. He expected to be the pursuer, not the pursued. In the latter case, desire all too easily turned to distaste. No matter how beautiful they might be, he had an aversion to women who, in his phrase, "won't leave me alone!"

During this period, a number of people who cared about Jackie spoke to her about her predicament and offered advice. Frank Waldrop, who thought of her as just a kid, warned that Jack Kennedy was too old and experienced for her. John White, though he was certainly no monk himself, worried about the sort of life she would have were she to succeed in ensnaring a fellow as sexually promiscuous as Jack Kennedy. Since the two men had hunted some of the same prey, White was in a unique position to know just how promiscuous that was. In one of their conversations at the cave, Kennedy had described himself to White as a sexual maximalist, determined to snatch as much pleasure from life as he could in his allotted time. As a husband, he would no doubt be as faithless as his father had long and notoriously been to Rose Kennedy. White counseled Jackie not even to think of marrying Jack Kennedy. When she refused to be turned from her purpose, he bet her a dollar the wedding would never take place anyway.

Janet Auchincloss also thought Jack Kennedy unlikely to marry her daughter, but in contrast to John White, she very much wanted him to, given all that splendid Kennedy money. In the aftermath of her daughter Lee's April 1953 marriage to Michael Canfield, who worked in publishing in New York and was rumored to be the illegitimate son of the Duke of Kent, Janet had begun to worry that Jackie had been using the wrong approach with Jack Kennedy. Jackie was always impatient to see him, always, as her mother lamented, much too obviously waiting for his call. On this one point, if on no other, Janet was in full-throated agreement with Black Jack, who had taught his daughters to play hard to get with young men and never to seem too eager or too available. In Janet's view, Jackie would do well to stand somewhat aloof, to show Jack Kennedy that she had an interesting life of her own quite apart from anything he had to offer. To that end, the concerned parent shared some news of

Jackie's old Newport set. In the summer of 1945, the wedding of Aileen Bowdoin, the elder sister of Jackie's friend Bow, to a returning serviceman and bearer of the Distinguished Flying Cross had been one of the premier events of the Newport social season. Many of the young people had attended the ceremony at Trinity Episcopal Church, and Jackie's then-aspiring boyfriend Bev Corbin had served as an usher. Aileen had since divorced and was in need of a companion to travel with to London for the coronation. Janet suggested to Jackie that the *Times-Herald* would probably be happy to send her over to cover the crowning of Elizabeth II. If Frank Waldrop refused to supply a ticket, Janet was prepared to pay for it herself as an investment in her daughter's future.

Jackie indignantly refused even to consider going abroad. Though it would not do to make Jack feel that he was being watched, she was not prepared to leave him entirely alone either. Besides, the trip would mean missing the wedding of Eunice Kennedy, with whom Jack had long shared messy and ill-furnished Georgetown living quarters that were said to resemble a fraternity house on the morning after an especially raucous party. There would never be any love lost between Jackie and "the Rah Rah Girls," as she snidely referred to Jack's sisters Eunice, Pat, and Jean, who mocked her in turn as "the Deb." Still, it was only natural that Jackie would have hesitated to miss such an important family event at a moment when she was so desperately maneuvering to become part of the family.

In the end, however, Janet, a proven expert in the art of hunting down a rich husband, prevailed, and Jackie sailed to England after all. The stratagem appeared to work, for by the time Jack Kennedy met Jackie's plane in Boston, on her return trip to the United States in June, he had proposed by telegram. There being considerable urgency on the Kennedy side to make the engagement public, Jackie supplied the same bridal portrait that had been used in the newspaper announcement of her engagement to John Husted. It could only be hoped that devotees of the society pages would not realize they had seen the picture before. In any case, as she was to discover, there would be plenty of time to take all sorts of interesting new photographs when she had her first joyous visit to Hyannis Port as Jack's bride-elect.

Jackie sailing with her future husband, Jackie affectionately mussing Jack's hair, Jackie discussing her recent marriage proposal with Eunice and Jean, Jackie playing softball and touch football with various Kennedy siblings, Jackie posing barefoot on the veranda—it is not too much to suppose that the happiness of the twenty-three-year-old woman in these images is authentic, though the situations were staged for the *Life* magazine photographers whom Joe Kennedy had wasted no time inviting in. Why should she fail to be pleased? Refusing to compromise or capitulate, she was finally about to get what she was after in life, was she not?

Not every aspect of the weekend was as bright as she might have hoped. Joe Kennedy had rather crassly transformed what ought to have been a private family celebration into a photo opportunity, and Rose Kennedy had condescended to lecture her on how to pose to maximum effect for the *Life* cameramen and even on how to pick out an engagement ring. Not for a moment, however, could Jackie afford to display any of the characteristic hauteur she had unrestrainedly shown in Bedford Hills the previous year. Writing afterward from Hammersmith Farm, she assured Jack's mother, "Very few people have been able to create what you have—a family built on love and loyalty and gaiety. If I can ever come close to building that with Jack I will be very happy. If you ever see me going wrong I hope you will tell me—because I know you would never find fault unless fault was there."

The photograph of the young lovers posed together on Jack's sailboat, perhaps the most striking image in the series, appeared on the cover of the July 20, 1953, issue of *Life* magazine, along with the heading "Senator Kennedy Goes A-Courting." Dedicated to Jackie's visit to the Cape the previous month, the generous four-page photo spread within was Joe Kennedy's way of blazoning to the world that "the handsomest young member of the U.S. Senate," as Jack was referred to in the text, was a frivolous playboy no more. The theme of the piece was that while their courtship had officially ended with the engagement announcement, young Kennedy was so ardent that he was still courting her in the days that followed. Forty-eighty hours after publication, Joe Kennedy acted to ensure that Jack did not promptly undo all this fine repair work on his image. Aware that in fact Romeo was planning a spree in the South of France as soon as the Senate adjourned, Joe assigned a friend of Jack's to watch out for him. "I am a bit concerned that he may get restless about the prospect of getting married. Most people do and he is more likely to do so than others," he wrote to Torby MacDonald, who had been Jack's roommate at Harvard, as well as a suitor of Kick's. "As I told you, I am hoping that he will take a rest and not jump about from place to place, and be especially mindful of whom he sees." Knowing that for his son such a trip inevitably meant girls, Joe Kennedy was determined that nothing be permitted to go wrong now that the countdown toward Jack's September wedding day had begun.

Meanwhile, Torby also had been drafted to accompany "jittery" Jack whenever he visited his fiancée at Hammersmith Farm, and on the less frequent occasions when Jackie came to see him in Hyannis Port. The constant, looming presence of the former captain of the Harvard football team, talking confidentially to Jack, telling jokes, discussing sports and politics, and otherwise dancing attendance on him, can have added little to the romance of these weekend encounters between the bride- and groom-to-be. Torby's mission on the impending trip to the South of France was clear. He was to protect Jack from exposure, an assignment that often meant picking up girls on his behalf and otherwise serving as a beard. But what exactly was there to shield Jack from at Hammersmith Farm? Apparently, the need to talk at any length to the partner of his future bliss. To his wife, Phyllis, who was pregnant at the time and not especially pleased about his prolonged absences, Torby spoke of his participation in these visits as if it were a solemn duty it had befallen him to fulfill. "You understand," he declared, "I have to be with Jack now." When they first saw Jackie, certain of Jack's other friends were mystified by how all this had come about. To Jewel Reed, the wife of Jack's Navy friend Jim Reed, she appeared "almost homely . . . an odd choice for him." Similarly, Betty Coxe Spalding, who was married to his friend Chuck Spalding and had shared an apartment with Kick in wartime Washington, expressed astonishment that Jack had selected a bride so unlike the strikingly beautiful women he tended to favor.

Whatever one might say about Joe Kennedy, there can be no denying he knew his boy. In August, when much-thumbed-through copies of the July 20 issue of *Life* magazine were informing a whole new audience in barbershops and doctors' waiting rooms throughout the United States that the recently engaged Senator John F. Kennedy was "like any young man in love," the senator himself was in Cap d'Antibes speaking of love to precisely the sort of individual his father had been worried about. That afternoon, at a moment when Jack Kennedy happened to be fleeing from yet another of the myriad women in his life who, to his perception, refused to leave him alone, he had met a languidly lovely, twenty-one-year-old Swede named Gunilla von Post. This time, he claimed, his persecutor was an Italian contessa who had been chasing him in Antibes on a Vespa scooter. "I don't know how to get rid of her. She's driving me crazy." Hours later, seated beside the delightfully less aggressive Swedish girl on the edge of a cliff overlooking the Mediterranean, Kennedy told Gunilla both that he had fallen in love with her in a matter of hours and that he was due to go back to the United States in a matter of days to get married. Not for the first time in his career, he emphasized that his destiny was what his father intended it to be. Portraying himself yet again as a reluctant participant in the signal events of his own life, Jack Kennedy wistfully declared that if only he had met Gunilla just one week before, he "would have canceled the whole thing."

As she made her way back from the altar on September 12, 1953, en route to face the swarm of press photographers outside, the newly minted Mrs. John F. Kennedy turned to look at something in the rear of St. Mary's Roman Catholic Church in Newport. There had been moments in recent weeks and days, even in the past few hours, when she too might have been tempted to call off "the whole thing" had it been possible. First, there had been the tense tango between her mother and Joe Kennedy. Janet insisted that the wedding be small, sedate, and, above all, private. Old Joe, of course, demanded big and splashy, with as much newspaper and magazine coverage as possible. It had hardly been a fair contest, for in Joe Kennedy Janet had finally confronted a superior will. By the day of the wedding, all of the various and tangled family factions seemed to be looking askance at one another. Jackie's mother and stepfather were indignant at the vulgarity of the show occasion that had been foisted upon them. Janet, who purported to be of an old and illustrious Southern family when in fact her Irish grandparents had come over at the time of the potato famine, left no doubt of her opinion that Jack Kennedy was "not good enough" for her daughter. The Bouviers, proud of what they misguidedly believed to be their own noble origins, shared Janet's view of the bridegroom's family as "social-climbing upstarts." But that did not prevent Janet, obsessed with ancient grievances, from communicating to her former husband that while she could hardly ban him from the church, he should know that he would be most unwelcome at the reception afterward at Hammersmith Farm.

Joe Kennedy, in turn, had contempt for the lot of them. For all the pains he had taken to show his son being welcomed into the bosom of the Wasp establishment, he sniffed that the wealth in Newport tended to be from a past era and that most residents were deeply in debt and just keeping up a front. Alert to any form of fakery because he was such a magnificent fake himself, he insisted that were one to pull the carpets up in many of the great houses, one was likely to find all the summer dirt swept underneath. The owners, it delighted him to point out, simply could no longer afford enough help to keep those enormous places running properly. On his son's wedding day, it fell to old Joe to notify the press that the bride's father had become ill at the last minute, requiring Hugh D. Auchincloss to walk her down the aisle in his stead. Joe mentioned something about the flu, but in truth Black Jack Bouvier had simply had too much to drink at his hotel the night before he was to face both sets of tormentors, the Auchincloss people and the Kennedy people, on enemy ground. Instead of providing courage for the fight, Bacchus incapacitated him before he reached the battlefield. Her father's absence was a source of sorrow to Jackie, and that sorrow unavoidably tinctured the proceedings until the strange pregnant moment shortly after the ceremony when the sight of a familiar pair of wild eyes in the rear of St. Mary's broke through the tension. The people around him began to laugh uncomprehendingly when John White waved a single dollar bill at Jackie, and soon the bride was laughing as well.

She had won the bet. She had brought it off. Jack Kennedy had married her after all.

Three

"How perfect it is being married," Jackie exulted at the close of her honeymoon stay in Acapulco.

In the weeks before the wedding, she had mentioned to her future father-in-law that she had once glimpsed a house that seemed as if it might be an ideal setting for a honeymoon. Jackie had spotted the pink villa, which sat atop a red-clay cliffside overlooking a bay, while she was traveling in Mexico with her mother and stepfather. The image had beckoned in her thoughts ever since, though she had only seen the place at a distance and had no idea of its precise location. Before long, however, Joe Kennedy had found the property and arranged with the owner, a former president of Mexico, for the newlyweds to have it, along with a staff of three servants—Noisette, Margarita, and Angelica—for as long as Senator and Mrs. John F. Kennedy might wish to remain. So this apparently was what life promised to be like now that Jackie had comfortably established herself under the warmth of the wings of the Kennedys.

The pink stone house when she saw it again did not disappoint. On the contrary, she judged it the most beautiful place imaginable. She and Jack were immensely happy there, though, as she wrote, her new husband did seem a bit shy about showing how much he liked it. Sensing that he might be nervous on his first honeymoon, she assured his parents that she was being careful to leave him alone a few hours each day. Otherwise, Jackie spoke of their two weeks in Mexico mainly in superlatives. To her, Jack was just "unbelievably heavenly." When they went deep-sea fishing together, the sailfish he caught was the most enormous seen in Acapulco all summer. When they water-skied around the bay, the sight of Jack leaping over the wake behind the boat prompted her to compare him to a lifeguard on the Riviera. (This, luckily, was one of those interludes when his unstable back was giving him a minimum of trouble.) She adored that the trio of Mexican maids found her husband beguiling and that for some reason the women refused to think the couple could really be man and wife. She delighted in the comic spectacle of Jack's unaccustomed helplessness whenever he needed something from the servants but had to wait for her to translate his requests. He in turn teased her about her anxiety over how she would look in their wedding pictures in the new issue of *Life* magazine, a copy of which he and Jackie had yet to see. He jested that he might have to leave her in the event that when they reached the West Coast, Jackie's appearance in the published photographs was not what it ought to be.

From Acapulco, the sojourners went on to Mexico City to attend a bullfight, before flying to Los Angeles, where Jack's father had arranged for them to have the baroque Beverly Hills hilltop residence of the film actress Marion Davies, who had been a guest at their wedding. There, they watched their first movie together as a married couple, a silent comedy starring Miss Davies, in one of the mansion's private screening rooms; took walks in the lush terraced gardens; and swam in a turquoise pool, which was bordered by ornate statuary and Venetian columns. The possibility that there might be a worm in the apple did not really present itself until the couple moved next to one of the vine-covered bungalows at San Ysidro Ranch in Santa Barbara, en route to San Francisco.

The worm seems to have appeared to Jackie by degrees. First, Jack arranged to join forces with another couple, his Navy friend Red Fay and Red's wife, Anita, abruptly and unilaterally ending the only sustained period he and Jackie had ever been alone together. Then he began to spend a good deal of time speaking confidentially to Red, much as he had huddled with Torby MacDonald at the time of the engagement. Then he suggested that Jackie return to the East Coast, while he stayed on for a bit in California. Jack may have been shy about showing how much he liked their honeymoon house in Acapulco, but he displayed no such bashfulness when proposing that his young bride go home without him.

Jackie related the story of his strange request to Anita Fay, though she knew Anita hardly at all.

"What shall I do?" Jackie asked.

In the end she refused to fly home by herself, but not two weeks after she had remarked on how perfect it was being married to Jack Kennedy, perfection was a memory at most.

When she and Jack arrived in Hyannis Port, it became evident that rather than buy a house of their own, Jack intended for them to live indefinitely in the poky room in his family's house that he had previously occupied by himself. He expected her to remain at the Cape during the week while he was off working in Washington. These living arrangements troubled her very much. Not only would she and her husband be apart most of the time, but also they would have no privacy when he came home for the weekend. Besides, to Jackie's eye that awful room was really "only big enough for one."

But none of this seemed to concern Jack. His priorities lay elsewhere. Now that he was a married man, suddenly everything in his political life was flying forward on greased wheels. He had accomplished little as a congressman, and his senatorial career to date had been equally undistinguished. Apparently all that was due to change, but rather than hear her husband's plans directly from him, Jackie tended to learn of them in overheard fragments of family conversation. No one would tell her anything, not even when she inquired. On one occasion during that fall of 1953, she walked in on Jack and his father at a moment when the men seemed to be speaking of the vice presidency. Afterward, when she asked Jack point-blank, "Were you talking about being vice president?," his only response was laughter. The ability to laugh at himself was part of Jack's charm. And in this case laughter adroitly deflected Jackie's query, as it no doubt was intended to do.

Though her questions went pointedly unanswered, it was hardly as if no one would talk to her. Joe Kennedy could scarcely have spent more time contentedly parleying with his new daughter-in-law. Indeed, he talked to her more than to his own daughters, which may have accounted in part for the Kennedy sisters' coolness toward her. Kick while she lived had been "the only one" of his daughters he believed he could really talk to. At least to all outward appearances, the other sisters "bored" him. Now he and Jackie regularly indulged in what an observer described as long "wonderful" conversations reminiscent of those he had once enjoyed with Kick. Whether or not John White's efforts to groom Jackie had had anything to do with it, old Joe seemed to have discovered in her something very much like "a substitute for Kick." She bantered. She teased. She presented herself as someone unwilling "to take any guff" from him or any other member of the Kennedy tribe. (A merciless mimic, Jackie perfected a cruel imitation of Rose Kennedy, whose voice was said by one family friend to call to mind "a duck with laryngitis.") At the same time she made it clear that she absolutely adored Jack's father, and he in turn left no doubt that he was enchanted by her.

As Jackie was to learn, however, behind her back he was capable of speaking of her in tones of arctic expediency. Once, when she overheard her father-in-law conferring with Jack and his younger brother Bobby about Jack's political future, she was surprised to hear herself mentioned as well. And the experience was by no means comfortable to her. "They spoke of me as if I weren't a person," Jackie said years later, "just a thing, just a sort of asset, like Rhode Island."

All her life, Jackie had been very picky, very proud. Inclined to believe that she ought to have things exactly as she wanted them, she had waited until she saw just the type of man she would like to marry. And when that man had proven to be rather less than eager, she had not rested until he made his move at last. All of her maneuvers and travails in the marriage market, all of her efforts to escape the traps that the world she grew up in had contrived to set for her, had finally landed her in this small, spartan room on the first floor of her in-laws' house where she slept alone most nights. A little bookshelf held certain of the volumes, many with mauve bindings, that Jack had first read when he was a sickly boy who was often confined to bed. These, she came to understand, were some of the books that had shaped her husband. Jackie could not help but be fascinated by them and by the tumultuous family drama in which they had played a part.

Early in life, Jack Kennedy had experienced what it is like to lay close to death. His first potentially fatal episode, a bout of scarlet fever, had occurred when he was just two years old. Rose Kennedy had been pregnant at the time, and having gone into labor on the day Jack's ordeal began, she had been unable to come to his room. Nor had she visited him afterward lest she or the newborn be exposed. In Rose's place, Joe had cared for the little invalid. He cradled Jack in his arms and faithfully lingered at his bedside. He left the child in no doubt that nothing else mattered except his survival and recovery. Joe subsequently reflected that he had been unprepared for the magnitude of his emotions when he grasped that it was possible Jack might die. Unable to comprehend why Rose had stayed away, the child bonded powerfully and permanently with his father. Rose may have had a reasonable excuse for absenting herself in this instance, but it was also the case that even in the best of times, she was just not physically demonstrative with her children. In later years, Jack would bitterly declare that he could not recall so much as a single hug from Rose. For parental affection, the boy had learned to rely on his father. Joe Kennedy, wonderfully, uninhibitedly emotional and tactile, was all that Jack had in this respect. To the child's dismay, however, he was by no means all that his father had. Joe Kennedy had dedicated himself to Jack's welfare when the boy was near death. Otherwise, more often than not he made the eldest son, Joe Junior, his priority. It was certainly not that Jack's father did not really love him, only that he seemed to prize the robust young Joe, twenty-two months Jack's senior, so much more.

To the father's thinking, young Joe was the model boy, healthy, handsome, and strong. In this regard, frail Jack, with his ever-lengthening record of illnesses both grave and routine, could scarcely compete. If old Joe did not overtly encourage the bullying to which the smaller, weaker brother was routinely subjected, he surely countenanced it. But Joe Junior was not the only instigator of these brutal encounters, which often ended with the older boy smashing the younger one's head against a wall. Despite the odds, Jack was known to incite countless fistfights with his brother. Jack longed to disrupt the pecking order by proving to their father that he too was the fierce, hardy kind of boy old Joe preferred. But in view of old Joe's maxim, "We want winners, we don't want losers around here," Jack's efforts were inevitably for naught. In these ludicrously ill-matched physical confrontations, he always seemed to get the worst of it. Yet, contrary to all reason, Jack, as stubborn as he was slight, kept rushing in for more.

Jack despised being restricted to bed, as he often was during his boyhood and teenage years. In any case, he managed to extract an advantage from these mortifying but unavoidable interludes. He used the time to read. The legends of King Arthur and the Round Table appeared on the shelf beside his bed. Then came works by Robert Louis Stevenson, Sir Walter Scott, and Thomas Babington Macaulay. And then, titles by Winston Churchill, John Buchan, David Cecil, Duff Cooper, Edmund

Burke, and others. Already physically out of harmony with the Kennedy atmosphere, Jack by his reading widened the breach. He also steadily, stealthily confirmed his belief that he was superior to his brother. Recasting delicacy in the form of refinement, he established himself, as Jackie would perceive years afterward, as the more imaginative of the two boys.

Still, it was regarded as "heresy" in the family to suggest that Joe Junior was in any way the lesser figure. Yet that was precisely what Kick, the sibling born in 1920 as Jack fell ill with scarlet fever, long and defiantly maintained. Kick's status as, in Rose's phrase, old Joe's "favorite of all the children" prevented her from being swatted down for daring to challenge the accepted order of things. She was permitted to speak out, but that did not mean her father was required to listen. He persisted in touting young Joe as the best of the boys, the Kennedy son for whom preeminence had been foreordained. When by the time Jack was about fourteen years of age he had failed to persuade old Joe to alter his views, the second son finally seemed to give up the fight. As both Kick and Lem Billings, Jack's prep school roommate at the time, understood, that did not mean Jack had abandoned his conviction that he was better than his brother. But, to all outward appearances, he did seem to put aside any hope of displacing him in old Joe's eyes. If their father persisted in thinking Jack inferior, the teenager thenceforth would gamely play along. Onstage, he cast himself as the sluggard Kennedy brother, whose lack of discipline and ambition his father never ceased to complain of. Offstage, Jack burrowed the more deeply into his reading.

Both tall, handsome brothers were in their early twenties when they appeared together in London at the time of old Joe's ambassadorship. The English debutantes dubbed Joe Junior "the Big One," by way of contrast with scrawny Jack. Known to speak often and openly of his confidence that Joe Junior would one day become America's first Irish-Catholic president, the ambassador encouraged the eldest son to write up his impressions of contemporary Europe as a way of generating the "international publicity" that could be so helpful when at last he was ready to launch himself in public life. The adoring father pitched Joe Junior's letters on travel and politics to leading periodicals. He urged him to find a way to stitch those letters together in the form of a book. He failed or perhaps refused to see that despite Joe Junior's ability to look and act the part of a rising man, his perceptions when set on paper tended to be second-rate at best. Meanwhile, Jack drew on his own European experience, as well as on the fund of knowledge laboriously built up in the course of years of reading, to produce the serious, successful political book that had been expected of Joe Junior. Written in less than six months, *Why England Slept*, about Britain during the run-up to the Second World War, became a surprise bestseller in the United States in 1940 and utterly altered Jack's standing in the family. At a moment when Joe Junior had managed to accumulate little more than a welter of notes and a stack of publishers' rejections, the second son had garnered the wide praise and prestige that was supposed to have been his brother's. Old Joe, who always loved a winner as much as he disdained a mere runner-up, was soon gaily citing Jack's bestselling opinions in public, whereas previously it almost certainly would have been Joe Junior he quoted.

After *Why England Slept*, the firstborn son never quite managed to regain his footing, whether it be in the family or in life. When Jack moved to Washington the following year, he began to speak, with his signature air of amused detachment, to an intimate circle including Kick, Inga Arvad, and Betty Coxe of the possibility that he might one day decide to seek the presidency. At the end of the war, when he returned to London on the eve of the 1945 general election, he left no doubt in the minds of his young English friends who were launching their political careers that he meant to study the electioneering with an eye to an impending run of his own in the States. In 1946, when the second son portrayed himself to voters as a most reluctant bearer of the family flag, that reluctance, like so much else in Jack Kennedy's complex demeanor, was a pose. In important ways, he had been fighting all his life, at moments literally with his fists, for the right to carry that flag. In suggesting that he would never have dared, or even wished, to attempt something like this had Joe Junior survived, he was advancing a biographical narrative that scarcely corresponded to anything that had actually happened in the privacy of his family. He was dissipating perceptions, as he had long found it useful to do, of the ambition that had fired him to surpass Joe Junior during the eldest son's lifetime.

Years later, when Jackie thought back to her early married life, it was the velocity she seemed to remember above all. Hardly had she reached her goal of becoming Mrs. John F. Kennedy when she found herself caught up in a new kind of momentum as her story intersected with Jack's. "Life with him was just so fast." She associated his high-vaulting ambition with one of the qualities she most prized in him, imagination. It struck her that had his older brother lived and been elected senator, Joe Junior, lacking anything like Jack's imaginative capacities, would simply have stalled there. But not Jack: "He never stopped at any plateau, he was always going on to something higher." The relentless propulsion Jackie later sought to evoke did not fully manifest itself to her until the couple acquired a first, albeit temporary, house of their own. In January 1954, they began a six-month rental of a fourteen-foot-wide "dollhouse" on Dent Place in Georgetown, which was owned by Auchincloss family friends who were traveling in Europe. During this period, there began the real work of recasting Kennedy's image, of which the decision to marry had been but an initial necessary step: The senator drew unprecedented attention with a principled but highly controversial vote in favor of the construction of the St. Lawrence Seaway, a stance that risked alienating constituents who protested that the bill would cost Massachusetts jobs. He delivered his first major Senate address, arguing against calls to send U.S. troops to Indochina. In the run-up to the 1954 midterm elections, he traveled extensively, campaigning on behalf of Democrats he might call on later to return the favor. He exhibited his nasal Boston twang to any print interviewer, and on any television or radio show that would have him. He and Jackie became regulars at the dinner parties, usually for ten or twelve, that were a staple of political life in the capital.

As a place of residence, Georgetown had been exceedingly fashionable during the Truman epoch. But the social geography of Dwight Eisenhower's Washington had since shifted, Georgetown having acquired the reputation in some Republican circles as a community of enervated eggheads and left-wingers that was best avoided in favor of more ideologically salubrious neighborhoods. Around the time Eisenhower was inaugurated, Joe Alsop had lamented that everyone he liked seemed to be going away, and no one he liked very much was replacing them. A year later, when Senator and Mrs. John F. Kennedy moved to Georgetown, they became part of an emergent social nexus that included the senators Stuart Symington, George Smathers, Mike Mansfield, and the Republican John Sherman Cooper, among others. On the one hand, it was unquestionably an advantage in this milieu for a politician to be married. On the other, as Jackie noted, some of the most valuable dinner party conversations tended to take place when the men had a chance to talk to one another afterward once they had peeled off from their wives. Before long, Jackie was presiding over such highly ritualized evenings of her own. As "Night and Day" and other tracks on the recording *The Astaire Story* wafted seductively through the tiny house, the Kennedys hosted their first candlelit formal dinner party in the narrow dining room at Dent Place. It was also during these months that they first returned in triumph to Dumbarton Avenue, where, before they were married, both had been known to attend the considerably more raffish gatherings at John White's. On the present occasion, however, the couple's destination was not the cave, but rather the distinctly different social and intellectual universe epitomized by the soirees at Joe Alsop's. After years of banishment, Jack Kennedy's invitation was a sign that he was finally projecting the gravitas that entitled a man to dine on Alsop's blue Sèvres china and to sip Pol Roger champagne from his monogrammed crystal glasses.

Meanwhile, early on, the young wife was confronted with aspects of marriage, or at least of her particular marriage, that she seems not to have anticipated fully. First, there was the matter of her husband's health. Here too the storm came on very quickly. Before the wedding, Lem Billings had made an effort to enlighten her on Jack's medical history. At the very least, she had often observed him hobbling about on crutches during their courtship. Still, by the time of the honeymoon, his back pain had subsided considerably, as the feats of water-skiing that his bride found so thrilling in Acapulco attest. But no sooner had the newlyweds begun their short-let than renewed pain caused him to seek advice from the surgical head at the Hospital for Special Surgery in New York. At a moment when Kennedy was about to embark upon a demanding program aimed at reinventing himself politically, the recommendation offered by Dr. Philip Wilson could scarcely have been more inopportune. Wilson urged him to undergo a double spinal fusion, noting that while there was no guarantee that the procedure would be effective, without it the senator would surely become incapacitated.

Quite apart from the disastrous timing, there was also a huge medical complication. Seven years previously at the London Clinic, Jack had learned that he had Addison's disease, a disturbance of the suprarenal glands known to produce extreme fatigue, nausea, weight loss, low blood pressure, and susceptibility to infection. Then, and on a subsequent occasion in Japan in 1951, he had nearly died. At the time of the initial episode, the London physician, Sir Daniel Davis, had predicted that Jack had no more than a year to live. Dr. Elmer Bartels, the endocrinologist at the Lahey Clinic in Boston who had overseen his treatment for Addison's disease since his return to America following the 1947 diagnosis, had been a good deal more optimistic provided that Kennedy, never the most compliant of patients, agreed to submit to proper management. Still, as Bartels never tired of pointing out, people with Addison's disease tolerate surgery poorly. For such a patient, the back operation Wilson was recommending in 1954 posed two grave risks. First, the trauma from the surgery might spark a new Addisonian crisis, which could lead to a loss of circulation in the legs and subsequent heart failure. Second, the operation could result in a fatal infection. So, almost from the moment Jackie began life in Washington with a new husband, their existence together was shadowed by death. To Jack, the specter was nothing new. She, on the other hand, simply had never had to absorb anything like that before. In any case, after the diagnosis at Special Surgery, Jack, having yet to decide about the spinal fusion, plunged back into the Washington fray. Though troubled additionally by problems of the stomach and urinary tract, among other physical woes, he strove to act before the world as though nothing were wrong. He had long "schooled himself" to live gracefully with pain, to exert what Chuck Spalding described as "an actor's control." When there was no choice but to speak of his medical misfortunes, he tended to make light of them as much as possible.

Nonetheless, by April 1954 the pain had become well-nigh intolerable and he entered the Lahey Clinic for additional consultations. By degrees, he lost the capacity to pick up a piece of paper that had fallen to the floor; to put on his own socks in the morning; to go up and down stairs normally. Navigating the marble floors between his Senate office and the Senate chamber; standing, as was required, to address the chamber—these and other routine tasks associated with his work were transformed into monumental undertakings. When, more and more, he found it necessary to use crutches, he scrambled to conceal them before anyone came into his office. From the time he first ran for Congress using the campaign slogan "The New Generation Offers a Leader," he had been keen to associate himself in voters' minds with the dash and vigor of youth. Now Evelyn Lincoln, his secretary, perceived that the incessant struggle to mask his condition made him snappish in private, so much so that at one point she considered quitting her job. When he returned to Dent Place at night, more often than not he was so drained, both physically and mentally, that all he wanted to do was go right to sleep.

Prior to the marriage, Lem Billings also had spoken to Jackie about

Jack's sexual habits. Nevertheless, according to Lem, until she was actually wedded to the man, she simply failed to comprehend "the depth of Jack's need for other women." Another old friend of Jack's, Jane Suydam, judged that in spite of anything Jackie had heard or seen in advance, "I don't think she anticipated a difficult marriage. We all thought we would change the man." Jackie, Suydam assessed, had entered married life with "eyes filled with dreams." In Lem's view, Jackie proved to have been unprepared for "the humiliation she would suffer when she found herself stranded at parties while Jack would suddenly disappear with some pretty young girl." Not even the wrenching back pain he was experiencing impeded his activities in this respect. On the contrary, the complicated stagecraft that was often necessary in these situations seems to have offered a welcome distraction. In addition to the women he compulsively targeted at Washington parties and otherwise pursued in the company of one of the married senators in his and Jackie's set, George Smathers of Florida, there were also the long-range fantasies that absorbed him more and more. Three months into the Kennedys' residence at Dent Place, he managed to track down the address of the statuesque Swedish girl whom he had met in Antibes on the eve of his wedding and had not seen or been in touch with since. "I expect to be in France in September," he wrote to Gunilla von Post on March 2. "Will you be there?"

That spring the women's magazine *McCall's* pitched a story to Senator Kennedy's office about young Mrs. Kennedy's adjustment to her new life in political Washington. "The Senator's Wife Goes Back to School" was to focus on Jackie's decision to sign up to study political history at Georgetown University's Foreign Service School. But hardly had the photo shoot begun in early May when it became evident that the senator intended for the piece to be as much about him as about his wife. During the course of five days, in locations ranging from Dent Place to the nearby cobblestoned streets of Georgetown to JFK's Senate office, *McCall's* generated nearly a thousand negatives. Almost a year had passed since

Jackie had posed for a comparable set of pictures at the time of her first visit to Hyannis Port as a bride-to-be. Whatever her unease had been when a private family event was transformed into a photo opportunity, the excitement and elation of the twenty-three-year-old woman portrayed in the *Life* photographs had no doubt been genuine. Whatever the calculatedness and cynicism involved in Joe Kennedy's decision to ask in the *Life* team, the images of a radiant young woman who adores the man who has finally asked her to share his life accorded with reality as Jackie Bouvier surely saw it in the spring of 1953. The *McCall's* shoot would prove to be another matter entirely.

Her husband by this time was very nearly at the point of having to use crutches constantly. Yet she is pictured cheering on a robust Jack Kennedy as he tosses around a football with his equally athletic brother Bobby. She had discovered that an evening out in Washington could be a mortifying ordeal when he routinely stole away with other women. Yet she is shown, dressed in a strapless evening gown, beaming at her no-less-adoring husband, also formally attired, at the outset of precisely such an evening. She had learned to resent the various men—Torby, Red, Lem, and others—who were forever interposing themselves between Jack and her so that she and her husband were, in her plaintive phrase, almost "never alone." Yet she is seen clowning merrily with Lem, as though nothing could delight her more than to have Jack's sycophants always about. She had found that Jack could scarcely be less interested in the academic studies she had undertaken to make herself a more engaging and useful companion. Yet she gamely appears in various shots on the Georgetown University campus. What makes these photographs so different from those generated by *Life* magazine the previous year is nothing in the pictures themselves. Rather, it is the freight of disillusioning knowledge on her part that makes her complicit in fashioning a public image so at odds with the facts. Last time she believed much of the hype. This time she countenances it. The boyishly coiffed twenty-four-year-old woman in the *McCall's* photographs is already amply acquainted with the stern, often squalid reality concealed behind this pictorial Potemkin village of happy young married life in Georgetown.

A salient feature of that reality was her husband's abiding restiveness. The month after *McCall's* rather charmingly photographed Jack and Jackie at his Senate desk serenely laboring together on his official correspondence, he sat in that same office drafting a letter of a decidedly more personal nature. "It now appears as though I shall be coming to Europe at the end of August," he wrote to Gunilla on June 28. "I thought I might get a boat and sail around the Mediterranean for two weeks—with you as a crew. What do you think?"

Four

For the rest of his life, Elmer Bartels would puzzle over Jackie Kennedy's behavior when he encountered her again in New York in October 1954. It was not the first time he had found her actions to be, in his phrase, "kind of strange." He had had a similar response to her at Hammersmith Farm the previous year when he was one of the approximately fourteen hundred guests at the Kennedy wedding. He noticed that every now and again the bride would disappear "behind the drapes" whenever she spotted someone on the reception line whom she presumably did not like or wish to see. But then, as the physician in charge of supervising Jack Kennedy's treatment for Addison's disease, Bartels had long perfected a disappearing act of his own. No one but Joe Kennedy and members of Jack's intimate circle knew that Jack had Addison's disease. No one but they were aware that the various bouts of illness described to the public as recurrences of malaria contracted in the South Pacific during the Second World War had in fact been Addisonian crises. No one had any idea about Jack's arrangement with Bartels, who was religiously available to him twenty-four hours a day, 365 days a year. Bartels attributed his willingness to give his patients so much of his time and spirit to the fact that when he was a boy in Ohio, the doctors had not been as attentive to his long-ailing mother as they might have been. Lest word of Kennedy's condition seep out, the senator always telephoned personally when he needed to see his endocrinologist. Nevertheless, on Kennedy's wedding day, there was Bartels—thin, balding, homely, and homespun—hiding in plain sight among the horde of reporters on whose presence Joe Kennedy had insisted despite the vehement objections of both Jackie and her mother.

Bartels, a staunch Republican who made a point of never discussing politics with the senator, prided himself on having managed to get Kennedy's Addison's disease under reasonably "good control." He sniffed at the catastrophic predictions made at the London Clinic before Kennedy initially came to see him in Boston. He was adamant that so long as Kennedy was fastidious about taking his medicine, avoided trauma and stress, and remembered that he would always be unusually sensitive to infection, there was every reason to believe he could enjoy a normal life span. He emphasized that when, as in Japan in 1951, Kennedy suffered a new, potentially fatal Addisonian crisis, it had been because the patient, who tended to be lax about such matters, had simply neglected or forgotten his medicine. The physician had a highly developed sense of duty and was inclined to blame himself severely when, despite his best efforts, patients acted recklessly.

A year after attending the Kennedy wedding, Elmer Bartels went to New York determined to prevent the senator from making a calamitous mistake. As late as August, Kennedy had been blithely telling Gunilla von Post that he planned to come to Europe in the fall. By September, however, Kennedy's health had gotten the better of him and he sent Gunilla a telegram claiming that, having been hospitalized on account of an injured leg, he was going to have to postpone the trip after all. In truth, unable any longer to endure his back pain, he entered the Hospital for Special Surgery on October 11, 1954, using the cover story that he needed to address an óld war injury. In fact, he was there to undergo the double spinal fusion recommended by the doctors in New York for the unstable back with which Bartels believed him to have been born. Bartels had previously attempted to talk him out of the procedure on the grounds that with Addison's in the mix, the surgery, which seemed misguided in any case, might have fatal consequences. When the Boston physician appeared in Kennedy's hospital room, time had very nearly run out. If Bartels was to talk Kennedy out of his purpose, it must be now or never.

But Jack Kennedy had another visitor as well. "The Senator's Wife Goes Back to School" had been published in the October issue of *McCall's* magazine, and Jackie had since been in touch with the photographer to acquire prints of some of the pictures. The magazine had already sent her a selection during the summer, but there had been a certain amount of confusion about the Kennedys' address. Since the Georgetown short-let had ended in June, the couple had been leading what Jackie ruefully described as a "nomadic" existence shuttling between their parents' homes and various hotels. The original package from *McCall's* therefore was presumed to have been lost in the mail. Now the replacement set had arrived and she fluttered about her husband's bedside, intent on sharing the numerous prints with him before the doctor had one last chance to make his case. For three-quarters of an hour, Bartels was left to stew in his own juices while Jackie laboriously commented in a babylike voice on each of the photographs in the pile.

Though it hardly seems possible, there was an even greater incongruity between those pictures and her day-to-day reality than had existed just five months previously. Since the couple left Dent Place, they had lacked even the illusion of having a home of their own. More than anything now she wanted roots, stability, "a normal life with my husband coming home from work every day at five." To judge by her remarks, the unadventurous life she had once regarded as a trap was beginning to look pretty good. Did the July 21, 1954, society wedding of John Husted to another Farmington girl, Ann Brittain, have anything to do with this change of heart? No doubt because prior to his hospitalization Jack had so often been away on political business, she dreamed of a time when he would at least "spend weekends with me and the children I hoped we would have." But here too she had been thwarted. Jackie suffered a miscarriage that fall. Whether or not it had anything to do with the loss of the couple's first child, these also had been the weeks when Jack finally had had to decide whether to risk everything in one desperate throw by consenting to a spinal fusion. Vehemently opposed, Bartels and his orthopedic colleagues at the Lahey Clinic militated for a more conservative course of treatment involving physiotherapy and exercise. Having lost one son already, Joe Kennedy also insisted that the danger was excessive. At a certain point, however, for all of Jack's stoicism, pain trumped every other consideration. Finally, at Hyannis Port, Jackie heard him tell his father: "I don't care. I can't go on like this."

The prints she maddeningly insisted on reviewing one by one when she came to see him that day at the Hospital for Special Surgery depicted two handsome young people beginning their life together. Now, a year into the marriage, the twenty-five-year-old woman who, to the physician's exasperation, persisted in babbling on about seeming trivia was faced with the very real possibility of imminent widowhood. Almost certainly she knew what Bartels had traveled from Boston to say. Surely Jack did. But at this particular moment, powerless though she might be to influence her husband on important matters, or even to get him to answer straightforward questions, the stage was hers for as long as she chose to command it.

When Bartels finally had his interview, he failed to convince Kennedy to cancel the operation. Doctor and patient had entirely different casts of mind. Bartels was cautious and conservative. Kennedy was a risk taker. Bartels was a plainspoken man who eschewed drama. Kennedy was byzantine and self-dramatizing. Though Bartels had assured him early on that it was possible for an Addison's patient to have a normal life expectancy, Kennedy had persisted in saying privately that he would not live past middle age. From boyhood, he had drawn a strange kind of sustenance from the proximity of death. Some observers believed that his brushes with mortality had in some curious way "liberated" him, forcing him to go after what he wanted in life earlier and harder than might otherwise have been the case. A sense of his own ending was the inner demon that drove him. Thus the dizzying velocity Jackie later sought to evoke in speaking of her early married life. As far as her husband was concerned, he had had to fight every inch of his road through life to this point, and the spinal fusion was just another of the obstacles he needed to surmount. In spite of anything his father, his endocrinologist, or anyone else said to dissuade him, Kennedy acted as if the operation were bound to be successful. As he awaited surgery, he made extensive plans for his political moves afterward.

At Hyannis Port in the weeks leading up to her husband's hospitalization, Jackie had been drafted to take notes when his great friend from prewar London days, David Ormsby-Gore, helped him begin to formulate certain of the policies and beliefs that would at length carry him to the White House and guide his actions as president. These unusually intense, fast-paced conversations continued in New York that October when the tall, gaunt thirty-six-year-old Ormsby-Gore, who had come to the United States the previous month as part of the British delegation to the United Nations General Assembly, visited the hospital room of the man he regarded as his "American cousin." Jack in turn characterized David to Jackie as, in her phrase, "the brightest man he'd ever met." And from the first, she too was powerfully drawn to David, who was to play an important role in her own life as well.

A decade later, when Jackie was a young widow, she judged that after Bobby Kennedy and herself, David had been the person who had been "the most wounded" by Jack's death. Whether or not that assessment was fair or correct, it suggests the depth of her emotional bond to David in 1964. "If I could think of anyone now who could save the Western world," she told Arthur Schlesinger Jr. in the aftermath of the assassination, "it would be David." Extravagant words, perhaps, but such was the significance she attached to the work that began when Ormsby-Gore visited Hyannis Port prior to her husband's back operation. Already, in 1954, David embodied certain of the strands she loved best in Jack—his bookishness, his conversational flair, his familial and philosophical ties to the British aristocracy, and not least the tragic-romantic backstory of which she had had her first tantalizing glimpses when she heard John White speak of his lost love Kathleen. For Jackie, the arrival of David added many crucial colorful bits of glass to the mosaic of her husband's early life.

David Ormsby-Gore, great-grandson of the Victorian colossus Prime Minister Lord Salisbury, had been a member of the set of young noblemen to which Kick Kennedy had gained entrée before her brother Jack, then a student at Harvard, joined her in London in 1938. He was the first cousin of Billy Hartington, the heir to the Devonshire dukedom with whom Kick fell in love and later married. David had been brought up virtually as a brother to Billy, as well as to Billy's younger brother, Andrew Cavendish. When Jack Kennedy arrived in London on the eve of the war, the young American was initiated into the second son's club, comprised of those like David and Andrew who were thought to have drawn the "short straw in life." As it happened, by virtue of their older brothers' early deaths, all three second sons were propelled to the position of "prime runner" in their families. Andrew became the 11th Duke of Devonshire, Jack his father's anointed to be America's first Irish-Catholic president, and David (whose elder brother, Gerard, was killed in an automobile accident in 1935) the heir to a peerage, as well as the eighth generation of Ormsby-Gores from father to son to sit in the House of Commons.

After the war, Kennedy's friendship with Ormsby-Gore deepened when David and his wife, Sissie, endeavored to look after Billy's young widow, who had chosen to remain in England. Jack, too, when he visited London in this period was treated by the Ormsby-Gores and other members of the set as if he were "another cousin"—no minor matter in that inbred aristocratic world. Jack and David had long reveled in each other's company, talking endlessly about jazz, reading, politics, history, and other shared interests, but a family connection intensified the bond and encouraged it to develop. When the friends met again in the autumn of 1954, David had much to tell about the strategic thinking on international affairs that had been taking place within Churchill's postwar administration.

Deprived of power in 1945, Churchill had again become prime minister in 1951, but as David spoke to Jack, the British leader was widely believed to be about to hand over power to his heir apparent, Anthony Eden. Certainly, Eden himself and various other Conservative leaders, as well as the administration in Washington, were eager for the old man to leave the stage. To some minds, the all-party eightieth-birthday tribute to Churchill set to take place in November seemed an ideal time for him to announce his retirement. Churchill, however, insisted that he needed more time in office. Furiously working to avert the third world war that in an age of nuclear weaponry threatened to destroy mankind, the PM remained intent on finishing the business left undone at Potsdam.

The year before, when Jackie, in her role as the Inquiring Camera Girl, asked people, "Malenkov said all issues between the United States and Russia are solvable by peaceful means. Do you agree?," the question touched on a key difference between Churchill's and Eisenhower's approaches to postwar East-West relations. Georgy Malenkov had been one of the new leaders in Moscow who had taken over after the March 5, 1953, death of Stalin. Churchill wanted to meet with the fledgling Russian leadership unconditionally and at once, not so much in the belief that they would immediately give ground on the Soviet presence in Eastern and Central Europe (and on other matters of contention) as that any contact between East and West inevitably helped to open up the heretofore hermetically sealed totalitarian society. In Churchill's view, each meeting, each agreement no matter how modest, each infusion of words and ideas from the West, was another step toward defeating the Soviet Communists without bloodshed. He argued that such contacts and infiltration were feared by everything that was evil in the Kremlin regime, and that by contrast Western leaders had nothing to fear from top-level talks so long as they approached those encounters from a position of military strength. Eisenhower, still bristling from having been lied to by Stalin over Berlin in 1945, took a sharply different view. He insisted that Stalin's successors demonstrate good faith by making specific concessions before he would agree to face them across a conference table.

As of October 1954, there the battle lines between the two chief Western Allies, Washington and London, remained. Churchill was still passionately fighting Eisenhower on the matter of a summit meeting, but time was clearly on the American president's side. Quite simply, the aged, ailing Churchill could not last long in office. When Ormsby-Gore spoke at length to Kennedy of the expertise he had been developing in disarmament negotiations, the context of his comments was the Churchillian policy of seeking the peaceful defeat of Soviet communism through contact and agreements. Ormsby-Gore suggested to his old friend some of the great things the latter might accomplish in the next phase of his political career—if only Kennedy, having reached what Disraeli called the fatal age of thirty-seven, the age that had snatched away Raphael and Byron, survived the October 21 operation.

At first it appeared he might not. Some seventy-two hours after the three-hour-plus operation, Kennedy developed a urinary tract infection. Before he lapsed into a coma, he called out for Jackie, who was waiting outside his room, but hospital staff declined to admit her. The incident led her to vow that she would never again permit doctors or nurses to keep her from her husband's side when he needed her. Meanwhile, Evelyn

Lincoln, when the hospital reached her at home at a late hour, was notified that the senator's physicians did not anticipate he would live until morning. Finally, Jackie joined other family members at his bedside as a priest administered last rites. Afterward, Jackie prayed, by her own account for the first time in her life. When next Mrs. Lincoln called the hospital, she was told that Kennedy had rallied in the course of the night.

Informed that the next ten days would be critical, Jackie read to her husband, clutched his hand, applied a moist cloth to his forehead, spoon-fed him—anything to help. When, though he was still gravely ill and in tremendous pain, the worst of the crisis seemed to have passed, Jackie, sitting not far from his hospital bed, wrote thank-you letters to various dignitaries who had sent good wishes to the senator. "It will be so long before he can write a letter or talk on the phone or anything," she wrote to Senate Majority Leader Lyndon Johnson on November 4, "and he wants you to know how much he appreciates your thinking of him and all the nice things you said." When Jack was finally well enough, he managed to undertake some correspondence of his own. Most other messages he could entrust to Jackie, but not the charming epistle he drafted on November 11. "I was terribly disappointed that at the last moment I was not able to come to Europe, especially when you were going to be in Paris and we could have had such a good time." The day after Joe Kennedy had publicly and not a little frantically denied a swirl of rumors in Washington that his son would never return to his Senate seat, Jack assured Gunilla von Post, and was probably also reassuring himself, that he would be back in Washington in January and would "without fail" come to Europe as soon as the Senate adjourned for the summer. As a sickly child in that tiny, bleak bedroom at Hyannis Port that Jackie would later share, he had often used the weapons of stealth, guile, and imagination to fight his battles. Now, dreaming of his reunion with the Swedish girl whom he had seen only once before in his life, it was as if he were willing himself to get better, projecting himself forward to a better time. Though Jackie was a constant comforting presence in his hospital room, it was Gunilla's face that, he wrote, haunted him still. Two months after the operation, Kennedy's doctors feared it had been a failure; indeed, that he might never walk again. In anticipation of being moved to the Kennedy family home in Palm Beach, he wrote again to Gunilla on December 18 to fantasize about his European summer plans and to suggest that in the meantime she write to him care of his father. Three days later, at a quarter past nine in the morning, a grim-faced Jackie walked alongside and whispered phrases of encouragement as her emaciated husband, supine beneath a plaid blanket, was rolled out of the hospital on a gurney en route to the ambulance due to transport the couple to LaGuardia Airport.

In the sprawling family house in Palm Beach, whose stucco facade was pocked with areas of mildewed peeling paint, and where a two-room suite on the first floor had been specially equipped with a hospital bed, Jack soon lapsed into a deep depression. It had been thought in New York that the move would be helpful to him. Instead, he was manifestly not improving. The pain from the metal plate that the doctors had inserted in hopes of stabilizing the spine was unceasing. The smelly, suppurating eight-inch-long wound failed to heal. The taped-down dressing had to be changed regularly, and he spent a good deal of time lying on his stomach because he could not tolerate any pressure on his back. After many months of frenetic political activity since the Kennedys' honeymoon, everything appeared to have come to a crashing, anticlimactic halt. It seemed to Jackie, who slept in an adjoining bedroom in case she was needed at night, that it was all Jack could do "just to keep from going mad." He grew bitter and dark in a way he simply had never been before. His father and others worried that, though it had not actually killed him, the botched operation threatened to destroy Jack as a man.

Which is why it was so important when he began to call for great numbers of books and other printed materials. Work tables were carried in, along with filing cabinets and a dictating apparatus. Jackie read to him, took notes on lined yellow paper, arranged for the professor who had taught her at Georgetown University to sign on as a researcher. The senator also had more than a little help with the actual writing of what slowly emerged as his new book. Trifles such as his letters to Gunilla he had no trouble producing on his own. More serious efforts were another matter. Though he responded powerfully, even viscerally, to great prose, he had always been an awkward writer, his ideas tending to outpace his ability to capture them on paper. Kick had known about this problem. So had Inga Arvad and John White. Thus, he had made it his habit of late to use a young senatorial aide named Theodore Sorensen to assist in the preparation of articles and other publications, in addition to the helper's myriad other duties.

On the book project, Kennedy himself appears to have been largely responsible for the introductory and concluding chapters, whereas Sorensen labored more extensively on the interior sections. The manuscript's underlying theme of political courage, however, and its application to present problems were entirely the product of Kennedy's thought and experience. In 1938, Jack had joined David Ormsby-Gore and the other bloods who comprised their London set in ardently debating the questions about leadership raised by Churchill in the newly published book *Arms and the Covenant,* a collection of his speeches since 1932. Alongside his accusations that the government of Stanley Baldwin had abdicated its duty by letting Britain "drift" while Germany systematically rearmed, Churchill had juxtaposed the prime minister's rejoinder in the House of Commons. Baldwin maintained that, given the temper of the electorate, had he pressed for rearmament—in the necessity of which he privately believed—he would have been defeated in the 1935 election. He made the case that his motivation for putting politics first had not been mere personal ambition, but rather his anxiety that the Socialists, whose statements and votes against defense measures were a matter of record, would triumph and that as a consequence things would be much worse than under his leadership. The marathon talkers in Jack's group went furiously back and forth about whether it was the duty of a leader in a democratic society to take action that, though to his mind right and necessary, jeopardized his political survival.

Sixteen years later, that question would be central to Kennedy's book *Profiles in Courage*. Writing out of his pivotal recent conversations with Ormsby-Gore, Kennedy suggested that a fresh approach to East-West relations, one likely to prove unpopular with a broad swath of American voters, was needed to beat a "foreign ideology that fears free thought more than it fears hydrogen bombs." That phrase owed much to Churchill's perception about the Kremlin's fear of words and ideas as a threat to their closed totalitarian society. Since boyhood, Kennedy had been steeped in the thought of the prewar Churchill. The passage, along with others like it, signaled that Kennedy had begun to engage the postwar Churchill as well. Churchill left office on April 5, 1955, before he had succeeded in initiating the new epoch in East-West relations he hoped would bring about the peaceful defeat of Soviet Communism. *Profiles in Courage* quietly suggested that in Churchill's absence from public life, that dream might yet be realized by others.

Meanwhile, Kennedy had regained his resolve but not his health. His pain was the greater now that he had endured the operation than it had been beforehand. When doctors determined that the oozing wound in his back was infected, he returned to the Hospital for Special Surgery to have the metal plate removed and to undergo a bone graft. In the course of a follow-up visit three months later, the endocrinologist associated with the hospital, Ephraim Shorr, who had assisted Philip Wilson at the time of the original surgery, admitted to Kennedy that he too had believed the operation ought not to have been performed. Why had he not said anything previously? Because he had felt that it was not his place to second-guess his orthopedic colleague. Had it been up to Shorr, he, like his Boston counterpart, Elmer Bartels, would have recommended some other course of treatment. Now that the operation had failed, however, he wanted Kennedy to see a new doctor in New York. Jackie, when she learned that a matter of professional etiquette had prevented Shorr from speaking up prior to the surgery, was furious. As far as she was concerned, it was "just criminal" that the operation had been allowed to be undertaken in the first place. Jack did not share her rage. It was to be typical of the marriage that whereas Jackie, perceiving some medical, political, or journalistic affront to her husband, would be indignant on his behalf, he tended to respond objectively and pragmatically. In this respect, she resembled Joe Kennedy Senior, who once remarked that, unlike Jack, when he had a bad experience with someone, he was inclined to "remember it forever." As Jackie came to understand and admire, Jack preferred to coolly regard certain people as if they were mere pieces "on a chessboard." The problem for Jackie, of course, was when he viewed her that way as well.

In May, after an absence of seven months, Jack Kennedy returned to Washington pretending to be almost fully recovered. He was richly tanned and he insisted to the reporters at the airport that he had discarded his crutches but a few days before. Beside him, Jackie, by contrast, appeared wan and tense, but then it was not Mrs. Kennedy whom the journalists were there to inspect. The senator delivered another demanding performance the following day, when he ascended the front steps of the Capitol, then pointedly walked, rather than rode, across the grounds to the Senate Office Building. He brought it all off to perfection, but the exertion cost him massively. Afterward, alone with Jackie, he retreated in agony to the hospital bed that had been set up for him at their hotel. Later that month when the Senate recessed for the Memorial Day weekend, Kennedy, on crutches again, secretly checked into the Cornell Medical Center at New York Hospital to begin receiving Novocain injections from Dr. Janet Travell, the pain specialist whom Ephraim Shorr had been urging him to see. He was back in the Senate on June 1, 1955, and Travell continued to treat him until the Senate adjourned in August. The Novocain injections were a partial fix at best, but they did at least allow him to live with the pain and to persist in acting before the world as if nothing very much was wrong.

In private, meanwhile, he delivered a second masterly performance, this time for his wife. The nervous young woman who, several months previously, had mystified and irritated an older, graver observer by chattering on about some magazine photographs when life-and-death matters urgently needed to be discussed had since incontrovertibly shown her mettle in the course of her husband's long, arduous, and not entirely successful convalescence. Now that Jack was somewhat better, he insisted she had done enough. He thought she deserved to have some fun. He felt confident that with the Novocain injections he was receiving, he was finally well enough to manage without her. He maintained that just because he had to remain in Washington until August, there was no reason she should be required to do the same. In truth, she was exhausted and did long to get away. After all those many months, the gift he proposed to give her was far from unwelcome. Jackie's sister Lee had moved to London, where her husband, Michael Canfield, had become a social secretary to the U.S. ambassador to the Court of St. James's, Winthrop Aldrich. Jack suggested that Jackie visit the Canfields in July. As soon as the Senate adjourned, he would join her for a real vacation together in the South of France. In the meantime, he was in a position to make the prospect of London even more alluring. Jackie had loved seeing David the previous autumn. In England, Jack would arrange for her to be entertained at dinners and country house weekends by other members of his prewar set of whom she had heard much but had yet to meet. He cast the trip as a gesture of gratitude and adoring self-sacrifice on his part. Actually, it was anything but that.

What he did not tell Jackie was that during all that time in New York and Palm Beach, he had been building castles in the air, writing and calling Sweden from his sickbed, presumably at those moments when his wife was out of the room. He urged Gunilla to send him her photograph. He obsessed aloud on the telephone about their lying on an Italian beach together. In a period when by any realistic measure such a trip remained well beyond his physical powers, he sought to arrange a rendezvous in southern Europe. Finally, when his Scandinavian pen pal, wary like Jackie before her of seeming too eager, demanded that he at least make the gesture of coming to her, he had little choice but to assent. As soon as the Senate adjourned, he could conveniently stop off in Båstad for a week en route to meet his wife in the South of France.

What he did not tell Gunilla was that, as in a farce, he was also arranging to have a backup, a married Swedish airline stewardess, waiting for him in Stockholm in the event that he chose not to remain the entire week in Båstad. At length, Jackie did travel to London, where the Canfields hosted a party in her honor at their Belgravia mews house, and where old friends of Jack's such as Hugh Fraser, Jakie Astor, and William Douglas-Home danced attendance on her. When, on account of her frequently being out to dinner with various grandees, stories circulated that she had left her ailing husband, it was Jack who tended to come off as the injured party. In fact, he had arranged to keep Jackie nicely distracted when, with Torby MacDonald accompanying him in the capacity of a beard, he sailed for Europe on August 5. Lest anyone think it frivolous of Senator Kennedy to schedule a luxurious European vacation with his wife so soon after his long absence from Washington, he traveled under the guise of a congressional fact-finding mission to Poland and the member nations of the North Atlantic Treaty Organization. In the official version, the senator was going abroad "to work and learn, not rest and play."

Jack Kennedy had long been calibrating the dates, venue, and other details of his love idyll. Such is the human comedy that the objectives of seeing the Swedish girl, on the one hand, and of completing a new book, on the other, were both integral to the story of his convalescence. Aboard the USS *United States* he by turns telegraphed Gunilla to say that he would soon be with her and contacted his father with the news that he was sending on the first and last chapters of the final draft of *Profiles in Courage,* Rose Kennedy having previously hand-delivered the rest of the manuscript when she joined her husband in the South of France at the start of their summer holiday. Also in the message to Joe, Jack fine-tuned the details of where he and Jackie would stay in Cap d'Antibes following the week he was to be on his own in Sweden. Eager that his wife enjoy herself on this second leg of her trip as much as she had during the first, he calculated that Jackie would like it best if they stayed at the Hôtel du Cap rather than in the rented house where Joe and Rose were in residence. That way, Jackie would be near her sister as long as Lee was there. Jack Kennedy seemed to have every element in place when, on crutches and in considerable pain, he arrived in southwestern Sweden on August 11. Soon, however, he found himself facing a good many more chess pieces than he can possibly have anticipated, Gunilla's mother and father, along with numerous other members of their large extended family, including the Swedish ambassador to Poland, cousin Eric von Post, also being on holiday in Båstad at the time.

What had begun as a tryst arranged in secrecy was suddenly transformed into a relationship conspicuously conducted in front of Mama Brita, Papa Olle, who was nearly two decades his wife's senior, and various other people. However improbably, the tumult of Jack's social life that week in Sweden nearly rivaled that which his wife had been delighting in elsewhere in Europe. Stranger still, all the Swedes seemed to know that Gunilla's lame lover was an unhappily married U.S. senator who aspired to be president someday. The senator, meanwhile, cunningly played his game. He assured Gunilla that he still loved her. He insisted to Brita that he wanted to leave Jackie in order to marry Brita's daughter. He pledged to discuss the matter with his father as soon as he left Sweden. Gunilla, speaking confidentially to Torby MacDonald, acknowledged that Jackie must love her husband and that she certainly seemed to have been kind to him throughout his ordeal. Torby replied that while Jackie had indeed visited at the hospital, "I don't think she was that concerned."

Jack and Jackie were reunited in Cap d'Antibes, where they made up a merry group with the Canfields and William and Rachel Douglas-Home, even as the senator diligently and discreetly maintained his Swedish contacts. On August 22, a day when he and Jackie, along with their companions, were lavishly entertained by the Kennedys' Palm Beach friends Charles and Jayne Wrightsman, Jack also managed to draft two letters, both in red ink on Hôtel du Cap stationery. In one missive, he reported to Gunilla that he had been doing nothing in the South of France but sit in the sun, look at the sea, and think of her. For some reason, he also felt the need to lie that he had just that day received word that his wife and sister-in-law were about to arrive in Cap d'Antibes, and to predict that when he saw them presently "it will all be complicated the way I feel now." In his second letter, lest the stewardess's door be closed to him in future, he politely sought to explain why he had failed to call her. Reporting that he had spent the entire week in Båstad, he emphasized that he had seen "nobody as nice" there as he had during his previous visit to Sweden, the latter a reference to an affair Kennedy had had with another airline employee, a close friend of the stewardess's, in Stockholm in 1949. There followed several calls to Gunilla, whom he hoped to persuade to meet him in Capri. He had already put in motion the plan that promised to free him up.

Due in Poland presently, he told Jackie that she must not accompany him because it would seem less than "serious" were he to arrive in Warsaw with his wife. No sooner had Jackie left Cap d'Antibes with her sister in anticipation of joining him later in his official travels than he headed directly for Capri. In the course of several phone calls, he implored Gunilla to come to him there. She, however, did not desire merely a second rendezvous with the senator. This time, she was playing for marriage. When Jack arrived in Warsaw, he went to the Swedish embassy to speak to Ambassador von Post both of his passion for Gunilla and of his desire to leave Jackie. It was a safe bet that the diplomat would pass on to his young cousin all that Jack said. Subsequently, on the phone to Gunilla, Jack claimed also to have spoken at last to Joe Kennedy. According to Jack, the old man had angrily refused even to listen to his reasons for wanting a divorce. Whether or not Jack had really had that conversation with Joe, the sad story in which he weakly (or was it shrewdly?) portrayed himself yet again as a mere pawn in the hands of his controlling father stirred the hapless, smitten Swedish girl, who finally agreed to meet him in Copenhagen. The senator, however, soon called back to cancel. Set to visit the NATO countries with his wife, he reported that Copenhagen was going to be, as they say, "difficult."

Jackie, when she traveled with her husband to Rome, Paris, and London, among other destinations, was beginning her third year as Mrs. John F. Kennedy. The marriage, it need hardly be said, was not everything she might have hoped for. Even in a period when the couple had seemed to achieve a modicum of tranquility as Jackie assisted him with his manuscript and otherwise ministered to his needs, the wheels in his brain had persisted in tirelessly spinning out plans for future assignations. Jack also kept significant other areas of his life carefully curtained off from her. As she later came to understand, in the period after the Kennedys returned to the United States on October 11, 1955, she had known almost nothing about how his mind was working with regard to the immediate political future. It was also during this time that the senator had made a point of instructing Janet Travell, when she came to see him in Palm Beach: "It's best if you don't go into my medical problems with Jackie."

All in all, then, Jackie was operating blind when she seized on the notion of acquiring a home near Merrywood, in McLean, Virginia, as a salve to the perturbations of her marriage. Originally, she had thought of building a one-story house atop a cliff on her mother and stepfather's land overlooking the Potomac. But the expense of bringing in water proved to be too great, and she abandoned the idea after Janet told her about a nineteenth-century Georgian-style brick house nearby that had come up for sale. Set on five acres, the property was known as Hickory Hill. Immediately, Jackie saw it as the anchor her marriage had been lacking, a place in the country where she could enjoy quiet weekends with her husband, who, she assumed, would welcome the opportunity to rest and recover from his public exertions. Jackie did not require a pain specialist to tell her what she already knew experientially: The senator's back problems were still far worse than he was prepared to disclose. After the couple purchased the property in October, she set to work overseeing the renovations with an eye toward Jack's comfort. In his bedroom and dressing room, for instance, drawers and shoe shelves had to be specially installed at a level that would not require him to lean over when he wished to get at them. But even as she was attending to all of this detail, she perceived that something was amiss. At the end of the workweek, instead of secluding himself with her at Hickory Hill, Jack was ever on the move again, chasing a new goal of which he had previously given her no inkling.

During the time that he had been in the South of France with Jackie, word had come from the States that he was under consideration to be Adlai Stevenson's running mate in the 1956 presidential election. Jack was, in his father's words, "very intrigued" by the rumors, whereas the old man for his part feared that being on a ticket with Stevenson could damage Jack's long-term presidential ambitions. Sorensen wrote to him at the Hôtel du Cap to report on a front-page story in the *Boston Post* confirming that the Stevenson people were indeed looking at him. When Jack returned to the States, he had wasted no time notifying Stevenson that he planned to formulate a public statement of support for the latter's candidacy, to be released whenever Stevenson judged it would be most helpful to him. Jack wanted the second spot, but he did not wish to seem too eager. Instead of staking his prestige on an open campaign for the number two position, he preferred that Stevenson make the gesture of coming to him. The challenge to Kennedy was how to get Stevenson to make his move. He therefore undertook what one presidential biographer has aptly described as a "surreptitious candidacy." He traveled, he gave speeches, he fought for control of the Massachusetts Democratic

Party. But he was loath to disclose his real objective, either to the public or to his wife.

As Jackie came to understand only after she established herself at Hickory Hill and began to spend solitary weekends there, Jack was already utterly caught up in the furious momentum toward the August 1956 Democratic convention. The battle for the Massachusetts party leadership, which pitted the senator against the present chairman, a plump, pugnacious onion farmer named William "Onions" Burke, was actually about who would control the state's delegation to the national convention. As Burke was opposed to Stevenson, were the current leader to be left in place, Kennedy would appear weak at the convention. Never before had Jack permitted himself to participate in a full-out local political mud-fight. But in the present emergency, it was clear that if he did not stoop, he could not conquer. His political operatives had never known him "so angry and frustrated" as he was during the fight, which came to a head when, at the close of a large fractious party meeting involving much booing, pushing, and grabbing at the gavel, and which threatened at several points to erupt in fisticuffs, the anti-Onions faction prevailed. At home as well, Jackie could not help but be struck by her husband's high agitation in the course of an internecine struggle that she gauged to be constantly in his thoughts.

Early in 1956, Jackie learned that she was pregnant. The baby was due in October, two months after the Democrats congregated in Chicago. News of the pregnancy was very pleasing to Jack, who made no secret of his desire for a large family like the one he had grown up in. Though Bobby and Ethel, who had four children and a fifth on the way, already enjoyed a substantial lead, Jack insisted that he and Jackie meant to catch up with them soon enough. For Jackie, children were integral to the life she hoped to have with Jack at Hickory Hill. She methodically set about assembling a nursery and otherwise equipping the house. For all of Jackie's great plans, however, her mother thought her just "too lonely" in the country, Jack being away so much. Nor, it turned out, did he intend to come home after Chicago. Whether or not he succeeded in becoming his party's vice-presidential nominee, he planned to go abroad immediately. The previous August, he had vacationed with Jackie in the South of France following his pas de deux with Gunilla. This year, as he wrote to his father on June 29, he expected to go with George Smathers right after the convention. When Jackie learned of her husband's plans, she asked him to forgo the trip, but Jack was unconquerable.

Finally, in a Chicago steak house on Friday, August 17, 1956, the last day of the weeklong Democratic convention, Jackie, twenty-seven years of age and seven months pregnant, broached the unhappy subject of the South of France with the big, brash, oily, jocose self-described "redneck" known to legions of Washington women as "Gorgeous George." Jackie disliked Smathers intensely. Smathers for his part had thought little of Jackie Bouvier when he first met her, and he had gone so far as to advise Jack that he believed he could do better, but the Florida senator had revised his opinion entirely when he saw the wonderful care Jackie Kennedy had given her husband during his long medical ordeal. In the recently published *Profiles in Courage*, which had been an immediate bestseller and a critical success, Kennedy had left unnamed the fellow senator who had unashamedly acknowledged to him that he always voted with the special interests in the expectation that they would remember him positively at election time and that the public would never know about, much less recall, his vote against their welfare. That politician had been George Smathers, now the chairman of the Florida delegation at the Chicago convention. He represented everything Kennedy had been writing against in his new book, yet it was he whom Kennedy asked to put his name into nomination at the International Amphitheater. Jackie's fraught encounter with Smathers took place after her husband, in the words of *The New York Times*, had come before the convention "as a movie star," when he narrated a slick Hollywood-produced documentary about the party; after Jack had nominated Stevenson in a speech painstakingly crafted to prove that the speaker was not just sexy but smart; after Stevenson had made the unexpected move of leaving the VP choice to the convention; and after the Kennedy contingent had stayed up all of Thursday night scrambling for delegates' votes.

Still rushing about on Friday, Jackie had paused to watch on a bank of television screens as her husband nearly secured the nomination, then lost to Estes Kefauver. Afterward, with one errant wing of his shirt collar inching upward as if he were a hastily dressed prep school student en route to dine with his parents, Jack faced the first failure he had ever known in public life. To make matters worse, he had to do it before an audience of 40 million at-home viewers. In a terse, gracious, gallant concession speech that Jackie sadly observed from a box in the Amphitheater, he asked that Kefauver be named by acclamation. Coming as it did at the close of a nail-biting real-life television drama, this affecting last little star turn consolidated what would henceforward be Kennedy's reputation as America's most telegenic politician. The vicissitudes of his unsuccessful bid for second spot on the ticket had riveted the nation, and in a matter of hours the modern-day alchemy of television had spun the name "Jack Kennedy" into political gold. Losing was far from delightful to him, certainly, but after his speech he left the hall in something very close to a haze of glory. "Don't feel sorry for young Jack Kennedy," proclaimed the *Boston Herald*. "He probably rates as the one real victor of the entire convention. His was the one new face that actually shone. His charisma, his dignity, his intellectuality, and in the end his gracious sportsmanship . . . are undoubtedly what those delegates will remember. So will those who watched it and heard it via TV and radio."

Following the great defeat, Kennedy and some of the people who were closest to him repaired to the steak house behind the Amphitheater. At the meal, Jackie, wearing a black dress and pearls, was crying openly. Eunice, said to look "like Jack in a wig," wept as well, but nowhere near as much as her sister-in-law. It had been thought wise to attempt to cushion Jackie somewhat from the hurly-burly of the politicking by having her stay with Eunice, who had a home in Chicago, while Jack roomed with Torby MacDonald, now a U.S. congressman. But in the end there really had been no protecting her. At one point during the convention, she had climbed up on a seat in her box to cheer Jack's nominating speech and to wave a Stevenson placard. At another, she had fled a reporter's questions by disappearing into a stairway that led to the bowels of the Amphitheater, then hiking up her dress and dashing across an underground parking garage. And on Thursday, she had stayed up through the night with other members of the (no-longer-"surreptitious") Kennedy campaign. In the course of the week, she had witnessed what might almost be described as her husband's apotheosis. She had seen the crowds of delegates press in on him from all sides wherever he went, heard the cheers and lavish praise for "her" Jack. She had watched the cup draw very near to his lips, but she had also been present when it was snatched away and given to another man. Clearly she had wanted this victory as much as Jack did, and at the steak house her demeanor left no doubt that she was, in the words of an observer, "very disappointed." So much so that Jack blamed what happened to her afterward on the frustrating outcome of the vice presidential balloting. "Jackie got too excited at the convention," the senator would tell his doctor in September. "It was all my fault for losing."

After the vote, Jackie was furious with Stevenson, who she believed had treated her husband shabbily at the convention. In contrast, by the time Jack reached the steak house, he was already contemplating what today's near-win might mean for the future. "I could really be president with a little more planning." Some people at the time saw Kennedy's decision to seek the vice-presidential nomination in 1956 as an important first break with his father. She who had had a chance to soak up the ether in Jack's childhood room at the Cape understood better than most that in fact his independence and ambition had taken root when he was a boy. Though it was solely in his imagination, he had been, as Jackie perceived, always moving, always charging forward, often in spite of his father's particular plans for him. The only real difference in Chicago was that the relentless momentum was suddenly palpable to everyone else as well. Now he meant to leave for the South of France, and as his wife had already discovered, in this matter as well there was to be no stopping him. Certainly nothing she said to Smathers when they faced each other at the steak house was going to change that. It sounds as if her words were flavored with irony when she told him: "Why don't you and Jack take a trip to the Mediterranean? He wants to go." With a flourish of faux-courtliness, Gorgeous George promptly "agreed," though in fact the yachting vacation had been arranged long before. Jack accompanied her as far as Massachusetts, where he declined to talk to reporters, with the explanation that he had had no sleep for three days. Not two hours later, he was gone.

On August 23 at Hammersmith Farm in Newport, Jackie began to hemorrhage. An emergency cesarean was performed at Newport Hospital, but the daughter whom she had planned to call Arabella was stillborn. Jack, on a chartered yacht with various young women who appear not to have been overly concerned with keeping their clothes on, was unreachable by phone or any other means. When at about two in the morning Jackie emerged from the vapors of anesthesia, the first face she glimpsed was that of Bobby Kennedy. After the convention, where Bobby had served as floor manager, Jack's thirty-year-old brother had left Chicago still fuming (Bobby seems ever to have been fuming) that the sole reason they had lost to Kefauver was that someone on the other side had "pulled something fishy." Directly, Bobby had gone off to rest at the Cape in anticipation of joining the Stevenson campaign, not because he had any particular love for the candidate, but rather because the experience would be helpful when Jack ran for president. And, whether Bobby liked it or not, his designated role was to be useful to Jack.

To this point in Jackie's story, Bobby has occupied a position at the margins of the narrative. Tonight, having raced from Hyannis Port, he appears center stage at Jackie's bedside with all of the fury and intensity that have long characterized the unhappy third of the original four Kennedy brothers. His "raging spirit," as Chuck Spalding would call it, was formed early in life as a consequence of Bobby's desire to "fight his way to the top" of a pecking order where his older brothers, who were both larger and personally more formidable than he, held sway. Scrape away the accumulated impasto of Bobby's ferocity, however, and there emerge reserves of tenderness and empathy that are suddenly on unrestrained display in his sister-in-law's hospital room. "Action Man," as someone dubbed him years later, takes charge immediately. He tells Jackie that she has lost the baby. He arranges for little Arabella's burial. He assures Rose Kennedy that he has chosen not to notify Jack because in view of Jackie's deep depression it would be best for them both if they did not see each other just yet. Convoluted reasoning, but given the supreme embarrassment of Jack's behavior, Rose seems eager to swallow it. In the older brother's absence, Bobby, who has not previously been especially close to Jackie, ministers to her needs as once she had for Jack when he was hospitalized.

Finally, on August 26, a day after the baby had been buried, Jackie heard her husband's voice on the telephone from Genoa. Directly—at the urging of George Smathers, who counseled him that to do otherwise would be disastrous for his presidential hopes—Jack returned to the United States. When he flew in to Newport on the twenty-eighth, an Auchincloss family member was waiting for him with a car. Even after Jack had been told about his daughter, he had been disinclined to return much before he was due to begin campaigning nationally for Stevenson in September, with an itinerary that promised to keep him busy until election day. Now, suddenly, he seemed frantic to reach the hospital. "I'll pay for any tickets," he said, pressing the driver to run stop signs and yellow lights en route. When at last he beheld Jackie at Newport Hospital, a week had passed since the convention, where it had been made manifest that the White House was suddenly achingly within their grasp. But a tremendous amount had changed in those few days. There could be no mistaking that he had come home to a wife who was angry, grieving, dispirited, confused about what came next. After two failed pregnancies, Jackie worried that she might never be able to have a child of her own, and after all those months of lovingly outfitting a nursery, she questioned whether she could bear to see Hickory Hill again, let alone live there in the future. To be sure, at this point she was as powerless to influence her husband's behavior as she had been when she spoke to George Smathers of the impending yachting holiday as though every fiber of her being were not ardently opposed to it. Yet for all that Chicago had done for Jack, she needed only to decide to walk away from the smoldering ruins of her marriage to destroy him politically.

Five

L et's face it. There are rumors going around in Washington about the senator and his wife, that they're not getting along, and that they've been separated. What about that?"

The woman asking the question was the *Look* magazine journalist Laura Bergquist. At work on a piece about the Kennedys, she was visiting the University of South Carolina campus, where the senator was about to deliver the commencement address. It was May 31, 1957; Dwight Eisenhower had begun his second term as president; and in the wake of the defeat of the Stevenson-Kefauver ticket, Jack Kennedy had decided to go after his party's 1960 presidential nomination. Following Kennedy's incandescent appearances in Chicago, so many speaking invitations had come in to his office as to fill the briefcase Ted Sorensen had presented him with after the ill-fated yachting holiday. In the intervening months, even when his campaign duties were done, he had been constantly in transit, coming home rarely, as Jackie later said, and then mostly to sleep. All the while, the political badinage at certain Washington dinner parties had begun to include talk about the senator and his wife. Newspaper coverage disclosing the family's inability to reach Jack on the Mediterranean while Jackie lay in Newport Hospital; the sudden, surprising sale of Hickory Hill to Bobby Kennedy; Jackie's having spent the better part of November 1956 abroad with her sister; the knowledge in Washington that she and her goatish husband were so often apart; and even a published story to the effect that in the aftermath of the stillbirth Joe Kennedy had paid Jackie a million dollars to remain in the marriage— all this had been responsible for the rumors that Bergquist had decided to raise with the Kennedy camp.

Though Sorensen, the upright, socially awkward twenty-nine-year-old senatorial aide to whom Bergquist had posed the question, did not in any obvious way resemble Kennedy, he was nevertheless oddly, even disturbingly, similar to his employer. Chuck Spalding judged that in the course of their professional association, Sorensen, whether unconsciously or by design, had by slow degrees "modeled himself, his gestures, his language, his thoughts" on Kennedy. Laura Bergquist perceived that Sorensen, whom she had known well prior to his association with Kennedy, had "picked up a lot of Kennedy's attitudes and mannerisms along the way." Given Sorensen's adoration of Kennedy, she described the process overall as an act of "passionate self-effacement." Joe Alsop, similarly, spoke of the aide's "self-abnegation." Of course, Sorensen needed to sound like the senator when writing for him. But before long, things had gone substantially beyond that. There came a point when, should the need present itself, Sorensen had no difficulty impersonating Kennedy on the office telephone. At such times, it was almost as if an alien spore had taken over Sorensen's body. But it was also the case that Sorensen had managed somehow to insinuate himself in Kennedy's head. The aide was proud of his ability, when conversing with Kennedy, to complete his boss's sentences and anticipate his questions.

Jackie found the dynamic creepy. Not without a palpable twinge of discomfort, she later insisted that she could remember when Sorensen began to ape her husband. She was sure the younger man had been blushing at the time. She perceived that he had "such a crush" on Jack and that that adulation was perilously rooted in feelings of "resentment" and "inferiority" on Sorensen's part. "I think he wanted to be easy all the ways Jack was easy." But then, her husband no doubt would have given much to possess Sorensen's easy way with a pen. McGeorge Bundy, later a national security adviser in the Kennedy administration, also picked up on the element of danger in, as he characterized it, "a relationship that was so close and so entangled and so full of worry to both" men. Indeed, that May of 1957, the relationship had been on the verge of imploding. Kennedy had just won the Pulitzer Prize for *Profiles in Courage*, and Sorensen had been making noises about town that in fact he had written a good deal of the book for the senator. Word of another man's considerable involvement in the preparation of a work for which Kennedy alone had won the Pulitzer seeped into the public discourse in the form of charges by the culture critic Gilbert Seldes, who wrote on May 15 in *The Village Voice* about the senator's having had a collaborator; and later and far more explosively by the political columnist Drew Pearson, who spoke on national television of Kennedy's having used the services of a ghostwriter. It is easy to see why in the wake of the literary award Sorensen would resent his position vis-à-vis Kennedy. Kennedy's abiding upset, as Bundy perceived it, about the need to employ a writer is also understandable. Finally, that month, Sorensen accepted a payment, which he regarded at the time as "more than fair," in exchange for his written agreement to back off from seeking public recognition of the extent of his role in Kennedy's writing life.

So in the end, contrary to rumor, it had not been Jackie who had had to be paid off lest she behave in such a way as to damage her husband politically. The real recipient of the hush money had been Sorensen, whom she would long persist in calling "sneaky." At a moment when Jackie was widely believed to be at odds with her husband, she cast herself, neither for the first time nor the last, as Jack's one-woman Praetorian Guard. Rather than futilely wax indignant about Jack's repeated betrayals of her, she found it much more satisfying to focus on what others had done to him. "Jack forgave so quickly," she later recalled, "but I never forgave Ted Sorensen. I watched him like a hawk for a year or so." Strange to say, the garrulous ghostwriter, whom her husband had meanwhile contrived to clutch with hoops of steel, also saw himself as Kennedy's impassioned defender. Sorensen responded to the question about marital rumors, as Bergquist remembered, "rather heatedly." "Well, that's not true," said Sorensen, who when speaking of his boss had a tendency to sound, at least to Bergquist's ear, a bit self-righteous. "As a matter of fact, I can tell you this in confidence. Jackie is pregnant and that's why she's not traveling with him." At the time Sorensen made that statement, Jackie was three months pregnant and had no plans to trumpet the news that she was expecting. If anything went wrong, the prospect of its being rehearsed in the press, as the stillbirth had been, horrified her. Additionally, Jackie had been eager to minimize any worries or pressures on herself for the duration of the pregnancy. So the gossip about her marriage, the gathering storm about the authorship of *Profiles in Courage*, and finally a series of newspaper items about the pregnancy, notably one by the Broadway columnist Dorothy Kilgallen, were especially unwelcome.

On August 3, 1957, Jackie, accompanied by her husband, rushed to Lenox Hill Hospital on the Upper East Side of Manhattan, but sadly by the time they got there, it was already too late. Moments before they entered the hospital, Black Jack Bouvier had died of cancer of the liver, aged sixty-six. While the Canfields, who had been in Italy at the time, traveled to the States, Jackie, now six months pregnant, oversaw the arrangements for the funeral service at St. Patrick's Cathedral on Fifth Avenue and the burial in East Hampton, Long Island. Confronted with the signature sunlamp tan from which the appellation "Black Jack" derived, the undertaker, assuming he was only doing what the family would want, painted the corpse over with flesh-toned makeup. Upon seeing the professional's handiwork, a dismayed Bouvier nephew—who as chance would have it possessed some competence in the mortician's art—set about to restore Black Jack to his customary swarthiness. There was a modest turnout at the funeral Mass, where the entire rear pew consisted of women in inky-black veils, who, though largely unknown to the family, were said to be some of Black Jack's lovers. Prior to the closing of the casket, "the most beautiful daughter a man ever had" undid a bracelet from her wrist and tenderly deposited the trinket, which Black Jack had given her as a graduation gift when she was a girl, in his hand.

Three months later, Jackie gave birth at New York's Lying-in Hospital on November 27, 1957. This time, her husband could hardly have been nicer or more attentive. It was Jack who wheeled in the newborn when Jackie first saw their daughter. "I don't think he really knew what loving someone was like until he had Caroline," remembered Betty Coxe Spalding. "He was adorable with her from the beginning." Jack was unreserved in his love for the child, intent, he later told his friend Debo Devonshire, on being physically affectionate, as Rose Kennedy had never been when he was a boy. As a parent, Jackie proved to be the more physically reserved of the couple. Nonetheless, a shared passion for their daughter, and subsequently for John Junior, would do much to help sustain the marriage in some exceptionally difficult times. The birth of Caroline was also politically useful. Senator and Mrs. Kennedy posed on the cover of the April 21, 1958, issue of *Life* magazine, with Jack holding the infant in his lap. The image satisfyingly, if belatedly, filled out the trajectory that had begun with the engagement pictures in *Life* and had been followed by the photographs in *McCall's* of the happy young marrieds at their rented Georgetown residence. By the time this new cover image appeared on newsstands, the Kennedys at last owned a home of their own, a three-story redbrick edifice on N Street in Georgetown, where more often than not Jackie remained with their daughter, while the senator traveled in anticipation of 1960.

It was during this signal period, from 1958 to 1960, that Jackie embarked on the next major phase of her Washington education. The first had taken place on Dumbarton Avenue, under the somewhat erratic but nonetheless highly effective tutelage of John White. This time her classroom moved across the street, where Joe Alsop, having recently returned from a year in Paris, proved eager to take her on. Hoping to serve Jack's interests by becoming the wife she believed he wanted and needed right then, Jackie in turn proved an apt pupil. Afterward, she remembered Alsop's tutorials with affection and appreciation. To look at, the curmudgeonly stager and the chirpy young Washington wife made a curious couple. Both used cigarettes, his ripped in two and screwed, at times a bit frenziedly, into a yellowing holder, as theatrical properties. Both spoke in an excruciatingly affected way, Joe's strangulated accent and intonation causing him to evoke, as someone once said, Charles Laughton essaying the role of Oscar Wilde; Jackie's mannered, whispery voice suggesting a repressed version of Marilyn Monroe. And, not least, Joe and Jackie were both perilously thin-skinned public people whose gifts of ridicule and raillery at once shielded and subverted them.

As Alsop surveyed a guest over his trademark massive circular dark horn-rimmed spectacles, he liked to cup his sagging, spotted face with his hands, giving him the appearance of someone suffering with a toothache in both jaws. At the outset, he saw Jackie as a "starter" who despite anything she had done or endured to date was suddenly at the very beginning of the particular race she had been designated to run in life. He judged that of all the starters he had seen and worked with in the course of his career, there had never previously been another who merited, in his phrase, "a higher handicap." Despite her immense potential, however, he also perceived that she possessed nowhere nearly enough self-confidence. That was where Joe came in. Joe, the cousin of Theodore and Franklin Roosevelt. Joe, the political and social arbiter. Joe, the aesthete and intellectual snob. Joe, who had briefly removed himself to Paris because he feared that his best years professionally might already be past.

Joe, who saw a Kennedy candidacy as a chance not just for the country's renewal, but, equally if not more importantly, for his own.

He was the person to go to for the facts and statistics regarding the deficiencies of Eisenhower's defense posture, but he was also the man who could tell you, with equal ardor, which restaurant was to be avoided because the owners did not systematically rotate the wine bottles in their racks. During Churchill's postwar administration Alsop had been the first newsman in Washington to learn that the prime minister had secretly suffered a stroke, but he could also be depended on to know all the choicest details about the European grande dame whose ornate dress had been intercepted by the customs authorities because of the danger of fowl pest being carried in its pheasant feathers. Such was the mentor who set about to help prepare Jackie Kennedy for what he was to call her "high role" in history. Now he spoke to her of power and politics, now of food and furniture. He gave her carefully chosen books, and regaled her with gossipy accounts of previous Washington wives who had experienced challenges similar to hers. Seeking to toughen Jackie against the myriad petty vexations of political life, he offered perspective when she was distressed; and, though known when upset to chew on his knuckles until they bled, he encouraged her to view her own challenges dispassionately. By turns, he sat with her, telephoned her, wrote to her, walked with her, and sailed with her.

Jackie had other counselors as well. A former Los Angeles shopgirl, Jayne Wrightsman was the the second wife of the Oklahoma oil tycoon Charles Wrightsman, whose social ambitions were said to be "as sizable as his fortune." Spurned by the old guard in Palm Beach in the 1940s, the couple set about to win social acceptance by reinventing themselves as free-spending connoisseurs of art and antiques, with an emphasis on eighteenth-century France. Mrs. Wrightsman, in particular, pored over art history books; conferred with curators, dealers, and other experts; and taught herself to distinguish between, in Alsop's words, "objects that are merely good of their kind, and objects of truly great quality." She imbibed the principle that the highest test of a collector is not whether the collection includes only things of the best quality, but rather whether the owner has composed the collection "as a true, independent work of art." And that, Alsop proclaimed of her Fifth Avenue apartment, where the decor fairly screamed magnificence and museum-quality, she had assuredly accomplished.

Alsop was no less in awe of Rachel "Bunny" Mellon, Jackie's other, even more significant adviser in matters of style and fashion. The Listerine mouthwash heiress, whose second husband, Paul Mellon, was the heir to a great banking fortune, subscribed to an aesthetic, if not to a form of snobbery, that could hardly have been more different from the Wrightsmans' approach. Jayne Wrightsman's personal narrative highlighted the infinite labor devoted to perfecting her taste and amassing her collections. Bunny Mellon, though equally painstaking and attentive to minutiae (such as the weeds she contrived to grow to precisely the right height between carefully irregular patio stonework), preferred to be admired for her ease and artlessness. She exemplified the idea that naturalness is perhaps the greatest affectation. Jayne Wrightsman's homes were all about show and splendor. Bunny Mellon lived by the dictum "Nothing should be noticed." Ostentation was anathema to her. Her raincoat was sable-lined, the fur being for her pleasure alone, not for display. Master gardener; art and rare-book collector; creator of beautiful, resolutely comfortable and serene homes in Upperville, Virginia, and other settings; devotee of the couturiers Cristóbal Balenciaga and Hubert de Givenchy, Bunny Mellon did not hesitate to pour vast sums of money into her projects—she simply thought it vulgar if the effort and expenditure were apparent. She also religiously shunned publicity as degrading to one's personal dignity, a notion that, however appealing to Jackie personally, was fundamentally at odds with the whole Kennedy ethos, indeed, with some of the practical advice Alsop was to offer her in this period.

As Jackie shed the last lingering vestiges of the "sloppy kid" that Bill

Walton fondly remembered her as having been during her John White phase, the question presented itself: Would the rarefied tastes and attitudes, the particular styles of dress and decor, that she had been cultivating help or hinder politically? There was no sense, as she made it clear to Alsop, in which she wanted to be perceived as acting "at cross purposes" with Jack. However it might sometimes appear, she really did mean to be a political plus. According to Walton, who, as an artist, was also known to advise Jackie on visual matters, she wanted so to please Jack: "She got elegant for him." But how would this increasingly chic young woman be received by the American people? What would voters make of her bouffant hairstyle, couturier costumes, and penchant for all things French? How would the country react to the sprightly remarks that always played so well in the deep-red-lacquered dining room at Joe Alsop's? Jackie's comments in this vein often had a lurking sting. What, someone wanted to know, did the French motto "Honi soit qui mal y pense" (Evil to him who evil thinks) inscribed in gold on her belt mean? "Love me, love my dog," she helpfully explained. Told of the religious prejudice that threatened to torpedo her husband's presidential hopes, she returned: "I think it's so unfair of people to be against Jack because he's a Catholic. He's such a poor Catholic. Now, if it were Bobby, I could understand it." Asked where she thought the upcoming Democratic national convention ought to be conducted, she deadpanned: "Acapulco." The matter of Jackie's political viability was fervently discussed within the Kennedy camp, and for all of her snark and sophistication, these conversations were capable of cutting her to the quick. When, in conference with his political team Dave Powers and Kenny O'Donnell, the senator wondered aloud if America was "ready" for Jackie, indeed, if it might be best to run her through subliminally in a quick-flash television spot so no one would notice her, she ran out of the room in tears.

The question of whether, in his oft-repeated phrase, Jack's wife had "too much status and not enough quo" would be merely academic, however, if he failed to make a compelling case for why Americans should vote for him. He began to find his voice as a presidential candidate in the summer of 1958, when, soon to run for another Senate term, he assailed Eisenhower for permitting the United States to become dangerously weak in the face of soaring Soviet military strength. In a landmark August 14, 1958, Senate address, Kennedy forecast (inaccurately, as it turned out) an imminent "missile gap" when Washington would cede nuclear superiority to Moscow. Alluding to Churchill's 1936 speech "The Locust Years," one of the addresses collected in *Arms and the Covenant* that had so fascinated Kennedy as a young man in London, he made the case that the Eisenhower years had been "the years the locusts have eaten." Kennedy argued that the present Republican administration had put fiscal security ahead of national security, and that that policy would soon bring the United States into even graver danger. Yet, he maintained, it was still possible to catch up. "In the words of Sir Winston Churchill in a dark time of England's history, 'Come then—let us to the task, to the battle and the toil—each to our part, each to our station. . . . There is not a week, nor a day, nor an hour to be lost.'" With the missile gap speech, Kennedy began to run for president, as Harold Macmillan later said, "on the Churchill ticket." Here and in subsequent addresses, the candidate asked voters to examine present international problems through the prism of interwar Britain, when the Nazi threat had been foolishly ignored. Kennedy portrayed himself as a statesman in the tradition of Churchill, prepared to tell the unwelcome truth and to demand the sacrifices necessary to guard American supremacy against the Soviets, who, he emphasized, hoped to bury the United States not only militarily, but also economically, politically, culturally, and in every other sphere of interest. He argued that under Eisenhower the United States had lost ground in each of these areas.

JFK finally had a chance to meet Churchill when he and Jackie vacationed in the South of France after the Senate adjourned. It is at this point that a celebrated or, depending on how one views it, notorious vessel, part secure residence, part floating pleasure palace, materializes however briefly in Jackie's story for the first time. The senator's unhappy encounter with the hero of his life took place aboard the *Christina*, the former wartime escort frigate owned by the Greek shipping magnate Aristotle Onassis. Churchill had first met Onassis at Roquebrune, near Monte Carlo, in 1956, when they were introduced at dinner by Churchill's son, Randolph. Two years later, Churchill, who had been staying in Cap d'Ail since the end of July 1958, was about to embark on his first cruise on the *Christina*, which was scheduled to begin in late September. Onassis had the well-earned reputation of a celebrity-hunter who loved to play host to the Greta Garbos of this world. For the moment, anyway, he regarded Churchill as the greatest trophy guest of them all. Churchill's physician, Lord Moran, wondered in his diary whether it was "the man or the yacht" that appealed to Churchill. "He is a little fellow," the doctor dryly noted of Onassis, "not as tall as Winston when they stand side by side." Clementine Churchill worried, by no means for the first time in a half-century of that difficult but delightful marriage, that her husband had fallen in with a bad element. She disapproved not so much of Winston's love of luxury as of his willingness to countenance the personal and ethical shortcomings of those in a position to provide the good things and surroundings he craved. Hilariously, Churchill's Cap d'Ail host Lord Beaverbrook, whom Clementine had been known to scorn for precisely this reason, shared, perhaps even exceeded, her indignation about Winston's new friend and benefactor, over whom such an air of disreputableness hung. Unmentioned in any of this, of course, was that a similar air had long hung over Churchill, who like his father before him had been widely regarded as an opportunist and adventurer.

In the course of a controversial and rampaging business career, Onassis had catapulted from penury in the aftermath of the Greco-Turkish War of 1922 to a personal worth estimated to be in the area of $500 million. Determined never to have to answer to shareholders or a board of directors, he individually managed about a hundred interlocking companies housed in a dozen nations. With Churchill, however, Onassis was always prepared, even eager, to abase himself symbolically. Metamorphosed into a devoted caregiver, he would tenderly brush the hairs from Churchill's coat collar and even spoon-feed him caviar, as one might feed an infant. These days, there were moments when the old man's bulbous, pink-veined eyes were blank and expressionless, other times when they gleamed again with interest and humor. Onassis, reveling in the luster that Churchill's presence seemed to confer upon him, was happy to dote on the former prime minister whether he was wonderfully alert and talkative or, as was often the case now, a mere shell of his previous self.

Unfortunately, Churchill was in the latter state when Jack Kennedy, attired in a white dinner jacket, and Jackie, in a white Saint Laurent trapeze dress, accompanied by the Gianni Agnellis, the William Douglas-Homes and some other friends, came to see him on Onassis's yacht. Weeks from his eighty-fourth birthday, the titan proved to be, at least on this particular occasion, quite beyond useful conversation. JFK had been, Jackie remembered, "so hungry to talk to Churchill at last," but it quickly became apparent that he had waited too long to approach him. Usually so calculatedly nonchalant, Jack could scarcely hide his upset afterward. Jackie saw and understood his immense disappointment, yet to all outward appearances she seemed to be inhabiting almost an alternate emotional universe when she mocked: "I think he thought you were the waiter, Jack."

When the Kennedys returned to the United States, they were greeted by disturbing political news. Presumably due to his stance on the St. Lawrence Seaway, his joust with Onions Burke, and certain other controversies during his first term, his vote count in the Boston senatorial primary was not all it ought to have been for a presidential aspirant. Presently, Jackie accompanied her husband during the statewide campaign, which she would remember as a blur of seemingly endless cars and hotels. "Just running, running." At length, the senator handily reclaimed his seat with more than 73 percent of the vote, the largest popular margin any political candidate in the state had ever received. And then, at least as his wife experienced it, he was gone again, away almost every weekend and more, as he sped from state to state in anticipation of 1960.

Meanwhile, Jackie endeavored to give him, in Bill Walton's words, "his first really marvelous house." Walton, who, like Alsop, enjoyed separate and distinct relationships with Jack and Jackie, had a unique take on the senator's visual predilections. Many people then and later assumed such things were of little concern to Kennedy. Not so, insisted Walton: "A big, rich, well-run house, he'd look at it with envy. He'd comment on it. He was always absolutely aware . . . what women wore, what service was on the table, how the place looked, totally aware. It always amazed me, the accuracy of his reporting about it." His parents' houses had never been of the sort he later came to admire, and his subsequent living arrangements as a Washington bachelor had been characterized by a certain dishevelment bordering on squalor. For many years thereafter, the fastidious Joe Alsop liked to tell the tale of his first alarming encounter with Jack in the Kennedy siblings' Georgetown house, which appeared to have suffered "from the ravages of a small, particularly unruly tornado." Jackie meant to provide Jack with something else, something she sensed he wanted very much. But her exertions were not to be understood solely in terms of his needs, or for that matter of the way in which he and his family had been known to live. Jackie's family was also a reference point. To Walton's eye, on N Street she was aiming at a level of refinement considerably beyond anything the mistress of Hammersmith Farm and Merrywood had ever accomplished. Jackie pointedly had never wanted to be what she saw as a Newport wife, and so it was now. "The Auchinclosses lived awfully well," Walton reflected, "but not with the elegance that Jackie eventually [attained]."

That aspiration went to the heart of the problem as Jack came to perceive it. For all of his family's wealth, he was nothing if not cheap. And the constant physical upheaval in the house, as Jackie chased an ever-elusive ideal of taste and charm, was indeed a tremendous source of irritation to him. Still, when he protested the expenditure; when he insisted that she return *objets* that had been sent over on approval; and when he was adamant that the high-Wasp decorator Sister Parish, a friend of Mrs. Mellon's, be fired partway through a new complete redo at N Street, there was a clear consistent subtext that transcended money and comfort. It was the old issue of political viability, of whether Jackie was not fast becoming too rare a bird to appeal to voters.

Nearly half a century later, Bunny Mellon said of her: "She knew all about the women, of course, but she stuck, and decided she was going to do a good job." Which no doubt made it so much worse when he balked at Jackie's efforts in that respect. Jackie saw a good deal less of him than she would have liked to in this period, yet when they were together, aside from the usual carping about furniture, wallpaper, and the like, he was often simply too fatigued to say very much. Finally, during a chinning session with Joe Alsop, Jackie questioned whether it was "really worth it" to have Jack seek the presidency. Calmly but authoritatively (though it cannot be guaranteed that at no point was Alsop tempted to lift his knuckles to his lips), he reassured her: "It's the only game that's worth the candle."

Set to take place in April 1960, the Wisconsin Democratic presidential primary, which pitted Kennedy against Senator Hubert Humphrey of the neighboring state of Minnesota, was to be the first major test of Kennedy's political strength. Beginning in January, Jackie joined her husband on the hustings. She cut a piquant figure, carrying the novel *War and Peace* under one arm of a beautifully cut red coat that proved to be a Givenchy copy. By turns, she complained that the people of Wisconsin were "really hard" and she conquered voters with her hushed voice and protestations of shyness. She despaired that the citizenry recoiled from her overtures, yet, on one occasion, she adroitly smoothed the feathers of an audience that her husband had kept waiting for an hour. It was said of her that she could be aloof and arrogant, but also that when she and Senator Kennedy worked opposite sides of the avenue, she always seemed to draw the larger crowds.

During this time, her reading, apparently, was by no means limited to Tolstoy. On election night, when she encountered a reporter named Miles McMillin who had written critically of her husband, Jackie, rather than follow Jack's example and be polite to the newsman, twice cut him dead. Following a huge win in Wisconsin, the Kennedys went on to barnstorm in West Virginia, where the senator scored another considerable victory. And then, almost imperceptibly at first, Jackie receded from public view.

At the cottage that she and Jack had on the Hyannis Port property, she secluded herself among the plants and flowers that Sister Parish had arranged to have sent over from a source in Boston. Excitedly, Jackie reported to the decorator that Jack had changed his mind after all about finishing the latest redo at N Street. The last time she had spoken to Mrs. Parish about any of this, Jackie had been nearly in tears; now her voice on the phone emanated the old enthusiasm. While she was at the Cape, she wanted Mrs. Parish to return to the charge at the couple's Georgetown house immediately. Meanwhile, in view of what had happened to her in 1956, Jackie hesitated to disclose even to Joe Alsop that she was pregnant again. In a phone conversation with her mentor shortly before the Democratic National Convention, she found that she still could not tell him why, alone among the Kennedy tribe, she would be absent from Los Angeles that July. Jack finally explained it all to Alsop in advance of a public announcement issued by his campaign. Once the news had been blazoned to the world, Dorothy Kilgallen, who was emerging as something of a specialist in the matter of Jackie Kennedy's pregnancies, insisted on maintaining a properly skeptical posture. She snidely suggested that Jackie was not really pregnant and that the senator's people had devised the ruse to sideline a wife who was simply too fey and fancy to be embraced by voters. The charges scorched, not because Jackie had been lying, but rather because the columnist had it right about the Kennedy campaign's ambivalence about the senator's spouse.

Following the convention, where Jack Kennedy became his party's

1960 presidential nominee, Alsop, who had been in Los Angeles to cover the proceedings, flew to Massachusetts to celebrate with the family at the Cape. He brought with him a gift for Jackie. It was a rare copy of *Manoeuvring*, an 1809 novel by Maria Edgeworth, about a woman whose stratagems in life produce results that are the very opposite of what she had intended. Amid the general rejoicing in Hyannis Port, Jackie greeted her guest in full war paint. In the course of several meals, as well as on a boat trip they took together, she spoke to Alsop of her discontent. She railed against the press. She protested the personal questions that reporters felt free to lob at her, and complained of the news photographers who seemed intent on transforming her daughter into, in Jackie's phrase, "a ghastly little Shirley Temple." She evinced irritation with her Kennedy sisters-in-law, who all seemed to "adore" the publicity process that Jackie had grown to detest in the years since her first photo shoot at Hyannis Port after Jack proposed.

Both in person and in a follow-up letter from Washington, Alsop pressed her to try to view the privacy problem unemotionally. He urged her to accept that as the wife of a presidential candidate she was just going to have to do things she would never have undertaken had she been, as Alsop archly put it, "plain Mrs. Kennedy of New York, London, and the Riviera." He suggested, for instance, that it would be wise if in addition to the relentless chatter in the press about her taste for European haute couture, there were also some articles about her buying her maternity clothes at the American department store Bloomingdale's. Though initially resistant to much of this, Jackie finally admitted to having been "unreasonable." In the interest of peace, she pledged to follow Joe's advice.

But peace, she discovered, was not so easily to be had. The newly anointed Democratic candidate's wife was pummeled by angry letter writers who mocked her hairstyle as a "floor-mop" and complained that she spent too lavishly on couturier clothes. The trade paper *Women's Wear Daily* and other publications similarly targeted her shopping habits.

Finally, the Kennedy people summoned reporters to the Waldorf Towers in New York, where, in keeping with Alsop's recommendations, Jackie dutifully modeled various inexpensive, American-made maternity dresses. For all of her forced cooperativeness and unctuous good cheer, however, a morsel of unalloyed snark did creep into her comments. Scoffing at reports that she spent $30,000 a year at the houses of Balenciaga and Givenchy, Jackie declared: "I couldn't spend that much unless I wore sable underwear."

Six

L ater, Jackie would tell the story of her marriage to Jack Kennedy in terms of his evolving sense of her political viability—a process that, as she saw it, was not complete until the very last hours of his life.

"I had worked so hard at the marriage," she told the Rev. Richard T. McSorley, a Jesuit priest who counseled her after the assassination. "I had made an effort and succeeded and he had really come to love me and to congratulate me on what I did for him."

Jackie constructed a similar narrative when she spoke to the society decorator Billy Baldwin of her sense of the state of the marriage at the time her husband was murdered, in 1963: "It took a very long time for us to work everything out, but we did, and we were about to have a real life together. I was going to campaign with him."

The couple had been married for seven years when Jack Kennedy defeated his Republican opponent, Richard Nixon, in the 1960 presidential election. JFK had at last reached the goal he had been hurtling toward for nearly the entire time he had been with Jackie, who was now thirty-one years of age. In the beginning, he had married for political reasons, confessedly and unabashedly so. The presidential hopeful had needed a wife, if only to eradicate his frivolous playboy image. But Jackie Bouvier, when he selected her, had had significant other advantages as well. She had not just been any attractive young woman, but rather one who, by virtue of her mother's advantageous second marriage, promised to confer upon Jack the luster of old Newport, Rhode Island, society that Joe Kennedy Senior so ardently desired for his boy.

From the outset of the marriage, Jackie had been accustomed to being spoken of by the patriarch and his surviving elder sons, Jack and Bobby, in tones of icy expediency. She had had to learn to navigate life with a man who was often absent, frequently ill, and perpetually unfaithful. She had had to live among people who, though most never mentioned the subject to her, were aware of her husband's infidelity, and who, fond of the young wife though they professed to be, could always be expected to put Jack's interests first. Along the way, she who had been brought in to help her husband politically had had to face the reality that he and his counselors had begun to wonder whether she might actually be doing him more harm than good.

Such questions about Jackie's usefulness remained very much in play at the time of JFK's narrow victory in 1960; indeed, they were amplified in the run-up to Inauguration Day, when a controversy over the first-lady-to-be's plans for the White House caused her husband to erupt in anger.

"Not one of my cabinet officers has had an interview," Jack confronted Jackie when he arrived in Washington on November 23, 1960, to celebrate Thanksgiving with her and their daughter. "Would you mind telling me what the hell Tish Baldrige is doing?"

In the weeks since the election, Jack had been at his father's house in Palm Beach, by turns resting and assembling his administration. Jackie had remained at their N Street residence in anticipation of giving birth by cesarean section at Georgetown University Hospital on December 12. In the meantime, she had hired an old friend, Letitia Baldrige, who like Jackie had attended both Miss Porter's and Vassar, to be her White House social secretary.

The Roman-nosed, six-foot-one Baldrige's tenure began calamitously when, on November 22, in response to reporters' questions, she affected a bantering manner that left it unclear at times whether she was speaking seriously or not. She announced that Mrs. Kennedy intended to make the White House a showcase of contemporary culture. She winked that the new first lady would enliven the premises with displays of current art. She jested that Jackie might even choose to temporarily hang certain twentieth-century works over paintings that had long been on exhibit. More often than not on this occasion, Baldrige's remarks were the lighthearted whim of the moment, but the journalists' pencils flew nonetheless. Also in this vein, Baldrige referred to the innumerable clubwomen across America who would soon be trying to meet her boss as "those great vast hordes of females." Even more interesting to the press people were her comments on Mamie Eisenhower's failure thus far to invite her successor to tour the White House before the thirty-fourth president and his wife moved out. It was not so much anything the new social secretary said about Mrs. Eisenhower that the journalists seized upon as it was the faint tone of mockery in which, to certain ears at least, she appeared to say it.

The next day's papers, which Jack read on the flight up from Palm Beach, rang with the incident. "Jack got so mad," Jackie later remembered. "It was the first set of bad, sensational headlines." On the one hand, the controversy was all rather absurd. Given the magnitude of the issues that had figured in the presidential campaign, the prospect of a new first lady's hanging modern pictures in the White House hardly seemed worth agonizing about. On the other hand, the tempest over Jackie's intentions reflected the unease in some quarters about the potentially tectonic cultural shift represented by the outcome of the 1960 presidential election. Politically, culturally, philosophically, Dwight Eisenhower really had been the ordinary heartland American portrayed in his TV advertising campaign when he ran for president in 1952. Eight years later, a good deal of the national nervousness about what the election of Jack Kennedy might mean for the country seemed to manifest itself in anxiety about Kennedy's wife.

Eager to make himself more palatable to voters, JFK, despite a lifetime of reading and study, often found it useful to play the yahoo to his supposedly more cultivated spouse. Still, at a moment when Kennedy remained acutely sensitive about his narrow margin of victory (the Democrat won the popular vote by a mere 118,574), he was furious about all the bad press Baldrige had drawn to the incoming administration. The intimation of contempt—for venerable White House traditions, for American clubwomen, for Mamie Eisenhower—that many listeners had detected in Baldrige's flippant comments seemed to confirm previous hints of Mrs. Kennedy's sense of cultural superiority.

Jack's upset spoiled what was supposed to have been a happy family reunion. As scheduled, he headed back to Florida the following day. The family-owned aircraft carrying the president-elect had nearly reached Palm Beach when JFK—who believed that the stresses of political life had been responsible for Jackie's 1956 stillbirth—found himself abruptly summoned back to Washington on the news that she had gone into premature labor. Delivered by cesarean section shortly past midnight on November 25, the couple's new six-pound, three-ounce son, John F. Kennedy Jr., had inadequately developed lungs and needed to be placed in an incubator. Over the course of the nearly two weeks that followed, as Jackie and the newborn remained in the hospital and Jack shifted his transition headquarters to Washington in order to stay close to his son, the Baldrige controversy dragged on in the form of newspaper articles that portrayed the "dim view" taken by Washington traditionalists of Jackie's White House agenda, as previewed by her social secretary.

Meanwhile, it turned out that JFK had not been the only prominent political figure whom Baldrige had annoyed. At a moment when Eisenhower was still stinging from JFK's relentless disparagement of his leadership, there was much distress at the White House about the attention that had been focused on Mamie Eisenhower's failure to receive Jackie. Directly, pressure from Mrs. Eisenhower led to Jackie's reluctant acceptance of a belated invitation, which came with assurances that a wheelchair would be available should she need one. The visit had to be squeezed in between the younger woman's discharge from the hospital, on the morning of Friday, December 9, and the flight to Palm Beach with her husband and children several hours thereafter.

In the event, the promised wheelchair never materialized, which meant that Jackie, still weak and in considerable discomfort following major surgery, was required to tour the mansion on foot. Whether that, or the failure even to ask her to sit down at any point, had been an oversight on Mamie Eisenhower's part or the expression of malice Jackie believed it to be, the ordeal robbed her of her last bit of strength at a moment when she felt as if she had almost none left. When Jackie finally got to Palm Beach, she lapsed into a "weeping fit" and spent the better part of the next two weeks in bed.

Jackie continued to be ill and dispirited on Inauguration Day, January 20, 1961. When, in the hours after her husband's hugely successful inaugural address, she awakened for the first time in the White House family quarters, where she had gone to rest, paralyzing muscle spasms gripped both legs. Dr. Janet Travell, summoned from the reviewing platform where she had been watching the inaugural parade with America's new thirty-fifth president, gave Jackie a Dexedrine in hopes the drug would help sustain her through the round of parties that were scheduled to begin at ten P.M. It would not be long before far more potent and dangerous medications would be required if the newly minted first lady were to fulfill her official duties.

In the meantime, an air of elation settled over the White House, where JFK was soon boasting of a 72 percent approval rating, numbers even better than Eisenhower had enjoyed after a single month in office. Kennedy's inaugural address had thrilled the nation with its soaring rhetoric and Churchillian themes. In the manner of Churchill, Kennedy took as his starting point the way in which the introduction of nuclear weapons at the end of the Second World War had made the world a very different place. "For man holds in his mortal hands the power to abolish all forms of human poverty and all forms of human life." Churchill in various postwar addresses had postulated exactly this choice. Like his political and intellectual hero, Kennedy urged East and West to "begin anew the quest for peace, before the dark powers of destruction unleashed by science engulf all humanity in planned or accidental self-destruction." Also like Churchill, the new young president insisted that it would be a grave mistake to tempt the other side with weakness. "For only when our arms are sufficient beyond doubt," said Kennedy, "can we be certain beyond doubt that they will never be employed."

Drawing on his pivotal conversations with David Ormsby-Gore about the policy of outmaneuvering Moscow through contact and agreements ("the strategy of peace," as candidate Kennedy had dubbed it), JFK declared: "Let both sides, for the first time, formulate serious and precise proposals for the inspection and control of arms." That longed-for crucial first agreement with the Soviets had eluded Churchill. For Kennedy, it was the "beginning" to which he had referred in the course of the campaign ("The problem is to find a beginning") and to which he repeatedly returned in his inaugural speech ("begin anew the quest for peace," "So let us begin anew," "But let us begin"). Kennedy's oratorical triumph suggested to many listeners, both at home and abroad, that he might indeed be just the man to reverse the humiliations (the downing of an American U-2 reconnaissance aircraft over the Soviet Union and the resultant breakup of the four-power Paris peace conference attended by Eisenhower and other world leaders) that had blighted the thirty-fourth president's last months in power and diminished voter confidence in Eisenhower.

The postinaugural euphoria did not last long, however. On April 20, 1960, Jackie observed something that, she later reflected, she had only seen once before, in 1954, when her husband had been so ill and depressed after the botched back surgery that nearly killed him. This morning, in their private quarters at the White House, she watched Jack drop his head into his hands and weep. He had previously authorized a CIA plan to overthrow the Cuban dictator Fidel Castro, which had been handed down to him from the Eisenhower administration. Now the attack, undertaken by a force of U.S.-trained Cuban exiles, had come to grief. Castro crowed that he had captured nearly two thousand prisoners and that the U.S.-backed invasion had been thwarted.

That day, President Kennedy, who had seemed so ebullient in recent weeks, had the appearance of a "shattered" man—like someone who had just endured "an acute shock." Within a few months of coming to office, he who had repeatedly cited the loss of power and prestige in the Eisenhower years had now himself overseen a debacle that had much of the world puzzling about what looked to be unprecedented new American incompetence. He who had excoriated Eisenhower for a failure to approach the 1960 four-power Paris peace talks from a position of strength would now himself have to embark on previously scheduled top-level meetings with France and the Soviet Union at a moment when American, not to mention JFK's own personal, prestige, had been badly tarnished. As a consequence of the failed invasion, France's leader, Charles de Gaulle, regarded Kennedy as "inept," and Russia's leader, Nikita Khrushchev, judged him to be "a soft, not very decisive young man" who had lacked the nerve to send in U.S. forces after the Cuban exiles failed. In the States, Eisenhower, when he conferred with Kennedy about the fiasco, seized the opportunity to privately humiliate his successor by cataloging the mistakes, both of planning and execution, that had led to defeat.

Jackie, for her part, found the spectacle of Jack's public failure almost unbearable to witness. "She was undone by it," remembered Betty Coxe Spalding, who spent the weekend with the Kennedys after the Cuban debacle, "and undone by the fact that he was so upset by it." Lest the first lady's depression prevent her from accompanying him to Europe, where protocol required her presence, Jack soon sent in a new doctor to see her. On May 12, at the Wrightsman estate in Palm Beach, where the Kennedys and the Spaldings were guests, Jackie received her first injection from Max Jacobson, otherwise known to a legion of celebrity patients as Dr. Feelgood. JFK, who had been introduced to the New York physician by Chuck Spalding, had himself secretly relied on the mood-enhancing injections at the time of his game-changing presidential debates with Richard Nixon. In the run-up to President and Mrs. Kennedy's departure for France, Jackie had several more doses of the mysterious elixir. Referred to by enthusiasts as Jacobson's "joy juice," the shots were a concoction of methamphetamine, steroids, calcium, monkey placenta, and other ingredients that the doctor steadfastly refused to disclose.

"It's not for kicks, only for people who have work to do," Jacobson was known to scold in a thick German accent that, according to one devotee, made him sound "like a caricature of Sigmund Freud." The president, after severely injuring his unstable back in the course of a tree-planting ceremony in Ottawa, also asked to be treated by Jacobson, though JFK had previously discontinued the injections because, he told Chuck Spalding, he did not like the feeling of being out of control that they gave him. Besides, though other patients attested to decidedly different results, JFK was convinced that the shots impeded sexual performance. Determined to disregard Dr. Travell's recommendation that he openly use crutches when he met with de Gaulle and Khrushchev in Paris and Vienna, respectively, Kennedy arranged for Jacobson to quietly accompany him and the first lady to Europe. Prior to takeoff on May 30 in New York, the unkempt doctor, who habitually stank of cigarettes and medicine and whose fingernails were stained black by chemicals, injected both Kennedys in the presidential stateroom of Air Force One.

In the course of their visit to France, Jacobson charged them up before their official appearances, and eased them down afterward in order that they might sleep serenely at night. His cocktail of drugs permitted President Kennedy to function in spite of an injured back, and it allowed the first lady to cheerfully and energetically perform public duties from which, almost certainly, she would otherwise have recoiled. It soon became apparent, however, that other factors were in play that made Jackie, in the phrase of the very political consultants who had previously doubted her appeal, "the hit of the show."

Immediately, the motorcade that carried the Kennedys, and their hosts President and Mrs. de Gaulle, from Orly Airport was greeted by cries of "Vive Jacqueline!" along the ten-mile route. It was certainly not anything Jackie had done on the trip thus far that stirred the crowds so much as it had been an interview with her, previously taped in Washington and aired on French television the night before. Speaking in very pretty French, Jackie had charmingly presented herself as a daughter of France. The broadcast caused a huge sensation, and the seventy-year-old de Gaulle, seated beside JFK in an open limousine, attributed the turnout of as many as a million people to the French public's fascination with Mrs. Kennedy. JFK, in turn, jestingly commented through a translator that he ought to be jealous. In fact he was pleased—up to a point, anyway—by the effect Jackie seemed to have, not just on the crowds, but on de Gaulle himself. One French newspaper satirized the latter dynamic in a political cartoon that depicted the famously puritanical de Gaulle asleep in a canopied bed dreaming of Mrs. Kennedy, whose image hovered above. Beneath the covers, the French leader's mousey wife, Yvonne, glared at Jackie and declared with outrage: "Charles!" At a luncheon at the Élysée Palace on the day the Kennedys arrived, Jackie, seated next to de Gaulle, delighted him with her command of his language and her knowledge of his country. The woman who in Newport in 1945 had dared not disclose how much she knew about such matters spoke unreservedly of them now to the hero of her youth. "Mrs. Kennedy knows more about French history than most Frenchwomen," de Gaulle presently informed JFK. When talks with America's prickliest ally went well, Kennedy remarked to aides (not perhaps without a dash of irony) that he and de Gaulle were getting on—"probably because I have such a charming wife."

The better part of two truckloads of baggage that the Kennedys had brought with them to Paris consisted of Jackie's wardrobe, which was comprised largely of costumes created for her by the American designer Oleg Cassini. On the occasion of the Kennedy–de Gaulle dinner on the second day of the state visit, however, she departed from her Alsop-inspired made-in-America rule and appeared at the Palace of Versailles in a beaded and embroidered white satin evening gown and matching coat designed by the French couturier Hubert de Givenchy. The next day's headlines blazoned the news of Jackie's triumph: "Paris Has a Queen" and "Apotheosis at Versailles." Addressing journalists at a fare-well press conference, JFK displayed the ability to laugh at himself that admirers had long found irresistible about him. "I do not think it alto-gether inappropriate to introduce myself to this audience," America's leader dryly declared. "I am the man who accompanied Jacqueline Ken-nedy to Paris, and I have enjoyed it." To some perceptions, however, afterward, JFK was not without ambivalence, even annoyance, about the tremendous amount of attention Jackie had received. Still, he seems to have been enough of a pragmatist to appreciate the advantage to him-self of her success.

In Vienna, Jackie drew more hyperbole and headlines. "First Lady Wins Khrushchev, Too," trumpeted *The New York Times*. "Smitten Khrushchev Is Jackie's Happy Escort," concurred *The New York Herald Tribune*. In what looks to have been a burst of mimetic desire, the crowds in the street were almost as eager to see Jackie as the French had been, though she certainly had never declared herself a daughter of Austria. On one occasion, as the president's car approached the Soviet embassy, a waiting crowd called for Jackie and was disappointed to discover that JFK and Secretary of State Dean Rusk had arrived without her. "Rusk," the president jested, "you make a hell of a substitute for Jackie!"

In London as well there was universal fascination with the first lady when the Kennedys arrived, ostensibly to attend the christening of the child of Jackie's sister Lee (now the wife of the Polish prince Stanislas Radziwill), but actually so that JFK might confer with Prime Minister Harold Macmillan about what de Gaulle and Khrushchev had told him. "In the pubs," reported *The New York Times*, "the talk is more of 'Jackie' . . . than of her husband and international politics." Joe Alsop encountered the Kennedys at the christening party at the Radziwill residence, and though Alsop had had much to do with preparing Jackie for public life, today it was a "visibly shaken" and "strangely preoccupied" President Kennedy who riveted the journalist's attention. In cryptic conversation with Alsop, JFK alluded to the threat that, as yet unbeknownst to the world, Khrushchev had made in Vienna. Determined never again to face a unified Germany, and most especially not a unified anti-Communist Germany, Moscow was threatening to cut off Western access to Berlin, even if that meant igniting a new world war. Kennedy, for his part, worried that his own lack of firmness in Vienna had lent credence to Khrushchev's opinion, formulated in the wake of the Cuban fiasco, that America's callow new young leader would accept almost anything to avoid a nuclear confrontation. In private, Jackie saw her husband lapse into "a gloom" that he refused to talk about, but which caused her on more than one occasion to feel what she later described as "a little shooting pain of fright" that even Jack would not be able to make this turn out for the best.

At the same time, she arrived back in the United States with new personal confidence and new clout. Confidence, because of the completely unexpected reception she had had abroad. Clout, because the trip had transformed her into a figure of international appeal. In the months that followed, she used the spotlight to help her husband's beleaguered presidency. She who had attracted the first negative press coverage of the administration reinvented herself as among its greatest public relations assets. She presided over exquisite state dinners and hosted high-profile arts events. Not so long before, candidate Kennedy had wondered aloud whether it might be best to run her through subliminally in a quick-flash TV spot. Now she starred in an immensely successful program aired on all three networks, *A Television Tour of the White House with Mrs. John F. Kennedy*, which showcased the work she had undertaken in collaboration with the French decorator Stéphane Boudin. Far from the iconoclast many people had feared early on, Jackie proved to be a champion of historical restoration and preservation. Far from striking America as too fey and too fancy, she delighted viewers with a full-out performance of the role she had been groomed to play at Miss Porter's: the cultivated wife who uses her painstakingly acquired knowledge and graces in the service of her husband.

In the present case, at least, the husband returned the favor by continuing to betray her with other women, often frolicking with them (JFK had a fondness for threesomes) in Jackie's own bed in the White House family quarters while she was at Glen Ora, the couple's rented country house in Virginia. He even embarked on an affair with a recent Miss Porter's graduate, Mimi Beardsley, whom he had met when the teenager came to the White House to interview Letitia Baldrige about Jackie for her proud alma mater's student newspaper. "It's not that he cheated on her," observed Larry Newman, one of the Secret Service agents assigned to guard Jackie, "but that everybody knew about it, and then she's got to appear with him." Nor did the president necessarily confine his sexual indiscretions to the times when his wife was away. In addition to the state dinners, Jackie arranged a number of dinner dances, which, according to Special Assistant Arthur Schlesinger Jr., she conceived "as a means of restoring a larger social gaiety to her husband's life. When several months of unrelenting pressure had gone by, she would feel that the time had come for another dancing party. . . . The President seemed renewed by them and walked with a springier step the next day." No doubt he did. At one such gala, on February 9, 1962, which was attended by Kennedy friends, administration members, foreign diplomats, and other Washington notables, Jackie danced the twist with defense secretary Robert McNamara in one of the crowded state rooms, while JFK enjoyed a tryst with another of his numerous mistresses, Mary Meyer, in his daughter's schoolroom upstairs.

The contrast between refinement and dissipation that was among this administration's salient characteristics began to play out in public with the juxtaposition of two lavishly publicized but otherwise distinctly different events in May of 1962. The first, held at the White House on the eleventh, was the Kennedys' dinner in honor of French Minister of State for Cultural Affairs Andre Malraux, who had been kind to Jackie at the time of the state visit to Paris. Jackie had long labored over the guest list, which, at the suggestion of France's ambassador in Washington, Hervé Alphand, included some of America's most esteemed artists. There were the playwright Tennessee Williams, the critic Edmund Wilson, the novelist Saul Bellow, the director Elia Kazan, the painter Mark Rothko, the dancer and choreographer George Balanchine, and the conductor Leonard Bernstein, among many others. The evening culminated the first lady's efforts over many months to establish "Kennedy Washington," as her mentor Alsop liked to call it, as the world capital of culture and taste.

Less edifying, perhaps, but in its way equally typical of the Kennedy years, was a Democratic fund-raiser in the form of a forty-fifth birthday tribute to JFK, which was held a week later in New York. Instead of Jackie, who chose not to attend, the star of the occasion was Marilyn Monroe. The actress sang "Happy Birthday" in a manner that Jackie's old nemesis, Dorothy Kilgallen, described to newspaper readers as "making love to the President in direct view of 40 million Americans" watching on TV. Marilyn had in fact been one of Kennedy's sexual partners, and his hubristic decision to allow her on that public stage seemed to dare journalists to investigate his philandering in a way that they simply had not before. Realizing the damage he had caused himself, he put out word to various press people that there was no truth to claims that he had slept with Marilyn. Unfortunately, however, the actress had shared his bed that very night at the Carlyle Hotel in New York, and she followed up with a series of frenzied calls to the White House in hopes of being invited to visit him in Washington. "He liked her," remembered George Smathers, "but she liked him *more*." And with Kennedy, of course, that "more" always presented a problem. Marilyn, having transformed herself into one of the countless women in his life who "won't leave me alone!", thereupon became persona non grata. Determined to stop her from phoning, the president dispatched Bill Thompson, one of his procurers, to Los Angeles to control her. In the meantime, Kennedy refused Marilyn's calls. Finally, "she quit bothering him," reflected Senator Smathers, "because he quit talking to her."

What did not quit, however, was the speculation in certain quarters about presidential promiscuity. In the past, both JFK and his father had been known to dismiss suggestions that his unfaithfulness to Jackie might damage him politically. Despite the swirl of rumors about the marriage that had materialized after Jackie's stillbirth in 1956, as well at other points, nothing substantive had yet to appear in print. Now the iconic image of Marilyn Monroe singing to JFK had put a familiar face on everything that people had heard or imagined. Suggestive of the sense of foreboding that pervaded Washington in the months that followed were the remarks about JFK that the French ambassador confided to his diary at the time: "He loves pleasure and women too much. His desires are difficult to satisfy without making one fear a scandal and its use by his political adversaries. This may happen because he doesn't take sufficient precautions in this puritan society." In a similar vein, there was mounting anxiety among the Kennedyites that Republicans would make JFK's womanizing an issue in the 1964 presidential campaign.

Rather than ask the president to restrain himself, however, his consultants cast a worried eye on Jackie. After a great deal of entertaining and additional foreign travel in her capacity as first lady (including two Latin American trips with the president, as well as a solo mission to India and Pakistan), she was planning to spend a few weeks in Italy with Caroline. In the present climate, his political experts worried that such a trip, undertaken for no reason other than Jackie's personal pleasure, would be read as evidence of unrest in the marriage. The White House sought to avert any such perception by announcing that her Italian sojourn had been scheduled to take place in a period when JFK, set to speak in various parts of the nation, would not be able to spend weekends with her at Cape Cod. The implication was that the first lady hoped to assuage her loneliness abroad.

In accord with White House instructions that she keep her stay in Ravello "low-key," Jackie made it clear to the limited staff accompanying her to the chic Italian resort that every possible propriety must be religiously observed. "She was very concerned about who she was and how she acted and how the people around her acted," recalled Mary Taylor, whom the U.S. embassy in Rome had assigned to be the first lady's assistant during her stay in Italy. "She wanted everyone to comport themselves in a good manner." Despite Jackie's best efforts, however, it soon became apparent that the advisers' anxiety had been far from unfounded. After the first lady, the Radziwills, and other friends were the guests of Gianni and Marella Agnelli on the couple's two-masted racing yacht, photographs appeared in the press that made it seem as if Jackie had been alone on the boat with Agnelli, with only a lone guitarist to serenade them. In fact, Agnelli's wife as well as various guests, not to mention Jackie's Secret Service protectors, had been there at all times, but the carefully framed and cropped photographs suggested to the world that Jackie and her host were having an affair. On the contrary, the Agnelli cruise had never been anything less than "a proper trip," attested Secret Service agent Larry Newman. "It was just beautiful people enjoying themselves." Newman, when he guarded President Kennedy, had been present on numerous occasions when JFK cavorted with other women. The agent found Jackie to be another story entirely: "I never saw anything of untoward desire or activity on her part toward another man." Nor, in his view, was she inclined to attempt to spite her faithless husband by misbehaving with Agnelli in Italy, as some would later represent her as having done. "She was above all that," Newman declared. "She didn't burn that kind of fire."

Neither JFK nor his team believed that Jackie was really misbehaving with Agnelli. They were, however, concerned about the potential political consequences of the pictures. Nor, importantly, can the press have believed any of it. Besides broaching the idea that all was not well in the Kennedy marriage, the contrived images appealed to popular sentiment that while it was acceptable for the first lady to use her rarefied tastes and graces in the service of her husband, it was another matter to play on her own, however blamelessly, among the international superrich. Ironically, at one point during the ensuing media tempest, JFK had been a guest at the Santa Monica residence of his brother-in-law the actor Peter Lawford, where, as was their custom, the president and Dave Powers diverted themselves with various women provided by their host. Meanwhile, it was Jackie whom a group known as the Concerned Citizens of America was threatening to picket when she returned to the White House. "Would you not better have served the nation and the President by remaining at home by his side?" Jackie's critics asked her in an open letter. "We have honored you greatly with the position of First Lady of our land. We ask only that you not violate the dignity of that title."

Jackie came home on August 31 to a husband who was indeed preoccupied with a series of surreptitiously taken photographs, though not the ones she had been hearing about. And, much as President Kennedy might have wished otherwise, there could be no doubting or denying the reality these new pictures disclosed. As it happened, hours before Jackie had been reunited with him, JFK had received hard evidence, in the form of photographic intelligence, showing that the Soviets were constructing missile sites in Cuba. Three months previously, as Kennedy frolicked with Marilyn Monroe in New York, the Kremlin had been quietly launching a plan to force JFK to agree to major concessions in Germany. That day, Khrushchev had spoken to Soviet foreign minister Andrei Gromyko and others of his idea of installing Soviet missiles in Cuba. As soon as Khrushchev had the missiles in place, he planned to appear in New York, probably in the latter part of November, and demand that Kennedy agree to pull Western troops out of Berlin, as well as abandon any idea of a reunified Germany. On the basis of Kennedy's weak performance in Vienna, where the American leader had been "savaged" by his Soviet counterpart, Khrushchev calculated that rather than risk all-annihilating war, Kennedy would quickly cave. JFK as yet knew none of this at the end of August, only that the missile sites were being built, and that he would soon have to make a decision about how, if at all, to react to the information.

Jackie would later speak of the autumn crisis, when a single miscalculation, either in Washington or Moscow, threatened to set nuclear weapons flying, as the period in the entire marriage when she had been the closest to her husband. "Please don't send me anywhere," she begged him. "If anything happens, we're all going to stay right here with you. Even if there's not room in the bomb shelter in the White House, please then I just want to be with you, and I want to die with you, and the children do too—[rather] than live without you." At length, by a combination of adroit negotiation, deft timing, and sheer nerve, JFK successfully resolved what came to be known as the Cuban missile crisis. In the end, it was Khrushchev who backed down, when he consented to remove the missiles from Cuba.

There followed a strange interlude in Kennedy Washington, when, amid the resounding chorus of praise for the president's strategic victory over Khrushchev, there was also, for the first time, significant open dissension among certain members of JFK's intimate circle about the sex parties, the mistresses, the prostitutes, the procurers, and the drugs that were regular features of his private life. "They had turned that place into a brothel, hadn't they?" said Betty Coxe Spalding of the debauched atmosphere that President Kennedy, Dave Powers, and their group had established at the White House. Spalding was one of those who finally decided that she could no longer countenance Jack's womanizing. "I didn't approve of the way he behaved," she recalled. "It was sick." Sissie Ormsby-Gore, who had herself known Jack since before the war when they were members of the same elite London set, also made it known now that she was "disgusted" by his betrayals of Jackie, to whom Sissie had become close during David's tenure in Washington. Presently, Sissie was one of the very few people to whom Jackie initially confided, not long after the missile crisis, that she was pregnant. Jackie's pregnancies had always been troubled, and now, as before, she was concerned from the outset that the baby might not survive. The first lady thereupon quietly withdrew from the active public role she had undertaken at a moment when her husband had needed her help.

For all of Jackie's precautions, however, the baby was born prematurely, with the same lung deficiency that had afflicted John Junior, except that in the present case the condition was much worse. At Children's Hospital in Boston, to which the four-pound, ten-and-a-half-ounce newborn, Patrick Bouvier Kennedy, had been moved, specialists, hoping to keep his lungs open, planned to try a pressure chamber typically employed in open-heart surgery. That night, JFK insisted on sleeping at the hospital, where the child visibly struggled to breathe. The president, wearing a white surgical cap and gown, held tiny Patrick's fingers for hours. He was still touching them when, shortly after four A.M. on August 9, 1963, the baby died. Directly, JFK went to Jackie at Otis Air Force Base Hospital, where, as she later described the scene, he knelt by her bed and sobbed. Afterward, Jackie told Betty Spalding that she had "never seen anything like that in him." He had reacted so heartlessly to the stillbirth of a daughter, seven years before. His response this time was entirely different, and Jackie, by her own account, was "stunned" and not a little hopeful that the ordeal might yet change him as a person.

At the same time, the child's death sent Jackie into a deep depression, news of which prompted an invitation, conveyed by her sister Lee, to cruise the Aegean as a guest on Aristotle Onassis's yacht. Previous European yachting holidays having been a big problem for this family on at least two occasions, the president initially did not like the idea of the new trip. For one thing, Onassis's history of legal skirmishes with the U.S. Maritime Commission and the Justice Department made it unseemly to accept the magnate's hospitality. More generally, his substantial business dealings with the U.S. government through Victory Carriers, a New York–based shipping company in which he held a large stake, posed conflict-of-interest problems. To make matters worse, there had been speculation in the press that Onassis was having an affair with Jackie's sister. The columnist Drew Pearson went so far as to suggest that Onassis was maneuvering to become the American president's brother-in-law, with all of the advantages that the familial status would provide. Under the circumstances, it seemed wisest to decline the invitation.

Still, Jackie wanted to go, and at length JFK conceded, as he said, that the cruise would probably be "good for her." Jackie insisted that there could be no question of accepting her host's offer to deflect some of the potential criticism by absenting himself from the yacht for the duration of her stay. So, in light of the misleading photographs that had been published at the time of her cruise with the Agnellis, JFK, at his wife's behest, drafted Undersecretary of Commerce Franklin Roosevelt Jr. to accompany her on the *Christina* in the role of a chaperon. The anticipated presence neither of Roosevelt nor of Stas Radziwill, who would be accompanying his wife, mollified those administration figures, Attorney General Robert Kennedy not least among them, who regarded the cruise as an ethical and electoral nightmare. As though there were any need to do so, Kenny O'Donnell warned the president that he had "an election year coming up." In a similar vein, the American ambassador in Greece, Henry Labouisse, urged the president to keep Jackie off of Onassis's yacht—not because her presence on the *Christina* would be wrong in itself, but rather because it was bound to leave "a poor impression."

Such criticisms were nothing, however, compared to the storm that erupted as soon as Jackie's trip was announced to the public. Angry letter-writers pelted the White House with protests. Some of the complaints were the work of the usual cranks, but a good many letters voiced the apparently sincere feelings of betrayal experienced by average citizens who had mourned the death of young Patrick and felt somehow mocked by Jackie's vacation on the playboy's boat. Why, they demanded to know, if she was well enough to go to Europe, did she not simply resume her responsibilities as first lady? Why not be a good wife and remain at home to help and care for her busy husband? The uneasy subtext of much of this was the question of whether people of her stratum of existence reacted differently to life's tragedies than everyone else did. The angry chorus intensified when Jackie turned up in Greece, where reports of all-night revelries on the *Christina* attended by the first lady and about a dozen other guests drew bitter protests from the American press and public. Jackie's cruise also caused JFK trouble in Congress, where Republicans branded the trip "improper" and asked why she did not simply choose to see more of her own country rather than gallivant about Europe.

Looking back at the episode in light of all that was so soon to follow, Jackie regretted her prolonged absence in Europe, as well as certain of her private behavior in the aftermath of her October 17, 1963, return to the United States. "I was melancholy after the death of my baby, and I stayed away last fall longer than I needed to," she would tell Father McSorley. "And then when I came back he [JFK] was trying to get me out of my grief and maybe I was a bit snappish; but I could have made his life so much happier, especially for the last few weeks. I could have tried to get over my melancholy." That, at least, is how she remembered it in 1964, when she was being counseled, by the priest among others, that it was time to "get over" the death of her husband. Interestingly, guilt feelings of a very different origin were already in the mix when she returned to the States on October 17, 1963, ten days after JFK had signed the instruments of ratification of the Limited Nuclear Test Ban Treaty, which, in close consultation with Harold Macmillan, he had at last secured with the Soviets—the "beginning" JFK had often spoken of during the presidential campaign, as well as in his inaugural address. So, unlike his hero Churchill, who had had to leave office before he could accomplish the great goal, Kennedy had managed to win the first precious postwar agreement with the Soviets after all.

Jackie, for her part, was uncomfortably aware of the political trouble her stay on the *Christina* had just caused him; he, coolly conscious of appealing to her "guilt feelings" when he asked her to accompany him, along with Vice President and Mrs. Lyndon Johnson, on an upcoming political trip to Texas. Jackie's assent, offered unhesitatingly, took the form of "a gesture of contrition" from a wife who, by her own account, had always been the partner in the marriage to make the first move toward conciliation.

Jackie had never accompanied the president on a domestic political trip before. Quite simply, it was not the sort of thing she relished or felt confident doing. Could she bring it off now, especially after the torrent of public criticism she had just drawn? Kennedy's political consultants saw Texas as a trial run for the 1964 presidential campaign. Despite everything that Jackie had accomplished to date as first lady, in the Kennedy camp there remained significant skepticism about quite how she would play there.

Hardly had she emerged from Air Force One in San Antonio, Texas, on November 21, 1963, however, when that skepticism evaporated. Dressed not like the jet-setter of recent controversy but rather like the conservative, though young and pretty, wife of a well-to-do American businessman, Jackie skillfully endeared herself to the crowd with what Lady Bird Johnson approvingly described as "a big, hesitant smile." That hesitancy seemed to signal Jackie's humble acceptance that whatever her past triumphs in Paris, Vienna, London, and elsewhere, today it was for the people of Texas to make up their own minds about her. Throughout the junket, she dutifully, strategically, played the part of the good, ordinary wife, ever doting on and deferring to her husband. Afterward, the first lady's press secretary reflected: "I think she wanted to be the woman to accompany John Kennedy to Texas." Ironically, that very determination to linger in the background quickly made Jackie, in the words of one press commentator, "almost the focus of the trip." That night, in their suite at the Texas Hotel in Fort Worth, the president assured her: "You were great today." The next morning, he humorously told an audience in the hotel's Grand Ballroom: "Two years ago, I introduced myself in Paris by saying that I was the man who accompanied Mrs. Kennedy to Paris. I am getting the same sensation as I travel about Texas." Back in the presidential suite afterward, before they flew on to Dallas, he asked her if she would accompany him on a campaign trip to California in two weeks.

"And, then, just when we had it all settled," Jackie recalled in conversation with Father McSorley, "I had the rug pulled out from under me without any power to do anything about it."

Of course, by the time she said that, sudden horrific events had inevitably and irreversibly made her a different person than the one she had been when her husband made his pitch about California. Still, what exactly did she think, or at least wish the priest to think, had finally been "settled" that last day of JFK's life? Certainly, whatever Jackie may once have hoped, the loss of a child had not changed him any more than marriage had. In both cases, he had soon reverted to past sexual habits. Had the assassination never taken place, Jackie would still have had to live among men who not only knew of the president's infidelity, but who in certain cases routinely shared girls with him. She would still have had to constantly face women—White House employees, journalists, members of her social circle—who at one time or another had slept with, or enjoyed somewhat briefer exchanges with, her husband.

From the moment in 1952 when Jackie had broken her engagement to another man in order to pursue a relationship with Jack Kennedy, politics had been both enemy and friend to her. Enemy, because, in the beginning, Jack's decision to seek a senatorship meant that he would often be away. Friend, because if Jack did manage to win a place in the Senate, given his particular ambitions he would soon no doubt require a wife. From the outset, their relations had been characterized by a good deal of separation and longing, the latter on Jackie's part anyway. At times, he had vouchsafed her little more than the voice heard amid a crash of coins in what she imagined to be some oyster bar on Cape Cod; the books, mainly British, that he left with her by way of suggesting how he saw himself intellectually; the French-language texts about Indochina, which she spent many late lonely nights translating in hopes that "he has got to ask me to marry him after all I have done for him." On their honeymoon she had been careful, as reported in a letter to his parents, to leave him alone a few hours each day. But even then, Jack had suddenly sent his young bride reeling when he suggested that she return to the East Coast, while he enjoyed a few extra days in California by himself. "What shall I do?" she had frantically asked another, older woman at the time. In one form or another, Jackie had been confronted with that very question over and over in the course of the decade of marriage that had followed.

But now again, politics, in addition to being the enemy, had also presented itself as a friend. Her brilliant reception in Texas thus far had finally persuaded Jack that America was "ready" for her.

Henceforward, when he went on the road, he wanted Jackie at his side.

Seven

During the long winter that followed, during the lonely nights that never seemed to end, the wakeful nights that no quantity of vodka could assuage, Jackie would relive the sliver of time between the first gunshot, which had missed the car, and the second, which hit both the president and Texas governor John Connally. Those three and a half seconds became of cardinal importance to her. In the course of her marriage, she had constructed herself as Jack Kennedy's one-woman Praetorian Guard—against the doctors, against the political antagonists, against the journalists, even against anyone in his own circle who to her perception would do him harm. So, again and again that winter of 1963–1964, she rehearsed the same brief sequence. If only she had been looking to the right, she told herself, she might have saved her husband. If only she had recognized the sound of the first shot, she could have pulled him down in time.

Jackie remembered that that initial gunshot, when she heard it, had seemed to be just some random backfire from one of the many police escort motorcycles. In the scorching sunlight, she had been sitting in the rear of an open midnight-blue Lincoln Continental convertible, smiling and waving to the crowds on her left. She had on a line-for-line copy of a pink wool Chanel suit with navy lapels, and white kid gloves buttoned at the wrist. A gold bracelet flashed and glittered on her left arm. Jack, seated beside her in the limo, had insisted that she not wear her sunglasses in order that the people of Dallas might see her face. The red roses she had been handed earlier at the airport lay on the seat between her and her husband.

When the initial shot was fired, Jack stopped waving and peered into the crowd. Briefly he turned to the left and glanced at his wife. By the time Jackie looked to her right, he had already resumed waving to onlookers. Then, like the president, she too turned back to the people on her side of the car and began to wave again. The sound of the first shot had been ambiguous. Secret Service agents traveling in the motorcade had similarly taken it for the gunning of motorcycles, or perhaps a firecracker. But there could be no mistaking the character of the second shot, which ripped through the back of the president's neck, exited below his Adam's apple, and hit the right shoulder of the governor, who was seated in front of Kennedy. Connally's cries, "Oh, no, no, no . . . My God, they are going to kill us all," caused Jackie to turn. Jack seemed to be reaching for his throat. First with her right, then with both hands, she tugged at his raised left arm in a desperate effort to pull him down, as Nellie Connally had succeeded in doing for her husband. Both of Jack's arms, however, were locked in place, and for five seconds Jackie struggled in vain.

She was looking directly into Jack's face when a third shot tore into the right side of his head. Upon contact, there was a loud thump, like a melon exploding on a pavement. A diaphanous pink cloud of brain and bone matter burst out of the wound, raining on Jackie's hair, face, and clothes. As he fell toward her, she screamed: "My God, what are they doing? My God, they've killed Jack, they've killed my husband, Jack, Jack!" Rising on her knees, she continued: "I have his brains in my hand." She might have been killed had the bullet's trajectory been slightly different, or she could easily have been slaughtered in the open vehicle afterward. Though she survived, deep, distinct memories of the interval between the first and third shots, and of certain of the incidents that followed, would color the rest of her life in ways over which she had no, or at best little, control, and which few observers appeared even to begin to comprehend. From then on, everything would be different for her because of a total of eight and a half at once evanescent and indelible seconds.

At the time of the second shot, Jackie's lead Secret Service agent, Clint Hill, had leapt off the sideboard of the follow-up car and begun running toward the presidential limousine. He had been struggling to climb onto the rear of the limo when the third shot split the president's head asunder. Suddenly, Jackie was crawling on hands and knees along the trunk of the now-speeding Lincoln. She appeared to be reaching futilely for a shard of her husband's head that had flown out the back. Dave Powers, in the follow-up vehicle, feared she was about to fall off and be ground under the advancing motorcade. Hill, as he drew near, sensed that she had no idea he was there. At last, he successfully propelled himself onto the trunk and pushed her into the rear seat, where he shielded her and the catastrophically wounded president with his own spread-eagled body.

Jackie cradled her husband in her lap. Tightly she held his head in both hands in a conscious effort to keep the brains from leaking out. "He's dead, he's dead," she heard someone shout. The pale blue interior of the limousine had been transformed into an abattoir. A hairy skull fragment lay beside Jackie's roses. As sirens roared and the car radio crackled, she muttered to Jack, asking if he could hear and repeating that she loved him: "Jack, Jack, what have they done to you?"

Six minutes later, the car halted at the emergency admitting platform in the rear of Parkland Hospital. Another agent, Paul Landis, found Jackie still holding her husband in her lap. Landis took her by the shoulders, attempting to help her up, but she refused to let go of the president's head. "No, I want to stay with him." Meanwhile, a hospital resident had appeared with a gurney. Surveying the interior of the car, he judged that the president was dead. He had never encountered anyone with a head wound of that magnitude, with so much brain matter strewn about, who survived. Finally, Clint Hill, sensing that Jackie did not want her husband to be seen like this, removed his own suit jacket and draped it over Kennedy's head and the upper portion of his chest. Thus reassured, she let go. A few ensanguined red roses clung to Kennedy's body as the agents removed it from the vehicle. Jackie's eyes gave the appearance of looking but not seeing. Yet when a nurse reached for the president's head in anticipation of lifting it onto the cart, Jackie pushed her out of the way and insisted on doing it herself.

As hospital staff raced the gurney to Trauma Room 1, Jackie dashed alongside, grasping her husband's hand. En route, the suit jacket dropped off his face. Initially, she refused suggestions that she wait in the hallway. In the belief that Jack was dead or dying, however, she did eventually allow herself to be lured out of the room, but shortly thereafter when a medic emerged with the information that the president was still breathing, she demanded to be allowed to return. Nurses had covered the floor around the cart with sheets to prevent slippage. Ignoring a Niagara of blood, Jackie dropped to her knees and prayed.

Doctors, meanwhile, were performing closed chest massage on the president, who had been stripped down to his undershorts and a back brace. Every time Kennedy's heart was compressed, a red geyser erupted from his skull and streamed down the right side of the table onto the floor. Neither chest massage nor a tracheotomy, which had been performed earlier, did much to improve his breathing. In any event, it was the head that had sustained the mortal wound, and when Dr. Kemp Clark, a neurosurgeon, saw the damage, he told Dr. Malcolm Perry, who was doing the cardiac massage, that there was no need to go on. When Perry continued notwithstanding, Clark stressed: "No, Malcolm, we are through." Jackie by this time had taken to pacing the trauma room, her hands clasped before her. Poking an anesthesiologist with her elbow, she hopefully presented him with a fragment of the president's brain.

Finally, Dr. Charles Baxter, the emergency room chief, told her that her husband was dead. She held Jack's hand beneath the sheet and softly joined in the prayers as a priest performed the last rites. When everyone else had left, she sat with Jack for a bit. Afterward, she waited in the hallway while nurses prepared his remains for the journey back to Washington. Since he was still oozing, they wrapped his head in four sheets, and when blood persisted in leaking through, they further insulated the casket with a plastic mattress cover. Jackie returned with the intention of depositing her wedding ring in the coffin. But when she attempted to remove her gloves, she discovered that the blackened white leather was so stiff with dried blood that she could not get them off without a policeman's assistance. Escorted by Dr. Baxter, she approached the dark red bronze casket, where she kissed Jack's toe, stomach, and lips. Then she attempted to put the wedding ring that she had worn for the past ten years on his hand. The ring too was bloody, and she managed to push it down no further than the joint of his little finger.

The corridor outside the emergency room was "deathly still" as the door opened and the casket appeared on a rubber-tired dolly. Jackie walked alongside, her left hand resting on the coffin. There was, said an observer, "a completely glazed look in her face. . . . If somebody had literally fired a pistol in front of her face . . . she would just have blinked. It seemed that she was absolutely out of this world." In the belief that any delay in removing the body from Dallas would have an incalculable effect on Jackie, Kenny O'Donnell and Dave Powers were eager to get the casket to Air Force One before local authorities enforced a state law that prescribed that an autopsy be performed in the jurisdiction where the homicide had taken place. The Dallas county medical examiner had already appeared at the hospital to warn that the body must stay where it was. Jackie was unaware of the controversy and thus, said O'Donnell, "perhaps confused as to the speed with which we were attempting to depart."

In the rear of the hospital, agents lifted the casket into a hearse and closed the vehicle's curtains. Declining suggestions that she ride in a follow-up car or even in the front seat of the hearse, Jackie insisted on sitting next to the coffin. The race to remove the remains continued at the airport. "We arrived . . . and we're all punchy now," O'Donnell recalled. "I'm concerned that the Dallas police are going to come and take the body off the plane and Jackie Kennedy's going to have a heart attack right in front of us there. I'm petrified." But when O'Donnell sent word to the pilot, urging him to take off immediately, the reply came back that Kennedy was no longer commander in chief. President Johnson was, and it turned out that he was already on the plane waiting to be sworn in prior to takeoff. In the meantime, when Jackie went to her bedroom for a moment, she found her husband's successor there. Immediately she repaired to the rear compartment, where Jack's coffin had been placed. At length, though Johnson had been assigned the presidential quarters when he boarded, he insisted that they ought properly to be occupied by the widow. Initially reluctant to return, Jackie finally acceded to the urgings of Lady Bird Johnson. Prior to the swearing-in, therefore, she had her first bit of privacy since the assassination.

In her absence from the presidential quarters, someone had laid out a white dress and jacket and black shoes, a tacit invitation to change her clothes. Gazing in the bathroom mirror, Jackie surveyed the blood on her face. No sooner had she wiped it off with a tissue than she sensed she had made a mistake. "Why did I wash the blood off?" she later remembered asking herself. "I should have left it there, let them see what they've done." This flash of anger points to one emotion the body had not shut down in its effort to allow her to do what she had to, both for her husband's sake and her own, in a situation of maximum stress. Presently, when

Jackie appeared at the swearing-in, she was still defiantly wearing the bespattered suit. Her stockings, as one observer described them, were "almost saturated with blood." Even her gold bracelet was horrifically encrusted. Jackie had just emerged from a kind of war zone where detachment, like anger, can be key to survival, operating as they both do to tamp down emotions that might diminish the warrior's single-minded focus. Thus, to Liz Carpenter, Lady Bird Johnson's press secretary, it was as though the murdered president's widow "were in a trance." Such was the figure who stood at Johnson's side during the ceremony in the sweltering stateroom, where a single jet engine's insistent low moan could be heard throughout. Afterward, the new president embraced the widow "by the elbows." Lady Bird Johnson pressed her hand and quietly declared: "The whole nation mourns your husband." Whereupon Chief Jesse Curry of the Dallas Police addressed Jackie for all to hear: "God bless you, little lady, but you ought to go back and lie down. You've had a bad day."

Lady Bird accompanied Jackie to the presidential quarters, where the new first lady pondered the incongruous sight of that "immaculate . . . exquisitely dressed" woman, as she said, still covered with JFK's blood. Also incongruous to Lady Bird was the ferocity with which Jackie refused her offer to send in someone to help her change. Echoing her private thoughts before the swearing-in, Jackie said: "I want them to see what they have done to Jack." Thereafter, she sat near the coffin with JFK aides for the duration of the flight.

When at length Air Force One reached Andrews Air Force Base in Maryland, Bobby Kennedy suddenly, mysteriously materialized on board. Having waited for some thirty minutes in the rear of a military truck out of sight of the press, he dashed up the ramp to the aircraft with all of the "raging spirit" that had long been associated with him. The sources of Bobby's fury on this occasion were manifold. He was grieving, of course, his face, as a witness described it, "streaked with tears." But he was also fuming at what he perceived to be the colossal affront of

Johnson's having insisted on being sworn in before takeoff, when to Bobby's mind it would have been so much more fitting and respectful to the Kennedy family had Jack been allowed to return to the capital as president. Ignoring the fact that, even in the absence of a swearing-in ceremony, the presidential mantle would have instantly transferred to Johnson when his predecessor died, the attorney general regarded Johnson as a usurper who had been in an unseemly rush to take over from JFK. Bobby's rage in this regard was not simply the product of a mind deranged by grief. Unlike Jackie, who had had a good relationship with the vice president, Bobby had long conceived of Johnson as an antagonist, and LBJ had loathed him in turn. The antipathy between the two men had been, in Joe Alsop's description, "a kind of chemical thing." And now the reality that Johnson was president seemed to offend Bobby's sense of prerogative. Said Alsop: "It was as though a ruling family had been displaced by unjust fortune." On Air Force One, Bobby pushed past Johnson and other passengers as though he did not see them or, LBJ feared, simply did not care to see them.

"Where's Jackie?" Bobby said. "I want to be with Jackie." Finally, recalled Liz Carpenter, "he pushed through and we got him to her." "Hi, Jackie," he said at last, wrapping his arm around his brother's widow. "I'm here." Bobby had a helicopter waiting to transport her to the White House while the remains were driven to Bethesda Naval Hospital in Maryland for an autopsy, but Jackie persisted in her refusal to be parted from the coffin. When at length she emerged into the lights and cameras on the tarmac, onlookers wept at the sight of her befouled garments and thousand-yard stare. The blood on the pink wool spoke to the suddenness of the tragedy and the impermanence of earthly dominion. Everything she had painstakingly created and made herself known for had been snatched away in an instant. This was a woman whose costumes always calculatedly drew attention, and never more so perhaps than now.

Seated across from her brother-in-law in the rear of the Navy ambulance where the casket had been taken, Jackie looked not into Bobby's face but rather at the closed gray curtain just behind his shoulder. Partaking of a ritual in which those returning from the battlefield have often engaged through the centuries, she began to tell the story of the horrors she had seen. She spoke of the motorcade, of the gunshots, and of the chaos that ensued. Like other people to whom Jackie would subsequently relate some version of this same story, Bobby perceived that whether or not he wanted to hear any of it, he had little choice but to listen. She needed to tell him this. She had to unburden herself. One must not interrupt. So, for approximately twenty minutes, Bobby sat in silence as Jackie talked on. At moments Bobby found himself peering through the curtains at the world flying past outside, but that was not an option for Jackie, who remained utterly preoccupied with the pictures that November 22 had etched in her brain.

To be sure, she and Bobby had their grief in common—deep, intense, gnawing grief—but in Jackie's case there was an additional factor, something that many people, then and in the future, would find it impossible to distinguish from grief. She was simultaneously bereaved and traumatized. Unlike her brother-in-law, she had had a direct experience of the bloodbath in Dallas, both as victim and witness. She had been rendered helpless in the face of overwhelming force. She had been powerless to save her husband and had been mortally threatened herself. She had, as she would say pointedly and repeatedly, held Jack's brains in her hands.

After Jackie had told her story to Bobby, she persisted in telling it to others when she reached Bethesda Naval Hospital. Over and over, she recounted the murder for the benefit of visitors to the seventeenth-floor presidential suite, where she had been brought for the duration of the autopsy, which was taking place elsewhere in the building. She described her husband's death to her physician, John Walsh; to Ben Bradlee; to Tony Bradlee; to Bob McNamara; to Charles Bartlett. Dr. Walsh referred to this episode as her talkathon. "She moved in a trance to talk to each of us," remembered Ben Bradlee. "She wasn't sobbing," recalled Charles Bartlett. "Tears were just a breath away, but they never came."

Initially, Jackie's doctor advised the others to allow her to talk herself out no matter how painful it might be to listen to her. Said Walsh: "Let her get rid of it if she can."

"Do you want to hear?" Jackie would begin. But, as had been the case in the ambulance with Bobby, she left them no choice really but to listen. Resisting her monologue would have been like trying to fight against the wind. RFK had asked Bob McNamara to come with him to the airport. Accordingly, the defense secretary had been waiting with Bobby when Air Force One landed. But he had declined Bobby's request that he accompany him onto the plane to collect Jackie. Now, when McNamara arrived at the hospital, he cut a commanding figure, the epitome of what one witness described as "naked strength." He was a man who always seemed to be operating on a strict schedule, and that remained oddly true on the present occasion. He had left his wife in their car in the expectation that his visit with the widow would be brief. But when it became apparent that Jackie preferred he remain, he instructed Marg McNamara to go on alone to collect their son from his Scout troop. Soon the towering defense secretary with the no-frills rimless wire spectacles; slicked-back, precisely parted hair; and dour Grant Wood countenance was seated on the floor gazing up at Jackie, who perched on a high stool. "She was in that suit with the bloody skirt and blood all over her stockings," McNamara recalled. "I felt I had to be calm for her and listen to her. . . . I was concentrating entirely upon her, because she needed me and I felt, the hell with the others; let them take care of themselves." To the hearer, it seemed as if Jackie's account of Dallas went on for hours.

Though dazed, she showed no sign of wanting sleep. She felt herself to be, in her phrase, "keyed up." Again and again, she reacted with an emphatic shake of the head to the urgings of visitors that she change her clothes. Meanwhile, Bobby Kennedy was overseeing the arrangements for Jack's funeral service at St. Matthew's Roman Catholic Cathedral and burial at Arlington National Cemetery, which were to take place on the twenty-fifth. There had been a time when Bobby had routinely issued orders in his brother's name. Tonight he repeatedly cited the authority of Jack's thirty-four-year-old widow. As the evening wore on and Jackie failed to wear out, Dr. Walsh suggested she try a sleeping pill. When the pill failed to take, he injected her with a strong sedative. Walsh anticipated that Jackie would fall asleep within no more than thirty seconds, but ten minutes later she was restlessly padding about the presidential suite in search of a cigarette. The physician, who had dozed off in a chair, was surprised to find her still on her feet.

In the preceding hours, she had refused to be parted from her dying husband. She had made it clear that she would not leave Dallas without his remains. She had declined to go on to the White House before the autopsy at Bethesda was completed. In the days that followed, she would be equally tenacious about a related matter. She intended to walk behind Jack's casket in the funeral procession in Washington, D.C. This posed a problem because of fears within the U.S. government that the assassination had been merely the beginning of a larger, Kremlin-based move against American power. Johnson himself suspected that the shooting could be the harbinger of a surprise attack in the manner of Pearl Harbor and that the missiles might start to rain on the United States at any time. The capture of Lee Harvey Oswald seemed to lend credence to such theories, for when Undersecretary of State George Ball ordered that Oswald's name be checked in the department records, it was quickly discovered that the suspected assassin had spent thirty-two months in the Soviet Union as recently as June 1962.

Though it had not been her intention, immediately Jackie's resolve to accompany the coffin on foot between the White House and St. Matthew's seemed to put pressure on high-ranking government figures, as well as on foreign dignitaries, to do the same. The Secret Service and the FBI urged that "under no circumstances should the American president take that risk." Dean Rusk and Undersecretary Ball worried over the possibility that an assassin might target one or more of the heads of state who had announced plans to attend the funeral. There was particular concern that Charles de Gaulle's height would make him an easy target for the assassins who had doggedly stalked him in the past. As the French leader had already survived at least nine attempts on his life, provisions had to be made in advance of his travels to refrigerate quantities of his rare blood type in the event that an emergency transfusion was required. Given the rumors of Communist involvement in President Kennedy's murder, there was also worry that an American revenge-seeker might go after Khrushchev's emissary to the funeral, Anastas Mikoyan, first deputy of the Soviet Council of Ministers, and thereby spark off a crisis, if there were not one already, between Washington and Moscow.

On Sunday, November 24, an already impossible situation became much worse. As the former first lady was preparing to attend a daylong public viewing at the Capitol, a mysterious killer shot Oswald while the latter was in police custody in Dallas. Observed on television by millions of Americans who had been waiting to see the cortege, Oswald's murder exacerbated fears that further violence might yet be planned. Still, Jackie resisted efforts to persuade her to abandon her plan to walk in the next day's funeral procession. Told that there was much concern about the danger to the heads of state and other dignitaries who might decide to walk if she did, Jackie replied: "They can ride or do whatever they want to. I'm walking behind the president to St. Matthew's." Concurrently, Dean Rusk attempted to persuade General de Gaulle to allow himself to be driven to the funeral, but he too refused. "I shall walk with Mrs. Kennedy."

On the twenty-fifth, though anonymous death threats on both de Gaulle and Mikoyan had been received that very morning, Jackie walked behind the casket to the cathedral, a distance of eight blocks. In her present state of detachment, the renewed peril, rather than daunting her, seemed almost to act as a spur, causing her to stringently narrow her attention to the objective of reaching St. Matthew's. Prepared to act in the event of another shooting, George Ball and Deputy Undersecretary of State for Political Affairs U. Alexis Johnson monitored events from a nearby office as Johnson, de Gaulle, Mikoyan, and other figures representing ninety-two nations followed the veiled, black-clad widow, who remained in the state of emotional lockdown that had kicked in when she and her husband were under high threat in Dallas.

Finally, as Jackie stood beside RFK at the grave site, a cemetery official leaned in to caution her that there was about to be a twenty-one-gun salute. Seven soldiers fired three volleys each. Every shot caused her to tremble anew, yet she sustained her outward composure throughout.

Rose Kennedy attended the funeral without the patriarch, who, having suffered a devastating stroke two years previously, was in no condition to travel to Washington. Jackie, when she arrived at the Cape on Thanksgiving Day, went first to the main house, where she asked to see old Joe. His nurse, Rita Dallas, who was upstairs with him when Jackie entered the house, could hear the widow's voice below as she addressed one or more family members: "From the tone of it, she sounded aggravated and determined. I could not hear what was being said back to her, but her voice was louder than I had ever heard it." "Please, please," Jackie nearly shouted, "leave me alone. I'm fine." At last, she forced her way up to the paralyzed old man's room, where she placed herself on a low stool beside his bed. By turns pressing and caressing his stiff, speckled hand, Jackie again poured out the story of Jack's death. She retold and relived it, said the nurse, "in total detail."

Like Joe Kennedy's nurse, the next person to hear Jackie's story, the *Life* magazine writer Theodore White, was struck by what he characterized in his copious notes that day as her "total recall" of her ordeal. When she evoked the killing, White later remembered, "the scene took over, as if controlling her." Ten years after she had come to Hyannis Port for what she anticipated would be a private family occasion, only to be confronted with the magazine people whom old Joe had invited in to publicize his son's politically advantageous engagement, now it was Jackie who had arranged to have a further story about herself published in *Life*. The day after Thanksgiving, at a moment when there was reason to assume that she had left Washington in quest of privacy, Jackie personally summoned an astonished Theodore White, who had just covered the assassination for *Life*.

In the week since Dallas, she had insisted on staying close to her husband's casket, sitting with it, riding with it, marching behind it. Today it was Jack's historical reputation she sought to guard. Frantic about the assessments of the Kennedy presidency that would no doubt soon begin to be published, Jackie had something she wanted *Life* magazine to convey to the nation, and she wanted Theodore White, whom she viewed as a friendly journalist, to be the one to write it. The Camelot myth is what tends to be remembered about White's Friday, November 29, visit to Hyannis Port. Not unfairly, Arthur Schlesinger would later say of Jackie's comparison of the late president and his administration to King Arthur and Camelot that it would likely have "provoked John Kennedy to profane disclaimer." White eventually had to admit that Jack Kennedy's magic Camelot never really existed, and even Jackie privately conceded that her metaphor had been "overly sentimental." Interestingly, it is the interview's assassination subplot, as detailed in White's notes but barely hinted at in the article printed in *Life* magazine on December 6, 1963, that was by far the more valuable contribution to the record. In the course of listening to the widow's message to America, White witnessed something extraordinary.

The limousine carrying the author of the bestselling campaign narrative *The Making of the President 1960* arrived at the Kennedy family property at half past eight at night in a cold, heavy rain. As he had done when he covered the funeral, White had asked that *Life* magazine not go to press until his story was ready. Indeed, in this case he was not even certain that there would prove to be a story. That depended fully on what the widow had to tell him. Since it cost some thirty thousand dollars an hour overtime to hold the presses on a weekend, he naturally felt a good deal of pressure to check in with his editors as quickly as possible.

At first, however, seated on a low sofa opposite the pale but utterly calm widow, he struggled to know where to begin the interview. Jackie asked how she could help him, a peculiar question, as it had been she, not the writer, who had requested a meeting. White attempted to direct their talk by picking up the thread of their telephone conversation earlier in the day. In rancorous tones, she had mentioned that several journalists were then at work on historical assessments of the Kennedy presidency and that she did not want her husband to be remembered in that way. How, White asked tonight, did she wish him to be remembered?

There followed some desultory talk on Jackie's part. She spoke of her intention to retreat from public life. "When this is over, I'm going to crawl into the deepest retirement there is." She touched on what had been her initial desire to return to her former house in Georgetown; on Bob McNamara's promise to her at Bethesda Naval Hospital that he would personally buy the property back for her; and on the thought that came to her immediately thereafter, that she could never go back to that bedroom. "I said to myself, 'You must never forget Jack. . . .'" The remark seemed to completely derail the original tenuous line of her conversation. Suddenly, without transition, she was speaking of something else she could never forget. This was the moment when, to her guest's perception, the "blood scene," as he called it, seized control. Images of the assassination poured out in a torrent, but even at the most brutal points in Jackie's narrative, White observed, "it was all told tearlessly, her wide eyes not even seeing me, a recitative to herself." It was almost as if the speaker had forgotten that anyone else was there.

Like others before and after to whom Jackie would describe the events, White sensed that he was about to hear more than he wanted to. And just as she appeared to have no choice but to recount them, the visitor saw no alternative but to listen.

Jackie began: "There'd been the biggest motorcade from the airport. Hot. Wild. Like Mexico and Vienna. The sun was so strong in our faces. I couldn't put on sunglasses. Then we saw this tunnel ahead. I thought it would be cool in the tunnel. I thought if you were on the left the sun wouldn't get into your eyes." She spoke of the gunning of the motorcycles, which she had heard throughout the motorcade, and then the noise she mistook for yet another backfire. She spoke of Governor Connally's outcry and of the instant when she turned to see Jack.

"Then Jack turned back, so neatly. His last expression was so neat. He had his hand out. I could see a piece of his skull coming off. It was flesh-colored, not white. He was holding out his hand. And I can see this perfectly clean piece detaching itself from his head. Then he slumped in my lap. His blood and his brains were in my lap." Skipping over the interval when she crawled along the rear of the speeding Lincoln, she cut abruptly to the endless ride to the hospital after Clint Hill had made his way to the car. "I kept saying, 'Jack, Jack, Jack,' and someone was yelling, "He's dead, he's dead.' . . . I kept bending over him, saying, 'Jack, Jack, can you hear me? I love you, Jack.' I kept holding the top of his head down, trying to keep the brains in."

White, listening to her evoke the rose-pink ridges on the inside of her husband's skull, felt as if he were paralyzed. While the editorial offices and printing plants waited through the night to hear from the *Life* reporter, time in the Kennedy cottage seemed to slow down. Jackie spoke "softly" with a "composure" and matter-of-factness that seemed at once to be at odds with and to give greater relief to the terrors she minutely detailed. "These big Texas interns kept saying, 'Mrs. Kennedy, you come with us.' They wanted to take me away from him. Dave Powers came running to me at the hospital. . . . My legs, my hands, were covered with his brains. When Dave Powers saw this, he burst out weeping. From here down"—she held her hand slightly above her forehead to indicate the spot—"his head was so beautiful. I'd tried to hold the top of his head down. Maybe I could keep it in. I knew he was dead. . . . They came trying to get me. They tried to grab me, but I said, 'I'm not leaving.' When they carried Jack in, Hill threw his coat over Jack's head. And I held his head to throw the coat over it. It wasn't repulsive to me for one moment. Nothing was repulsive to me."

She spoke of standing in the hall outside the trauma room; of forcing her way back in; and of the doctor, Malcolm Perry, who wanted her to leave. "But I said, 'It's my husband. His blood, his brains, are all over me.' . . . There was a sheet over Jack. His foot was sticking out of the sheet, whiter than the sheet. . . . I took his foot and kissed it. Then I pulled back the sheet. His mouth was so beautiful. His eyes were open. . . . When he was shot, he had such a wonderful expression on his face. You know that wonderful expression he had when they'd ask him a question . . . just before he'd answer. He looked puzzled. And then he slumped forward."

As Jackie talked on, White perceived, "she lived the horror of the hour." In a strange sense, for her it was as if it were all happening again right then.

What exactly was it that her visitor was witnessing? The sudden loss of conscious control to a flood of hellish images; the abundance of vivid detail; the incongruously calm, detached style of narration—all point to an instance of traumatic memories being summoned from the brain's limbic system, which processes violent, highly distressing, and life-threatening events. This more primitive, "reptilian" part of the brain is located beneath the cerebral cortex, where rational thinking takes place. Certain extreme experiences—helplessly watching the death of a person one cares for; nearly being killed oneself; handling human body parts—carry a greater neurological punch than routine events. The brain stores this emotionally fraught material more deeply and in a much more concentrated form than it does other memories. Were one to face a similar high threat later on, the brain is able to instantly call up these images for purposes of warning and guidance. The process is involuntary, and it may be set off at moments when there is no authentic danger. Then, far from enhancing survival, the flashbacks make one a helpless victim of the brain's animal responses.

Soldiers returning from battle are often racked by intense intrusive memories of certain of the episodes they have endured. So was the slain president's widow, who, in another context, compared the experience to the opening of "floodgates." For some veterans, the painful pictures begin to fade in the fullness of time; for others, they do not.

Suddenly that night in Hyannis Port the floodgates closed, and Jackie, speaking in a different register, returned to the subject that she had broached on the telephone several hours before. "I want to say this one thing. It's become almost an obsession with me." She evoked Jack's nightly habit before going to sleep of playing some records on the old Victrola they had owned for a decade. She explained that the song he loved best came at the end of a recording of the Broadway musical *Camelot*. She proposed that his favorite line from that recording might serve as a fitting epitaph to his presidency: "Don't let it be forgot, that once there was a spot, for one brief shining moment that was known as Camelot." This was the message she wanted *Life* magazine to convey before other authors sought to define her husband's administration. She wanted people to think of the Kennedy years as Camelot. She wanted the public to understand that though there might be other great presidents in the future, "there'll never be another Camelot again." Whether or not the Camelot metaphor was valid, a desire to put it out there was the rational reason she had had for summoning White in the first place. The rest of the strange session had been something else entirely.

Jackie went on to evoke the picture of Jack that she had created to anesthetize herself during those first solitary nights in his room at the Cape shortly after their honeymoon. She spoke with much tenderness of the "lonely sick boy" who as he lay in bed had read about the Knights of the Round Table and about Winston Churchill's ancestor the 1st Duke of Marlborough. She communicated her sense that what she arrestingly referred to as the "satin-red history" (i.e., the violent, blood-drenched stories of heroes and warriors) that Jack had devoured in youth had made him the man he was.

But then, moments after she had offered these reflections, suddenly, to White's sense, she "reverted to the assassination scene again." Was it the phrase "satin-red history" that had stimulated this new outpouring of blood imagery? For whatever reason, she was back on Air Force One, where others were urging her to wipe off Jack's blood in anticipation of his successor's swearing-in ceremony.

At midnight, White withdrew to a servant's room in the cottage to type his story. He had just witnessed a mesmerizing spectacle. The handwritten notes he had taken of the approximately three-and-a-half-hour session were so disturbing to him that, by his own subsequent account to Jackie, it would be three weeks before he could bring himself to transcribe them. And when he did, he refrained from sharing any of it even with his wife or his secretary. Five months hence he would send Jackie a "rough-typed" transcript, which he characterized as "historical material," along with the strong suggestion that she show it to no one with the possible exception of Bobby Kennedy. On the night of the interview, however, White worked swiftly to produce a very different sort of document for his editors. He shaped an account that protectively eliminated all of the widow's most searing images of the assassination and made no reference to the oddly affectless manner of her narration.

Forty-five minutes later, he presented Jackie a first draft of the *Life* magazine piece for her approval. Whereupon another remarkable thing happened. The widow's pencil left not a single paragraph of his prose untouched. She transposed words and lines. She added phrases and beats. She slashed whole passages. In certain instances, not satisfied to draw a line through the offending material, she made a point of laboriously blacking it out. The typed pages when she returned them to the author were buried beneath an avalanche of her insistent markings. The wan, whispery figure whom White had just seen succumb on at least two occasions to an involuntary rush of agonized flashbacks had moved emphatically to seize control of his copy. With the vigilance she had often displayed when she perceived her husband's interests to be at stake, she hovered nearby as White dictated his story to New York from a kitchen wall phone at two A.M. Though Jackie could not hear what was being said on the other end, she shook her head with displeasure when she gleaned that his editors wanted to tone down the Camelot theme.

Responding to her signal, White insisted that Camelot dominate the published article.

And so in the end it did.

Eight

I just wanted you to know you were loved by so many and so much. I'm one of 'em," said Lyndon Johnson, whose Texas twang oscillated between the fatherly and the flirtatious, sometimes suggesting both attitudes at once, as he talked to Jackie on the telephone.

It was Monday, December 2, and she and the children had returned from Cape Cod the night before in anticipation of moving out of the White House family quarters at the end of the week so that Lyndon and Lady Bird could move in. She had initially hoped to be ready to go on Tuesday, but the move had had to be put off until Friday. She was to move temporarily to a borrowed house on N Street in Georgetown, three blocks from the house where the John F. Kennedys had lived at the time he was elected president. Packing had begun in Jackie's absence, but in the course of the next few days she planned to pick through her husband's wardrobe herself in order to determine which items to keep and which to disperse. Helpers laid out the president's clothes on sofas and racks for her to inspect. Seeming to connect the irrational death of her young husband and the loss of the two babies, Arabella and Patrick, she also planned to immediately reinter the latter beside their father's grave. As far as she was concerned, there was not a moment to be lost. The secret burial was set to take place that week under the auspices of Bishop Philip Hannan, who, at Jackie's request, had given the eulogy for President Kennedy at St. Matthew's. It remained only for Teddy Kennedy, youngest of the Kennedy brothers, to fly in the remains of both children on the family jet.

In the meantime, an affectionate letter from LBJ had been waiting for Jackie when she came in on Sunday, but, as she told him now on the phone in a hushed, impish voice, she assumed he would be so busy that she "didn't dare bother" him with a written reply.

"You got some things to learn," said Johnson, slathering on the down-home schmaltz, "and one of 'em is: You don't bother me, you give me strength." As far as the notion of a written response was concerned, LBJ had a better idea: "Don't send me anything! You just come over and put your arm around me. That's all you do. When you haven't got anythin' else to do, let's take a walk. Let's walk around the backyard. And let me tell you how much you mean to all of us and how we can carry on if you give us a little strength."

Johnson, who was speaking to her from the Oval Office, went on to talk of an earlier time in his political life when everyone but his mother, his wife, and his sisters seemed to have given up on him. "You females got a lotta courage that we men don't have. So we have to rely on you and depend on you. And you've got somethin' to do. You've got a president relyin' on you. And this is not the first one you've had. There're not many women, you know, runnin' around with a good many presidents!" This last remark prompted an explosion of girlish gaiety from Jackie: "She ran around with two presidents, that's what they'll say about me!"

To judge by her reaction to Johnson in this and certain other recorded conversations at the time, it is hard to imagine that she did not derive some grain of genuine comfort from their talks. Still, was LBJ really just being kind to the young widow, whose voice cracked piteously at one point in the December 2 exchange when she said that she now had more letters in his hand than she had in Jack's? Or was he simply jockeying to get her on his side in the toxic struggle that had erupted when Bobby Kennedy brushed past him on Air Force One on his way to collect Jackie? In the ten days since Dallas, tremendous accretions of ill will had rapidly built up on both sides of the eternal LBJ–RFK conflict.

Bobby Kennedy was convinced that Johnson had shown the most appalling disrespect for Jackie in Dallas, appropriating her bedroom on Air Force One, calling her "honey" when he offered his condolences, unconscionably postponing the departure of the presidential jet, contriving to have her photographed beside him as he took the oath. The political iconography of the latter images was especially distressing to RFK, who believed them to be grossly exploitative of his sister-in-law at a moment when he had not been there to protect her. It is a fact that, thereafter, Johnson surreptitiously taped his calls with her. And while it is true that he recorded calls with other people as well, in Jackie's case he went considerably further: In the course of the Christmas holiday of 1963, when she and the children traveled to Palm Beach, Johnson sought to demonstrate the intimacy of his relationship with the martyred president's widow by allowing four reporters to secretly listen in on a call he placed to her from the Cabinet Room. In private, he certainly was blunt about how helpful she could be to him. A month after the assassination, he mentioned the idea to Pierre Salinger, the press secretary whom he had inherited from his predecessor, of appointing Jackie ambassador to Mexico. "God almighty!" the president went on. "It'd electrify the western hemisphere. . . . She'd just walk out on that balcony and look down on 'em, and they'd just pee all over themselves every day." When Salinger suggested that he needed time to consider the proposal, Johnson returned defensively: "You think they'd think we were trying to use her or something?" Salinger confessed that that indeed was his concern.

Confronted with charges that he had treated Jackie improperly, even exploited her, Johnson always insisted that on the contrary he had been unfailingly respectful, holding her up on a pedestal and treating her with dignity and deference. To LBJ's sense, it had been Bobby Kennedy, the "little shitass" as he was known to call him, who had been outrageously disrespectful to him on Air Force One in Maryland, rushing past "so that he would not have to pause and recognize the new president." Johnson had been indignant when Bobby ushered his sister-in-law off the plane, leaving the president to make his exit without any of the customary courtesy being directed toward him. In later years, Johnson reflected that from day one of his new presidency he had dreaded the moment when RFK would openly announce his intention "to reclaim the throne in memory of his brother."

Jackie Bouvier's aura of the Wasp patriarchate had greatly appealed to old Joe Kennedy when Jack first brought her to meet the family. Now, because more than any other person Jackie possessed the aura of JFK, she became from the first a critical prize in the post-assassination struggle for place and power. Her natural allegiance was emphatically with Bobby, who, in his capacity as new head of the Kennedy family, had assumed the role of powerful protector at a moment of supreme need on her part. In the days immediately after the assassination, Bobby had been "the one person" who seemed capable of soothing her. "Shall we go visit our friend?" he had asked on the night of the funeral after everyone else had left them alone at the White House. A midnight trip to the grave, where they knelt in the enveloping darkness to pray, was only the first of many such emotionally charged visits to Arlington Cemetery together. Late afternoons in the cold months that followed, as she observed a one-year period of mourning, Bobby would sit with her near the firelight in her Georgetown living room and talk. Compared to RFK, Johnson was clearly the underdog in their contest for the widow's imprimatur. Still, as Jackie's fond, often mirthful conversations with LBJ attest, she was by no means impervious to his Big Daddy charm. More importantly, the fact that she and Johnson had both been in Dallas at the time of the assassination was a tremendous bond; in later years, they communicated about what had happened on November 22 in ways that leave little doubt of the sincere empathy each felt for the other. But that empathy did not prevent Johnson from endeavoring to use to personal political advantage a bond that had been forged in tragedy. He was not altogether without hope of prevailing with Jackie, and as a consequence even his seemingly most earnest and well-intentioned exchanges with her have the capacity to bristle with ambiguity and subtext. Motives tend to be mixed in such matters, yet it is worth asking whether, when in this early period Johnson told her to tell her children that he wanted to be a "daddy" to them, it was their interests he was thinking of primarily or his own.

At the same time, behind the wasted face and haunted, sleep-deprived eyes, Bobby Kennedy in these weeks was not exactly artless himself. The impact on him of his brother's death had been palpably physical. "I don't think I ever saw human grief expressed as in the face of Robert Kennedy after the assassination," remembered William vanden Heuvel. Pierre Salinger described him as "the most shattered man I had ever seen in my life." Nevertheless, two full weeks had yet to pass since the assassination before Bobby was speaking about the possibility of seeking the vice presidency. And before the end of December, he too was already contriving to use Jack's widow to personal political advantage. JFK's purpose in traveling to Texas had been, in Charles Bartlett's phrase, "to set the stage for 1964." A month later, again it was the impending presidential election that was in play, but with a significantly altered cast of characters. Oddly, one constant was the sense that Jackie's participation could be of immense benefit to the Democratic presidential candidate. As yet undecided about whether he would prefer to be vice president or secretary of state in 1964, Bobby saw her as a crucial negotiating chip with Johnson in either case.

Arthur Schlesinger was an ardent supporter of what he already understood to be RFK's long-range presidential ambitions. Yet he expressed skepticism when Bobby spoke to him of what he was certain would be their "bargaining power" with Johnson in advance of the next election. Schlesinger maintained that whether or not Johnson gave Bobby the particular job he wanted in 1964, Bobby and his supporters would have little choice but to play a role in LBJ's presidential campaign or "be finished forever in the party."

"Yes," Bobby replied, "but there is a considerable difference between a nominal role and a real role. We can go through the motions or we can go all out. It may make a difference, for example, whether Jackie appears with Johnson at the last big rally, or whether she goes to Europe in the autumn for her health." Bobby's implication, of course, was that he would be in a position to dictate his sister-in-law's decision in the matter.

Jackie was, as she later said of herself at this point, "not in any condition to make much sense of anything." In spite of that, she had yet to move out of the White House when she was confronted by the need to take an immediate decision about the first of the assassination books to be commissioned. Author Jim Bishop, whose previous titles included *The Day Lincoln Was Shot* and *The Day Christ Died*, was first out of the gate with his planned *The Day Kennedy Was Shot*, but other writers no doubt were soon to follow. Appalled at the prospect of this same painful material, as she said, endlessly "coming up, coming up," she decided to block Bishop and others by designating one author who would have her exclusive approval to tell the story of the events of November 22. At length, she settled on a writer who, curiously, had voiced no interest in undertaking such a project and had no idea he was under consideration. Nor, at the time Jackie chose (she later used the word "hired") William Manchester, had she ever even met him. Manchester was a forty-one-year-old ex-Marine who had suffered what his medical discharge papers described as "traumatic lesions of the brain" during the carnage on Okinawa in 1945. Among his seven previous books was a flattering study of JFK called *Portrait of a President*, galleys of which Manchester had transmitted to the White House in advance of publication so that the president might have an opportunity, should he desire it, to alter any of his own quotes. Now, at a moment when Jackie could do nothing to stanch the flow of her recollections of Dallas, she selected Manchester because, she judged, he at least would be manageable.

Prior to the move to N Street, Jackie, along with Bobby, her mother and sister, and a few others, gathered at night at Arlington Cemetery to reinter Arabella and Patrick. She and Bishop Hannan deposited the heartbreakingly small white caskets on the ground near Jack's freshly dug grave. Given what he saw to be the state of her emotions, the bishop elected to say only a short prayer, at the conclusion of which Jackie sighed deeply and audibly. While he walked her back to her limousine, she broached certain of the conundrums that had been torturing her since Dallas as she struggled to comprehend events that, after all, could not be explained in any rational terms. To the bishop's perception, she spoke of these things "as if her life depended on it—which perhaps it did."

As he and the widow were not alone, he wondered whether it might not be, in his words, more appropriate if they continued their talk elsewhere. He thought perhaps it would be better to meet in his rectory or at the White House, but Jackie continued to pour out her concerns notwithstanding. She did not care who else heard her speak of such intensely private matters. Her behavior in this respect was sharply out of character for a woman who, as her mother said, tended to cover her feelings, but she had all these urgent questions and she demanded answers: Why, she demanded to know, had God allowed her husband to die like this? What possible reason could there be for it? She emphasized the senselessness of Jack's being killed at a time when he still had so much more to offer. "Eventually," the priest recalled many years later, "the conversation turned more personal." Jackie spoke of her unease with the role that the American public had thrust upon her in the aftermath of Dallas. "She understood that she was forever destined to have to deal with public opinion, the differing, not always flattering feelings toward her. But she did not want to be a public figure. . . . Already, however, it was clear that the world viewed her, not as a woman, but as a symbol of its own pain."

The unanswerable questions that Jackie had posed to Bishop Hannan continued to preoccupy her when, on December 6, she moved to the house that Undersecretary of State W. Averell Harriman had provided for her use until she was able to acquire a property of her own. "Jackie's bedroom was on the second floor and she seldom left it," remembered her secretary Mary Gallagher. "I was constantly aware of her suffering." She wept. She drank. By turns unable to sleep and oppressed by recurrent nightmares that caused her to awaken screaming, she lacked even the solace of safely withdrawing into unconsciousness. Trying to make sense of the assassination, she lay awake, endlessly going over the events of November 22. By day, she told and retold her story to Joe Alsop (who clutched her hand throughout her narration), Betty Spalding, and numerous others. She pinballed between being, in her phrase, "so bitter" about the tragedy and futilely enumerating the things she might have done to avert it. Though she had no rational reason to feel guilty, she second-guessed her every action and reaction that day. She pounced on every missed opportunity and pondered how it all might have been made to happen otherwise. Again and again in these scenarios, it came down to some failure on her part: If only she had not mistaken the sound of a rifle shot for the gunning of motorcycles. If only she had been looking to the right, "then," as she later described her line of reasoning, "I could have pulled him down, and then the second shot would not have hit him." If only she had managed to keep his brains in as the limo sped to Parkland Hospital. She even dwelled on the red roses with which she had been presented when the presidential party arrived at Love Field in Dallas, whereas at previous stops she had been given yellow roses of Texas. Ought she to have recognized them as a sign?

Two days after Dallas, Bobby Kennedy had phoned the British embassy to ask David and Sissie Ormsby-Gore to spend the day with Jackie, who, he explained, had had another bad night. In Jackie's view, of all the people who had been close to Jack, David had been, next to Bobby and herself, the one who had been "the most wounded" by his death. As did Bobby, David regarded it his bounden duty to help care for Jack's widow. Nineteen years previously, he and Sissie had felt similarly responsible for Jack's sister Kick after her young husband died. Sitting with Jackie in the traumatic aftermath of the assassination, hearing her repeatedly recount the evil hour, was a wrenching experience for the Ormsby-Gores, who were both of an exceptionally sensitive, even fragile, cast of mind. Sissie had grown tremendously fond of Jackie in the course of David's ambassadorship. Both wives were accomplished horsewomen; both were Catholics; both were noted for their panache in matters of dress and decor. In the words of McGeorge Bundy, during the presidential years Sissie had been "company and friend for Jackie in a way that very few official wives were." Sissie's daughter Alice, though older than Caroline, had played with Jackie's daughter, and following the widow's move to N Street, the Ormsby-Gores had volunteered to host Caroline's school at the embassy when it could no longer be located in the White House. In mid-January 1964, David and Sissie accompanied Jackie on a visit to the Georgia plantation of the former U.S. ambassador to Britain John Hay Whitney. Afterward, Sissie, feeling half mad herself, reported to a friend that listening to Jackie's eruptions of violent imagery, usually the same episodes involving blood and brains, often in nearly the identical words, invariably in a flat tone of voice, was becoming well-nigh unbearable; yet listen she must.

At other times, conversations with Jackie were like skating on a pond of thin ice, with certain areas designated dangerous. Easily provoked to anger, she bristled when a woman in her social circle praised her bearing during the memorial services. "How did she expect me to behave?" Jackie remarked afterward to Arthur Schlesinger with what struck him as a certain contempt. Jackie was, in her word, stunned when other friends said they hoped she would marry again. "I consider that my life is over," she informed them, "and I will spend the rest of my life waiting for it really to be over." She became indignant when, however well-meaningly, people suggested that time would make everything better.

She found it too painful to see so much as an image of her husband's face—the face she had been looking into when the fatal bullet struck. The single photograph of Jack that, by her own account, she did have with her at the Harriman house was one in which his back was turned. Paintings as well were problematic. When Bob and Marg McNamara sent over two painted portraits of JFK and urged her to accept one as a gift, Jackie realized that though she especially admired the smaller of the pair, which showed her late husband in a seated position, she simply could not bear to keep it. In anticipation of returning both paintings, she propped them up just outside her bedroom door. One evening in December, young John emerged from Jackie's room. Spotting a portrait of his father, he removed a lollipop from his mouth and kissed the image, saying, "Good night, Daddy." Jackie related the episode to Marg McNamara by way of explanation as to why it would be impossible to have such a picture near. She said it brought to the surface too many things.

For all that, she did everything she could to sustain an atmosphere of normalcy, threadbare though it might be, for Caroline and John. Before leaving the White House, she held a belated third birthday party for John, whose actual birth date had coincided with his father's funeral. In Palm Beach at Christmastime, she was determined to make it, in the words of the nanny, Maud Shaw, "a good time for the children," putting up the familiar lights, stars, and baubles, hanging stockings over the fireplace, and repeating other of the little things they had done as a family when Jack was alive. And when she purchased an eighteenth-century fawn-colored brick house across from the Harriman residence on N Street, she showed the decorator Billy Baldwin photographs of the children's White House rooms and specified that she wanted their new rooms to be precisely the same.

At midnight on January 31, 1964, on the eve of her move, Jackie wrote to former prime minister Harold Macmillan, who was then two weeks from his seventieth birthday. Macmillan had left office on account of illness in October 1963. Still unwell by the time of President Kennedy's funeral, he had designated Andrew and Debo Devonshire to represent him there. Bobby Kennedy had spoken to Macmillan on the phone recently; and Jackie's intention in writing to him, as she said, was to tell him how much Jack had loved him. But, as was often the case with her these days, her original aim was soon derailed. Hardly had she begun to write on her black-bordered mourning stationery when she found herself speaking of the bouts of bitterness that continued to vex her; of her failed efforts to find religious consolation; and of her sense of life's unfairness and of its being the best people who were made to suffer.

Still, at a time when Jackie was yet darkly insisting to friends that her future had died with her husband, she expressed the tender hope to Macmillan that the next day's move might actually be the start of "a new life." During her two months as a recipient of the undersecretary of state's hospitality, the crowds that regularly stood vigil outside, sometimes shivering in the snow, had been a source of distress to Jackie. At a moment of national catastrophe, people had anointed Jackie a heroine. In a time of mass confusion and anxiety, they had invested her with almost magical powers to hold the nation together. They had seized upon the widow's demeanor of emotional control at the funeral to transform her from a symbol of helplessness and vulnerability to a symbol of resolute strength. Jackie for her part was irritated by the chorus of public praise for her conduct in the aftermath of tragedy. "I don't like to hear people say that I am poised and maintaining a good appearance," she resentfully told Bishop Hannan. "I am not a movie actress." Nor did she feel like much of a heroine. On the contrary, she remained privately preoccupied with the notion that she had missed one or more chances to save her husband.

The crowds outside her house were upsetting to her in another way as well. Confronted with the throngs on N Street, she feared that real danger might suddenly spring forth, as it had on November 22. Easily startled, she felt her body tense for another attack, and grew exceedingly alarmed when people attempted not only to see but also to touch the woman who had survived the slaughter in Dallas, or when certain of them broke through the police lines in an effort to kiss and hug the slain president's children. As January waned, the numbers on the sidewalk, instead of diminishing, seemed only to swell in anticipation of the widow's move across the street. Every time Billy Baldwin came from New York to check on the paint, curtains, and other details, it struck him that there were even more people lined up outside the new place, straining to look in the huge windows.

Soon the problem was not just the crowds. Cars and eventually even tour buses began to clog the narrow street. At Arlington National Cemetery, an average of ten thousand tourists visited President Kennedy's grave every day. Many made the pilgrimage to inspect the widow's new house as well. By moving day, N Street had established itself as "one of the tourist sights of Washington." The new residence, which Jackie dubbed "my house with many steps," perched high above street level. Nevertheless, Billy Baldwin recalled: "I was shocked at how easy it was to see inside the house, despite its great elevation. Once I arrived in late evening, and the lights inside the house were making a doubly interesting show for the spectators." After dark, Jackie had no choice but to draw the voluminous apricot silk curtains lest she be on full view to strangers who loomed adoringly, expectantly, until all hours.

Jackie's first month of residence there coincided with the opening sessions of the Warren Commission, a seven-man bipartisan panel convened by the president to review and reveal all of the facts and circumstances surrounding the assassination and the subsequent killing of the alleged assassin. Oswald's death had left the nation in suspense about who had been responsible for the murder of President Kennedy. Among Johnson's aims in establishing the commission was to restore order by reassuring Americans that the crime had been fully investigated and solved, responsibility for the cataclysm firmly fixed. Johnson was also eager to terminate the speculation about Soviet involvement that persisted in many quarters. He worried that Moscow, were it to grow fearful that Washington planned to retaliate, might make a first strike.

Beginning on February 3, the day when Marina Oswald, the alleged assassin's widow, appeared before the committee, the panel took the testimony of 552 witnesses, including associates and acquaintances of both Lee Harvey Oswald and his killer, Jack Ruby; doctors; bystanders; policemen; journalists; and Secret Service agents. Five months into the proceedings, Jackie would testify as well. In the meantime, it was almost impossible to look at a newspaper or turn on a radio or television without encountering further talk of the assassination. At a moment when the country was frantic to learn definitively and at last who killed President Kennedy, Jackie discovered that she had little interest in that particular whodunit. "I had the feeling of what did it matter what they found out?" she later reflected. "They could never bring back the person who was gone."

Another problem for her was that every media reference to the official inquiry had the potential to cause a new flood of uninvited memories. She had acted at once to try to stop precisely this sort of provoking material from "coming up, coming up" (not by chance, her phrasing in this respect reflected the involuntary nature of these onerous recollections) when she moved to exert personal control over the books about the assassination. Suddenly, however, it became impossible to fully shield herself against the steady blast of information from the Warren Commission.

Approximately three weeks after Jackie sent off her letter to Macmillan, she received a fifteen-page answer written in the barely decipherable scrawl that was a result of his having been shot through the right hand during the battle of Loos in 1915. Jackie later said that no letter in her life "could ever have been" what that letter was for her. She called it "the rock that I went back to over and over" throughout the winter of 1964. A year and a half later, she would insist that she could still almost remember it "word for word." And even after four years had passed, there would be moments when, she avowed, a sentence from Macmillan's long letter came "crashing back into my head—and I could see the page it was written on as I did the first time—the color of the ink and paper."

Macmillan told her that he had "read & re-read" her own message and "pondered deeply about it." Though he did not mention it to her, prior to responding he had also conferred with his longtime aide Philip de Zulueta and learned what he could about Jackie's present circumstances from David Ormsby-Gore. In the end, however, it was Macmillan's formative personal experience of having, as he said, "lived through two wars" that would shape his February 18, 1964, reply. That personal history allowed him to make an imaginative leap. It encouraged him to look beyond Jackie's status as a grieving widow and to take into account certain other factors that were also crucially in play. It allowed him to view her ordeal through the unexpected lens of the stories of warriors whose overwhelming experiences on the battlefield, like hers in Dallas, had forever set them apart.

As a captain in the Grenadier Guards in the First World War, Macmillan had been severely wounded in the left thigh during the Battle of the Somme. He had lain for hours surrounded by the dead and screaming wounded. He had been in shock and very nearly died himself. As he told Jackie in his letter, the casualties in that war had been "on a frightful scale." By 1918 he had had "scarcely a friend or relation alive, of military age, except those who had been too ill or weak to go." He too had felt much bitterness. He too had been moved to ask "Why—oh, Why" in an effort to make sense of the senseless. He too had suffered bouts of depression. It struck Macmillan that in important ways Jackie's tribulations had been even worse than his own, for soldiers at least have the consolation of feeling that their sacrifices are for something. "But this," Macmillan wrote, "what has happened to you and (in its way) to all of us. How can we accept it? How can we explain it? Why did God allow it? I am sure you must say this to yourself (as I do) over & over. Such a waste! Such folly! Such bad workmanship! Can there really be a God, who made & guides the world?" He admitted that there were no satisfactory answers and that the only thing to do was to try somehow to retain one's faith in the face of what had occurred.

At the heart of Macmillan's letter was his offer to serve as "a sort of safety-valve or lightning conductor" for Jackie. He encouraged her to view him as a kindred spirit to whom she could write of her anguish in the expectation that he at least would understand.

"You have shown the most wonderful courage to the outer world," he wrote. "The hard thing is really to feel it, inside."

Many times in the course of that winter, Jackie undertook to write back to Macmillan. But when in the morning she reviewed the night thoughts that she had committed to paper, she concluded that it would be wisest not to let anyone see them. So she discarded what she had written. At last, Jackie asked David to explain to Macmillan why he had yet to hear from her.

In the meantime, she promised herself that eventually, perhaps when spring came and things were "a little better," she would manage to produce a letter that actually went off to Birch Grove. Then she would tell the former prime minister that he had helped her more than he would ever know by spurring her to produce all those unsent letters.

The act of writing them, she later said, had been a release for so much that would have destroyed her had she kept it all inside.

During this same period, Arthur Schlesinger made the first of seven official visits to N Street, where he set up his tape recorder and proposed that Jackie answer his questions about her late husband and his administration as if she were speaking across the decades to "an historian of the twenty-first century." These interviews, conducted between March 2 and June 3 of 1964, were part of a larger effort undertaken by a team of historians to record the memories of individuals who had known President Kennedy. The tapes would at length be transcribed and deposited in the archives of the projected John F. Kennedy Library in Boston. The concept behind the emergent academic discipline of oral history was that in an epoch when people were producing fewer letters and diaries, historians had better interview all the players directly lest precious details that would previously have been committed to paper be forever lost to posterity. Jackie's willingness to participate in the oral history project was predicated on two stipulations. The first was that her reminiscences would remain sealed until sometime after her death. The second was that in any case, she would be free to strike anything from the transcript that on reflection she did not care to be part of the historical record.

Thus, whenever she instructed Schlesinger to turn off the machine so that she could ask, "Should I say this on the recorder?," the bow-tie-wearing historian invariably reminded her of the original agreement. "Why don't you say it?" he would reply. "You have control over the transcript."

For Jackie, control was all important in interviews that offered a chance to fashion a narrative not just of her husband's life and presidency, but also, more problematically, of their marriage. It had long been Jack's plan that when he left office, he would tell his story as he saw it and wished others to see it. Now, she believed, it fell to his widow to attempt to do it in his stead, if not in a book, then in the form of these conversations. Still, the undertaking presented a formidable challenge, not least because JFK had had so many secrets. At moments in the tapes, Jackie clearly is not quite sure how much she ought to disclose about her husband's precarious health. She whispers, she hesitates, she requests that there be a pause in the recording. The tapes therefore are often as interesting for their ellipses as for their content, for the intervals when the machine has been urgently turned off as for when it is actually running. On the matter of her marriage, Jackie's task is even more complicated. One observes her proceeding gingerly, testing to see what she can feasibly claim to have been the case to an interlocutor who, on the one hand, knows full well about Jack's dissolute sexual habits, and, on the other, is likely though by no means sworn to go along with the lie.

At times, when the subject matter is especially sensitive, as when she finds herself compelled to comment on Jack's friendship with George

Smathers, Jackie stumbles in the thicket of her own desperately contorted phrases. The thicket is filled with thorns, and at every turn they draw blood. First she insists that the friendship took place "before the Senate." Then she says, no, it was indeed in the Senate but "before he was married." Then she suggests that Smathers "was really a friend of one side of Jack—a rather, I always thought, sort of crude side. I mean, not that Jack had the crude side."

When the subject matter is less personal than political and historical, the challenge that confronts her is no less of a minefield, for, more often than not, she is addressing subjects that she would never have dared or been even remotely inclined to pronounce on while her husband lived. Not only is Jackie doing something that she never anticipated having to do, she is operating in the worst imaginable circumstances—when she is unable to sleep, self-medicating with vodka, tyrannized by flashbacks and nightmares. For Jackie, the principal point of these interviews is to burnish her husband's historical reputation. She certainly does not want to do him any damage, yet there is always the chance that inadvertently she will accomplish precisely that.

There were other potential pitfalls in her talks with Schlesinger, who, in addition to his chores as an oral historian, had recently embarked on the preparation of a much-ballyhooed book about the Kennedy presidency for the publisher Houghton Mifflin. Given the recent upheaval in Schlesinger's professional circumstances, he had an awful lot at stake in the book project. At a time when Johnson had been frantic to retain as many Kennedy people as he could, the new president had scarcely concealed his disdain for Schlesinger, whom he had systematically isolated within the administration. Not inaccurately, Johnson viewed Schlesinger as being in league with RFK. When Schlesinger submitted his resignation, it was accepted, to his perception, with alacrity. Schlesinger in turn was surely no admirer of Johnson's, yet the president's eagerness to see him go stung nonetheless. To make matters worse for Schlesinger, Johnson was intent on inducing the other Kennedy administration insider said to be planning a book, Ted Sorensen, to remain in the administration. Unlike Schlesinger, whom Johnson regarded as a useless intellectual, Sorensen possessed the invaluable skill of being able to write in JFK's voice.

So Johnson was hugely disappointed when at the end of February, Sorensen resigned to produce his own literary take on the Kennedy years. With considerable fanfare, Harper & Row announced the So-rensen book on March 1, the day before Schlesinger's initial oral history interview with Jackie, whose friendship and favor Schlesinger could not but regard as a glittering prize. During the White House years, he had been a social friend of President and Mrs. Kennedy's, a status to which Sorensen could make no comparable claim. Further, Jackie was not alone in disliking and distrusting Sorensen; Bobby, who early on in the speechwriter's tenure had exhibited a certain jealousy of his relation-ship with JFK, had long been cool to Sorensen as well. In any case, as Schlesinger and Sorensen competed to be first with a book in the stores, could Schlesinger really be trusted to scrupulously forget everything the widow told him in the course of their supposedly privileged interviews? Would he even be inclined to do so?

Potential problems in this regard were not limited to the fact that he was simultaneously at work on a book. Given Schlesinger's status as a player in the post-assassination power struggle, might certain of Jackie's remarks, though made with the assumption that they would long remain under seal, suddenly become ammunition in that fight? Once Schlesinger had extracted certain critical information about, say, JFK's private views on Johnson, or the late president's intentions as to whether or not to re-tain Dean Rusk as secretary of state after the '64 election, could Jackie reasonably expect that that information would not somehow find its way into the present political fray?

At length, when Jackie commented that the oral history interviews had been an excruciating experience, it is a safe bet that she was referring not merely to the exertion involved in dredging up from memory so many details about JFK. As she faced Schlesinger, she also had to make spot judgments about which of those details to cover over and conceal— from posterity, from her interviewer, and even at times from herself.

The oral history tapes spanned the late president's life from boyhood on, with the freighted topic of the assassination deliberately left out. In the course of a brief discussion of JFK's religious beliefs, Jackie did touch on certain of the "Why me?" questions that had absorbed her of late. "You don't really start to think of those things until something terrible happens to you," she told Schlesinger on March 4. "I think God's unjust now." Otherwise, she preferred to leave the events of November 22 for her impending talks with William Manchester, whom, by design, she had still yet to meet. As Jackie later said, if Manchester's book were ever to be published at all, she imagined that it would be "bound in black and put away on dark library shelves." The image is immensely suggestive. At moments, Jackie acted as if once she had spoken for the book, the oppressive recollections could be filed away in some densely shadowed corner of the mind where they would never be able to intrude upon her consciousness again. In a sense, her cooperation with Manchester may be seen as an attempt to master material that heretofore had proven impervious to anything like conscious control.

Until the moment when Jackie actually had to face Manchester, she contrived to deal with him through various emissaries. On February 5 she had reached out to the Connecticut-based writer via a phone call placed by Pierre Salinger. On February 26, Bobby Kennedy met with Manchester at the Justice Department to detail her wishes. When Manchester proposed that it might be a good idea to see the widow before he signed on, RFK assured him that there was no need. As the attorney general had been doing since that first night at Bethesda Naval Hospital, he made it clear that he spoke for Mrs. Kennedy. In the present negotiations, if at this point Manchester's dealings with the family might even be called that, he proved to be as deferential as he had been when he invited JFK to alter his own quotes. After various decrees from on high had

been transmitted to Manchester by both Salinger and RFK lieutenant
Edwin Guthman, the author unflinchingly signed an agreement that
provided that his final text could not be published "unless and until approved" by both Jackie and RFK. Presently, Manchester's eager offer to
come to Jackie in Washington at any time on just a few hours' notice fell
flat. So did his request for a quick meeting the better to know what to say
in response to press inquiries once the book deal had been announced.
On March 26, the day after the attorney general's office released the
news of Manchester's appointment, Jackie went off for the Easter weekend with Bobby and Ethel, and both sets of children, to ski in Stowe,
Vermont. Manchester, meanwhile, assured the press that he intended to
see her as soon as possible while her recollections were fresh.

Presently, Jackie, Bobby, Chuck Spalding, and the Radziwills assembled in Antigua, where they were due to spend a week at the waterfront
estate of Bunny Mellon. The group swam and water-skied, but as Spalding remembered, an "overwhelming" air of sadness pervaded the trip. It
struck him that the immense beauty of the setting, which overlooked
Half Moon Bay, merely highlighted "everybody's terrible sense of dejec-
tion." Jackie had brought with her a copy of Edith Hamilton's *The Greek
Way*, which she had been studying in an effort to learn how the ancient
Greeks approached the universal questions posed by human suffering.

Bobby, who had been troubled by questions of his own since November 22, borrowed the Hamilton book from her in Antigua. "I remember
he'd disappear," Jackie later recalled. "He'd be in his room an awful lot
of the time . . . reading that and underlining things." To Spalding's eye,
Bobby was depressed nearly to the point of paralysis. Unable to sleep,
frantic that his own actions as attorney general against Cuba or the
Mob might inadvertently have led to his brother's murder, he had lost an
alarming amount of weight, and his clothes hung loosely from a frame
that called to mind a Giacometti figure. For all of Bobby's acute suffering, however, he was also worried about Jackie. Though in the course of
a March 13 interview he had assured the television host Jack Paar that

she was making "a good deal of progress," it was evident in private that she was not. After they came back from the Caribbean, Bobby, concerned about Jackie's abiding mood of despondency, asked a Jesuit priest with whom he and Ethel were close to talk to his brother's widow. First, however, in response to a new handwritten note from Manchester requesting a meeting, Jackie finally consented. When, shortly before noon on April 7, the edgy, rumpled, ruddy-faced author beheld her at last in her book- and picture-filled living room, she told him that her emotional state made it impossible to be interviewed just now. Manchester had no choice, really, but to be patient.

Before Jackie received Manchester again, she began to see Father Mc-Sorley. The flimsy pretext for these sessions, which began on April 27, was that the priest, who also happened to be an expert tennis player, had signed on to help Jackie improve her game. Almost immediately that first day on the tennis court at Hickory Hill, she broached certain of the preoccupations she had previously spoken of with others. On this and subsequent occasions, Father McSorley recorded her comments afterward in his diary. Today there were the unanswerable questions: "I don't know how God could take him away," she told the priest. "It's so hard to believe." There were the feelings of guilt at what she perceived to have been her failure to act in time to prevent Jack's death: "I would have been able to pull him down," she said remorsefully, "or throw myself in front of him, or do something, if I had only known." But it was not until the next day, when Jackie and the priest faced each other again on the tennis court, that she began to speak overtly of suicide.

"Do you think God would separate me from my husband if I killed myself?" Jackie asked. "It is so hard to bear. I feel as though I am going out of my mind at times." When she asked the priest to pray that she die, he responded: "Yes, if you want that. It's not wrong to pray to die." Jackie went on to insist that Caroline and John would be better off without her: "I'm no good to them. I'm so bleeding inside." Father McSorley countered that the children did indeed need her. He argued that, contrary to anything Jackie said, Caroline and John certainly would not be better off living at Hickory Hill, where Ethel Kennedy could hardly give them the attention they required. "She has so much pressure from public life and so many children," he said of Ethel. "Nobody can do for them except you."

Six days after Jackie confided to Father McSorley that she had been contemplating suicide, she finally sat down with Manchester to talk about the assassination. Jackie asked him: "Are you just going to put down all the facts, who ate what for breakfast and all that, or are you going to put yourself in the book, too?" Manchester's reply, that it would be impossible to keep himself out, seemed to please her. Nonetheless, in important ways, she and the writer were and would remain at cross-purposes. She longed to stop reliving the horror. He was determined to experience it himself, the better to enable readers to experience it as well. She needed to relegate November 22 to the past. He aspired by his craft to make it vividly present. Manchester's aesthetic, which, then and later, emphasized sensations, impressions, and the minutely detailed moment-by-moment reconstruction of events, reflected his wartime experiences as a marksman for whom everything seen over his sights had had, in his words, "a cameolike quality, as keen and well-defined as a line by Van Eyck." At his most acutely intense, Manchester brought to the act of writing the hyperawareness that soldiers experience in the war zone when the body, faced with high threat, diverts blood to the limbic neurons in a concentrated effort to locate and dissipate danger.

Curiously, when Manchester encountered JFK's widow, he was still years away from being able to write about the war, his war. "It lay too deep," he later said. "I couldn't reach it. But I had known it must be there. . . . Some recollections never die. They lie in one's subconscious, squirreled away, biding their time." Manchester was, by his own telling, "a troubled man who, for over thirty years, repressed what he could not bear to remember." By contrast, Jackie's memories of Dallas, some of them anyway, were readily, plentifully available, indeed, too much so for her comfort, if not for her sanity.

"It's rather hard to stop once the floodgates open," Jackie was to say ruefully of the Manchester interviews, which the author captured on a tape recorder that he arranged to place out of her sight, though she knew it was running. Lest the floodgates close at any point, Manchester fed her daiquiris, which he poured liberally from large containers. RFK, unlike his sister-in-law, refused to take a drink when interviewed; as a consequence, Manchester lamented, the attorney general's replies were "abrupt, often monosyllabic—and much less responsive." From the interviewer's perspective, in Jackie's case it also helped that before talking to her he had already interrogated others connected with the assassination. Crucially, he came to her with an abundance of detail culled from other sources. The episodes he repeatedly guided Jackie over were already familiar terrain to him. He also gleaned, from the widow herself, that she devoted many sleepless nights to obsessively turning certain of these episodes "over and over" in her mind; she knew that brooding was useless now, yet she was unable to stop herself. For Manchester, rather than have to start from scratch, it became a matter of cuing her properly and inserting himself in an agonizing process she had been through many times before.

Various people, from RFK on, who had heard Jackie speak of Dallas had sensed that they were about to be told more than they wanted to hear. Manchester, by contrast, could never seem to get enough detail. He did not just want objective information; he wanted to know how it all had felt at the time. "He must be there, and he must be there then," Manchester once said of the imaginative act that has to occur if a nonfiction writer is to succeed in recapturing the past. In the present instance, he required Jackie to take him there. For literary reasons, he needed her to reexperience the assassination, whereas for personal reasons, she needed to learn somehow to tell her story without wholly reliving it. The Manchester interviews were exceptionally painful to her, and at moments her voice dropped so low that he feared his tape recorder might not have captured every word.

It is not too much to suppose that further intensifying the emotional-ism of these sessions was that certain of the experiences she talked about proved to have been uncannily like Manchester's own during the battle for Okinawa, the very material he had yet to be able to resurrect in his own mind. Strange to say, in the Pacific theater he too had been spat-tered with blood and brains when someone nearby was killed. He too had narrowly escaped being slaughtered himself. He too had felt guilt at having survived. So, when Jackie spoke of such matters, it had to be fas-cinating, even stimulating, to Manchester for sheerly personal reasons as well.

"I just talked about the private things," Jackie was to say with regret of her sessions with Manchester. "Then the man went away, and I think he was very upset during the writing of the book."

Their meetings that month took place on May 4, 7, and 8. By the nineteenth, Father McSorley found himself growing fearful that Jackie, as he wrote, "was really thinking of suicide." The priest had briefly hoped she might be doing better, but the way she talked now spurred him to take a different view. Speaking again of the prospect of killing herself, Jackie told him that she would be pleased if her death precipi-tated "a wave" of other suicides because it would be a good thing if peo-ple were allowed to "get out of their misery." She disconcerted the priest by insisting that "death is great" and by alluding to the suicide of Mari-lyn Monroe. "I was glad that Marilyn Monroe got out of her misery," JFK's widow maintained. "If God is going to make such a to-do about judging people because they take their own lives, then someone ought to punish Him." The next day, after Father McSorley strove to persuade Jackie that suicide would be wrong, she reassured him that she agreed and that she would never actually attempt to kill herself. Still, it was clear from all she had said previously that she was not improving—far from it.

Jackie described herself in this period as having tried "to climb a little bit of the way up the hill," only to abruptly discover that she had rolled back down to the bottom again. She was speaking of her feelings during a May 29 memorial Mass at St. Matthew's, presided over by Bishop Hannan on what ought to have been President Kennedy's forty-seventh birthday. Jackie later remembered that as she stood "in the same place in the same church" she had been in in November, she felt "as if time had rolled back six months." When the bishop approached her afterward to exchange the peace of Christ, Jackie discovered that she could not bear even to look at him, for she doubted that she would be able to restrain her tears. Following the Mass, she told David Ormsby-Gore (who had become Lord Harlech on the recent death of his father) that she was no closer to being reconciled to events than she had been in November. Later in the day, Jackie flew to Hyannis Port, where she and RFK participated in a satellite television tribute to President Kennedy, which also included contributions by former prime minister Macmillan, speaking from England, and other world figures.

The next morning brought unsettling news. It was reported in the press, erroneously as it would turn out, that the Warren Commission's findings were expected to show that, contrary to much previous opinion, the first bullet had struck both the president and the governor and that the last of the three shots had gone wild. That certainly was not how Jackie remembered it. She had been there. The mental pictures with which she continued to be inundated were so sharp and detailed. Yet here was new information that seemed to challenge the validity of her memories. Nor was this the first vertiginous discrepancy between what she thought she remembered and what she subsequently read or saw. Similarly disorienting had been film stills of Jackie crawling on the rear of the presidential limousine. Try as she might, she could recollect no such episode. She did not deny that it had taken place, but it had no particular reality for her either. As Jackie prepared to deliver her widely anticipated testimony before the Warren Commission, it was becoming apparent, even to her, that despite the many times she had retold and relived the events of November 22, she was less certain than ever of what had actually occurred.

Back in Washington on June 1, Jackie told Bishop Hannan of the sense she had had at the birthday Mass that her recovery efforts to date had been "for nothing." She pledged to try "so hard" for her children's sake in the years that were left to her—"though I hope they won't be too many," she added pointedly and poignantly. Following two days, June 2 and 3, of further interviews with Arthur Schlesinger, she received representatives of the Warren Commission at her home on the fifth. Facing Chief Justice Earl Warren and the commission's general counsel, J. Lee Rankin, along with the attorney general and a court reporter, in her living room late on a Friday afternoon, Jackie asked for the umpteenth time: "Do you want me to tell you what happened?"

On countless occasions since the night at Bethesda Naval Hospital when she had greeted visitors in her bloodied garments, she had related this same story, often in nearly identical phrases, to friends and interviewers. "Let her get rid of it if she can," the physician had urged, yet for all the words and images that had poured from Jackie's lips, there could be no denying that, six months later, the horror was still very much with her. The assumption at Hickory Hill, and increasingly in various other quarters, was that Jackie needed to try harder to, in her brother- and sister-in-law's phrase, "get out of the doldrums." "Sorrow is a form of self-pity," Bobby counseled her. "We have to go on." Even Jackie seemed to ascribe the absence of progress to some personal weakness of her own. In conversation with Father McSorley, she bitterly lamented that she lacked Bobby and Ethel's drive and energy. She blamed herself for, among other failings, spending so much time in bed in a mist of depression; some mornings, she required as long as ninety minutes to wake up fully. Still, when RFK, Father McSorley, and others urged her to stop brooding and to get on with her life, they were asking her to do something that in ways they seemed never to comprehend was simply beyond her capacity. When Jackie had spoken of feeling as though she were losing her sanity, Father McSorley appears to have interpreted her remarks exclusively in terms of a widow's longing for her husband. When she talked repeatedly about taking her own life, it seems not to have occurred to the priest, focused as he was on her recent bereavement, that she might be responding as much, if not more, to the pain of living day to day with all that was still going on inside her head.

Jackie had hoped to start a new life when she moved to a house of her own on N Street. But how was she to do that when memories of November 22 kept invading and usurping the present? She had an abiding need to endlessly go over the sequence of events in Dallas. She persisted in having nightmares and otherwise finding it hard to sleep; in feeling, even hoping, that she had no future; in perceiving herself to be constantly under threat; and in perpetually seeking to avoid things that might call up recollections of the assassination.

In 1964 there was as yet no name for what she was enduring. At the time, Harold Macmillan perhaps came closest to intuiting the character of her post-Dallas ordeal when he compared it to the experiences of war veterans like himself. Macmillan could not precisely identify the problem, but he suggested exactly the right frame within which to begin to think about it. In the following decade, the efforts of Vietnam veterans and a small number of psychiatrists sympathetic to their plight led to the 1980 inclusion of posttraumatic stress disorder (PTSD) in the American Psychiatric Association's official manual of mental disorders. Subsequent study of the effects of trauma on a wide range of subjects, including veterans of Iraq and Afghanistan, added a profusion of invaluable detail to the picture. In every significant respect, Jackie's ordeal conforms to the portrait that has gradually emerged of the effect of overwhelming experiences on body and mind. Symptoms of PTSD include reliving the traumatic event; avoiding situations that threaten to provoke memories of the event; feeling numb; and feeling keyed up. Among other hallmarks are suicidal thoughts; nightmares and sleep disturbance; obsessive ruminations; and a significant spike in distress around the anniversary of the traumatic event.

Not everyone who has experienced a traumatic event—such as combat exposure, assault, sexual abuse, or a natural disaster—will later suffer the thralldom to the past that characterizes PTSD. For some people, the painful pictures really do begin to fade when the trauma becomes assimilated as an extreme experience in their personal past that, so long as they have been removed from the threatening environment, is unlikely to recur. A crucial distinction between people who are temporarily stressed and those who develop PTSD is that, at a certain point, the latter start to painstakingly organize their lives around the trauma. A diagnosis of PTSD requires that the symptoms be in play for at least a month. When they last as many as three months, the disorder is said to be acute. When they persist beyond that point, it is described as chronic. People who have witnessed the violent death of someone they loved are at especially high risk for developing PTSD.

Central to the traumatic experience is the acknowledgement of humankind's existential vulnerability that it forces upon us. The notion that much of life is random and beyond our control is almost too uncomfortable to acknowledge. We look for any way around it. We ask the unanswerable questions. We blame ourselves, however unjustly and irrationally, for the unspeakable thing that has occurred, aiming to shore up, even at our own expense, the fragile illusion of human mastery. It is characteristic of PTSD that whereas certain episodes are recollected in rich, vibrant limbic detail, others, often those in which we were confronted with our own powerlessness to alter the course of horrific events, we may remember not at all.

Nine

I think we gotta give a little thought to our vice president," said Lyndon Johnson. "You know who's campaigning for it, and that's gonna be a knock-down drag-out probably. With Miz Kennedy nominating him and all the emotions . . . you can't tell what'll come there."

It was July 3, 1964, a month before Democrats were due to assemble in Atlantic City to name their presidential and vice-presidential candidates. Johnson, at the LBJ Ranch for the weekend, was on the phone talking to John Connally about what White House aides had taken to calling "the Bobby problem." As Johnson's remarks made clear, he was haunted by visions of Jackie appearing at the Convention Center and effectively closing the deal for her brother-in-law by nominating him for the number two position.

In the immediate aftermath of the assassination, Bobby had been far from the only one to consider the possibility of a Kennedy vice presidency. Also by December 1963, LBJ too had begun to reflect on the suitability of RFK as a running mate. In private, the president left no doubt that the prospect of anointing Bobby was abhorrent to him. "I don't want history to say I was elected to this office because I had Bobby on the ticket with me," Johnson declared. "But I'll take him if I need him." Seven months later, the president's superb approval ratings, coupled with preliminary poll numbers suggesting that he would handily obliterate any Republican adversary in November, indicated that he did not need his enemy on the ticket after all. Besides, the Republicans when they assembled in San Francisco in mid-July seemed likely to nominate the ultraconservative senator from Arizona, Barry Goldwater. One Washington wag quipped that should Goldwater be the candidate, LBJ could choose Mickey Mouse as his running mate and yet be assured of victory.

Accordingly, LBJ's Bobby problem went from deciding whether he needed RFK to determining how best to cut him from contention. At this point it was something the president was going to have to do soon, but he was exceedingly nervous about what might happen afterward. From first to last, the specter of Jackie's intervention loomed large in LBJ's perfervid calculations. Johnson had worked hard to get his predecessor's widow on side, or at least to convey the impression that she was on side. Having failed in both respects (a particular disappointment had been her unwavering refusal to visit Johnson at the White House, because, she said, "I'm so scared I'll start to cry again"), he shifted his energies to at least preventing Jackie from speaking for RFK in Atlantic City. The day after Johnson had talked to John Connally about his fears of precisely such a setback, the president called Jackie at the Cape, where she and the children had been installed since mid-June. Rather than request anything of her directly, LBJ, in the course of the customary affectionate banter, clutched her with hoops of steel.

The woman to whom LBJ imputed an almost mystical capacity to influence great events in Washington was, when he called her on July 4, about to make a public announcement of her decision not to return to the nation's capital. Her effort to start anew there had already folded its wings. Spring had come and matters were not even "a little better," as she had once anticipated. Washington aroused too many unwelcome recollections. The new residence had quickly become contaminated by the trauma, her words and images in the course of various interviews having worked their way into the freshly white-painted living room walls like wood smoke. And not least, there had been the problem of those enormous windows overlooking N Street, and of an adoring, but also somehow threatening, public's access to her there. Jackie's Warren Commission testimony ("I was trying to hold his hair on. From the front there was nothing—I suppose there must have been. But from the back you could see, you know, you were trying to hold his hair on, and his skull on") proved to be her Washington swan song.

Echoing the phrase she had used on the eve of her previous move, Jackie told Marg McNamara of her intention to attempt to start a new life in New York. In Washington, she acknowledged, she had been becoming more and more of a recluse. Along with Father McSorley, who continued to advise her, she hoped that the move to a new city would, among other advantages, help her to stop brooding. But, whatever Jackie and the priest may have wished, it would not be so easy to escape the traumatic memories that, wherever she went on earth, would long persist in causing havoc in her life. She and Father McSorley both believed her to be suffering from an inability to get over her grief. He went so far as to suggest that Jackie felt guilty about getting better and that she needed to divest herself of that guilt. But in ways he simply did not grasp, Dallas had burdened her with a condition that was not so much psychological or emotional as physiological. As she was soon to discover, her problem was not something that she could just choose to leave behind in Georgetown as though it were a sofa she preferred not to take with her to Manhattan because it might clash with the new decor.

That July, the assassination inevitably pursued her to Hyannis Port in manifold guises, among them the persistent person of William Manchester, whose visits to N Street had been so disturbing to her. The author turned up at the Cape to interrogate Rose Kennedy, Pat Lawford, and the widow herself. Unbeknownst to him at the time, his July 20 session with Jackie would be his last. Lest she further allow Manchester, by his highly detailed questioning, to repeatedly hurl her back to the events of November 22, Jackie arranged never to be interviewed by him again. To his monumental frustration, henceforward whenever he contacted Jackie's office, he would be referred to RFK's secretary, who in turn would pass him on to various aides.

Jackie's dealings with *Look* magazine, which was preparing a special JFK memorial issue in conjunction with the upcoming first anniversary of the assassination, were a good deal more complicated because of the clashing Kennedy interests in play. She had previously rejected the idea of an upbeat story about her life since Dallas that the photographer Stanley Tretick wanted to do for the memorial number. Tretick had pitched her unsuccessfully on May 21, two days after Father McSorley had begun to fear that she might actually be about to kill herself. And she remained opposed when Tretick re-pitched her on July 12. "My feeling," Tretick wrote, "is that in the context of the Memorial Issue it would not be harmful to show that [JFK's] children . . . are getting along fine with the help of his brother and some of the rest of the family. And that Mrs. John F. Kennedy (even though the scar will never heal) is not in the depths of deep despair, that she is working hard to preserve the fine image of President Kennedy and that she is building a new life for her and her children."

For Jackie, the problem with saying no to this was that Bobby was cooperating enthusiastically with the magazine, which he had already invited in to photograph at Hickory Hill. At a moment when Bobby's immediate active options included not only the vice presidency, but also a Senate seat from New York, a *Look* feature that showed him assuming his brother's political mantle, as well as looking after JFK's widow and children, was not to be turned down lightly. At length, Bobby persuaded her to participate.

Though RFK had briefly considered abandoning, or at least taking a hiatus from, politics after Teddy Kennedy was severely injured in a plane crash in June, the attorney general had since enthusiastically recommitted himself to public life. A June 24–July 1 trip that he and Ethel had taken to Germany and Poland had been immensely successful, particularly the visit to Cracow and Warsaw, where Bobby seemed to discover in lighthearted exchanges with adoring crowds of young people a new, easier, more effective public persona. The cheers that greeted RFK in Poland appeared to sandblast away the despair that had accrued to him since his brother's death. Back home he returned to a spate of press articles conjecturing about what he planned to do next politically. Among these articles was a major piece in the July 13 *U.S. News & World Report* titled simply "Bobby Kennedy's Future."

By some lights, RFK never entirely emerged from his depression. "When did he come out of that?" his sister Jean would say many years later. "I don't think he ever came out of that." Still, at the time, a certain perceptible change for the better does seem to have occurred. Ethel Kennedy referred to it, characteristically, as a matter of "getting Bobby over the hump." And Chuck Spalding would later say: "It seemed to me that that mood [of dejection] prevailed right up until the time that Bobby just rid himself of it, as everybody else had to sooner or later . . . And then I think that probably time doing what it does it removes these things from you. You simply . . . can't exist like that, and you begin to fill in your life with other things and that becomes a memory. What formerly held your attention so completely becomes a memory and fades."

Jackie, by contrast, seemed to experience no such improvement. "I am a living wound," she said of herself at the time. Heretofore, she and RFK had seemed at moments to be almost a unit apart from other people. The electric intensity of their bond (which, then and later, persuaded many people that they must be having an affair) derived not only from her great need, but from his as well. In lavishing care and attention on his brother's widow, he was fulfilling the role of family leader he had coveted all his life but had never had reason to believe would ever be his, though he naturally despised the manner in which it had come to him. So how to account for the disparity in their respective aspects and outlooks that began to be noticeable that spring and summer of 1964? In incipient form, it had already been present in the ambulance to Bethesda Hospital, he intermittently peering through the curtains at the world flying past outside, she riveted to the ghastly images inside her head.

Eight months later, instead of fading out, or even beginning to lessen in immediacy, November 22 remained powerfully present to her. The floodgates were constantly in peril of reopening, which is why the photographic session at Hyannis Port, with all of the chaotic feelings it threatened to incite, was just not something she wanted to do. But Bobby needed her to pose with the children, and at last she consented out of loyalty—loyalty to her brother-in-law, but also to Jack, whose agenda RFK pledged to keep alive.

As July drew to a close, the question of how far Jackie would go the following month in support of RFK remained paramount at the White House. The Republicans had indeed anointed Barry Goldwater, whose strength lay in the Southern states, precisely where RFK was weakest. Even with the numbers emphatically on Johnson's side, however, the president was frantic Bobby might yet outmaneuver him. "He's got the lady [Jackie] thinking about going to the convention, and he put that out yesterday," LBJ complained on the morning of the twenty-ninth. "He thinks that most of the delegations are for him, and this is the thing he wants more than anything else in his life. If he's denied it, it'll be 'very cruel.'" When Johnson spoke those words, he was bracing himself to face down Bobby, who was due in the Oval Office later in the day. Even when RFK seemed to react calmly to being told that he would not be on the ticket after all, the president continued to worry. On the thirtieth, a news report that JFK's widow did indeed plan to come to Atlantic City, where she would press delegates to support Bobby's vice-presidential bid, sent Johnson into a new fit of agitation. "There have been stories this morning that Teddy wanted him [to fight for the second spot on the ticket] and Miz Kennedy was going to the convention," the president lamented to Dean Rusk, ". . . and that this means a war."

Word that Bobby had invited key political advisers to Hyannis Port that weekend further inflamed the president. Did the summons mean that RFK and his supporters were indeed planning to stampede the convention? In fact, the meeting with former New York governor Averell Harriman and other boosters proved to be, in Ethel Kennedy's words (citing news accounts), "a turning point for Bobby"; he emerged determined to run for the Senate now that the vice presidency was no longer in play. McNamara, who prided himself on maintaining extremely close personal contacts with the Kennedys though he continued to work for LBJ, assuaged the president's fears somewhat when he reported that Bobby was indeed going to seek a Senate seat. That was good news for the Johnsonites, as it meant RFK would be less likely to disrupt the convention.

McNamara had encouraging news about Jackie as well. By this time, she had taken the children to Hammersmith Farm, where she planned to leave them with her mother while she traveled by yacht along the Dalmatian Coast of Yugoslavia with the Wrightsmans, the Radziwills, and the Harlechs (as David and Sissie Ormsby-Gore were now known). McNamara told LBJ that he had talked to her and that she wanted no part of any RFK–LBJ showdown. Besides, she was to be in Europe throughout the critical run-up to the Democratic National Convention. "I hope she'll stay a little longer than planned," McNamara went on, ". . . and that will keep her out of it." McNamara himself had been urging RFK to pursue the Senate seat, and he assured Johnson that he had asked Jackie "to push him" as well. McNamara's private conversations with Jackie before she left the United States on August 5, and his willingness to report on them to the president, epitomized the vulnerability of a woman who could rely on none of these figures—McNamara, RFK, or LBJ—to advise her in terms of her interests alone. Each man spoke to her in a manner that was kind, warm, and understanding, yet each had his own interests at heart and did not scruple to use her to further those interests. Which is not to suggest that they failed to care for her deeply and sincerely, only that politics and careers were ever in the mix of their dealings with her.

While Jackie was abroad, the Kennedyites examined how most effectively to employ her to further RFK's chances in New York, where some key politicos, New York City mayor Robert Wagner not least among them, regarded Bobby as an interloper. A tribute to JFK was scheduled in Atlantic City, which LBJ had insisted take place after both he and his chosen running mate, Hubert Humphrey, had been nominated, lest Bobby and his supporters use the opportunity to storm the convention. LBJ's recurrent Jackie nightmare notwithstanding, there had never really been any question of her appearing at the Convention Center. Like Johnson, she too feared the outpouring of emotions her presence there would elicit from the delegates, but whereas the president dreaded the potential political impact of those feelings, she worried about the effect upon herself.

Given the Kennedyites' inability to position Jackie at RFK's side on the evening of the tribute, when he was scheduled to introduce a short film about his late brother, their next-best idea was to produce her at an invitation-only afternoon reception hosted by Averell Harriman at a nearby hotel, where she and RFK would greet delegates together. Soon, however, a telephone call that Johnson placed to Bobby in Maine on the morning of August 12 scrambled calculations within the Kennedy camp. Due to meet with Mayor Robert Wagner later that same day, Johnson unexpectedly offered to help Bobby in New York. "I just want to make it clear that I want to do what you want done," said Johnson, binding to him a man he despised and who was known to loathe him in turn. "I think that would be damn helpful," said Bobby, for whom Wagner had hitherto loomed as a—perhaps the—major obstacle.

But how would Johnson react when he learned that Jackie was indeed coming to the Jersey Shore? Might he fear that an insurrection was yet in the works? The president was capable of bringing in Wagner and other key figures, but he could just as easily assure their opposition to a Kennedy candidacy. In an effort to forestall such a disaster, Teddy Kennedy was delegated to call Johnson on the thirteenth. "Mr. President," said the Massachusetts senator, who was still convalescing after the plane crash, "we have had a very nice invitation from Governor Harriman to have a reception at the convention on Thursday after the selection of the presidential and vice presidential candidates . . . for Mrs. Kennedy. Jackie has indicated that she would be delighted to accept this, but of course we wanted to have this in complete accord with your wishes."

What could Johnson do but assent, though it is hard to imagine he was delighted when he said: "I want to do anything and everything I can at any time to make her as happy and as pleased as she can be, under the circumstances." LBJ's strategic countermove was to invite Jackie to sit with him in the presidential box during the nationally televised tribute to her late husband; that way, if she really had to be there, at least the luster of her presence would be conferred upon Johnson.

In the event, Jackie preferred to fly into Atlantic City for the day only, and to leave well before the evening tribute. At the August 27 reception in her honor, she, along with Bobby, a pregnant Ethel, and other Kennedys, greeted some five thousand delegates in three shifts. The husband-and-wife actors Frederic March and Florence Eldridge read a program of excerpts from some of JFK's favorite literary works, much of it about death and dying young, which Jackie had selected for the occasion. Introduced to the audience by Harriman, Jackie spoke in a scarcely audible voice: "Thank you all for coming, all of you who helped President Kennedy in 1960." If possible, her words were even harder to make out when she continued: "May his light always shine in all parts of the world." In the course of the five-hour reception, Jackie twice appeared on an exterior balcony, first with Bobby, then with Ethel, to wave to excited crowds on the Atlantic City boardwalk.

By design, she was safely back in Newport that night when RFK received a rapturous sixteen-minute ovation in the Convention Hall when he came out to introduce the documentary about his brother. Bobby concluded his own remarks with a passage from Shakespeare's *Romeo and Juliet* that Jackie had suggested: "When he shall die / Take him and cut him out in little stars / And he will make the face of heaven so fine / That all the world will be in love with night, / And pay no worship to the garish sun." Then and later, many people would note the thrust, as Arthur Schlesinger called it, of the last line.

Was the reading a deliberate jab at LBJ? Not likely. Two days previously when Bobby, with Mayor Wagner at his side, announced his entry into the Senate race, he had noted that President Johnson had pledged to campaign for him in New York. RFK was hardly about to do anything at the convention to jeopardize that crucial White House support.

Afterward, Jackie wrote to Joe Alsop that she ought never to have watched the filmed tribute to JFK on television in Newport, where the last photographs of him and John on the beach had been taken nearly a year before. Having successfully ducked one situation likely to unseal disturbing recollections, Jackie had promptly and calamitously placed herself in another. As it happened, viewing the documentary in this particular setting had provoked a whole separate chain of anguished associations.

To make matters worse, when she read Alsop's August 28 account of his own deeply felt response to the JFK film, which he had seen at the convention, his letter, she reported, "opened the floodgates" anew. Nine months after the assassination, rather than diminishing, the potential triggers of trauma-related memories and emotions seemed only to proliferate. She had come to a point where even a letter meant to be helpful, as Alsop's plainly was, was capable of setting off strong feelings of distress.

Simply by causing her emotions to surge, Alsop's remarks had plunged her back into the trauma. Jackie replied to Alsop on the thirty-first by observing that contrary to what people said about time making everything better, it was proving to be "just the reverse" for her. She noted that every day she had to steel herself, as she put it, took a little more out of her that she needed for her task of making a new life. Jackie's abject suggestion that JFK's death had left her to be the "miserable self" she had long been seeking to escape horrified her former mentor.

"You have never had nearly enough self-confidence," Alsop passionately retorted. ". . . Your self is not 'miserable.' " Reminding Jackie that when she first came to him, he had given her the highest handicap he had ever bestowed on any starter, Alsop urged her to concentrate on all that faced her presently when she endeavored to start over again.

Jackie had a fantasy of what might be possible in New York, where she was to take up temporary residence at the Carlyle Hotel while an apartment that she had purchased at 1040 Fifth Avenue was being prettified. As she told Treasury secretary C. Douglas Dillon, whose purview included the Secret Service, she longed to be able "to walk around the city, take taxis, do all the little daily things, without two people always following." On her first day in Manhattan, Monday, September 14, the indications certainly seemed positive. She took both children rowing in Central Park, where few people appeared to notice them. This was nothing like Washington, where she had needed only to appear at her front door for onlookers to call her name and snap photos in rapid succession. For a few halcyon hours it seemed as if New Yorkers might actually afford her a modicum of privacy, but the picture changed abruptly the next day.

After she delivered Caroline to her new school at the Convent of the Sacred Heart in Carnegie Hill, Jackie and young John visited RFK's midtown campaign headquarters. Bobby's staff had notified the press (though not the local police station) that his brother's widow was to be there greeting campaign volunteers, and a battery of photographers

Queen Deb, age eighteen.
©*Condé Nast Archive/Corbis*

At the *Washington Times-Herald*, 1952.
Courtesy of the Everett Collection

Wedding day, Newport, Rhode Island, September 12, 1953. Behind the newlyweds are JFK's siblings Bobby, Pat, Eunice, Teddy, and Jean.

Photograph by Toni Frissell in the John F. Kennedy Presidential Library and Museum, Boston

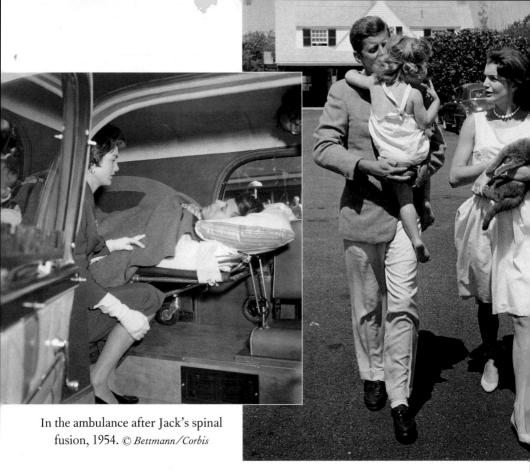

In the ambulance after Jack's spinal
fusion, 1954. © *Bettmann/Corbis*

Presidential candidate JFK holding daughter
Caroline. Jackie was then pregnant with John Jr.
Hyannis Port, August 1960. © *Bettmann/Corbis*

With French President
Charles de Gaulle on
the European trip that
made Jackie a figure of
international appeal.
© *Bettmann/Corbis*

In Fort Worth, Texas, the morning of November 22, 1963. © *Bettmann/Corbis*

Dallas. *Zapruder Film © 1967 (Renewed 1995), The Sixth Floor Museum at Dealey Plaza*

With RFK at Andrews Air Force Base in Maryland, November 22, 1963.
Associated Press

With Lady Bird Johnson and RFK at a reception in Jackie's honor at the 1964 Democratic National Convention in Atlantic City. © *Bettmann/Corbis*

With John Jr. and
Caroline in New
York. © *Condé Nast
Archive/Corbis*

With Harold Macmillan at
Birch Grove, 1965.
*Photo by David Cairns/Express/
Getty Images*

With Bob McNamara
prior to the christening
of the aircraft car-
rier *John F. Kennedy* in
1967. *Photo by Michael
Ochs Archives/Getty Images*

In Cambodia with David Harlech, 1967.
© *Bettmann/Corbis*

With Caroline and John Jr. (*to Caroline's left*) at St. Patrick's Cathedral after Bobby Kennedy's death, 1968. © *Bettmann/Corbis*

Marriage to Aristotle Onassis, Skorpios, 1968.
© *Bettmann/Corbis*

Pursued by paparazzo Ron Galella.

Photo by Ron Galella/Premium Archive/Getty Images

At Lord Harlech's funeral in Wales with Teddy Kennedy, 1985. *Photo by Tom Wargacki/WireImage*

With Ari.

© Bettmann/ Corbis

With Maurice Tempelsman. *Photo by Bettina Cirone/Time & Life Pictures/Getty Images*

With John in 1989. *Photo by Time & Life Pictures/Getty Images*

Photo by Time & Life Pictures/Getty Images

downstairs on East Forty-second Street attracted a crowd of some four hundred people. When Jackie, holding young John by the hand, emerged from the campaign office after about ten minutes, the friendly, cheering crowd surrounded her. Amid the chaos, there was a bit of pushing. More than once, as campaign workers attempted to clear a path, Jackie seemed as if she might be about to fall. In the end, she and her son reached the car safely. Still, it was the sort of episode that, after Dallas, could not but propel her into heart-pounding, adrenaline-pumping high alert. She had yet to spend forty-eight hours in the city when the visit to Kennedy headquarters had thrust into stark relief the conflicting needs of Jackie and the brother-in-law whom she depended on and adored. At a time when he was seeking public office there, New York was almost certainly among the last places in which to search for any kind of peace.

The timing of her move proved inopportune in other ways as well. The findings of the Warren Commission were scheduled to be made public later that month in hopes of providing resolution before the first anniversary of JFK's death. The panel's assessment that a crazed lone gunman had been responsible offered no comfort to Jackie, who would have preferred for her husband at least to have died for some great cause such as civil rights. Instead, the official ruling merely highlighted the senselessness of the tragedy. That left her with no way to rationalize his violent death in terms of some higher meaning. At any rate, as she told Alsop, she was determined to read nothing that was written in the run-up to November 22. Given the degree of public interest in the assassination, however, it was one thing to actively attempt to avoid reminders of Dallas and quite another to succeed when the volume was so immense. The uncertainty about where and when they might suddenly materialize transformed Manhattan, even her own hotel suite, into an anxiety-laden obstacle course.

And it was not just the reminders themselves when they popped out at her, often in the form of words and pictures, that were so upsetting. The very anticipation of encountering some new trigger could be acutely painful, as when, in this period, Jackie worried at the prospect that she would one day be confronted with a book titled *The Day Kennedy Was Shot*. "The idea of it is so distressing to me, I cannot bear to think of seeing—or of seeing advertised—a book with that name and subject," she wrote on September 17 to Jim Bishop, whose work-in-progress she had thus far failed to obstruct by commissioning another book on the same subject. Jackie went on: "This whole year has been a struggle and it seems you can never escape from reminders. You try so hard to avoid them—then you take the children to the news shop—and there is a magazine with a picture of Oswald on it, staring up at you." Without mentioning that she was already fleeing from Manchester, she repeatedly cited his forthcoming authorized account in a renewed effort to stop Bishop. Jackie begged Bishop not to proceed with his book, noting that its very existence "would be just one more thing that would cause suffering."

Bishop countered by pointing out that his book was only one among a great many on the subject. He cited various other accounts that had already been published or were even then (in case Jackie had not yet visualized the process herself) "being set in type." "This morning," Bishop helpfully continued, "ten thousand newspapers throughout the United States published a re-creation of November 22, 1963. Next week, Bantam books will place 500,000 copies of it in the bookstores. The Government Printing Office has a backlog of orders for the Warren Commission report. G. P. Putnam's John Day sent an announcement to me that they were publishing the European bestseller: 'Who Killed Kennedy?'" Far from assuaging her, these and similar details were the equivalent of a red rag to a bull. Jackie, meanwhile, sent copies of this fraught correspondence to Manchester, who, far from being pleased by her emphatic reiteration of his favored status, balked at Jackie's reference to having "hired" him and to her assumption that so long as he was "reimbursed for his time" she had the right to decree that his book ought not to be published.

In the midst of further frantic back-and-forth with Bishop and his publishers, Jackie forgot to call off the delivery of her newspapers at the Carlyle before the September 28 release of the Warren Commission report. "I picked them up and there it was," she said at the time, "so I canceled them for the rest of the week." She soon learned that that would not be protection enough. Living with PTSD is a bit like inhabiting a country that has been besieged by terrorists. One has no idea when the next attack will occur or the precise form it will take. It may come in a place one had every reason to expect to be safe. Jackie was at her hairdresser Kenneth's when she saw a copy of the October 2 issue of *Life*, whose lead story concerned the Warren Commission report. The stills on the cover, extracted from amateur footage of the assassination filmed by Dallas resident Abraham Zapruder, showed Jackie futilely struggling to pull her wounded husband down to safety in the moments before the fatal bullet struck.

"It was terrible," she said of her brush with that particular magazine. Then she added: "There is November to be gotten through . . . maybe by the first of the year . . ." When she made these comments, a week had passed since the Kenneth's incident, and Jackie was at home at the Carlyle having drinks with Dorothy Schiff, the publisher of the *New York Post*, whose endorsement RFK was then scrambling to secure. Early on in the New York Senate race there had been expectations both among the Kennedyites and in other quarters that by this point in the campaign the late president's brother would have established a decisive lead among voters. With less than a month to go before the election, however, major polls showed RFK lagging behind the incumbent, Senator Kenneth Keating, a moderate Republican. It was said that Bobby was not as popular as Democrats tended to be among Jewish and Italian-American voters in the state, that many New Yorkers were as uncomfortable with him as they had been with Richard Nixon four years previously, and that a surprising number of people who had supported JFK in 1960 might well split their ticket and vote for Keating this time. Even certain of RFK's backers worried that their man was running a lackluster campaign, that the more accessible public persona he had discovered in Poland was no longer in evidence, and that overall Bobby seemed somehow woefully ill-cast in his new role. An additional complication was that though Bobby publicly portrayed himself as JFK's rightful political heir, he privately resented the necessity to dwell so much in the shadow of his late brother. On one occasion, as RFK looked out at a large crowd of New Yorkers who had come to see him, he protested to an aide: "They're for him. They're not for me."

At a moment when the New York press appeared to have united against his candidacy, RFK was eager for a nod from the politically liberal *Post*. Dorothy Schiff privately likened Bobby to Sammy Glick, the ruthless, backstabbing protagonist of the Budd Schulberg novel *What Makes Sammy Run?*, but she also was keen to have Jackie sign on as a *Post* columnist. Hence the October 10, 1964, meeting that RFK engineered between the two women. The previous week he had promised to produce Jackie when Schiff mentioned how much she wanted to meet her. Still, the publisher had assumed until virtually the last minute that the meeting would never actually occur. But Bobby's campaign was in trouble, and it fell to Jackie to emerge from her private hell in order to secure the endorsement herself. Jackie's desperation in trying to help her brother-in-law when she was hardly in any condition even to try was reflected in the odd character of certain of her remarks about him. "He must win. He will win. He must win," she said. "Or maybe it is just because one wants it so much that one thinks that."

More usefully, perhaps, Jackie assured her guest that while many people called Bobby "ruthless and cold," in fact he had "the kindest heart in the world." Otherwise, she talked disjointedly about, among other subjects, her need to get away from Washington because of the many reminders there, and her apprehensions about moving to a new apartment, which suddenly seemed a good deal less welcoming than when she had first seen it.

"People tell me that time will heal," she burst out. "How much time?"

It was then that she spoke of her disastrous mistake the other day in forgetting to cancel her newspaper delivery, of the episode at Kenneth's, of the new trials that faced her in November, and of her hope that things might be better in 1965.

The meeting with Dorothy Schiff was far from the only instance of Jackie's permitting herself to be rolled out in support of Bobby's candidacy. On one occasion, she even allowed him to produce young John, clad in a white sweater and red short trousers, at a photo opportunity in Riverdale, the Bronx, where Joseph P. Kennedy Sr. had once owned a home. By reminding voters that Bobby had lived in New York when he was a boy, the visit aimed to counter the carpetbagging charges that continued to vex his campaign. He might have taken any of his own children to Independence Avenue that day, but it was more politically advantageous by far to be pictured with JFK's son. Lest there arise a perception among voters that Bobby alone enjoyed the favor of President's Kennedy's widow, LBJ, when he came to New York in keeping with his promise to campaign with Bobby, asked to be taken to see Jackie in her new apartment.

It was a maxim of LBJ's that "when you get 'em by the balls, their hearts and minds are sure to follow." What could Bobby do but acquiesce at a moment when, humiliatingly, his best hope for being elected seemed to be a big win on Johnson's part, and when he needed to tie himself to Johnson at all costs? In the event that Johnson beat Goldwater by a huge margin, it was statistically unlikely that there would be enough ticket splitting to make the difference for Keating. Much was made of the lack of fanfare in advance of Johnson's October 14 meeting with Jackie. There had been no prior announcement of LBJ's stop at 1040 Fifth Avenue, to which he was transported in an unmarked car, but that did not mean that the strategic thirty-minute visit arranged by Bobby was not prominently reported in the papers the next day, which was all that the president needed to reaffirm his ties to JFK.

In the end, Bobby was elected to the U.S. Senate on November 3, the apparent beneficiary of a Johnson landslide. To certain of RFK's admirers—perhaps best described by McGeorge Bundy as that "circle of people who felt that their happiness and hopes died on the twenty-second of November unless they could be revived by the younger brother"— the victory marked day one of the push to secure a Kennedy restoration in Washington. Jackie attended the election-night festivities at Delmonico's along with Sissie and David Harlech, but Bobby's triumph, much as she had wanted and worked for it, did nothing to alter her own situation as the first anniversary of November 22 drew near. More than ever, Jackie was privately preoccupied with armoring herself against all that the anniversary promised to bring—the tributes, the requiem Masses, the television dramas and documentaries, the magazine and newspaper articles.

Uneasily, she hung suspended between a determination to try, in her phrase, "to put [JFK] out of my mind," and a sense that it was her duty to memorialize him. Though she did not intend to join Bobby, Ethel, Eunice, and the rest at Arlington National Cemetery on the twenty-second, or indeed to participate in any public tributes prior to that date, one last decision about JFK's burial place still faced her. Jackie had yet to ratify the final plans for the grave design. Once she had done that, John Warnecke, the architect whom she and Bobby had appointed in the aftermath of the assassination, could call a press conference, as seemed fitting, in advance of the first anniversary of President Kennedy's death. According to Warnecke, a six-foot-two, 220-pound former college football star who had then been in his mid-forties, on the same day Jackie gave her final approval to the grave design, she also went to bed with him. Given the signal conjunction of these two events, was the latter an effort on her part to jump-start the process of forgetting that, in another context, she spoke of consciously endeavoring to begin?

Finally, Jackie, who had noticeably lost a good deal of weight in the weeks since Bobby's Senate race, remained in seclusion on the twenty-second. Her children and a few other family members were with her at the fieldstone house overlooking Long Island Sound that she had recently taken as a weekend retreat. When the last of the church bells had tolled, she sat up late into the night scribbling letters, which she tore up afterward because, as she said, she feared they were overly emotional.

Her one-year period of mourning at an end, she planned to appear at a pair of charity events immediately thereafter, a Washington, D.C., screening of the film *My Fair Lady* to benefit the Kennedy Center for the Performing Arts and the International Rescue Committee, and a fundraising dinner for Cedars-Sinai Hospital in Los Angeles. As early as the twenty-fourth, however, it became apparent that even now there was to be no relief from the emotional triggers that could come at her unexpectedly at any time. Days before her Warren Commission testimony had been officially scheduled to be released, Jackie opened the newspaper to discover extracts of her remarks, including a description of her efforts to second-guess her actions in Dallas.

Whereupon she canceled her impending appearances. A spokesperson announced that Mrs. Kennedy had hoped to attend both events: "However, due to the emotional strain of the past ten days she feels unable to participate in any public engagement."

Ten

I just heard that you were probably going to go to the memorial to the president," LBJ told Jackie on the phone.

When Johnson called her on March 25, 1965, she had only just arrived in Hobe Sound, Florida, a few hours previously. In the four months since the November 22 commemorations, Jackie had moved about a great deal; moved about almost compulsively. She had sojourned in Aspen, Colorado, and Lake Placid, New York. She had traveled to Mexico. Now she had taken a house for ten days at the Jupiter Club in Hobe Sound. After that, she was off to New Hampshire and Vermont. The question being not whether the mind's floodgates might suddenly, spontaneously, reopen, but rather how best to keep those inevitable occasions to a minimum, she had persisted in shunning all public appearances since she canceled the two charity events in late November.

Finally, however, Jackie had nervously accepted one invitation, if only because it had come from David Harlech, who had recently resigned his post as ambassador in Washington and was back in England. On May 14, Queen Elizabeth was due to dedicate to JFK's memory a parcel of land at Runnymede, where in 1215 King John had met with his rebellious barons to sign Magna Carta, the foundation of constitutional government. It was the dedication ceremony honoring President Kennedy that LBJ had called to discuss with Jackie in Florida.

"I wanted to suggest that if you cared to, that you and your party take one of the 707s. And I think that I might ask Bobby and Teddy if they wanted to go to represent me. . . . You just let me know and I'll have it all set up for you."

"Oh, that's so nice, but that's wasting taxpayers' money!" said Jackie, whom Alsop had recently warned against allowing Johnson to put her in his debt.

LBJ, for his part, denied that flying the Kennedy party to England would be a waste of tax dollars. On the contrary: "It's very important to us, and very important to the country."

"Oh, listen, I just don't know what to say," Jackie returned.

"You don't say anything."

"That's the nicest thing I ever heard of."

"Just quit being so elusive. It's been too long since I saw you," said LBJ, suggesting by this rejoinder the character of his anxiety and calculations. "And whenever, wherever I can do anything," the president went on, "you know I'm as close as the phone, dear."

Perhaps he was, but three days later "Dear" chose to reply in writing to his offer. "I did not know if I could steel myself to go on one of those planes again," Jackie told the president. On reflection she had decided to accept: "But please do not let it be Air Force One." Lest the familiar ambience carry her back in memory to November 22, 1963, she preferred not to be confronted with the particular plane in which she had flown home with her husband's remains. Nor would it be enough to keep clear of the plane itself. Though in her rational mind Jackie would know that she was not on the actual aircraft, even the palest reminder, imperceptible though it might be to other eyes, threatened to set her off, and once the images and emotions began to flow, there would be no stopping them.

"Please," Jackie implored, "let it be the 707 that looks least like Air Force One inside."

So Jackie and her children, along with JFK's surviving brothers, flew to London on one of the other presidential planes. The day of the Runnymede ceremony was hot and sunny, the soft white tree-fluff that wafted in the air causing one commentator to think of "snow in May." By three in the afternoon, approximately five thousand guests, some wearing impromptu hats of folded newspapers against the glare, had gathered in the meadow, which was flecked with the gold of buttercups and dandelions. That, at least, was the bucolic scene that most people would have observed. But Jackie no longer perceived the world quite as most others did. To her biased vision, Runnymede was an emotional minefield, not least of the dreaded reminders being the sight of Harold Macmillan. At the time David Harlech first broached the idea of the memorial, Jackie had told him that she could not conceive of traveling to Runnymede unless Macmillan was asked to speak. In the event, however, Macmillan's hoary presence on the speakers' platform, where she too was seated, proved to be too much for her. By this point, she associated Macmillan not just with her late husband, but also with the magnificent fifteen-page February 18, 1964, letter about herself, which had spurred so many unsent letters of her own. In Atlantic City, Jackie had spoken in a barely audible voice. At Runnymede, even that level of performance would be beyond her.

As Macmillan addressed the audience, Jackie became so overwrought that she realized she could not possibly deliver her own remarks. This was the same woman whose demeanor at the time of JFK's funeral had so endeared her to her countrymen. Days after the assassination, she had still been in the warrior-like state of emotional lockdown into which she had been plunged in Dallas. As she said, there had been moments when she had wanted to cry but found that she could not. Eighteen months later, Jackie cried all too easily, and once she began, there was always the danger that she might not be able to stop. On this particular occasion, given her decision not even to try to speak, the text of what she had intended to say, a meditation on the way in which English literature and history had shaped JFK "as did no other part of his education," was published in the London press instead.

Two days after Runnymede, Jackie was similarly affected in the course of a private Kennedy family visit to the Macmillan family at Birch Grove. The many mementoes of President Kennedy about the house, the special rocking chair he had used during his 1963 stay, the gifts that Jackie had helped select at the time for both the prime minister and Lady Dorothy, the various framed photographs of JFK and Macmillan together, along with the sight of their host steering Bobby into his library and closing the door in anticipation of the sort of private colloquy he used to conduct with JFK—all of it had the effect of sending her into what an observer described as "a very low mood."

That mood persisted the next day when she was too upset even to get out of bed. Having missed the chance for anything like "a proper talk" with Macmillan though previously they had communicated so feelingly and unrestrainedly on paper, she set out to write a new long letter to him in which she spoke of the intensity of her emotions at Birch Grove; of her unsuccessful efforts since moving to New York to banish Jack from her thoughts for the sake of his children; and of the children's role in giving her a reason to live in order that she might make them the people Jack would have wished them to be. "Probably," she darkly suggested, "I will be too intense and they will grow up to be awful." Again when she read over what she had written, she felt embarrassed by her words and judged that it might be best not to send the letter off, but when she tried to produce another letter, the result was so stiff and formal that, as she told Macmillan, she took a deep breath and dispatched both missives to Birch Grove in hopes he would understand.

Jackie had suggested in the original May 17, 1965, message to

Macmillan that the things her husband most cared about were no longer priorities in Washington and that there was nothing she could do to affect that. Meanwhile, others at home, notably LBJ, took a different view of what a pointed word or gesture from her might mean just now in the political sphere. Despite his landslide victory in the 1964 presidential election, Johnson persisted in the belief that he had to continually paint himself as his predecessor's legitimate heir, a leader determined to pursue the policies of President Kennedy. To some perceptions, Johnson had even been willing to politicize his presidential proclamation on the first anniversary of November 22 when he underscored that "the vision of John F. Kennedy still guides the nation." Did it really? Or was LBJ, who had his own exceedingly ambitious agenda for the country quite apart from anything JFK had been prepared to pursue, merely seeking to reassure the American public that all was as it would have been? As far as Johnson was concerned, the White House could ill afford for RFK ever to be viewed as being more in sync with his late brother's ideas than Johnson was. Especially now that RFK had left the administration, Johnson was ever striving to seem somehow more Kennedy than Kennedy.

LBJ's blood had risen shortly before his January 1965 inauguration when he learned of rumors emanating from certain of the Kennedyites that he blamed America's troubles in Vietnam on JFK's immaturity and poor judgment. "Have you ever heard me blame Kennedy for anything?" LBJ demanded of Bob McNamara, who replied reassuringly: "No, no, absolutely not! . . . I have mentioned this to Jackie several times." Johnson was under intense pressure from McNamara and McGeorge Bundy to choose between two alternatives in Vietnam, either to escalate U.S. military involvement there or to withdraw. Lest he damage himself with voters, the president had put off any decision until after the presidential election. Now that Johnson was in again, he had a new concern, that controversy over Vietnam could jeopardize the Great Society domestic program that was so dear to him. At the same time, LBJ did not wish to come under attack from RFK and his supporters on the grounds that he had neglected to pursue his predecessor's Vietnam policy. The fact that there was no clear agreement among the various sects of the religion of Kennedy as to exactly what that policy had been added immeasurably to LBJ's challenge.

In early June, a cable from General William Westmoreland, U.S. military commander in Vietnam, calling for extensive additional combat troops to pursue the conflict there led McNamara to conclude that a choice could no longer be postponed. While he waited for the president to make a decision at last, he repeatedly volunteered to run interference with his friends the Kennedys. At the moment, it seemed as if his best chance of bringing over at least one prominent Kennedy was to work a little more on Jackie.

He certainly was not without influence on her. Jackie called McNamara the Kennedy cabinet member who "gave the most . . . as much as Jack's own brother Bobby gave." She regarded him as one of the very few friends who had not failed her when she tried to start over in Georgetown after the assassination. Freshly reeling from her experience of absolute helplessness in the face of overwhelming events, she had responded strongly, welcomingly, gratefully, to this forceful figure who always seemed so sure of what needed to be done and so certain that he was the man for the job. It was McNamara who on the night of the assassination had immediately offered to buy her the old house in Georgetown where she had once lived with JFK; McNamara who had argued that the president needed to be buried not in Massachusetts as family members seemed to favor, but in a national cemetery; McNamara who had chosen the particular spot where JFK was laid to rest. She anointed McNamara her shining knight. She credited him with having saved her from drowning. She later said that in her dark times he had always been the one who helped her.

Among other things, he liked to read to Jackie Henrik Ibsen's *The Master Builder*, a play that explored some of the very questions she had been struggling with since Dallas. The picture of Bob McNamara, technocratic manager par excellence, staunch believer in man's capacity to intelligently and rationally control events, speaking the impassioned lament at life's randomness and unpredictability that is at the heart of the play—"Oh, that such things should be allowed to happen here in the world!"—is a riveting study in contrasts. The play's protagonist broods about the deaths of his two infant sons after a fire that occurred more than a decade before, a tragedy that still gnaws at him day and night. Seeking to make sense of the senseless, he alternates between blaming God for the deaths and holding himself responsible, though intellectually he knows he is not at fault. At times, these preoccupations appear to have deranged him. When he falls to his death at the close of the third act, whether or not he has taken his own life remains an open question.

It is well to remember that McNamara was referring to a woman who saw him, and to whom he had indeed acted, as a loyal, loving friend, when he crisply, confidently assured LBJ, not long after she had returned from Europe: "I'm planning to have dinner with Jackie tonight in New York. I can do something on that front, if I can't on Bobby." Paranoid though Johnson often was, his anxiety that Jackie might be displeased with his administration, whether wholly or in part, was not without factual basis. In private she had already written in a negative vein to both Macmillan and Alsop about the way things were proceeding under her husband's successor. The danger for the White House was almost certainly not that she would say such things publicly or even that, à la RFK, she would leak any views she might have to the press. But there was always the chance that she could speak to a friend or an acquaintance who would in turn communicate to others that the widow was, in her word, disenchanted.

So LBJ was very keen on the idea of McNamara's undertaking to influence Jackie over dinner in a new push to align her with the White House. Evidently, William Manchester was not alone in his willingness to use alcohol to get what he needed from Jackie. The president, seeming rather to relish the prospect, went so far as to suggest certain points Mc-

Namara might put off making to her until after they had had their second drink.

Nor was the June 17 dinner the end of it. McNamara continued to work on her in the weeks that followed. After a reconnoitering trip to Vietnam that led to his final recommendation to put in more troops, he turned up at the Cape bearing a gift for Caroline and John: a stuffed Vietnamese tiger, which America's ally, the despotic, Hitler-worshipping new Vietnamese prime minister General Nguyễn Cao Kỳ, had given him in Saigon. Jackie responded with an elegant thank-you note in the form of a watercolor that the tiger had inspired her to paint. A delighted Mc-Namara had the picture mounted and framed. While the widow and the defense secretary diverted themselves in this charming manner, fifty thousand American soldiers had been dispatched on the president's orders, with many more troops to follow. In response to Johnson's decision to commit American combat forces, Norman Morrison, a Quaker from Baltimore, Maryland, immolated himself some forty feet from McNamara's office window at the Pentagon. Morrison had had his year-old daughter with him at first, but as onlookers begged him to let her live, he threw the child to safety. McNamara later wrote: "I reacted to the horror of his action by bottling up my emotions and avoided talking about them with anyone—even my family. I knew Marg and our three children shared many of Morrison's feelings about the war, as did the wives and children of several of my cabinet colleagues. And I believed I understood and shared some of his thoughts. There was much Marg and I and the children should have talked about, yet at moments like this I often turn inward instead—it is a grave weakness. The episode created tension at home that only deepened as dissent and criticism of the war continued to grow."

While McNamara had been wooing Jackie on behalf of LBJ, she proved to be considerably less malleable in her dealings with two other Kennedy administration veterans. It would scarcely have helped Arthur Schlesinger or Ted Sorensen to offer Jackie a second drink as both men vied for official approval of the manuscripts they had been racing to finish in time for publication before the looming second anniversary of November 22. Unlike their mutual friend William Manchester, neither writer had a contractual obligation to the family. But, as both former JFK aides hoped for a role in any impending Kennedy restoration, what other option did they have but to seek Jackie's and Bobby's blessing?

Her assent was by far the more difficult to secure. She called for excisions and alterations, and then when she had been given everything she asked for, she indignantly insisted on still more. Her complaints ranged from a well-founded objection to Schlesinger's comment that JFK came to the presidency knowing more about domestic matters than foreign affairs, to the stipulation that the particular rooms she and JFK had inhabited together not be described. She sniped that she had shared those rooms with him, not with Book-of-the-Month Club readers. In view of the many Kennedy books being produced, the same woman who longed somehow to stop thinking about her late husband was also eager to stockpile certain private details that she alone would possess.

Though Manchester later claimed to have devoted two hours to begging Sorensen to be firm, Sorensen, who billed his book as a substitute for the one JFK would have written had he lived, quickly caved. He yielded to Jackie on "point after point," in Manchester's judgment "weakening what should have been a great volume." When Sorensen's book, titled simply *Kennedy*, was published that fall, the author publicly conceded that he had, in his word, softened the text. Arthur Schlesinger, by contrast, did put up something of a fight. In this he was aided by Manchester, who wrote to Jackie on his fellow author's behalf, arguing that history ought not to be turned into bland custard by removing too much.

In the end, Schlesinger left Manchester with the impression that besides consenting to delete a single passage derived from his taped oral history interviews with Jackie, he had refused to budge elsewhere. Schlesinger's own August 10, 1965, letter to Jackie, written apropos of her upset over the prepublication serialization of his book in *Life* magazine, tells a different story. Schlesinger maintained that the fundamental problem was that he had been trained all his life to be an historian, and that it was the Hippocratic oath of his profession to come as close as possible to the truthful reconstruction of past events. He therefore had set out to write *A Thousand Days: John F. Kennedy in the White House,* as his book was called, using the same kinds of materials and the same standards as in his previous works about the Roosevelt and Jackson administrations. Schlesinger continued: "I see now that I was mistaken, and that it is just not possible to write an honest account so close to the events. Accordingly when I get the proofs, I propose to go through the book and comb out everything (not yet published) which would produce a headline in a newspaper—controversies, personalities, intimacies, everything else." Schlesinger said he feared that removing all of this material would give the book a certain blandness as history, but he consoled himself by asserting that the core of the story, which was the character of the president, would remain in any case. Even after the historian's abject capitulation, Jackie fired back with demands for further revisions. When Schlesinger sent RFK a final batch of pages on September 4, he reported that he had decided practically to cut Jackie from the book.

In the course of these negotiations, Jackie had been resolutely pursuing what she described as a "mindless existence" dedicated to physical sensation—sun, food, exercise—first in Hyannis Port and then in Newport. Given her battle with the biographers, however, her summer at the shore was plainly neither as tranquil nor as grounded in the here and now as she liked to suggest. Still, on her final morning at Hammersmith Farm, September 14, 1965, before she returned to New York, where school was due to begin the next day, she judged herself to be in better condition than at the same time the previous year. In a new letter to Harold Macmillan, she rejoiced that she had pulled herself together enough to be of help to her children. Jackie felt a determination, "almost a rage," she declared, to keep it up until she herself found some peace.

But could she keep it up? In the months ahead, would it really be possible not to brood, not to endlessly recall and replay the events of November 22? That she was worried about this is suggested by something else she told Macmillan: "When winter starts—you have to think again."

At first she seemed determined to ward off the thoughts that promised to set her back. That autumn, squired by Bill Walton, she presided over a large, loud, lavish party for JFK's ambassador to India, John Kenneth Galbraith, at the Upper East Side restaurant the Sign of the Dove that spectacularly marked the widow's return to active public social life. Late-night passersby, looking beyond the police barricades and through the open street-level French windows, caught glimpses of Jackie performing the new hip-swinging fad dance the Frug with Galbraith, McNamara, and other partners amid shadowy torchlights. In the weeks that followed, New York witnessed a good deal more of the same. She visited the discotheques Arthur and Le Club. She hosted a dinner at the chic restaurant Le Pavillion. She appeared at parties and at theater and ballet events.

Gradually, however, in anticipation of another November 22 (the very date, like September 11 in a later era, exerted a strange malevolent power of its own), she began rerouting her life around this year's anniversary coverage and commemorations. And even then, she could not reasonably expect to be able to bypass every trigger.

"There is November to be gotten through," Jackie had told Dorothy Schiff the year before, and so it would be again.

And again.

And again.

To explain what promised to be her conspicuous absence from the parties and receptions in honor of Princess Margaret and her husband, the Earl of Snowdon, who were due in Manhattan in November, Jackie, employing a euphemism she was to use for the rest of her life, put out word that their visit coincided with her "difficult time" of the year.

Eleven

In keeping with Bunny Mellon's detestation of publicity, the arrangements for Jackie's thirty-seventh birthday celebration, to be held belatedly at the Mellons' Osterville, Massachusetts, estate, on August 5, 1966, began in a haze of secrecy. Given the guest list, however, which included prominent figures from the worlds of politics, media, and the arts, the national press was soon trumpeting an occasion described by turns as "the event of the summer on Cape Cod" and as Jackie's "farewell to sadness and . . . emergence definitely into a new life." Throughout the early part of 1966 she had been widely photographed and chronicled as she traveled, rode, danced, dined, and appeared on the arm of various men, single and married, straight and gay. On the basis of all he had seen in the papers recently, William Manchester, who, it need hardly be said, had often had occasion to think of Jackie in the two years since they last met, concluded that she must be "fully emerged from mourning" at last.

RFK, who continued to represent her interests in the family's dealings with Manchester, knew better. At least since the time of the 1964 dinner party in her honor, after which she had spoken to Arthur Schlesinger of the flight back from Dallas and of the efforts made to persuade her to change her clothes, she had often told listeners in various moneyed Manhattan settings some of the identical stories she had related to Manchester. "That's the trouble," Bobby had been heard to remark on one such occasion of late. "She lives in the past too much."

Nevertheless, Bobby was unprepared for the violence of her reaction when, shortly before the Mellon party, he walked over to her Hyannis Port cottage on a Sunday evening to inform her of the sale to *Look* magazine of prepublication excerpts from the recently completed Manchester book for the record sum of $665,000. Jackie, who had spent the early part of the summer in Hawaii (a portion of that time in the company of John Warnecke), had just arrived from Newport, where she had celebrated her actual birthday, July 28, and attended the wedding of her Auchincloss half sister, Janet. In the turbulent weeks and months that followed Bobby's July 31 talk with Jackie, he would regret having delegated the vetting of the voluminous manuscript to lieutenants rather than read it personally. "It's really mostly my fault," he would say. "I just never wanted to spend the time on that." He would regret what he came to see as his failure to shield his sister-in-law from additional suffering, and he would regret the mighty political trouble he thereby had brought upon himself at what was looking to be a watershed in his career.

But up to that moment at the Cape when he conveyed to Jackie that, acting on her behalf as well as his own, he had already conferred his written assent to Manchester ("Members of the Kennedy family will place no obstacle in the way of publication"), he simply had not foreseen the extremity of the emotions that the news would elicit from her. There had been every reason to assume that she wanted to have as little as possible to do with the book. Had she not appointed Bobby her agent in all matters pertaining to it? Had she not conspicuously sought to avoid

Manchester at almost every turn? Had she not been inclined to ignore Manchester's letters, and, as recently as early 1966, had she not refused to read his manuscript on the explanation, which RFK passed on to the publisher Harper & Row, that it would only stir up difficult memories?

In spite of all that, when Jackie absorbed that the first extracts were scheduled to appear on newsstands in October, she was like a sea traveler who suddenly perceives the bow of another ship fast approaching through the fog. The fabulous price fetched at auction for the magazine rights suggested that the book itself, rather than languish "on dark library shelves" as she had allowed herself to imagine it would, was guaranteed to be major news. For many months, it would be impossible to completely avoid the book and the innumerable other potential triggers, in the form of publicity and comment, it was sure to engender. Jackie had once told Jim Bishop apropos of his work in progress *The Day Kennedy Was Shot* that she could not bear the thought of seeing, or of seeing advertised, a work with that title and subject. Now again, though Manchester had begun work at her behest, the very anticipation of being confronted with *The Death of a President* proved unbearable to her. She left Bobby Kennedy in no doubt that she wanted the enterprise stopped at once. He would do that for her, wouldn't he? Had it not been his self-appointed role since Dallas to do such things for her?

For Bobby, the timing of all this could scarcely have been more unfortunate. Though the assassination had instantly altered his place in the universe, it had only really been in the past few weeks that his closest supporters had started to seriously contemplate a presidential run in 1968. There had been a time when LBJ feared that Bobby would criticize him for a failure to take strong action in Vietnam. Now the danger seemed to be any word from RFK that Johnson had gone too far. Among the Kennedyites, the president's apparent commitment to widening the war in Vietnam, a war that had spectacularly belied McNamara's cocksure initial forecasts, seemed to make the idea of an RFK candidacy, as Schlesinger cheered in his diary, "both possible and necessary." To this point, the senator's people, when they vetted the Manchester manuscript, had striven to tone down evidence of the author's flagrant dislike of LBJ, a bias that could reflect badly on RFK in a book known to have been sponsored and approved by him. Now a whole new problem presented itself. In the aftermath of Bobby's bestowal of family approval, any move to suppress publication threatened to fuel the charges of arrogance and ruthlessness with which he had been vexed throughout his public life.

Though RFK let it be known at Harper & Row that Jackie was distraught, he did not yet go so far as to ask that the book be scratched. For Manchester, matters remained in this rather maddening state of limbo when, presently, the Bobby Kennedys, the Teddy Kennedys, the Bob McNamaras, the Averell Harrimans, the Leonard Bernsteins, the William Paleys, and many others feted Jackie at the Mellons' Osterville home. The guest of honor was seated between Paul Mellon and the director Mike Nichols, the latter a frequent escort of Jackie's during this period. Mrs. Mellon lived by the maxim that nothing should be noticed, and tonight, at least as far as the impending battle of the book was concerned, nothing was. Arthur Schlesinger, the Mellon party guest whom Manchester had delegated to learn how Bobby's and Jackie's minds were working, managed to glean no significant information from either source. It was not until five days later that Bobby suddenly notified Harper & Row of his view that *The Death of a President* ought neither to be published nor serialized: "I would appreciate it if you would inform William Manchester."

During the past two years, Manchester had worked twelve-, fifteen-, sometimes twenty-hour days, seven days a week. He ate little, and if he slept at all, he dreamt of Dallas. At a certain point, he later said, time seemed to have stopped for him on November 22. "The book had become an obsession with me; I was possessed by it." Manchester sought to live in the shoes of the slain president, of his killer, and of the president's widow. He retraced JFK's itinerary through Texas, leading to Parkland Memorial Hospital. He crawled across the roof of the Texas School Book

Depository and gazed out at the world from the point of view of Oswald's sixth-floor hiding place. He located and opened the carton where the first lady's pink suit had been stored away. He undid the white towel containing the stockings she had worn that day, and he noted how, in the intervening months, President Kennedy's blood had dropped off the sheer fabric in flakes that now rested on the nap of the towel in the form of tiny brittle grains.

Manchester also amply fulfilled his pledge to put himself into the account, though in ways that neither he nor Jackie might have anticipated at the outset. The few "flickers" of memory that remained of his own traumatic episodes on Okinawa were "blurred" because, he later judged, "there was so much that I did not want to remember." It was not until years afterward that those memories came rushing back with the "blinding" clarity, as he called it, that eventually allowed him to compose his 1980 memoir of the Pacific War. To examine that memoir, *Goodbye, Darkness,* side by side with *The Death of a President* is to begin to sort out quite how much of himself he had written into the Kennedy story and quite how much of the latter he subsequently wrote into his own.

Such, at any rate, was the intensity with which Manchester labored in 1965 that he gripped his pen so tightly, blood oozed from beneath his thumbnail, sullying the pages of text. The finger became infected and needed to be lanced on three occasions, but Manchester kept writing nonetheless. Schlesinger informed mutual friends that he feared poor Manchester might be about to crack. Indeed, on the second anniversary of the assassination, Manchester had been at work on the section of his narrative devoted to the killing of Oswald when his pen stopped dead and he found that he simply could not will himself on. Four days later, he was admitted to a Connecticut hospital to be treated for nervous exhaustion. During the latter part of his hospitalization, Manchester completed much of what remained to be written of the book. "When I awoke this morning," he informed RFK after he had finished, "I felt as though I had emerged from a long, dark tunnel." Manchester was convinced that he had produced a masterpiece. This, then, was the man whom RFK had advised the publishers to notify that his book was to be canceled.

Notwithstanding anything Harper & Row might decide, there remained the problem of the serial sale. Manchester, when he faced off with RFK in Washington after learning of the latter's decision, maintained that he had signed a contract with *Look* from which he could not now simply withdraw. The meeting degenerated into a suffering contest. Manchester alluded to his recent hospitalization and noted that he remained under a physician's care. RFK flashed out: "Do you think you've suffered more than Jackie and me?" And so it went, all to absolutely no avail.

Jackie, when she learned that *Look* still planned to publish, angrily blamed RFK for the mess. She had cried out for help, yet he had failed her. As far as she was concerned, controlling Manchester was a life-and-death matter, and she had absolutely relied on her brother-in-law to do what was necessary. Hence her fury at what most other people would probably regard as a mere lapse on Bobby's part in the context of all that he had done for her in the past. Seeking to distance herself from the written approvals Bobby had conferred, Jackie claimed to *Look* publisher Gardner Cowles that her brother-in-law did not really represent her. What was his role, then? "He sort of protects me," she said. It is hard not to feel the irony of Jackie's "sort of." Unspoken was that Bobby had not protected her very well this time, thank you very much. In conversation with Manchester, whom she invited to the Cape in a futile effort to personally persuade him to withdraw from the *Look* deal, she went further in her mockery of Bobby, acidly comparing his behavior of late to that of "a little boy who knows he's done wrong."

Manchester, for his part, grew troubled and confused when his hostess's conversation digressed from publishing matters to what struck him as a completely irrelevant topic: the problem that had arisen over President Kennedy's grave site at Arlington National Cemetery. For Jackie, however, the two subjects were far from unconnected. It had long been planned that the bodies of JFK and the two babies buried alongside him would be moved to new permanent graves, some twenty feet downhill from the temporary site, as soon as construction of the Kennedy Memorial had been completed. In the meantime, a disagreement about the landscaping at the final grave site had developed, with Jackie and Bunny Mellon on one side and the Army Corps of Engineers on the other. Jackie, who like many people with PTSD had a tendency to catastrophize, was absolutely convinced that she saw another "disaster" coming.

Frantic at what she regarded as RFK's ineptitude with Manchester, she turned the landscaping dispute over to Bob McNamara. The can-do man promptly and smoothly settled the matter of the grave site to Jackie's complete satisfaction. Afterward, she insisted that as a consequence of his intervention she felt "peaceful and optimistic" for the first time in many months. At a moment when Jackie had begun to lose confidence in her brother-in-law, the episode immeasurably deepened her attachment to and dependence on McNamara. The defense secretary, in turn, appears to have especially welcomed the involvement with her at a moment when he had begun to lose confidence in himself.

The Bob McNamara of 1966 was no longer the person who had cut such a commanding figure at Bethesda Naval Hospital on her return from Dallas. The escalation he had championed in Vietnam, the use of ground forces, the bombing, had not accomplished what he had said they would. McNamara had had to acknowledge that his vaunted computer printouts had failed him and that the military commanders he believed himself to have managed so adroitly had misled him. This man who had always been so sure that every problem was solvable had finally come up against one problem (Jackie called it "more complex than any dark hell that Shakespeare ever looked into") that challenged all of his most fundamental assumptions. Confronted by the evidence of his own fecklessness, the architect of the Vietnam War became a man at war with himself.

RFK and Schlesinger found it puzzling that when McNamara conversed with them, he was an advocate for limiting the war, though publicly he remained the administration's spokesman for widening it. Such was McNamara's duality of mind that he delivered a controversial address in Montreal that appeared to give succor to critics of the war, a speech in which he painted himself as a utopian dreamer, a seeker, like his beloved Ibsen character the Master Builder, of the impossible. Then, not long afterward, he disowned those remarks as childish, adding that as a sitting defense secretary whose job it was to motivate men to fight, he ought never to have permitted himself to say such things.

At home, he agonized; he wept; he ground his teeth in his sleep, keeping his wife awake at night. Presently, also like the Ibsen character, McNamara sought solace in the companionship of another woman, one who believed in him utterly, and not a little misguidedly; a woman to whom he found that he could speak as he could not to his wife. At the same time, he was not always sure of what to make of his confidante; of the extremity, even the violence, of certain of Jackie's feelings and actions.

One night after he and Jackie had dined together at her Fifth Avenue apartment during this period, they were seated on a sofa in her library. McNamara had come up to New York to see her while Marg was traveling. By this point, Jackie had become depressed by and critical of the Vietnam War, carnage-filled images of which it was almost impossible to escape being inundated with on the nightly news, so much so that Vietnam came to be called "television's war." But it was not Vietnam he and Jackie were speaking of when McNamara witnessed the outburst that, in his phrase, "so overwhelmed" him that he would puzzle about it for years to come. Jackie and her guest had been discussing the Chilean poet Gabriela Mistral, specifically her poem "Prayer," a plea to God to forgive the compulsively unfaithful man she loved ("You say he was cruel? You forget I loved him ever. . . . To love . . . is a bitter task"). Suddenly, McNamara saw a change come over Jackie's body. She seemed to grow so tense that she could scarcely speak. Erupting in anger and tears, she directed her fury at him. Pounding McNamara's chest with her fists, she demanded that he "do something to stop the slaughter!" Long afterward, McNamara reflected in his memoirs: "Whether her emotions were triggered by the poem or by something I said, I do not know."

Had talk of Gabriela Mistral's beloved called to mind Jackie's similarly unfaithful late husband? Had the war, which trailed McNamara wherever he went, become for her a trigger that elicited feelings and perceptions associated with the slaughter in Dallas? Had the violent images on TV become intertwined with the violent images in her head? In some strange way, when she implored McNamara to stop the slaughter, was she referring not just to Vietnam, but also to the troubling memories she found herself unable to escape? Whatever it was that set this particular episode in motion, the image of Jackie hitting McNamara's chest encapsulates a critical feature of advanced PTSD. The terrifying inability to control the responses of body and mind to an ever-expanding network of triggers traumatizes the sufferer anew. The present sense of helplessness echoes the powerlessness experienced during the original traumatic incident. Interestingly, McNamara was not the only person close to Jackie to be confounded by her sudden physical and emotional outbursts. Her sister Lee spoke to a friend, the photographer and diarist Cecil Beaton, of the manner in which Jackie would suddenly, inexplicably, hit her across the face.

Along similar lines to those who struggled to comprehend such behavior, throughout the autumn of 1966 RFK's people tried to make sense of Jackie's frenzied reaction to the Manchester manuscript. What exactly was it in the sprawling text, which she appeared not even to have read, that was upsetting her so? Which of Manchester's nuggets of detail would have to be excised before she would give her assent? In deference to her anguish at the prospect of the magazine extracts appearing on newsstands during her "difficult time," Gardner Cowles had agreed to put off serialization until January 1967, with the book to follow in March. Jackie, when she secured that concession, basically turned the negotiations back to Bobby, whose lieutenants used the breathing space provided by the postponement to scour the manuscript with an eye toward assuaging her concerns.

Would she be happy if they managed to remove this image, or that vignette, or some other morsel they had yet to seize upon? Theirs was a guessing game, really, and necessarily a futile one because it was founded on a false premise. In this one area at least, Manchester had a more acute understanding of his antagonist than the Kennedyites did. To the author's sense, it was not any particular fact or constellation of facts that Jackie objected to; it was the entire manuscript. In short, no number of cuts would ever satisfy her. "The only thing Jackie wanted, and the one thing she couldn't have," Manchester judged, "was no magazine series, no book; just one big blank page for November 22, 1963."

In any case, when the third anniversary of the assassination had passed, and the twin disasters of the magazine serialization and the book continued to draw near, Jackie, emerging from her customary seclusion during her "difficult time," sought out a new protector. Cass Canfield, the chairman of the executive committee of Harper & Row, who also happened to be her sister's former father-in-law, agreed to notify Manchester that if he did not immediately make all the changes that had been demanded on Jackie's behalf, Canfield would cancel publication. Jackie, for the moment, seemed to focus on the publishing executive's willingness to speak in terms of cancellation, rather than on any interest he might have in forcing through a list of edits that would satisfy her once and for all. Persuaded that Canfield would never allow the book to go to press in the absence of her approval, which of course she would never give, she relaxed and began to make plans for Christmas. Bobby's Washington office announced that she intended to spend the holiday with him and his family in Sun Valley, Idaho.

Manchester, in the meantime, expressed indignation at the publisher's ultimatum. "I have reached the point where, if the integrity of my manuscript is violated, I have no wish to go on living," he told his agent, Don Congdon. "It sounds vainglorious, I know, but I am ready to die for this book." Rather than a refusal to negotiate, however, that was merely Manchester's histrionic way of instructing Congdon to do it for him.

With the agent in charge, there was suddenly a good deal of progress in the editing. At length, Canfield notified Jackie that as far as he was concerned, all of the legitimate requests for changes that had been made in her name had been satisfied, and the Manchester manuscript was finally ready to be published.

That, of course, was far from what she'd had in mind. Over Bobby's strong objections, Jackie instructed her lawyer to sue Manchester, the publishing house, and the magazine. RFK, advised by an aide that a lawsuit was a terrible mistake, replied: "Yes, it is a terrible mistake, but nothing can be done about it." His partisans would later maintain that loyalty to the widow had trumped any practical political considerations on his part, but it was also plainly the case that—like Bob McNamara and Lee Radziwill when Jackie's fists began to fly—RFK was powerless to stop the woman whom he privately and not a little ruefully referred to as "my crazy sister-in-law." Though it was soon widely known in Washington that he had urged Jackie to refrain, his public posture was to support her wholeheartedly in her impending court fight. In an effort to bolster Jackie's charge that Manchester had exploited the emotional state in which she had recounted her recollections to him in early 1964, Bobby regretted to the press that it had been he who had counseled her to tell the whole story to Manchester in the first place. In view of RFK's conferral of written approval the previous August, Jackie's other accusation, that Manchester had violated his contract, was decidedly a weak point in her case. Bobby, in an affidavit to the court, sought to explain away his telegram by claiming that he had sent it only after Harper & Row told him that Manchester had been becoming ill with an obsession that his manuscript might never be published. According to Bobby, the purpose of his telegram had been nothing more than a kindly desire to allay the writer's fears.

Still the damning document existed, and there was reason to believe that the magazine, at least, would prevail in court. Under pressure to settle with *Look*, Jackie attended what was to have been a clandestine meeting at the Wall Street office of the magazine's attorney. Methodically, dispassionately, she reviewed the proofs of the upcoming serialization, noting numerous personal details that she wanted expunged. She was smiling as she left the meeting, but her eyes moistened at the sight of waiting reporters. Manchester had not been present at the attorney's office, but when he learned of the disparity between the calm countenance Jackie had worn during the proceedings and her tearful public display afterward, he judged the latter to have been nothing more than a pretty piece of theatrics.

From the moment that word of the gathering storm over the Manchester book first reached the White House, LBJ had been tracking it with immense interest and concern, not least because of rumors about the author's relentlessly negative portrait of him. The psychological atmosphere in the Johnson camp approximated that of a bunker as the president, Lady Bird, and Johnson appointee to the U.S. Supreme Court Abe Fortas strategized on how best to respond to the charges of gross insensitivity to Jackie and the Kennedys that were about to fall on the White House like so many bombs. Intermittently, the president would break away from this anxious conversation, the better to concentrate on the latest news about the debacle in Vietnam from his perpetually blaring television set. The fact that such an unflattering account of his behavior in the aftermath of Dallas was about to be published was especially unwelcome at a moment when the nightmare that had haunted LBJ since day one of his presidency—that RFK would move to reclaim the throne—was threatening to become a reality.

For all that, it soon appeared as if the controversy might actually benefit the president as well. Reports of the internecine disagreement over whether to sue the author and his publishers appeared to offer Johnson the long-sought opening to detach Jackie from RFK. On December 16, the very day it was announced that Jackie would not be joining Bobby and his family in Sun Valley for Christmas after all, a carefully crafted letter that was deeply sympathetic to her court battle ("Lady Bird and I have been distressed to read the press accounts of your unhappiness about the Manchester book") went out to her from LBJ. The president said he had seen accounts of her displeasure with certain passages in the manuscript that were unfavorable to Lady Bird and him. "If this is so," Johnson wrote, "I want you to know while we deeply appreciate your characteristic kindness and sensitivity, we hope you will not subject yourself to any discomfort or distress on our account. One never becomes inured to slander but we have learned to live with it. In any event, your own tranquility is important to both of us, and we would not want you to endure any unpleasantness on our account."

The December 16 letter was in fact a group effort. It had been Abe Fortas who composed the text and it had been Lady Bird's idea for her husband to write to Jackie in his own hand. The often heavy-handed Johnson liked the letter so much that at one point he considered whether it might not be advantageous to release a copy to the press, but Fortas advised against it.

By the time Jackie replied to LBJ, on December 21, she had reluctantly settled with *Look*. The magazine had agreed to the edits she and her representatives had demanded. Yet she was still miserable, because, she made clear, she objected to all that remained as much as she did to the material that had been taken out. And what, after all, was the point of a lawsuit when no court, or out-of-court settlement, had the power to accomplish what she really wanted and needed—to make the floodgates close forever?

In the process of going to law, she had hurt people she cared about, and for what? "I am sick at the unhappiness this whole terrible thing has caused everyone," Jackie told the president. "Whatever I did could only cause pain." Though in the past she had been warned to guard against Johnson's brazen attempts to manipulate her, Jackie, in her anguish, readily opened her heart to him now. She related that since her return from Hawaii the previous August, she had been constantly pleading by letter or telephone or in person with one or more people on the other side, or agonizing over what step to take next with the individuals who were helping her. To Jackie's mind, the author and publishers had repeatedly broken their word, and she had finally come to understand that that was precisely what they intended to keep on doing—play cat and mouse with her until she was exhausted and they had managed to go to press.

Now, ostensibly, she was winning, but, as disclosed to LBJ, her victory struck her as hollow, with everything she had objected to in the book being printed all over the press anyway thanks to the twenty-five copies of the manuscript that had circulated to magazine editors in anticipation of the serial sale.

"I am so dazed now," Jackie declared, "I feel I will never be able to feel anything again."

Twelve

On December 20, 1966, the North American Newspaper Alliance sent out over the newswire an article "For Immediate Release," accompanied by a note to the editors of ninety papers: "This may be the first article in newspapers that is openly critical of Jacqueline Kennedy's posture in America—above and beyond her involvement in the Manchester dispute."

Written by Vera Glaser, the syndicate's Washington bureau chief, the piece made a striking claim: Jackie's actions to obstruct the publication of *The Death of a President* served "to prolong the nation's trauma." Glaser noted that since Dallas, "The nation's heart has gone out to her in love, sympathy, and protectiveness. Reams have been written applauding her courage." But now, Glaser said, people were ready "to take a fresh look at the former first lady." Glaser wrote of "a surfeited nation"; of "former admirers" who had begun to regard Jackie as "a professional

martyr"; of critics who maintained that she was enjoying her preroga-
tives "beyond a reasonable statute of limitations."

"Meanwhile," Glaser went on, "it is worth noting that since November 22, 1963, more than six thousand Americans have met violent death
in Vietnam. Like John F. Kennedy, these young men were young, stal-
wart, full of dreams and promise. Their mutilated remains have been
shipped back in aluminum cases to grieving widows, most of whom are
not beautiful and wealthy. Their courage as they struggle to rear children without fathers, cope with finances, pay mortgages and hunt jobs
goes largely unsung." Unlike Jackie Kennedy, the author suggested,
these widows bravely "try not to look back."

In the ensuing weeks and months, the Vera Glaser piece, which had
appeared nationally under the headline "Uneasy Rests the Crown of
JFK's Jackie," was followed by other severely critical articles in a variety
of publications. As before, Jackie was charged with sabotaging press
freedom and with treating the history of her late husband's administration as her personal property. But, like Glaser's, these new articles also
hit hard at her personally. By turns, Jackie was assailed for wallowing in
self-pity, and well-nigh accused of faking her pain in the interest of getting her way in the lawsuit. Scored for her spending and partying, she
was portrayed as spoiled, frivolous, and imperious. "For the first time . . .
Mrs. Kennedy has her back to the wall," reported Mary McGrory in the
New York Post. "The sympathy and understanding which the world has
accorded her since her superlative demeanor during the tragedy is be-
grudged her." Commenting on the opprobrium that was suddenly, stun-
ningly being heaped upon his formerly sacrosanct sister-in-law, Bobby
Kennedy, in a letter to *Washington Post* publisher Katharine Graham,
protested the relentless derision of "a girl who hadn't committed any
great crime but who day after day was being attacked and pilloried in all
kinds of scandalous ways." Jackie, said RFK, was "so upset and really
crushed" by all the public criticism.

What caused Jackie to go from being idealized to stigmatized? The original Vera Glaser piece comes as close as any to spotlighting Jackie's root transgression. It was, in the journalist's phrase, "to revive the sadness and pain" associated with the Kennedy assassination. Glaser spoke to what she saw as the country's desire for all that sadness to be at an end. Before Air Force One had even left Dallas on the day of the assassination, a fresh white dress and jacket and black shoes had been suggestively laid out for the widow by unseen hands: a tacit invitation to at least begin the process of distancing herself from the bloodshed. Since the time, four months later, when RFK assured TV viewers that Jackie was already making "a good deal of progress," many had been the announcements and intimations that she was about to start a new life at last. Now, however, three years after her husband's murder, her suffering was yet too raw and unprocessed for many people's comfort. At a moment when Americans, still hungry for resolution, were devouring fresh details of Dallas in reports of the upcoming *Look* magazine serialization (both what had been left in and what had been cut), they began to turn against her en masse.

Jackie was far from the first traumatized person in history, and certainly not the last, to be treated in this manner. In a later era, for instance, the 9/11 New York City firefighters, originally lauded as heroes, were subsequently repudiated when they, like Jackie vis-à-vis the assassination, failed to recover quickly enough to satisfy the needs of a society determined to expunge the memory of suffering. These twenty-first-century fallen idols would be charged with offenses that included alcohol and substance abuse, brawling, and sexual misdeeds. Injured people may be used, as Jackie had surely been used by both Lyndon Johnson and Bobby Kennedy, for political purposes. Yet so upsetting is it to have to contemplate human helplessness in the face of overwhelming events that at a certain point we may go so far as to indict the victim for reminding us of things that we prefer to suppress and forget. This rejection of the sufferer is what theorists refer to as the "second injury," and at length it can prove to be even more damaging to the individual than the original traumatic episode.

The day after Christmas, Jackie went off to Bunny Mellon's Antigua estate, hoping, by her own account, to temper her upset. On the evening of her first full day there she had gone for a swim when a pair of news photographers materialized in the crystalline waters near her hostess's supposedly secure private beach. After Jackie's Secret Service protectors chased the intruders off, a spokesperson issued a regal-sounding public statement of the former first lady's extreme displeasure: "Mrs. Kennedy is irked. She has demanded complete privacy." Irked? Demanded? That something had changed in press attitudes toward JFK's widow was reflected in the often lighthearted coverage of the episode. The quotation marks in the *New York Times* headline, "Mrs. Kennedy 'Irked,'" injected what looked to be a note of irony, suggesting that in the wake of the battle of the book, America's patience with her haughty attitudes and locutions had begun to fray.

Jackie did not see the newspapers in Antigua, but in the course of her stay there she did find herself reading a story in a weeks-old magazine about the very controversy she had expressly traveled to the Caribbean to escape. The article reported Manchester's assertion in the book that Jackie had objected to LBJ's calling her "honey." When she read that, she wrote to Johnson on her last day in Antigua: "All the rage that I have been trying to suppress and forget down here boiled up again." At a moment when she was being widely criticized, Jackie, noting that "honey" was an affectionate word, insisted she would like to hear it more often. At a time when a great many people seemed to have altered toward her, Jackie emphasized the constancy of her feelings for Johnson, though she acknowledged that he too might be about to change. Predicting that she would no doubt wish she had torn this letter up as soon as she sent it off, Jackie explained that her purpose in writing it was to express "the fondness I will always feel for you—no matter what happens, and no matter how your feelings may change for me. Once I decide I care about someone—nothing can ever make me change."

Two days before the first installment of the *Look* magazine serialization was due to appear on newsstands, Jackie returned to New York on the evening of Sunday, January 8, 1967, to find the entrance to her Fifth Avenue apartment building aglow in TV camera lights. Her hand reached up to shield her eyes against the glare as she entered the lobby, while reporters vainly shouted questions about "the book." That same Sunday, the page-one headline of the city edition of the *World Journal Tribune* was "Jackie Comes Off Her Pedestal," the first of a multi-part series. Calling the to-do over the Manchester book "tasteless, undignified, and ultimately pointless," the writer Liz Smith declared that whether one agreed or disagreed with Jackie's actions, it was clear she would not emerge from the episode "unscathed": "From now on, she would never again appear in the limelight with quite all that queenly dignity intact. Things were being said, innuendoes repeated." An accompanying page-one piece by Larry Van Gelder reported on "first details" from *The Death of a President*.

But taken by themselves, prepublication tidbits, no matter how alluring, offered little hint of the particular literary form Manchester had conceived for the material that *Look* had chosen for its premier installment. Perhaps it was his knowledge of the many nights Jackie had spent replaying the assassination in her thoughts that led him to tell this part of the story quite as he did; perhaps, too, it was that he had had something of the same experience himself after Okinawa. In any case, the author structured his narrative around a series of implicit what-if questions that did much to give the piece its unique psychological power. What if President Kennedy had not rejected the use of a bubble-top on the presidential limousine? What if one of the other proposed sites for the president's speech had been chosen, which would have made it unnecessary to pass the Texas School Book Depository en route from the airport? What if the warnings to avoid Dallas altogether had not been ignored in Washington? What if some of the Secret Service agents had not stayed out late the night before? What if Marina Oswald had told her friend about Lee Harvey Oswald's rifle? What if Marina, who had left Lee, had agreed to return to him? What if she had not humiliated him the night before President Kennedy's visit to Dallas? By repeatedly posing the question of how the outcome of November 22 might have been different had a single detail been altered, part one reflected the abiding human desire to believe that people are capable of controlling their own destinies. Like the obsessive ruminations of the PTSD sufferer, Manchester's narrative allowed the reader to seek in his own mind to undo the chain of events that had led to the traumatic incident, and thereby to reestablish the illusion of control.

Hours after the issue containing the first installment went on sale in New York's Times Square, an estimated four thousand copies had been purchased in that venue alone. In the course of the heavily ballyhooed four-part serialization of what *Look* was calling "the most important book of 1967," the magazine sold the highest number of copies per issue in its history. Overall circulation jumped from 7.5 million per issue to 9.5 million. Newsstands, where sales spiked from 500,000 to 2 million an issue, could scarcely keep the magazine in stock, prompting *Look*'s admen to launch a poster campaign based on the slogan "If you can't buy it, borrow it." Meanwhile, Governor Connally and other players in the assassination saga suddenly and conspicuously entered the fray with complaints to the press about their various disagreements with Manchester's account.

Also crowding the newspaper columns were reports of the refusal of the West German magazine *Stern,* which had purchased the serialization rights, to follow the edits agreed to by *Look.* The first German-language installment included a letter written by Jackie to her husband while she was in Europe during the summer of 1963. The contents of that letter were among the personal details she had demanded be stricken from the *Look* magazine excerpt. Now, however, *The New York Times* published the letter in the context of the paper's coverage of the *Stern* matter. The episode imparted new meaning to Jackie's perception, previously communicated to LBJ, of the hollowness of her victory. A month after the

Times's James Reston had suggested in his column that she was futilely "holding up her hand to [an] avalanche," she sadly agreed to settle the lawsuit that had done so much to help publicize the very work she had hoped to suppress. Whereupon Manchester, whom Harper & Row had hitherto been rather keen to restrain, felt free to publicly assail the woman he regarded as the author of his latest woes.

His blasts against her, both spoken and written, went on for weeks. Challenging the widely held assumption that the imprimatur of the slain president was Jackie's to confer, Manchester suggested that, despite the widow's complaints, he had told the story exactly as JFK would have wanted it written. He insisted that JFK was the only Kennedy he needed to please. He noted that Jackie's air of fragility had always been deceptive and that she had become increasingly strong-minded since Dallas. He argued that "nothing in her new life discouraged this tendency." He maintained that she was isolated from the world by her wealth and by the sycophants who danced attendance on her in hopes of assuring their own political futures in an RFK administration. He encouraged the public to view her as an accomplished tragic actress. "She must be seen to be believed," Manchester insisted. "When she turns on the charm, it's incredible." Jackie was also, he suggested, quite capable of turning on the tears, as she had when she spotted reporters on the day of the *Look* settlement talks. The implication in all of this was that the figure who had exerted such impressive emotional control at her husband's funeral was similarly the master of her effects now, and that Jackie's public display of anguish over *The Death of a President* had been a performance to cover her own grasping, imperious nature.

In the book, by contrast, Manchester portrayed Jackie as the heroine whose conduct at JFK's funeral had, as he wrote in another context, "held us all together . . . and . . . rekindled our national pride." It is suggestive that Manchester believed his final chapter, covering the events of November 25, to be the best and most important he had written. As an artist and a storyteller, he aimed to deliver the "redemption" that the more clumsily and haphazardly presented offerings of the Warren Commission had failed to provide. ("So far as I know," Manchester wrote, "no committee has ever composed a brilliant symphony, produced a stunning painting—or written a memorable book.") In terms of his book's architecture, he conceived of the penultimate scenes, presided over by the widow, as a "catharsis," which somehow invested the "ghastly futility" that had gone before with meaning. The fact that Manchester in his public remarks about the lawsuit was now gleefully and not a little rabidly comparing that same heroine to Marie Antoinette and Mao Tsetung did provoke some skepticism. Still, the consensus of opinion favored Manchester, the underdog who came off as a brave battler for press freedom against the woman who would capriciously deny the nation the resolution it deserved.

At the close of January 1967, both the Harris and Gallup polls made it clear who the loser had been. According to the former survey, one in three Americans thought less of Jackie as a consequence of the Manchester dispute. No doubt the public stoning to which she had been subjected in the press, from Vera Glaser on, had had an effect on people's perceptions as well. Having previously assured Jackie that her tranquility was paramount to Lady Bird and him, LBJ rejoiced at national polls that documented the self-inflicted damage wrought by her lawsuit, both to her personal reputation and, even more delightfully, to RFK's 1968 presidential ambitions. "God, it just murders Jackie and Bobby both!" the president exulted when he reviewed the latest poll numbers. "It just murders them on this thing!"

Jackie's sense of beleaguerment in this period bonded her the more strongly to Bob McNamara. She felt a sense of imaginative kinship with the defense secretary, whom she saw as similarly misperceived and menaced over Vietnam. Then and later, Jackie focused on those moments when McNamara seemed dangerously under assault from, on the one side, antiwar activists and, on the other, his opponents in government, who, in her view, hoped to snuff out McNamara's light bit by bit "for their own misguided ends." By this time, McNamara's personal crisis had deepened to the point where he was taking pills to sleep, his nights vexed by brooding reveries and bad dreams that Jackie associated with her own. Shortly after the last of the *Look* extracts had run, a major profile of McNamara in *Parade* magazine brought Jackie to tears whose authenticity not even William Manchester, had he known about them, could be tempted to doubt, as they had been shed in private. Recalling JFK's line "One man can make a difference," Jackie asked herself apropos of McNamara's solitary struggle: "When has one man ever made such a difference?"

She who had just failed in her efforts to hold back an avalanche of reminders wrote on March 7 to tell McNamara how proud she was of him: "With all the grinding power of government, of military against you—and just you, trying to hold it all back, trying to stop the nightmare." She who had often lain awake at night dwelling on what she felt certain had been her errors in Dallas assured this man who now privately acknowledged the miscalculations that had cost so many lives in Vietnam: "I know how much you must give up in the dark." She who had sought on countless occasions to imaginatively undo the tragic past avowed: "I feel so close to you in the times I know must be difficult for you—because in my dark times you were always the one who helped me. I wish I could change the world for you."

Jackie wholeheartedly bought into McNamara's self-justificatory sense of himself as laboring passionately and selflessly to alter American foreign policy from within the present administration, where he could operate so much more effectively than if he simply quit. Where many others viewed McNamara as a symbol of the American war machine, Jackie saw a man single-handedly attempting to end the war. Where strangers in the street greeted him with angry cries of "Murderer!" and "Baby burner!," Jackie wondered how many people would one day "owe their lives, or any peace they might know in their lives or their children's lives," to him. Where a legion of skeptics saw a carnivorously ambitious individual endeavoring to hold on to power under Johnson while jockeying to assure that he would have a position in a new Kennedy administration, Jackie beheld a figure determined to do the right thing at whatever personal cost.

She once told him apropos of his efforts to stop the Vietnam War: "You are the Master Builder." Strange to say, in her relations with McNamara, Jackie replicated the role of the fanciful young woman in the Ibsen play who thinks that she alone understands the Master Builder ("Oh, no one knows him as I do!") and perceives the heights he is capable of attaining.

In April 1967 came the tsunami of publicity surrounding the 600,000-copy first printing of, depending on one's perspective, the long-awaited or long-dreaded Manchester book. For a woman who still needed to find a way to relegate the assassination to the past, Jackie's challenge was made the more difficult by the fact that her husband's murder was again incessantly in the news. During this period, she lapsed into a frenzy of anticipation of a public event she was scheduled to attend, the christening of the aircraft carrier *John F. Kennedy* in Newport News, Virginia. At the ceremony, as at Runnymede, Jackie would inevitably confront a host of traumatic triggers, this time in the form of numerous familiar faces associated with her White House years. As the day drew near, she was conscious of dwelling in a self-protective state of emotional numbness, which she described afterward to Marg McNamara as "a kind of trance."

When she actually encountered all those faces at the May 27, 1967, dockside ceremony, the trance, by Jackie's own account, became all the more intense. That day, it fell to Bob McNamara to steer her through the crowd on her arrival and to extricate her as soon as possible after LBJ's brief but barbed speech. The president's remarks proved to be a thinly veiled attempt to claim JFK's authority for the current administration's pursuit of the Vietnam War. Among his listeners at the event was Bobby Kennedy, who, a few weeks before, had outraged him with a speech that called on the administration to seize the initiative in Vietnam by halting the bombardment of the North and announcing Washington's readiness to negotiate. RFK had been worried that such a move on his part would be too risky politically, but he had been under acute pressure from within his own circle to speak out. In view of all this, the prevailing narrative of the spectacle that unfolded in Newport News highlighted current presidential politics.

For Jackie, by contrast, from first to last the occasion had been about something else entirely, her abrupt early departure following the ceremony far from the tacit expression of displeasure with Johnson's Vietnam policy, and of familial solidarity with RFK's, that some observers took it for. Desperate to escape before the floodgates opened, Jackie, as she later told it, held her breath while McNamara cunningly sent Johnson on to the reception area with the assurance that she would be right along. This was one of those moments when the need to remove herself from public view was very strong in her. The unbidden memories and emotions, when inevitably they came forth in a rush, were not anything she cared to endure in front of other people. So, before the president had had a chance to realize that he had been cheated out of a photo opportunity with his predecessor's widow, McNamara had hurried Jackie and the children off to the helicopter waiting to take them to their small jet. On her return to Hyannis Port it was evident that, though she had gotten out in time, the day had been an excruciating experience. "I have reached the point where I cannot go through any more public functions," Jackie said to old Joe's nurse, the unfortunately named Mrs. Dallas. "Today was heartbreaking . . . and I cannot keep it up."

Still, she had little choice but to try. Seventy-two hours later, Jackie was suddenly arranging to travel to England with RFK and other Kennedy family members for the funeral of Sissie Harlech, aged forty-five, who had been killed in an automobile accident in Wales. Since Lord and Lady Harlech's departure from Washington, David Harlech had accepted a position in Edward Heath's shadow cabinet as deputy leader of the House of Lords. Meanwhile, he had been a frequent visitor to the

United States, where he had been prominently associated with both Harvard's rechristened Kennedy School and the planned Kennedy Library where JFK's presidential papers were to be housed. He also had served as a trusted adviser to Bobby Kennedy, as well as to Jackie. Following Sissie's funeral, he arranged to visit Jackie in Ireland, where she was to stay for six weeks. "They were like two wounded birds together," said his daughter Jane Ormsby-Gore of the widow and widower. "Ghastly things had happened to them."

Another ghastly thing very nearly occurred in the course of Jackie's stay. Evenings, without telling anyone, including the Secret Service agents who had accompanied her and her children abroad, Jackie would slip out of the house she was staying in and drive herself to a cove where she could have a long, solitary swim across the channel and back. One afternoon, she was out picnicking on a sandbar with some others when she felt the familiar urgent need to escape. In the belief that no one in the party had seen her go off, she walked along the beach for approximately half a mile to her secret spot. Jackie, veteran of many summers at East Hampton, Newport, and Hyannis Port, was an expert swimmer. In an earlier time, she almost certainly would have recognized that the waters she was about to enter were at high tide, perilously so. But, focused by turns on her demons and on the process of numbing herself to them, as she tended to be these days, she was oddly oblivious to the danger. Midway across the channel, Jackie was caught in an overpowering current so icy that she could not keep her fingers together as she swam.

Greatly fatigued, helpless against the mix of cold and current, she feared she was about to slip past the spit of land opposite and be flung into the twelve-mile-long bay. Suddenly, however, "a great porpoise," as she later described her rescuer, materialized at her side. It proved to be a Secret Service agent who, unbeknownst to her, had followed her to the cove night after night. Today, fortuitously, he had broken away from the party of picnickers in order to pursue her here. Setting his shoulder against hers, he guided her to shore, where she sat on the beach for a long while, coughing up seawater. Had the agent not been there, Jackie would likely have drowned. During the previous few months, she had privately characterized herself as dazed; as uncertain whether she would ever be able to feel anything again; as existing in a kind of trance. While she certainly had not chosen to live in this manner, body and brain had withdrawn, the better to concentrate on avoiding painful memories and emotions. In Ireland, however, a posture designed to spare her a certain amount of anguish had almost had fatal consequences. Being, in effect, dead to the world so much of the time had nearly cost her her life.

Another consequence was that she often found herself suppressing not just painful feelings and perceptions, but potentially pleasurable ones as well. It was as though any stimulation were dangerous; as though the only safety were to be found in the complete absence of feelings. At the same time, she longed to feel and enjoy, to make herself, in her phrase, "interested in things again." Expressly to that end, in this period she had conceived of a journey to inspect the temples of Angkor, the seat of an empire that flourished between the ninth and fifteenth centuries. It was quite the sort of trip Jackie would have found exhilarating when she was first lady. Might it be that for her again? Might a visit to the ruins help free her from the tyranny of the past? Reaching Angkor would be no simple undertaking. Cambodia, where the temples were located, had severed relations with the United States two years previously due to the Vietnam War and other sources of friction.

She asked McNamara to see what could be arranged. At length, he discovered that not only would Cambodia's chief of state, Prince Norodom Sihanouk, agree to a visit, he actually welcomed it. President Johnson, evidently, was not the only world leader eager to be photographed at her side. For Sihanouk, playing host to an American president's widow would be a way of irritating China, his erstwhile ally in the region. The prince also seems to have viewed the invitation as an overture of friendship toward Bobby Kennedy, whom he thought likely to occupy the White House one day very soon. In any case, McNamara's successful efforts to gain entry for Jackie into a nation ostensibly hostile to the United States caused her to affectionately liken him to Harry Lime, the roguish character played by Orson Welles in the 1949 film *The Third Man*, who miraculously produces a passport for a beautiful young actress portrayed by Alida Valli. Jackie extracted McNamara's promise to screen *The Third Man* while she was in Cambodia, but she was soon flirtatiously lamenting the prospect of his falling in love with Alida Valli.

In other ways as well, *The Third Man*, which Jackie had first seen as a college student in Paris in 1950, figured prominently in her imagination that tempestuous fall of 1967. She told McNamara how, seventeen years previously, the movie had inspired her to make a side trip to Vienna, where Soviet troops patrolled the streets with machine guns, and where she had been scared as never before in her life. Proposing, curiously, that present-day America was very much like the era depicted in *The Third Man*, Jackie seemed to suggest that she was similarly fearful now. The occasion for these fraught reflections was a newspaper photograph she had seen of McNamara gazing out his office window at many thousands of demonstrators, who had converged in Washington on October 21, 1967, determined to shut down the Pentagon. In consultation with LBJ, McNamara had surrounded the building with a cordon of rifle-bearing troops. Because of all that firepower, any confrontation with the missile-hurling demonstrators, not a few of whom seemed intent on provoking the troops, threatened to ignite major violence, the culmination of months of national disquiet that had included not just rising anti–Vietnam War protests, but also the urban race riots known as the Long Hot Summer of 1967.

By this point, McNamara's standing in the administration had decayed markedly since the time, shortly before the christening of the aircraft carrier *John F. Kennedy*, when he had advised the president that the Vietnam War was not winnable and that it would therefore be wisest to negotiate a peace, however unfavorable. In the course of pursuing this war, Johnson had clung to the fact that his advisers had been JFK's counselors as well. Now that such a key adviser had unequivocally taken a dissenting view, LBJ oscillated between blaming McNamara's conversion on the corruptive influence of Bobby Kennedy and suggesting that the defense secretary had grown mentally unstable. "He's a fine man, a wonderful man, Bob McNamara," Johnson effused. "He has given everything, just about everything, and . . . we just can't afford another [James] Forrestal," the latter a pointed reference to the Truman-era defense secretary who, in a bout of depression, had committed suicide by jumping to his death from a hospital window. Might McNamara be about to crack as well? Might he too be about to take his own life? Johnson was not the only figure in Washington to regard McNamara as "an emotional basket case." Burdened with a heavy load of guilt about the many lives that had been sacrificed in Vietnam, but also about the wife whose severe ill health due to an ulcer he felt similarly responsible for, the Bob McNamara of these months was a gray, gaunt figure, who, according to one White House aide, seemed to be barely "hanging on by the fingernails." On the day of the Pentagon march, McNamara showed a tortured visage to the world as he surveyed the angry crowd from his window, but Jackie emphatically did not perceive him that way. Putting on a cast recording of the Broadway musical *Man of La Mancha*, which she and McNamara had often listened to together, she wrote to assure the embattled defense secretary that she had never seen "anything so brave" as he.

Whether that was quite the way to describe him became a matter of passionate discussion within the Kennedy camp when, presently, LBJ, in response to another dovish screed from McNamara, undertook to maneuver him out of office by nominating him to lead the World Bank. Bobby Kennedy implored McNamara not only to refuse the new post, but also to resign as defense secretary with a public announcement to the effect that he could no longer continue to serve this administration in good conscience. Bobby urged him to go out "with a hell of a blast at Johnson." McNamara's principled defection, though no doubt costly to himself in the short term, would lend a certain legitimacy to Bobby Kennedy's antiwar posture. On the other hand, a decision by McNamara to acquiesce to the president's efforts to silence him would be, in the words of one RFK supporter, "a big blow" to Bobby politically. In the end, McNamara's willingness to servilely accept the World Bank post seemed to confirm the view of him as a man who was less interested in principle than in place. RFK, responding to an aide's tart analysis that McNamara, when he chose "safe submission," had permitted Johnson to "break him into nothing" and "tear out his spine," commented sadly: "That's about right." By contrast, Jackie saw no reason to revise her heroic conception of McNamara. Later, recalling all that he had accomplished during his tenure as defense secretary, she said she wondered if he knew how many lives he had saved—beginning with her own.

On October 18, 1967, Jackie and an entourage finally flew to Rome on the first leg of her Cambodian journey. In Italy, she was joined by David Harlech, whose diplomatic flair promised to be useful when, presently, she was the first American to be received with high state honors since Cambodia had broken relations with the United States. On various occasions, both she and McNamara had attempted to leave Sihanouk in no doubt that she wanted to keep the visit private. In deference to her host's political needs, Jackie had consented to major press coverage on her arrival in Cambodia as well as on her departure. Otherwise, she stipulated that it would be sufficient for Sihanouk's personal photographer to take a single picture of them both at Angkor, which the prince would be free to distribute afterward. Whatever hopes Sihanouk and others had invested in her trip, she persisted in viewing it primarily in personal terms.

Hardly had Jackie and her party landed in Cambodia on November 2, 1967, however, when her great plans unraveled. The waiting crowd of ten thousand; the welcoming rituals involving the prince, various Cambodian officials, and members of the diplomatic corps—it was all somehow too much for her. At length, Jackie was shown to her rooms, where she and David Harlech quarreled over her insistence that she was too tired to attend Sihanouk's dinner in her honor that night. Unlike McNamara, who had grown accustomed to Jackie's outbursts and who saw it as his role to do whatever she appeared to require of him at the moment, Harlech, with his finely honed sense of duty to matters greater than oneself, was furious at behavior he perceived as childishly selfish.

Jackie finally consented to go to the palace dinner, but before she gave in, she and Harlech had quite a row, at the end of which he said something unexpected. Widowed but six months previously, JFK's great friend selected this most peculiar of moments to ask Jackie to marry him. His proposal was incongruous, embarrassing, and not a little odd, yet she had to respond. Speaking in general terms, she told him that she did not want to marry and have her heart hurt again.

Despite this rejection, Harlech did not abandon his efforts to make Jackie his wife. Thereafter, he saw her frequently in New York, where his youngest daughter, Alice Ormsby-Gore, went to school. He and Jackie were also to take another trip together, to the Georgia plantation of their friend, former U.S. ambassador to Britain John Hay Whitney, which they had previously visited when Sissie was alive. But, though he repeatedly raised the issue of marriage, Jackie continued to put him off. Her line about not wanting to be hurt again appears to have been a gentle way of saying no without having to raise any specific objection to a man she sincerely admired and held dear. As long as David Harlech lived, she seems never to have wavered in the conviction, expressed soon after Dallas, that he might be just the figure "who could save the Western world."

As she wistfully suggested many years later, however, it had been David's capacity to make one person in particular feel safe that had been in doubt. That person, of course, was Jackie herself.

Thirteen

On Sunday, February 18, 1968, the sound of revolver shots automatically tripped off the security system in Jackie's brain. Cecil Beaton, who had escorted her to the New York City Ballet that evening to attend a rare performance by the choreographer George Balanchine in the title role of Don Quixote, watched her nearly jump out of her seat and over the rail of the dress circle. It was a false alarm, the gunfire being part of the show. But since the assassination, Jackie had been wired to react instantly, without so much as a moment's reflection. Ever on guard for a repetition of the trauma, the limbic memory, kicking in independently of her conscious control, reacted to the staged gunshots as if Jackie continued to be threatened with annihilation. At that moment, it was as if the violence she had experienced in 1963 were about to be played out all over again.

For many months Bobby Kennedy had vacillated about whether or not to challenge Johnson for their party's 1968 presidential nomination. He worried that from the point of view of his own ambitions it might be best to wait until 1972; that a decision to take on Johnson would appear to give credence to those who had long insisted that RFK was motivated not by principles but rather by a sick personal vendetta against his brother's successor; and that even a fruitful bid on RFK's part for the Democratic nomination would only divide the party and elect Richard Nixon or some other Republican.

Suddenly, however, beginning in late January of 1968, the Vietcong's massive Tet offensive within South Vietnam, launched mere weeks after General Westmoreland had confidently prophesied that U.S. gains in 1967 would be increased manyfold in 1968, scrambled political calculations in Washington. Suddenly, the "bang-bang coverage" (as the footage of troops shooting at one another in Vietnam was known in TV industry parlance) on the nightly news seemed to underscore enemy strength and resilience, and thereby to call into question the veracity of an administration that had emphatically portrayed the Communists as in no condition to essay anything like a major offensive.

Tet transfigured the antiwar candidacy of Senator Eugene McCarthy, who came within three hundred votes of beating LBJ in the March 12, 1968, New Hampshire Democratic primary. In one fell swoop, McCarthy had proven that an insurgent bid could be viable; yet it was Bobby Kennedy who, at least by some calculations, still seemed to have the better chance of vanquishing Johnson. Four days after New Hampshire, speaking in the very Senate Caucus Room where JFK had announced his own presidential bid eight years before, Bobby Kennedy declared his intent to challenge Johnson.

From the first, he made the violent tenor of American life in the waning 1960s a campaign theme. "Every night we watch horror on the evening news," the senator told an audience in Kansas on the eighteenth. "Violence spreads inexorably across the nation, filling our streets and crippling our lives." He maintained that the Johnson administration offered no solution to the war—"none but the ever-expanding use of military force . . . in a conflict where military force has failed to solve anything."

The specter of violence was much in Jackie's thoughts as well when she contemplated the prospect of her brother-in-law's candidacy. She was in Mexico to view the Mayan ruins in the company of former U.S. undersecretary of defense Roswell Gilpatric, a married man who frequently escorted her in public, when reporters asked her about Bobby's decision to seek the nomination. "Whatever Senator Kennedy will do, I know it will be all right," she said. "I will always be with him with all my heart. I shall always back him up." Still, the greatest fear of any traumatized individual is that the instant of horror will be reprised. Contrary to anything Jackie said in public, that fear tinctured her anguished private remarks about RFK's presidential bid. In the course of a dinner party at the home of *Vogue* magazine editor Diana Vreeland on April 2, 1968, Jackie asked Arthur Schlesinger: "Do you know what I think will happen to Bobby if he is elected president?" Schlesinger indicated that he did not. "The same thing that happened to Jack," Jackie went on. "There is so much hatred in this country, and more people hate Bobby than hated Jack. That's why I don't want him to be president." Jackie had spoken of her concerns directly to Bobby on several occasions, but he had pressed forward notwithstanding. Certain of the senator's aides also were known to worry about his safety, but again and again he refused to take the precautions that were urged upon him.

Two days after Jackie confided her sense of foreboding to Schlesinger, she attended the installation of Archbishop Terence Cooke at St. Patrick's Cathedral on Fifth Avenue. LBJ, who had recently announced that he did not intend to seek another term and that in the meantime he hoped to negotiate a settlement in Vietnam, was also present at the installation ceremony. By this point Johnson felt as though he had been "chased on all sides by a giant stampede": race riots and peace protests; the Tet offensive and McCarthy's stunning performance in New Hampshire. Finally, however, it had been the realization of the fear that had possessed him since November 22, 1963, that Bobby Kennedy would openly move to seize the crown, that seems to have driven Johnson from office. To judge by the serene atmosphere in and around St. Patrick's, the placard-wavers known to taunt and torment him wherever he went no longer saw any reason to show up. The picture of the ruined president chatting pleasantly with Jackie at the cathedral on April 4, 1968, proved to be the quiet between the heaves of storm.

That same day, Martin Luther King was assassinated in Memphis. Cities across the United States erupted. Neighborhoods burned. Businesses were looted, Molotov cocktails thrown. The nation that had recently chided Jackie to let Americans put the past behind them was suddenly, ineluctably, hurled back into that very past, as commentators linked the civil rights leader's murder to the assassination of President Kennedy. "Have four and a half years really gone by since Dallas?" asked the *New Yorker* writer Michael Arlen. To Bobby Kennedy, it seemed as if his brother's assassin had "set something loose in this country." Whatever narrative resolution or redemption, if any, the Warren Commission Report and *The Death of a President* had managed to provide vanished along with the waves of gray smoke that rose from countless torched buildings on the evening news.

No longer alone in associating present-day bloodshed with the events of November 22, 1963, Jackie released a public statement of sympathy for King's widow and children. "When will our country learn that to live by the sword is to perish by the sword? I pray that with the price he paid—his life—he will make room in people's hearts for love, not hate. Some people would never kill—but even to speak of another with hatred is the same and causes death." But would Jackie attend the slain civil rights leader's funeral in Atlanta on April 9? Coretta Scott King broached the subject of the former first lady's participation with Bobby Kennedy, who planned to march in the next day's funeral procession, as well as attend the church service.

RFK replied: "This would be very hard because of her own experiences, but if it meant anything to you perhaps she would try to come." When Mrs. King indicated that it would indeed count for a great deal, once again RFK arranged to produce Jackie. As he had foreseen, she did not want to go to Atlanta. She dreaded the crowds and the inevitable reminders of President Kennedy's funeral. A new burst of violence in American cities over the weekend, the likes of which had not been experienced since the Civil War, had led to anxiety in some quarters about what might happen in Atlanta on the day of the funeral. Still, Jackie agreed to fly in that morning because Bobby had asked her to be there.

When Jackie arrived at Ebenezer Baptist Church, where great numbers of chanting, weeping people had gathered in oppressive eighty-degree heat, she looked tense and terrified as, caught up in a surging crowd, she found herself being "pulled and pushed" into the church, which had but 750 seats. During the memorial service that ensued, Jackie, in one of the pews, scrutinized the faces of certain of her fellow mourners. The objects of her roving gaze were black Americans, who, she later remembered thinking, knew death—that is, violent death—because they saw it "all the time" and were "ready for it." Her perceived affinity with them was based on the fact that she too knew death; she too was ready. On her return to New York, Jackie predicted that the national outpouring of sympathy for the King family that had been manifest in recent days would not last. "Of course people feel guilty for a moment," she sardonically observed to Arthur Schlesinger. "But they hate feeling guilty. They can't stand it for very long. Then they turn." That repudiation was something Jackie had experienced firsthand.

Since he had been Jackie's host in 1963, Aristotle Onassis, reluctant to abandon such a splendid connection, had telephoned at intervals, as well as dined with her privately. On Jackie's side, there had always been a certain amount of guilt attached to her interlude on the *Christina* after the death of baby Patrick. Still, there could be no denying that Onassis had acted beautifully to her after the Kennedy assassination. Immediately, he had appeared in Washington to attend the funeral in the company of the

Radziwills. More recently, he had cut an incongruous figure at the christening of the aircraft carrier *John F. Kennedy*, where Jackie had been surprised and, apparently, not a little pleased to spot him among all those familiar Washington faces. As her sister Lee was to say of Onassis in another context: "For him, life was a chess game. . . . His patience was enduring." In the anxious aftermath of the King funeral, Onassis seemed to perceive his opening at last. He offered to transport Jackie and the children on his private jet to Palm Beach, where she was due to spend the Easter holiday. She gratefully accepted. At a moment when she and the Kennedy assassination were again much in the news in connection with her dramatic and much-noted presence in Atlanta, the flight would at least spare her the ordeal of traveling in public view on a commercial airline. Not incidentally from Onassis's perspective, it also afforded him an opportunity to personally accompany her on the jet, before continuing on to Nassau, where he was to meet his daughter. A month later, when most other Kennedy family members were out campaigning for RFK in the Democratic primaries, all of which Bobby had insisted he must win, Onassis offered Jackie a refuge in the form of a four-day cruise of the Virgin Islands on the *Christina*, beginning May 25. In advance of her arrival, the consummate host had adorned the saloon, the smoking room, and the teak-paneled study with silver-framed photographs of President and Mrs. Kennedy. But the pictures were promptly taken down when Jackie's maid, who had come on board beforehand, informed Onassis that the widow still could not bear to have images of her murdered husband about.

By this point, Bobby Kennedy had triumphed in Indiana and D.C. on May 7 and in Nebraska on the fourteenth. His concern with those members of society who are without power and privileges had finally allowed him to formulate a distinctive political identity apart from his late brother's. Still, RFK's numbers thus far had not been sufficient to eliminate Eugene McCarthy. Oregon and California loomed, and McCarthy seemed poised to do well in both critical contests. Jackie would later recall that she had spoken to Bobby of her concerns about his safety—"several times." Nonetheless, more than ever after the death of Martin Luther King, RFK seemed weirdly intent on disregarding the danger to himself. Certainly he acknowledged the existence of that danger. Had he not remarked in the hours after the King assassination, "That could have been me"? Yet, a week later, when the Kennedy campaign was notified that a gun-wielding stranger had been observed on a nearby rooftop, RFK balked at an aide's efforts to lower the blinds in the candidate's hotel suite. "If they're going to shoot," Bobby said chillingly of any would-be assassins, "they'll shoot."

Jackie disembarked from the *Christina* on Tuesday, May 28. That day, McCarthy won Oregon. RFK, while seeking to downplay previous statements about what a single loss might mean, suggested that if he did not win the following Tuesday in California he would withdraw. After what the *Los Angeles Times* was calling Oregon's "body blow" to the Kennedy campaign, California emerged as "the ultimate test." Even a modest win by McCarthy threatened to poison Bobby Kennedy's chances not just in 1968, but in 1972 as well. During the whirligig final week of campaigning, Jackie persisted in her unwillingness to join other family members on the hustings. Like them, however, she understood that, for Bobby, it might well be now or never. So on June 4, despite her abiding fears for him, she was thrilled to learn that he had won California. Jackie was in New York, where it was three hours later than on the West Coast. She went to bed before she could watch him speak on TV at midnight Los Angeles time.

It was about four A.M. in Manhattan when the light on Jackie's night table telephone flashed on. The caller proved to be Stas Radziwill, who was in London.

"Isn't it wonderful?" Jackie asked him, still fueled by the enthusiasm and expectancy of the past few days. "He's won. He's got California."

Stas countered: "But how is he?"

"Oh, he's fine. He's won."

Stas persisted: "But how is he?"

"What do you mean?"

Many nights in this very bed, she had struggled with intrusive recollections of her husband's murder. Many nights she had helplessly, endlessly relived the assassination in the form of dreams and reveries. But what Stas went on to tell her, about the gunman who had been waiting for Bobby Kennedy after he delivered his victory speech at the Ambassador Hotel in Los Angeles, was no nightmare from which Jackie would eventually awaken screaming. The shots that had rung out that night had been all too real.

Lee Radziwill, also in London at the time, spoke to Cecil Beaton of the effect this new shooting was likely to have on her sister's already tortured state of mind. "You don't know what it's like being with Jackie," she explained. "She's really more than half round the bend! She can't sleep at night, she can't stop thinking about herself and never feeling anything but sorry for herself! 'I'm so unprotected,' she says. But she is surrounded by friends, helpers, FBI. . . . She takes no interest in anything for more than two minutes. She rushes around paying visits but won't settle down anywhere or to anything. She can't love anyone. . . . The new horror will bring the old one alive again and I'm going to have to go through hell trying to calm her. She gets so that she hits me across the face, and apropos of nothing."

Immediately, Jackie flew to Los Angeles, where Chuck Spalding, now Bobby's fervent supporter as once he had been Jack's, met her at the airport. "I took her to the hospital," Spalding later recalled. "And the whole thing had that whole same feeling for everybody of just being replayed again, just the business of going through with it . . . everybody overwhelmed by the repetition of the same event." In the hospital room, Bobby, near death, lay in a tangle of medical equipment. Ethel Kennedy, pregnant with their eleventh child, was beside him. Teddy Kennedy, on his knees, prayed at the foot of the bed. The attack by a young Palestinian who had been in the United States for more than a decade had left

RFK with irreversible brain damage. There was no improvement, no hope. In the course of a twenty-four-hour vigil, each time press secretary Frank Mankiewicz emerged to issue an update to the TV cameras, his face seemed somehow more ravaged than before.

At one point when Jackie and the press secretary were alone in the corridor, she mused about some of the people she had observed two months previously at the funeral of Martin Luther King, people who, she explained, really knew death because they saw it constantly and were ready for it to happen again. As she had following her husband's murder, she spoke disturbingly of the attraction that dying held for her as a consequence of what had happened: "Well, now we know death, don't we, you and I?" she told Mankiewicz. "As a matter of fact, if it weren't for the children, we'd welcome it."

Jackie was at RFK's bedside when he was pronounced dead, nearly twenty-six hours after he had been shot. Bobby had been known to lament that Jackie lived in the past too much. But after he too had been murdered, how could she ever get unstuck from the past? How could she ever learn to see the first Kennedy assassination as an isolated episode that, whatever brain and body persisted in telling her to the contrary, was unlikely to recur? How could she accept the events in Dallas as an instance of life's randomness, when the killings of Martin Luther King and RFK seemed, along with JFK's, part of an emergent pattern, which she was far from alone in perceiving? What did it mean any longer for Bobby to have called Jackie his crazy sister-in-law when so many other people—sane, reasonable, responsible people—suddenly shared her sense of dread?

David Harlech, set to be a pallbearer at Bobby's funeral, publicly decried the violence that was igniting late-1960s America as "an international scandal." Lyndon Johnson and Teddy Kennedy both worried that the same tragic fate awaited them as had befallen JFK, King, and RFK. Since the death of her husband, Jackie had been tensed in expectation of another assault. In view of what had happened to Bobby, she feared she was the next target. Under the circumstances, who could say with confidence that she was wrong?

Johnson sent a presidential jet to transport RFK's remains, along with Ethel, Jackie, Teddy, and the rest of the Kennedy party, to New York, where there was to be a requiem Mass at St. Patrick's Cathedral. Jackie, when she arrived at Los Angeles International Airport, initially refused to board in the mistaken belief that the aircraft was the one on which she had accompanied Jack's coffin from Dallas. It was characteristic of the day, however, that she was not the only person to be painfully reminded of that earlier journey. The scene at LaGuardia Airport in New York, where some of the people who had been at Andrews Air Force Base had gathered again, was all too familiar, Arthur Schlesinger observed in his diary; the identical sadness penetrated everything. In 1963, Bob McNamara had been waiting with RFK in the rear of a military truck. Knowing Bobby's temperament as he did, however, McNamara had declined to accompany him onto Air Force One to collect Jackie. McNamara's decision to stay behind spared him from being immediately drawn into RFK's inevitable struggle with LBJ, who was the defense secretary's new boss after all. In 1968, though it was Bobby who lay in a maroon-draped mahogany casket, that struggle absurdly continued. At a time when Johnson was already seeking to prevent his old foe from being buried near President Kennedy at Arlington National Cemetery, McNamara quietly appealed to him to let RFK be interred in keeping with his survivors' wishes. But all of that was merely the frenetic offstage action. As the aircraft from Los Angeles came in, McNamara, who also had been asked to serve as a pallbearer at the funeral, lingered in a nearby automobile, out of sight of the TV cameras. Finally, in the words of an onlooker, "he leaped out of the car, dragging his wife after him." He rushed to Jackie, who dropped her head on his shoulder and wept. Surely, that night it was he who wished he could change the world for her.

Later that evening, at St. Patrick's Cathedral, Rose Kennedy attempted to comfort Jackie by wrapping both arms around her daughter-in-law's shoulders after the younger woman exploded in tears over Bobby's casket. Rose and Ethel Kennedy alike were sustained by the power of their faith. Andrew Devonshire, who attended RFK's funeral, later remembered feeling nothing less than jealous of the unshakable religious convictions that allowed Rose Kennedy to react so calmly to the loss of yet another of her children. During the time that RFK's body remained on public view in the vaulted nave, Jackie would have occasion to remember something Ethel Kennedy had told her after Jack died: "At least you have the comfort of knowing that he has found eternal happiness." Now as then, much as Jackie might have wished to, she simply did not share Rose's and Ethel's steadfast beliefs. As she was soon to suggest, for her there was no consolation, no hope.

After a sleepless night, Teddy Kennedy, aged thirty-six, made a vivid impression when he delivered the eulogy at his brother's June 8 funeral. "My brother need not be idealized or enlarged in death beyond what he was in life," Teddy said, eyes downcast, "but be remembered as a good and decent man who saw wrong and tried to right it, saw suffering and tried to heal it, saw war and tried to stop it." In private, however, Teddy, like Jackie, palpably lacked the tranquility of Rose and Ethel. He had loved and depended on Bobby, whose existence had been one final buffer against a role that, unlike RFK or JFK, Teddy had never coveted. Teddy, the cosseted baby of the family, the beloved purveyor of joy and mirth, had long been content to leave it to his brothers to carry the Kennedy flag. Bobby had grieved deeply and at length after Dallas, but it is also indisputable that he had been quick to reconnoiter the newly altered political landscape in terms of his own long-range presidential ambitions, as well as to coolly calculate how JFK's widow might prove helpful in his negotiations with LBJ. Four and a half years later, Teddy showed no comparable inclination when, less than an hour after his brother had been pronounced dead, Allard Lowenstein, a liberal Democrat and founder of the Dump Johnson movement, approached him in a hospital elevator to earnestly communicate that he, Teddy, a man whose senatorial candidacy had not too long ago been widely regarded as a joke, was all that the party had left.

In the days and weeks that followed, when other prominent Democrats sought to persuade him to take up his brother's fight by running against Richard Nixon in 1968, Teddy tended to be no more receptive to their overtures. In a time of national anxiety about the madness that had already taken place that year and about the madness yet to come, party leaders saw Teddy as a link to what now looked to be a simpler and more optimistic era, the years when a Kennedy last inhabited the Oval Office. At length, Mike Mansfield would go so far as to say that Teddy Kennedy had no choice about whether to accept the leadership role in the party that Mansfield characterized as "preordained . . . a matter of destiny." Given the myth of Jack Kennedy's reluctance to take over from Joe Junior after the war, Teddy's acquiescence to a long-entrenched family narrative that he, like Bobby before him, appears never to have questioned seemed preordained as well.

All of this put what proved to be an impossible burden on Teddy. In Jackie's telling, he sailed Nantucket Sound that summer "with this terrible look of not real gaiety on his face—and his lips cracked with red wine . . . as he took Bobby's sons and Jack's son to sea." She portrayed these voyages as a Celtic ritual, akin to Jack's having taken Teddy sailing after Joe Junior died. But, as she well understood, they also served the purpose of facilitating the senator's escape from the prominent public role that was being urged upon him. National polls suggested that the Kennedy name on the ticket, whether it be on the top or at the bottom, might assure Democrats a landslide, in contrast to the toss-up that was otherwise prophesied for November. In early July, however, when Schlesinger, over drinks at Jackie's cottage in Hyannis Port, so much as suggested the possibility that Teddy might run, she was quick to reject the idea. Jackie was convinced that if Teddy took a more conspicuous part in public life, he too would be shot.

To Jackie's mind, Teddy was being terribly brave under the circumstances. He unflinchingly embraced what he saw as his duty not only to serve in loco parentis to Jack's and Bobby's children, but also to comfort and care for his slain brothers' widows. Nonetheless, he was far from the force in Jackie's life that Bobby had been after Jack died. Beset by visions of her own annihilation as Jackie confessedly was, her perceived need at this point was for the powerful protector that it was simply beyond poor troubled Teddy's capacity to be. Jackie compared the family atmosphere after the second Kennedy assassination to the milieu of the White Russians in Paris, grand dukes who drank and despaired all day, despair being the element in which they swam and breathed. But at night, she emphasized, they "have their music—and there is this wild moment of defiance and despair and laughter." Such was the moral and emotional disarray that greeted Aristotle Onassis when he came to see Jackie less than two weeks after Bobby Kennedy's funeral.

When they realized the magnitude of what Onassis had methodically accomplished during the four strange months that followed, even some of the people who had observed him then, in Hyannis Port, Newport, and New York City, were astonished. How had he brought it off? How had he successfully courted JFK's widow at a time when both the Kennedys and the Auchinclosses, not to mention Jackie herself, were still reeling from Bobby's murder? No one could later accuse Onassis, with his chunky gangster-style dark glasses, brilliantined hair, and enveloping cloud of Montecristo cigar smoke, of having failed to operate in plain sight. There had been nothing subtle or secretive about the gift boxes containing, all told, several million dollars' worth of diamonds, rubies, emeralds, and pearls that had persisted in being delivered throughout the period when he was seeking to make Jackie his wife. The jewelry itself, in the form of bracelets, tiaras, necklaces, and the like, had been so ostentatious that it would be hard to accuse the sender of having failed to disclose his intentions when he had fairly screamed them to anyone who cared to see or hear. Turning the teachings of Bunny Mellon on their head, Onassis seemed to believe that everything should be noticed.

Nevertheless, Rose Kennedy, though she certainly had entertained

Onassis at the Cape that summer (as well as received an expensive bracelet from him, which she had promptly had appraised in the mistaken suspicion that it must be a fake), appears to have been sincerely "stunned" and "perplexed" when, in the autumn, she finally learned of the impending marriage. Rose was troubled by the disparities in age (Onassis claimed to be sixty-two, though he was rumored to be even older) and religion—and certainly by the fact that he was divorced. She confided to her diary that David Harlech would have been the more logical choice by far because he was so much more intellectually compatible and because of his considerable history with the family. David was not a Catholic, of course, but at least he had been married to one. Janet Auchincloss, whom Onassis had similarly visited (and lavishly gifted) early on at Hammersmith Farm, later reacted hysterically to the news that she would soon have him as a son-in-law. There was perhaps no greater indication of Janet's displeasure than when she evoked the detested name of Black Jack Bouvier. After she failed to turn Jackie from her purpose, the mother wept that her eldest daughter had finally found a way to punish her for divorcing Black Jack. Arthur Schlesinger had met Onassis that summer at the New York nightclub El Morocco. Onassis flattered Schlesinger by saying that he had heard a great deal about him from Jackie and would like to talk. But when the magnate went on to praise the new Greek military dictatorship that had seized power in Athens the previous year, Schlesinger excused himself. Subsequently, the former Kennedy adviser thought that Jean Kennedy Smith must be jesting when she informed him that Jackie was about to marry Onassis. Disbelief shaded into horror as he realized that it was true. Schlesinger's opinion, that Jackie's marriage to this unapologetic supporter of the Greek colonels would be an insult to JFK's memory and a betrayal of everything the late president had represented, epitomized the view of a good many Kennedy-administration veterans. Finally, Jackie's decision to accept this man with whom she had such emphatic differences in matters of intellect, style, politics, and much else besides prompted Bunny Mellon to ask her point-blank: "Why are you doing this?"

"I have no choice," Jackie replied. "They're playing Ten Little Indians. I don't want to be next."

In a similar vein, speaking in later years of her unlikely second marriage, Jackie would reflect of the aftermath of RFK's murder: "I wanted to go off. I wanted to be somewhere safe."

Never perhaps did it seem clearer that Jackie could no longer find safety under the warmth of the wings of the Kennedys than when she and Teddy traveled to Greece as Onassis's guests at the beginning of August. Teddy delivered a cringe-worthy performance on Skorpios, Onassis's four-hundred-acre private island in the Ionian Sea, near Greece's west coast. At best Teddy's mission had been to head off the marriage, at worst to negotiate a financial settlement in the widow's favor. At length, he proved to be no match for Onassis, who, in advance of their parley, plied the younger man with ouzo and girls. In the course of a party aboard the *Christina*, a journalist who was thought to have insinuated himself among the hired bouzouki players (but whom some people later suspected of having been planted by Onassis) photographed the pink-shirted, flush-faced married American senator as he caroused with a young blonde. Teddy thereupon alternated between furious but futile demands that the reporter hand over the film and empty threats to destroy the fellow's career. Onassis later made a show of using his influence with the rightist government to have the reporter arrested in Athens, where the authorities forced him to surrender the film that had the potential to cause such embarrassment to Jackie and her in-laws. So in the end, Teddy, who had landed on Skorpios as Jackie's putative protector, had had to be protected himself—and by Onassis and the Greek colonels no less. Such, at least at this point, was the mortifying ineffectualness of the Kennedy family's new leader, who returned alone to the United States, where calls had intensified that he make himself available to lead America. Ten days after Teddy's departure from Skorpios, Jackie followed him home with a sense that Onassis, with his island kingdom, seventy-five-man armed security force, warship-sized yacht, and privately owned airline, could afford her the insulation she required against what she pointedly began to refer to as "the outside world."

At the time, the latter seemed a very threatening place indeed—not just to her, but to anyone with a TV set. Jackie had returned to an America that was riveted by images, similar in form to the bang-bang coverage from Vietnam with which those pictures were interspersed, of young Americans being bludgeoned and tear-gassed in the streets of Chicago, where the thirty-fifth Democratic National Convention was then in progress at the International Amphitheater. Some ten thousand antiwar protesters were set upon by more than double that number of helmeted Chicago police and Illinois National Guardsmen, the latter with instructions to shoot to kill should it prove necessary. Deploying an array of weapons ranging from defense spray Chemical Mace to billy clubs and rifle butts, the authorities indiscriminately attacked people on the street. Following months of assassinations, civil unrest, and overall lawlessness, the images from Chicago depicted a society gone to smash.

The chaos was closely monitored in Hyannis Port, where Teddy Kennedy, meanwhile, pondered how best to respond to the Draft Kennedy movement that was being lashed together at the convention. On the one hand, Teddy reflected that his family had "a hell of an investment" in 1968, and on the other he acknowledged a strong feeling that 1968 was not his year. Eugene McCarthy, Bobby's former antagonist, lacked the votes necessary to mount an effective challenge against the all-but-anointed Hubert Humphrey. Should Humphrey become president, he seemed likely to continue Johnson's policies in Vietnam, where the casualty count had spiked since LBJ's decision not to seek another term. McCarthy offered to swing his support to Bobby Kennedy's kid brother, but at last Teddy chose to remove himself from the race. He spoke, halfheartedly it seemed, of preferring to run later, when he had had a chance to establish himself "to some degree as in control of events." As it was, the nation had veered so perilously out of control since Bobby Kennedy presented a filmed tribute to President Kennedy at the 1964

Democratic National Convention in Atlantic City that Teddy dared not appear in person in Chicago to introduce a similar documentary about RFK. Instead, Teddy's voice had to be transmitted to the convention hall from Cape Cod.

A little over a week later, Jackie returned to Newport News, Virginia, for what would prove to be her final public appearance in the United States as Mrs. John F. Kennedy. The occasion was the commissioning ceremony at which the aircraft carrier named in honor of her late husband was officially handed over to the Navy. Teddy Kennedy spoke briefly, but the main address was delivered by Bob McNamara. Jackie found Mc-Namara's paean to JFK, with its echoes of Pericles's funeral oration on the slain young warriors of Athens, to be an emotionally shattering experience, not least because she believed that of all the works Jack had admired, the Pericles text had been closest to him philosophically.

Late that night at Hammersmith Farm, after everyone else had gone to bed, Jackie wrote to tell "dearest, dearest Bob" that only his speech brought hope—"or rather it makes us all comrades of love and blood in a time of absence of hope." As the violent and tumultuous summer of 1968 drew to a close, Jackie feverishly wrote of Teddy's wine-cracked lips, of the certainty that she, Teddy, Bob McNamara, and the rest would "all be annihilated in the end," and of what she took to be Pericles's message that rather than seek consolation or hope it is best simply to accept "the terrible way things are."

Blood, the red on the last surviving Kennedy brother's lips, annihilation: This nexus of associations provides a fascinating window into how her mind was working in the weeks before she rocked the world anew by her decision to become Jacqueline Kennedy Onassis.

Fourteen

On the rainy evening of October 20, 1968—to a chorus of squawks and screams from frustrated journalists aboard the many hired fishing vessels that the junta had prevented from coming too close to Skorpios while the Greek Orthodox wedding ceremony was in progress—Jackie began the latest iteration of what she persisted in calling "my new life."

There had been a time, shortly after Dallas, when she questioned whether she wanted JFK to be able to see what had become of the world following his death. Five years later, she felt certain that could he "see and know all that has happened . . . since he died," he would have understood her decision to marry Aristotle Onassis. Indeed, Jackie maintained, the marriage was "what Jack might have wished for me" under the circumstances.

Few other people viewed things as she did, however.

"Jackie, Why?" demanded one international headline. "Jackie, How

Could You?," "Jack Kennedy Dies Today for a Second Time," "America Has Lost a Saint," and "Jackie Marries Blank Check" proclaimed some others. *The New York Times* suggested that "it was almost as though an American legend had deserted her people."

Jackie's plunge from grace at the time of the Manchester controversy had been as nothing compared to what happened to her after the October 17 public announcement of her marriage plans. Much had changed in American society since she had been assailed in print for a willingness "to prolong the nation's trauma." Following on a year of assassinations and urban riots, including the so-called "police riot" at the Democratic National Convention in Chicago, Richard Nixon was seeking the presidency on a campaign pledge to restore law and order to the United States. In this fraught climate, JFK's widow, who had played such a prominent part at both the King and RFK funerals, became an even more inconvenient symbol than before. A nation that was weeks away from electing Nixon proved more eager than ever to distance itself from a woman who, in her unabated suffering, was a living reminder of the tragedy and trauma of the 1960s that her countrymen were so impatient to leave behind. In a sense, the very turmoil at home that had caused Jackie to seek safety on Skorpios led many Americans to welcome the opportunity she had provided to cast her out. Looked at from that angle, it was perhaps less the American legend who had deserted her people than it was the other way around.

By contrast, instead of viewing Jackie as tainted by the trauma, the Greek colonels could scarcely wait to embrace her. At the time she married him, Onassis was in talks about a business partnership with the Greek government that, the Onassis organization calculated, had the potential over the next ten years to make him the world's richest man. From the perspective of the bridegroom, his spectacular marriage seemed likely to elevate him in the dictators' eyes and assure the success of his new undertaking. From the perspective of totalitarian Athens, Jackie's presence in the mix promised to soften the eighteen-month-old regime's international image, perhaps even to lure some of the coveted U.S. investment dollars the strongmen had so far failed to attract. Eager, like LBJ and RFK before them, to bask in the aura of JFK, the junta sent in the Greek police and coast guard to smooth Jackie's approach to Skorpios in advance of her nuptials. The military government also kept all non-Onassis shipping at a safe distance from the island on the joyous day itself.

The shipping ban, however, did nothing to stop the excluded reporters' disembodied cries from competing with the chants of the black-bearded, gold-brocade-wearing prelate who performed the marriage ceremony amid gusts of incense before an audience of twenty-one guests in a tiny, candlelit eighteenth-century chapel. Clutching ceremonial candles, John, aged seven, and Caroline, aged ten, stood on either side of the couple. Unlike the journalists who longed to be allowed onto the island, certain of the invitees would surely have preferred not to be there at all. Janet Auchincloss continued to be inconsolable. In the conspicuous absence of Teddy Kennedy, two of JFK's sisters, Pat and Jean, represented the late president's family, which was known to have made repeated efforts to prevent the wedding. Onassis's children, Alexander, aged twenty, and Christina, aged seventeen, who had hoped that their father might yet remarry their mother—whom he had forsaken in 1960 in favor of an affair with Maria Callas—looked on miserably as Jackie and the old man exchanged rings and sipped red wine from a silver goblet. The father had informed neither birdling of his marriage plans until days before the wedding.

Following the ceremony, more shouts from the fishing boats punctuated the festivities on the *Christina* until Onassis finally invited some of the excluded press people aboard. At moments, Jackie seemed terrified of all the clicking cameras. Still, the consensus among press and public, then and later, was that she had brought the media onslaught upon herself by callously, calculatedly marrying a man old enough to be her father. Five years after she had epitomized human vulnerability and terror as she crawled along the rear of the speeding Lincoln in the iconic images seen by all the world, her unlikely marriage made it possible to conceive her completely anew: as the adventuress who, far from being helpless, had helped herself very nicely to Onassis's fortune.

Two days after the wedding, Jackie's children were flown back to New York, where, still in school, they would be looked after by a governess and the Secret Service detail that continued to be assigned to them. Their mother, on the contrary, automatically forfeited her Secret Service protection when she remarried. Within forty-eight hours of the children's departure, Jackie found herself alone on the *Christina* when Onassis traveled to Athens to resume his business talks with the junta's top dog, George Papadopoulos. Henceforward, she was to be guarded by her husband's private security force, but no number of armed men would be sufficient to protect her against the incubi that had slipped through Onassis's and the dictators' bulwarks combined when the bride-elect arrived on the island the week before.

Thus the strangely lighted scene that Billy Baldwin observed one evening soon after Jackie was wed. She and the decorator, whom she had summoned from Manhattan, were on the *Christina* when they heard the roar of a seaplane's engine. At first, Jackie remained motionless, scanning the sky for the aircraft on which her husband was due to return from Athens. When she saw the plane at last, she waved happily. But then her body froze, rigid with tension and dread. So long as his client remained like that, Baldwin dared not utter a word. Only when, at length, she heard the splash of the landing did she finally appear to relax. "Thank God he's safe," Jackie declared. Though Onassis had landed without incident many times in the past, Jackie's experience of the two Kennedy assassinations had upended fundamental assumptions about safety and predictability, as well as burdened her with the expectation of imminent danger and doom.

Disconnected from the present, she was constantly, helplessly looking forward in time—or backward. Also during the "honeymoon" period that fall of 1968 when Onassis was frequently off to dicker with Papadopoulos, Jackie spoke to her husband's sister, Artemis Garoufalidis, of the memories of Dallas that continued to vex her. On one such occasion, Artemis had noticed that Jackie seemed sad and uncommunicative. Asked if anything was wrong, Jackie began to weep. "I know I should be happy now," she said after the tears had ceased, "but all I can think about today is my first husband and what happened to him in Texas." The difficulty proved to be a good deal more complicated than the intrusive recollections themselves. "Sometimes I think I will never be able to be truly happy again," Jackie went on. "I try but I cannot forget the pain. And when I am feeling happy, I am just waiting for it to return."

That last sentence was key. Though the memory might not actually be before her at a given moment, Jackie, by her own account, was ever anticipating its reappearance. The here and now, to the extent that she was able to experience it, was ceaselessly, insidiously eroded by the trauma. The sense of apprehension disclosed to Artemis was not a matter of anticipating an encounter with some new external trigger, as when the very thought of seeing the Bishop or Manchester books, or references to them in the media, had proven so distressing. In this case the dreaded event was strictly internal. Jackie had come to Skorpios in search of protection from the dangers that loomed in the outer world. But, as her words to her new sister-in-law suggest, her inner world was no less of a danger zone than the violence and chaos she had fled. Sometimes her deeply etched memories took the form of physical sensations, such as the intermittent, at moments unbearable throbbing in her neck that, she explained to Artemis, was the result of nerve damage suffered as she held President Kennedy's head in both arms after the shooting.

On November 1, 1968, Onassis called a news conference in Athens to report that the government had indeed designated him to build the complex of industries—an oil refinery, an aluminum plant, a thermoelectric power plant, an air terminal, and myriad other entities as yet unspecified—that he touted as the largest individual investment ever made in Greece, as well as proof of the stability of the Papadopoulos regime. In closing the deal, Onassis had outmaneuvered his longtime personal and business rival, Stavros Niarchos, who also had been keen to establish himself as the commercial partner of a dictatorship that routinely imprisoned and tortured anyone who dissented from its policies. But no less important to Onassis's self-image as a man at the apex of his powers—"the sun king," as an associate characterized him in this period—was his having single-handedly overcome the monumental opposition of the Kennedys, the Vatican, and world opinion combined when he married Jackie. For Onassis, the outraged and bewildered international headlines had merely underscored the magnitude of his accomplishment in having persuaded Beauty to marry the Beast. In the wake of his press conference, he hosted a celebratory dinner party in honor of Papadopoulos. Jackie, attired in a snug black gown and a diamond necklace, was later reported to have been the evening's "pièce de résistance."

Afterward, the newlyweds embarked on a weeklong cruise of the Sporades Islands in the northwest Aegean Sea, at the conclusion of which a stopover in England to visit the Radziwills was marred when a jewel thief entered a second-floor-bedroom window of the house where the Onassises were staying and removed various gems. Jackie, escorted by one of her husband's senior executives, flew to New York on November 18 in order to be with John and Caroline on their respective birthdays, his on the twenty-fifth and hers two days later. As always, Jackie spent the anniversary of the JFK assassination in seclusion, this time at Wind Wood, her rented country house in Peapack, New Jersey. Onassis, who had arranged for the property to be surrounded by guards, flew in from Paris to join her there that night. Two days later, Jackie was walking alone on her property, as she liked to do, when a French photographer suddenly leapt out and pursued her across a field as he attempted to take her picture.

The jewel thief, the photographer-trespasser, not to mention the grenade- and pistol-wielding hijackers who commandeered an Onassis-owned Olympic Airways jetliner on November 8 in protest against the Papadopoulos regime: As early as the second month of the Onassis marriage, these episodes already suggested that no location, however carefully guarded, was impregnable. So it was a measure of Jackie's need to idealize her new husband that, at this point, she asked the Secret Service to reduce considerably the government protection afforded to her children, both in New York and on their visits to Europe. Part of this, to be sure, was the old privacy issue that had long been so dear to her, as well as the sense, expressed soon after Dallas, that it was essential to give the children as normal a life as possible. But Jackie struck a new note in a December 11, 1968, letter to Secret Service director James Rowley, when she insisted that the security measures Onassis had previously put in place for his own purposes would amply serve her and the children's needs as well. At a moment when Jackie had been much excoriated for betraying the memory of President Kennedy, she maintained that, with regard to John and Caroline, she was only doing what JFK would have wanted: "The children will never be safer than they will be on Skorpios or the *Christina*. . . . As the person in the world who is most interested in their security, and who recognizes most what threats there are in the outside world, I promise you that I have considered and tried every way, and that what I ask you for is what I know is best for the children of President Kennedy and what he would wish for them."

At a glance, Jackie's request seems paradoxical in view of recent incidents. But the very sense of helplessness and terror that had led her to put herself under Onassis's protection after the second Kennedy assassination persisted in fueling her need go on believing in this particular tutelary deity. She clung to the illusion of mastery—the notion that Onassis could foresee and forestall any potential dangers—that had drawn her to Skorpios in the first place. Rowley for his part urged her to take a more realistic view. Alluding to the episode the year before in Ireland, shortly after the death of Lady Harlech, when Jackie's strange blindness to certain forms of danger had nearly caused her to be drowned, Rowley proposed that she reflect on what might have happened had the agent on duty not disregarded her wish to be left alone. The director suggested that security was a less clear-cut affair than Jackie imagined, and that not every danger was capable of being anticipated and averted if only the right thought processes were applied. As far as Rowley was concerned, it was the function of security "to guard against more than only the obvious and the foreseeable threat." Implicit in all of this was that Onassis must inevitably fail to live up to her idealized expectations. In the end the Secret Service prevailed with regard to specifics, even if the director did not succeed in actually changing Jackie's mind.

For the moment anyway, her illusions, threadbare though they might be, did often seem to sustain her. At such times, she appeared "serene and happy." Or so Joe Alsop judged her to be when, in New York in the spring of 1969, he saw Jackie again—scrutinizing her, it may be imagined, over his large round horn-rimmed spectacles—for the first time since her controversial second marriage. Alsop, who made a point of assuring her that he had "always" liked "Ari," was no longer the arbiter he had once been. His raving advocacy of the Vietnam War, not only in print but also at table, had led him to be regarded in certain circles as the thing he most detested—a bore. In dread of Alsop's tirades about Vietnam, a good many people made a point of declining all invitations to the deep-red-lacquered dining room that had once been an important gathering place of the Washington tribe. Such was the dizzying degree to which the political world of JFK, and even of RFK, had already vanished that Alsop, once the high priest of the religion of Kennedy, had found himself uncomfortably welcoming the November 1968 election of Richard Nixon.

Despite Alsop's fall, to Jackie he remained the adored preceptor, the man who had gripped her hand as she spoke of Dallas, the rare friend who had not abandoned her when she sought to start anew in Georgetown early on. As she fondly acknowledged, he had loved both Jack and Bobby, though in the end he had assailed RFK for having betrayed what

Alsop believed had been President Kennedy's unambiguously hawkish position on Vietnam. Writing to Alsop in the weeks before she remarried, Jackie had made it clear that she would never be able to love or care about anyone again, and that whatever she may once have hoped, she knew now that grief was an element she would always live in—"like sea or sky or earth." So, less than a year after she had expressed those sentiments, Alsop had been pleased and no doubt relieved to find her apparently so contented and so well. He compared the happiness she radiated in Onassis's company to "a good fire" in a cold English room.

Strange to say, at this juncture the prototype for the newlyweds' relationship was perhaps less Onassis's fiery liaisons with Maria Callas (whom, it later turned out, he was still seeing on the side) and other inamoratas as it was his role as devoted caregiver to the aged Winston Churchill. Far from ignoring or minimizing the injuries that had propelled Jackie into this marriage, Onassis made it his mission to rescue her from what he liked to call her "years of sorrow." Early on, he communicated to his staff and intimate circle that his emotionally fragile bride was going to require special care. "It was as if Mr. Onassis had married an injured creature," his longtime private secretary Kiki Feroudi Moutsatsos recalled, "and we were all responsible for helping her wounds to heal." The doting husband whispered to Jackie, laughed with her, told her stories, sang to her, and otherwise danced attendance. These days, she was ever bedizened with the jewelry he lavished upon her, such as the heart-shaped ruby earrings and matching raspberry-sized ring that obscured the entirety of her rather large knuckle and had to be removed whenever she made a telephone call. Though some observers were put off by the extent to which Onassis flaunted his sex life with his younger, taller wife (pawing at her in ways that seemed at odds with his insistence on her fragility), not all of his gestures were as desperate and self-serving. The man who mobilized planes and police on her behalf was also capable of more intimate demonstrations of concern and affection. A heavy smoker himself, he tried to make Jackie smoke less by snatching at her cigarette pack whenever she reached for it. He rarely succeeded in preventing her from lighting up, but his attempts, often accompanied by a display of mock exasperation, were among the couple's fond private jokes, as well as a sign to others of what looked to be his sincere solicitude.

Crucially, Onassis took marvelous care not just of Jackie, but also of John and Caroline. When the children came to spend their first summer in Greece, he toured them about his scorpion-shaped island, which included an untamed, heavily forested area, where he pointed out the unique animals and plants that thrived there. He escorted the boy and girl on motorboat rides and fishing expeditions and, in a voice said to resemble "soft gravel," regaled them with tales of his own childhood. Though John and Caroline were accompanied by Secret Service agents, Onassis insisted that his private security men be responsible for the children.

Jackie, who turned forty that summer, spent her days swimming, water-skiing, walking, painting, reading, and studying. In flight from a previous identity that she regarded as dangerous, she sought to reinvent herself. She learned Greek. She studied the history and culture of her new home. She elicited the guidance and advice of various experts and connoisseurs. She accompanied her husband on long, leisurely walks about his island kingdom, during which Onassis, between puffs on his cigar, declaimed poetry to her in Greek. She arrayed the old house that he had had painted pink for his new bride with carefully chosen Greek furnishings and art. To explain her obsession with redoing the edifice and its environs, she declared that there were many things in the world that she could not change, but that when it came to such matters as furniture and draperies and flowers, it was quite within her capacity to make all the changes she desired. And that, she emphasized, was very satisfying to her.

Despite everyone's efforts, not least of them her own, this relatively tranquil first phase of the marriage proved to be short-lived. Jackie had considered enrolling one or both children in school in Switzerland after the summer, but at length she decided that New York was still best. Accordingly, she was back in Manhattan with John and Caroline in the early autumn as they began the new academic year. Though Jackie certainly did not recognize it then, the afternoon of September 24, 1969, was the start of something very important. No sooner had mother and son exited through the cast-iron front door at 1040 Fifth Avenue, en route to ride their bicycles together in the park, than a photographer leaped out from behind the canopied limestone building's sidewalk plantings. Six years after the first Kennedy assassination, Jackie continued to be easily startled, and she later remembered feeling terrified when the lone cameraman began shooting.

Still, the encounter, however unpleasant, was in itself nothing unusual. The marriage to Onassis seemed to have obliterated any respect for her widowhood that the press had retained following the Manchester controversy. Ironically, the union that was supposed to have shielded Jackie's privacy had done much to further erode the belief that she was entitled to any such thing. Eleven months previously in Greece, Billy Baldwin had been stunned and not a little frightened by "the bedlam of professional Jackie-watchers and photographers" who crowded furiously in on her whenever she was in public. When Baldwin went so far as to admit that he feared for her life, she assured him that the best possible response to all those aggressive press people was simply to smile at them. In the course of the September 24, 1969, incident, however, when the lensman who had just alarmed her outside her New York residence reemerged, jack-in-the-box-like, from some shrubbery in Central Park, causing John to swerve his bicycle, Jackie was no longer inclined to smile.

Nor would a staged response have been likely to satisfy the thirty-eight-year-old Bronx-based freelancer Ron Galella. He defined himself as an artist, had studied art photography, and considered the type of camerawork he practiced to be unique. He wanted something more than just contrived expressions from the famous people he stalked. Aiming to capture, in his phrase, "the full range of human emotions," he depended on the element of surprise. He frequently camouflaged himself, but when at last he did pop out of hiding, rather than look through a view-finder, he preferred to lock eyes with his prey. Far from posing a problem, a subject's discomfiture, involving as it did the revelation of authentic emotions oozing through the carefully composed celebrity veneer, was hugely desirable. Galella prided himself on his intrepidity. So when, at Jackie's instigation, John's Secret Service guards had the photographer charged with harassment, the result was far from what she seemed to have intended. Hardly had the charges been dismissed in Manhattan Criminal Court in October 1969 when a defiant Galella returned for more of the pictures he passionately believed he had every right to go on taking. Thereafter, he maintained a vigil in front of Jackie's building and otherwise pursued her on foot and by automobile and aircraft. To be sure, other paparazzi hunted and haunted her in these years, but none perhaps with Galella's Manchester-like doggedness and sense of personal mission.

Galella had something else in common with the author of *The Death of a President*. Manchester's intensive interviewing technique, which encouraged Jackie to minutely relive the events of November 22, 1963, had repeatedly, disastrously, hurled her back into the trauma. Galella's aesthetic, with its emphasis on surprise and provocation, instilled her with feelings akin to the sense of vulnerability and powerlessness she had known in Dallas. From 1969 on, Jackie, by her own account, lived in fear of Galella's sudden, startling intrusions in her daily life. She could never be certain how or when he would spring out at her, only that eventually he would and that there was really nothing she could do to stop him. True, he sought merely to take Jackie's picture; but in important ways, she responded to his presence as if she were being attacked again. In this respect, her behavior with the paparazzo may be compared to that of Pavlov's dogs. Faint reminders had been transformed into conditioned stimuli for the summoning up of unbearable feelings and associations that properly belonged to the past.

Galella's many "candid" shots of Jackie were a new iteration of her shifting relationship with a society still struggling to suppress the painful emotions attached to an earlier set of images produced by a very different photographer. Compare, on the one hand, Abraham Zapruder's raw, visceral film stills of her as she drags herself along the rear of the presidential limousine in an apparent state of dissociation and, on the other hand, Galella's emblematic image, "Windblown Jackie," in which, caught unawares on Madison Avenue, she turns to direct a "Mona Lisa smile" at her pursuer. In both the Zapruder and the Galella pictures she has been ambushed—by an assassin in the former and by a paparazzo in the latter. In the work of both photographers, she is depicted in what looks to be a state of flight. But in the Galella, the material disarray to which the moment has subjected her is limited to the filigree of hair that prettily streams across her face. For all of Galella's talk of spontaneity, he was also a painstaking craftsman with a fine sense of pictorial composition. As he would point out, in "Windblown Jackie" he had captured not just any moment, but rather the precise instant when the smile has begun to form. "When you see the teeth," Galella clinically explained, "it's too late and not as great."

By producing an emotionally distanced and highly aestheticized version of certain of the cardinal elements (victimhood, powerlessness, attempted escape) in the Zapruder footage, Galella in "Windblown Jackie" and numerous other images tapped into conservative impulses in the society that aimed to defuse and disavow the collective memory of suffering. Jackie expressly intended her scintilla of a smile to deny Galella the display of emotions he contrived to provoke. He, in turn, used her facial expression to give credence to the claim, central to his legal and aesthetic argument, that Jackie, far from being harassed and terrified, really "loved" being pursued and photographed by him.

So, he went on startling her with flash guns, chasing her along dark

Manhattan streets, and compelling her to resort to exiting her apartment house through a rear entrance. Wearing fake mustaches, wigs, and other disguises, her tormentor materialized suddenly in restaurants, nightclubs, theaters, and shops where Jackie, whether alone or with her husband and children, happened to be. On one signal occasion, Galella even managed to get past Onassis's private security force in order to surprise Jackie on Skorpios. Thereafter, the island kingdom touted as the place where her children would be safest no longer seemed so secure.

In the course of one of the walks with her husband that had formerly been so pleasing to her, Jackie panicked when the couple found themselves trapped in some especially dense foliage on the untamed patch of Skorpios. "I was frightened by the lizards and the mice," she subsequently recalled, "but mostly, I was terrified that someone would harm the two of us." When they failed to return to the *Christina* in the gathering dusk, staff members went out to search for them. So thick was the brush in which the couple had become entangled that employees had to use a hatchet to free them. Safely back on the yacht afterward, Jackie continued to be acutely agitated. Onassis scoffed at her apprehensions, adding, RFK-like, that if someone wanted to kill him the attacker would surely find him no matter what preventive measures had been taken. Whereupon Jackie shook her head in anger and walked off. The episode crystallized her growing sense that the supposedly omnipotent rescuer she had turned to after the second Kennedy assassination was scarcely capable of protecting himself, let alone her.

In other ways as well, Onassis was manifestly no longer the figure he had seemed to be at the time of the wedding. The U.S. investors that his marriage to an American legend was supposed to have attracted had failed to materialize. Perhaps it was the hubristic negotiating positions he had taken in the aftermath of having snared both Jackie and the prized government deal. Perhaps it was simply that the brutal Papadopulos regime proved to be a tougher sell to U.S. investors than Onassis had imagined. Even after—to Onassis's fury—the junta had insisted on bringing Stavros Niarchos into the picture, the efforts of the two Greek business titans combined could not save the mega-deal. As disillusioned with his trophy bride as she was with him, Onassis began more and more to be seen in public with Maria Callas, to whom he felt he could speak of his troubles as he could not to his wife. On Skorpios, he and Jackie quarreled fiercely and often, and she increasingly gravitated to New York, where he visited her at intervals.

By early 1972, Jackie publicly described herself as a wife and mother who spent the school year in America and summers and school vacations in Greece. The occasion for this statement was her testimony in federal court in lower Manhattan, where she was seeking legal protection against what she painted as Ron Galella's relentless persecution of her and her family, both in the United States and abroad. Galella, for his part, was suing her for interfering with his livelihood. In what amounted to Jackie's first extended public testimony since she addressed the Warren Commission in 1964, she spoke of being terrified anew. On the witness stand in the fifteenth-floor courtroom, which overflowed with people who lined up in the morning to see her and left en masse as soon as she was done, she portrayed the deleterious effect on her of knowing that Galella was ever following her about. "He lunged at me," she recalled one encounter, "and he was grunting and he was saying, 'Glad to see me back, Jackie, aren't you, baby?' And then he took his camera strap and was flicking me on the shoulder."

Had Jackie not been desperate to stop Galella, she would never have exposed herself day after day to intense public scrutiny, as she did in the course of the February–March 1972 legal proceedings. Still, the tone of the copious and colorful press coverage ranged from mirthful to disparaging. *The New York Times* dubbed the trial "the best off-Broadway show in town" and *Life* magazine dismissed it all as a case of "staggering pettiness." Public sympathy certainly seemed to favor Galella, who portrayed himself as merely doing his job when he photographed "the number one cover girl in the world," a woman he characterized, again à la Manchester, as "snobbish and cool."

Given popular attitudes toward her after she became Mrs. Aristotle Onassis, Jackie's claims against Galella would likely have elicited a good deal of skepticism and derision in any case. But she had the misfortune to have gone to law at a cultural moment when Americans were especially anxious to distance themselves from the nation's recent violent past as a new presidential election drew near. Jackie had been an inconvenient symbol in 1968. And so, four years later, she proved to be again. In 1972, politicians such as Hubert Humphrey, George McGovern, Edmund Muskie, and George Wallace, as well as President Nixon himself, would make a point of risking exposure to large crowds in an effort to establish that the violence of the 1960s was over and thereby to restore national confidence and pride. The presidential primaries were already in progress when the most prominent survivor of the carnage in Dallas struck a dissonant note by insisting upon her dread of a new tormentor, who threatened to emerge from the shadows at any time.

Jackie could not exactly be rendered invisible, as many injured people are when they attempt to speak out. Like others with posttraumatic conditions, however, she did find herself subjected to myriad questions and suspicions about the authenticity of her suffering: Was she really as terrified as she claimed to be? Or as Galella's attorney, Alfred Julien, maintained in his opening statement, had she "grossly exaggerated" when she catalogued her fears? In court, Julien displayed a photograph his client had taken at the airport in New York. "Does it show a frightened or alarmed Mrs. Onassis?" he demanded of her. "I can't say, sir," she responded. Seeking to establish the former first lady's "anguish threshold," as he curiously called it, Julien inquired whether books or other writings about herself and her family published during the past few years had distressed her. Federal judge Irving Cooper upheld an objection from her lawyer, Martin London. But even in the absence of Jackie's reply, the suggestion lingered that given her well-known complaints about Manchester and other authors, this was a woman who had cried wolf before.

Meanwhile, as Jackie's court battle dragged on, pressure was building on Teddy Kennedy to join the race for the Democratic presidential nomination. After the Chappaquiddick episode of 1969, when Teddy drove a car off a bridge, leaving a young female companion to die in the submerged vehicle, he had pledged not to seek the presidency in 1972. But, as the historian James MacGregor Burns wrote in *The New York Times* in April 1972, the senator might yet end up in the grip of forces and events beyond his control, such as a deadlocked convention and the inability of the party's left wing to produce a strong candidate. No sooner was the prospect of a new Kennedy candidacy openly discussed than the specter of assassination was spoken of as well. Burns quoted a school friend of Kennedy's on the effect that the slaying of another Kennedy brother would have on national morale. Still, the dissatisfaction in certain quarters with the field of Democratic candidates made it seem possible that Kennedy might yet be tempted to come in.

Until, that is, a May 1972 assassination attempt on Governor George Wallace scrambled everyone's calculations. The dreaded thing had occurred. Another shooter had sprung forth. The madness and anarchy that Americans had been frantic to leave behind was still demonstrably a factor in public life. No one seemed surprised when President Nixon, upon learning of the nearly fatal attack on Wallace, who was left paralyzed for life, immediately directed that Secret Service protection be assigned to Teddy Kennedy, though the senator was not a candidate. Two months later, Teddy, citing "personal family responsibilities" both to his own family and to those of JFK and RFK, declined the number two spot on a presidential ticket headed by Senator George McGovern.

On November 7, 1972, Nixon won reelection by a huge margin, bringing to an end a campaign season that had been shadowed by apprehensions of further bloodshed. Five days later, Jackie sat in her Fifth Avenue home watching William Buckley's television interview with Harold Macmillan, who was promoting a new volume of his memoirs. To her, the world was again characterized by chaos and looming disaster. Thus, when she wrote to Macmillan immediately after the program, she evoked a society in which, paraphrasing William Butler Yeats, "the center does not hold." Those words, as the bookish Macmillan would surely recognize, were an allusion to Yeats's "The Second Coming." Studded with images of blood and anarchy, the 1919 poem depicts a world in the process of splitting asunder.

In the end, the federal court had relieved Jackie of at least one of her anxieties, when, public sympathy with Galella notwithstanding, Judge Cooper directed her nemesis to always remain at least fifty yards from her and seventy-five yards from John and Caroline. But hardly had Jackie prevailed in this respect when she was confronted with the fresh terror that was to grip her for years to come. She adored Teddy Kennedy, the very idea of whose presidential candidacy she had ardently opposed in 1968. Now again, the notion, increasingly in play in high Democratic circles, that Teddy, who had amply confirmed his popular appeal when he campaigned for McGovern, should be the front-runner next time, was anathema to her. Also as in 1968, she was again no longer alone in discerning a pattern in the violence that had afflicted America since Dallas. Henceforward, the possibility of a third Kennedy assassination would be routinely broached whenever political commentators assessed the surviving brother's prospects in 1976. Besides Chappaquiddick, fears for Teddy's physical safety emerged as among the senator's principal liabilities as a potential candidate.

Importantly, on November 12, 1972, Jackie had not viewed the Buckley broadcast alone. As she told Macmillan, she had watched it in the company of Onassis and eleven-year-old John. She and Ari had recently celebrated their fourth wedding anniversary with a party at El Morocco, attended by, among others, most of the Kennedys, with the exception of Teddy, who had been in Newark that evening, chasing votes for McGovern. The Callas affair and other trials notwithstanding, Jackie persisted in her considerable affection for the second husband who, as she later said, had "rescued me at a moment when my life was engulfed in shadows." She particularly appreciated his many ongoing kindnesses to her children, especially John, who had grown immensely fond of his stepfather. Onassis's relationship with his own beloved son was fraught, not least because of Alexander's abiding resentment of Jackie. At the same time, Ari seemed to enjoy and certainly excelled at being the formidable figure JFK's son needed in the absence of his real father. The quiet commonplace scene of Jackie, Ari, and John watching Macmillan speak of President Kennedy in tender phrases, which, she rejoiced, the boy was old enough to understand, offers a telling snapshot of the frayed yet still oddly viable Onassis marriage two months before the sudden tragic event that was to forever destroy it.

On January 21, 1973, a plane carrying Alexander Onassis went down in Athens, critically injuring Ari's son. In the wake of Alexander's demise twenty-seven hours later there began to be nervous whispers among the Greek populace about "the curse." Jackie had been accused of many things since the first Kennedy assassination, but nothing of the magnitude of what began to be said about her now. The death of Alexander Onassis took Jackie's experience of the second injury to a whole new level, as the woman who had fled the United States in hopes of escaping annihilation found herself accused of transporting the very seeds of annihilation to Greece. While it is true that Christina Onassis, like her brother, had long resented Jackie, at this point Christina was merely reflecting the suspicions of many of her countrymen when she pointed out that prior to Jackie's arrival, the Onassis family had been strong and well. "Before she came to us, she was by her American husband's side when he died," Christina railed. "My unlucky father had to go find her and bring her to our shores. Now, the curse is part of our family and before long she will kill us all."

Jackie later reflected that when his son was killed, it had seemed as though Ari suddenly became old. Along similar lines, his secretary judged that the ordeal aged him by twenty years. In the end, this man who had amassed such great wealth and power had been powerless to protect his boy. Night after night on Skorpios, he would haunt Alexander's burial place, bringing with him a bottle of ouzo and two glasses, one glass for the father and the other for the son. Addressing the grave as though the deceased were yet capable of hearing his laments, Onassis would ask, over and over again, if it were possible that such an accident should ever have occurred. Refusing to regard Alexander, let alone himself, as a mere victim of the world's randomness, Onassis insisted that the fatal crash had to be the result of sabotage. Endlessly, obsessively, and not a little guiltily, he reviewed the precise circumstances of his son's demise in hopes of determining who among his many many personal and professional enemies could be responsible.

When two major formal inquiries, one conducted by the Greek courts and the other by a respected British accident investigator in Onassis's private employ, concluded that the crash had been accidental, Onassis indignantly rejected their findings. Frantic to wrest back control, or at least the sustaining illusion thereof, he offered a $20 million reward for information about the cause of the tragedy. He alternated between fighting to keep the inquiry open and insisting that he wanted to die. Such was Onassis's demeanor that when Anthony Montague Browne, formerly Churchill's private secretary, encountered Onassis again in this period, he feared for the unfortunate man's reason.

In the meantime, Jackie and her husband seemed to have eerily exchanged positions. Now it was he who was the injured creature and she who strove to help his wounds to heal. She arranged a cruise from Dakar to the Antilles, a holiday in Mexico. When, in the course of the latter trip, Ari, as was his wont, suddenly began to sob, "Jackie put her arms around him, just like the Pieta, and held him," remembered the fashion publicist Eleanor Lambert, who witnessed the scene at Loel and Gloria Guinness's in Acapulco. "She let him cling to her for what seemed like ten minutes." Still, nothing appeared to work. Hardly would Onassis return to Skorpios when his raging nocturnal soliloquies at Alexander's grave would resume.

To make matters worse, though initially inclined to silence his daughter when she criticized Jackie in his presence, more and more the deeply superstitious Onassis found himself resignedly listening to Christina's theory that it was Jackie—the "Black Widow," as she called her—who was responsible for the ill fortune that had lately befallen the House of Onassis. Nor did the family's afflictions cease with Alexander's demise. Tina, the mother of Onassis's children, died. The Onassis organization lost control of Olympic Airways. Several impending business deals soured. Onassis's health decayed markedly due to the neuromuscular disease myasthenia gravis, lending credence to the view of Jackie as a contaminated carrier of catastrophe.

On the flight home from Mexico, Onassis rewrote his will in his daughter's favor, leaving his widow a yearly income of $200,000 plus $25,000 a year for each of her children until they reached the age of twenty-one. And, three months before his death, he contacted the American lawyer Roy Cohn about his intention to divorce Jackie. When it became evident that Onassis did not have long to live, however, the divorce plans were abandoned. Jackie, Christina, Artemis, and other family members maintained a vigil at his bedside in the Paris hospital where he lay for weeks. Finally, assured that her husband's condition was stable, Jackie went off to see the children in New York, where, on March 15, 1975, she learned that Onassis had died in her absence.

A smile wreathed Jackie's face when the paparazzi greeted her at Orly Airport in Paris. Was her facial expression a conscious contrivance? A reflex action? A bit of both? In any case, coming on top of the fact that Jackie had not been with her second husband as he lay near death, that smile, a version of which she had often used to cover over her emotions, was now widely taken to suggest that she was oddly devoid of emotion— though not so oddly, perhaps, were she indeed the cold-blooded adventuress she had been portrayed as in 1968.

Again, when Jackie left the hospital after viewing her late husband's corpse, she smiled fixedly as she passed through a gauntlet of jostling

press. And again, at Lefkada Airport, near Skorpios, the widow's countenance contrasted markedly with the unrestrained torment of Christina
Onassis, who (rumored to have attempted suicide immediately after her
father's death) stood beside her as the body was removed from the aircraft in anticipation of a burial service at the same chapel where Jackie
had been wed.

Fifteen

ven before Aristotle Onassis died, David Harlech had judged that Jackie, aged forty-five, seemed somehow to have, in his phrase, "turned a corner." The acute tensions in her marriage following the death of Alexander Onassis, when the second husband who was supposed to have been her rescuer and protector became, however unthinkably, her accuser, had finally led her to conclude that she needed to do something to help herself. But what?

After the funeral, during which various mourners' bitter remarks about "the curse" had wafted through the tiny chapel on Skorpios, Jackie struck Letitia Baldrige, her former White House social secretary, now the head of her own public relations firm, as "depressed and lethargic." Back in New York full-time, she again confronted the task of trying to begin "a new life," whatever exactly that might mean after so many futile attempts in the dozen years since Dallas. Baldrige proposed that Jackie, who had previously looked to powerful men as protectors, try a different approach this time. "Who me, work?" Jackie exclaimed when Baldrige suggested that her particular interests and abilities well suited her for employment as an editor at a New York publishing house. Baldrige urged her to talk to Thomas Guinzburg, the head of Viking Press, whom Jackie had known for years.

Baldrige's advice about Jackie's career prospects seemed to have a distinctly feminist cast. And so she meant her comments to be taken, though by her own account she sensed that Jackie was personally no feminist. Jackie, who had come of age in a milieu where a woman of her caste was expected above all to marry well and thereafter to be an asset to her husband, had lived to see the emergence of the women's movement and all that flowed from it. By the time Baldrige prodded her to find a job, more than a decade had passed since the landmark publication of Betty Friedan's manifesto *The Feminine Mystique*, which argued that women ought to pursue meaningful employment outside the home that makes full use of their intellectual powers. Not at all inappropriately, many authors have sought to tell the story of Jackie's entry into the world of work in terms of the dramatic changes that were taking place in the mid-1970s in attitudes toward women's roles in society.

But there is another, very different prism through which to usefully examine the career that Jackie built for herself in the latter part of her life, a prism that did not really become available until the late-twentieth- and early-twenty-first-century proliferation of knowledge about trauma and trauma survivors, notably the understanding that a principal objective of any course of trauma recovery must be the retrieval of a sense of control. In this perspective, it is not that Jackie's work failed to be empowering, but rather that that empowerment had less to do perhaps with any generic feminist narrative than with her experience as an individual still struggling with the legacy of trauma.

Concurrently with the women's movement, another massive upheaval was then taking place in American life. In April 1975, the U.S. military presence in Vietnam concluded when Saigon fell to North Viet-

namese forces, and all remaining American military and civilian person-
nel had to be evacuated. Jackie's latest effort to start afresh was occurring
at a moment when Americans were struggling to resolve the wrenching
historical episode she had once described to Bob McNamara as "more
complex than any dark hell that Shakespeare ever looked into." As it
happened, part of that national ferment involved the campaign launched
by Vietnam veterans and a small group of sympathetic psychiatrists to
secure formal recognition of PTSD as a psychiatric diagnosis. To be
sure, previous generations of warriors had been known to manifest postwar problems designated by such names as shell shock and combat fatigue. But the impact of Vietnam, specifically the incidence of PTSD,
estimated in 1990 to have afflicted more than a quarter of returnees,
did seem extraordinary in its magnitude. Upon their homecoming the
vets were urged, much as Jackie had been after Dallas, to get over their
anguish and thereby permit the nation to move on. Some vets were
retraumatized when they faced public reproach and rejection for their involvement in a discredited war that had lacked popular support from
1968 on. Suspected of exaggerating or altogether faking their claims, returnees were routinely informed that drugs and alcohol, not the war, were
really to blame for their problems. Significantly, it was not the civilian
population alone that endeavored to draw a curtain of forgetfulness on
the vets' suffering. The House Committee on Veterans Affairs and the
Veterans Administration were dominated at the time by Second World
War veterans, who, on the principle that the Vietnam generation should
not require benefits and services its predecessors had failed to enjoy,
were reluctant to acknowledge the existence of a condition described by
turns as war neurosis, post-Vietnam syndrome, and PTSD.

Meanwhile, Tom Guinzburg's announcement that Viking had signed
Jackie to begin work that fall of 1975 as a consulting editor, her first ordinary job since she toiled at the Washington *Times-Herald*, was met
with a good deal of incredulity from press and public. For many people,
Jackie's strange smiles in the aftermath of Onassis's death had served as

ocular proof that, precisely as had been suspected in the first place, the marriage was a sham. Was her new job also not quite what it was purported to be? Was it a publicity stunt on Viking's part? A whim on Jackie's? Obviously, she did not need the $200 weekly salary; her representatives were then in hard-driving negotiations with the Onassis estate to substantially augment her financial settlement. Viking's other consulting editor, the novelist, poet, and critic Malcolm Cowley, had been responsible through his various endeavors at the house for significantly revising the reputations of William Faulkner, F. Scott Fitzgerald, and Sherwood Anderson, and for the breakthrough publication of Jack Kerouac's *On the Road*. What could it mean, then, for a woman known in recent years more as a shopper than a litterateur to suddenly hold the identical title as that distinguished book man? There was speculation that Jackie had been brought in principally to lure other celebrities to pen their autobiographies, even that she might be about to produce a memoir of her own.

So, when Jackie reported for her first day at the publisher's Madison Avenue offices on September 22, 1975, she encountered the same skepticism that had faced her twenty-three years before at the *Times-Herald*. Now she insisted that she meant "to work, not to play." She planned to devote her first months at Viking, as she said, to "learning the ropes" of the business. There had been a time when it had fallen to her to show America that she was the good, ordinary wife, ever doting on and deferring to JFK. Now she confronted the rather different task of proving herself an independent working woman. As Onassis's wife, she had known the advantages of vast wealth. As his widow, she waited on line at the office copying machine like other Viking employees, prepared her own coffee, placed her own telephone calls, and did much of her own typing. She came to the office four days a week and religiously phoned in to collect her messages on Mondays, her days off.

As she adjusted to the altered habits of her life, she had the benefit of regular sessions with Marilyn Monroe's former psychoanalyst, Dr. Marianne Kris, whom Jackie had quietly begun to see. Though in important respects Jackie was substantially better than she had been seven years before when, beset by visions of annihilation in the aftermath of Bobby Kennedy's murder, she fled to Skorpios in quest of security, she continued to be vexed by premonitions of some terrible thing waiting to occur, of the plane crash that would end her life or the New York City taxicab poised to mow her down. The old invasive memories, nightmares, and "difficult times" persisted, as did those strange moments when, exclusive of any act of will on her part, intimations of danger and doom became manifest in her body, which "remembered" what had happened in 1963 and 1968, and therefore remained in a permanent state of alert for the next attack in whatever form it threatened to take. Jackie's decision to seek psychiatric treatment was a huge step, an important acknowledgement that she needed help.

The motherly, empathetic seventy-five-year-old Kris had had a prior connection with the Kennedy family. During the Second World War she and her husband, the psychoanalyst and art connoisseur Ernst Kris, had been among the beneficiaries when Ambassador Joseph P. Kennedy made it possible for various members of the London circle of Sigmund Freud's youngest daughter, Anna Freud, the founder of child analysis, to emigrate to the United States. In the late 1950s and early 1960s, Monroe, recommended by her then-husband Arthur Miller's former psychoanalyst Rudolph Loewenstein, had been Marianne Kris's patient, often going directly from her analyst's office to the quarters of her acting coach, Lee Strasberg, in the same Beaux Arts pile on Central Park West at Seventy-third Street. After Monroe's death in 1962, the bulk of the actress's estate went to Kris and Strasberg jointly, with the stipulation that the analyst use the legacy to further her own work.

When, concurrently with the start of Jackie's Viking job, Caroline Kennedy went to London to pursue a full-time, ten-month visual and decorative arts course at the international auction house Sotheby's, Kris asked Anna Freud to make herself available should the seventeen-year-old need someone to talk to at any point. Clearly, the New York psychoanalyst reached out to her London counterpart as much for Jackie's sake as for her daughter's. Kris's gesture was nothing so dramatic as what Onassis and the Greek colonels had undertaken when they sent in the police and coast guard to guarantee Jackie's safety. In the present instance, the idea was simply to reassure her that were the need to materialize, there would be a professional in place for her daughter. Additionally conducive to the parent's serenity of mind was that Caroline was to be housed in the Kensington residence of JFK's friend Hugh Fraser. The Conservative member of Parliament lived in the same neighborhood as David Harlech, now remarried, who also could be counted on to take an interest in Caroline's well-being. But all this was merely to provide the illusion of control, not the thing itself, which, however much human beings plan and prepare (and confer with their therapists), remains ever elusive.

On the morning of October 23, 1975, Fraser, who made it his habit to drop Caroline off at the building near Oxford Street where her school was located, paused to speak on the telephone to another MP before leaving his home at the regular hour. He asked Caroline to wait in another room until the call was finished. He was still on the line when a passerby's dog sniffed the wheel of Fraser's red Jaguar automobile, which was parked outside on steep, tree-lined Campden Hill Square. Whereupon an IRA bomb exploded, killing both the dog walker, a noted physician and cancer researcher who resided in the area, and his pet. Debris from the vehicle shattered windows and pocked the facades of nearby Victorian houses. The blast was the latest in a series of terrorist attacks to rock London at the time, including a September 5 explosion at the London Hilton, which had left two people dead and another sixty-three injured. Scotland Yard theorized that, though the London terrorists tended to strike at random because that approach proved to be the most frightening and disruptive, Hugh Fraser had been the target of the October 23 explosion due to his prior public statements against terrorism. Apparently, there had been no intent to harm Caroline. Still, had Fraser not hesitated at the precise moment he did, both she and he almost certainly would have died.

Although the episode would have been a severe trial for any parent, it was all the more so for Jackie, who needed to rebuild precisely the sense of safety and predictability that this new sudden act of violence had done so much to subvert. In the aftermath, she was often on the phone to the Harlech residence, where Caroline had been transported after the incident, as well as to other members of London's aristocratic cousinhood from whom she sought reassurance about her daughter. Adding to Jackie's pressures, her first six months at Viking also coincided with a fresh burst of press revelations about President Kennedy's womanizing, specifically his liaisons with two of his many mistresses, Judith Campbell and Mary Meyer. That JFK had been a philanderer was scarcely news to Jackie, but public disclosure was always very grievous to her, not least in a period when she was oppressed by an unusual amount of close daily, at times moment-by-moment, scrutiny in conjunction with her new employment. She was monitored not just by the photographers and sundry other gawkers who always seemed to be lurking in the vicinity of the publisher's midtown offices, but also by Viking coworkers, who, love her or loathe her, could hardly help wonder about, in Guinzburg's phrase, "this giant celebrity" in their midst. Jackie bore it all beautifully, determined, Tish Baldrige perceived, to finally be in a position "to rely on herself rather than a man." When in the autumn Bob McNamara, who by this time had led the World Bank for seven years and seven months—six months longer than he had served as secretary of defense under Johnson and Kennedy—seemed eager to resume the role he had played in her life after the death of JFK, Jackie, devoted to McNamara though she remained, showed no inclination to revert to the old arrangement.

In the Russian Style, scheduled to be published in conjunction with a Metropolitan Museum of Art exhibition focusing on Russian costumes of the eighteenth and nineteenth centuries, was touted as "Mrs. Onassis's first major assignment" at Viking. And, though Jackie's name would be prominently displayed on the book, from first to last there was wide speculation about how much work she actually had done on the project.

The honest answer was: a huge amount. She undertook prodigious research. She hunted down obscure volumes. She interviewed experts. And, when Diana Vreeland, who was organizing the Met exhibition, returned from a trip to Moscow without certain of the prized objects that she and Jackie both desperately wanted for the show and the book, Jackie volunteered to approach the Communist authorities herself.

Directly, she flew to Paris to meet up with the Met's director, Thomas Hoving, who was to accompany her to the Soviet Union. On their way to dinner that first night in Paris, Jackie seemed in high spirits, "bubbling with enthusiasm" for her impending journey to a nation she had never visited before. But their cab had hardly reached the Left Bank restaurant where Hoving had reserved a table when everything changed. The doorman at her hotel had informed the press about her evening plans. "Jackie! Jackie!" the cameramen shrieked as they rushed in on all sides. "Somehow, we made it into the restaurant," Hoving remembered, "and the proprietor guided us into the back and flung himself against the door to stop the full horde from rushing in. Flashbulbs were popping; people were screaming. I thought Jackie was going to crawl under the table. She was shaking." Briefly, it seemed as if the Russian trip would have to be canceled, when Jackie protested that she would not go if this was the kind of reception she could expect to receive. Hoving assuaged her concerns when he pointed out that the one nice thing about a Communist state was that the government-controlled press would take a single picture when she arrived and another when she left.

Jackie's ability, for good or ill, to draw a crowd fascinated the museum director, who was known, not always favorably, for his Barnum-like skill at luring great numbers of people to the Met. Hoving reflected that were Jackie to parachute into the wilds of Madagascar, Murmansk, or Mozambique, crowds would have gathered in advance of her arrival in hopes of securing photos and an autograph. He well understood that her status as possibly "the most famous face and personality on earth," though not without its drawbacks, might also be used to significant advantage. Never was that clearer than during Jackie's nine-day Soviet sojourn, in the course of which, Hoving's protests notwithstanding, their hosts persisted in addressing her as "Mrs. Onassis Kennedy." That peculiar appellation no doubt reflected the glamorous aura of the Kennedy era in Washington that still hung about her, but also perhaps the Russians' understanding, though it might already have been largely forgotten in the United States, that the easement in Soviet-American relations known as detente had had its origins in the first major postwar East-West agreement, the partial test ban treaty. Shortly before President Kennedy was assassinated, he had spoken to David Ormsby-Gore, as he was then, of his intention to visit the Soviet Union following his reelection, in hopes of sustaining the momentum toward the further contact and agreements at the heart of his strategy of peace.

Fittingly, now it was Jackie who had come to the Soviet Union to pursue the sort of cultural contact that Churchill had envisioned as marking the beginning of the end of the closed Communist society. As Macmillan liked to observe, many Russians longed as much as, if not more than, anyone in the West to see the barriers brought down. Thus the ambivalence with which Jackie's requests for the release of certain treasures from the Soviet archives were met. On the one hand, when she asked for the costumes of Czar Nicholas and Czarina Alexandra, both of whom had been slaughtered on Lenin's orders, the Communist bureaucrats were adamant that that would be impossible. On the other hand, there was on the bureaucrats' part a certain palpable, even impish, desire to make an unprecedented gesture to Jackie. Finally, the Soviets surprised and delighted her by agreeing to send over the green-velvet-upholstered sleigh and lap robe of Princess Elizabeth, the daughter of Peter the Great and Catherine I. Hoving wryly called Jackie's triumph "a thrilling moment in detente—and for the Russian costume show."

Shortly past 8 P.M. on the evening of December 6, 1976, Jackie, attired in a white strapless Mary McFadden dress that contrasted markedly with the workaday image she cultivated at the office, was the focal point of attention on the receiving line at the opening-night party for the *Glory of Russian Costume* show at the Met, for which she served as chairman. Tapes of Mussorgsky, Rimsky-Korsakov, and Tchaikovsky blared, and pungent clouds of Chanel's "Russian Leather" perfume filled the air, as Diana Vreeland, at the top of her lungs, implored the many social figures in attendance—Lee Thaw, Françoise de la Renta, Marella Agnelli, and C. Z. Guest among them—to buy a copy of Jackie's new book, which had been released that day. Soon after this, Viking hosted a small press luncheon at the Carlyle Hotel to publicize *In the Russian Style*. Lest any of the journalists violate his stipulation that all questions for Mrs. Onassis be confined to the book and nothing but the book, Tom Guinzburg hovered protectively about the fledgling editor, who wore a black turtleneck sweater, checked trousers, and a soupçon of makeup. Her bald, broad-shouldered boss scoffed at suggestions that she had had little role in the production of the volume. "Jackie wouldn't have allowed her name to go on the book if she hadn't been the prime mover behind it," Guinzburg broke out. He added pointedly that she was not merely "a Hollywood type of star, with a double doing the hard part of the job."

All in all, the publication of *In the Russian Style* was a supremely happy moment for Jackie. The book's very existence testified to the success of her latest effort to try to fashion a new life, as she said, out of the "old anguish." As far as Jackie was concerned, her career was well launched. She was involved in the preparation of various other Viking titles as well. Her books there would include a novel about Thomas Jefferson's mistress, an anthology of Russian fairy tales, a biography of Mayor Richard Daley, a celebration of American women's lives in the eighteenth century, and a collection of Matthew Brady's photographs of Abraham Lincoln. Under the tutelage of Bryan Holme, head of the Studio Books imprint, she would develop an expertise in the production of illustrated volumes. Meanwhile, Tom Guinzburg's robust remarks at the press luncheon, along with his gentlemanly determination to shield her from inquiries about any subjects that might prove distressing to her,

can have left Jackie in no doubt that she enjoyed her publisher's appro-
bation and support. Thus perhaps the magnitude of the blow when, a
month later, Guinzburg told her of a novel Viking planned to publish
that depicted a conspiracy to assassinate a newly elected President Teddy
Kennedy, who has managed to unseat President Carter in the 1980 Democratic presidential primaries. The plot was the stuff Jackie's nightmares
were made of.

There were times when Jackie's abiding revulsion at the idea of a
presidential run by the surviving Kennedy brother was palpable without
her needing to utter so much as a word. When the previous year Carter
had emerged as a contender for the 1976 Democratic nomination, Teddy
had oscillated wildly between imagining that he would or would not
challenge the Georgia governor whom he and other party liberals feared
and distrusted. In the end, Teddy, exuding a melancholy sense that history might finally have passed him by, had decided to stay out of the
race. After Carter became the nominee, he appeared to seize every opportunity to distance himself from the family of JFK and RFK, as if to
demonstrate that he could win the election without them. The Kennedys
in turn were pointedly disdainful of him. In the course of an October
1976 telephone conversation with Arthur Schlesinger, Jackie was tread-
ing familiar ground when she spoke of her displeasure with the Carter
candidacy. Schlesinger commented without thinking that should Carter
lose they could at least console themselves that Teddy would likely be
the Democratic candidate in 1980. Immediately, upon hearing the elo-
quent intake of breath on the other end of the line, Schlesinger recognized his mistake.

Four months later, when Guinzburg entered Jackie's office and shut
the door after him so that they might speak in private, she responded
instantly, viscerally, involuntarily, to his account of the assassination plot
in the British author Jeffrey Archer's new novel *Shall We Tell the President?* "It was just as though I hit her," Guinzburg remembered years afterward. "She winced." In that moment, all of the control that Jackie had

painstakingly begun to retrieve in the course of her brave apprenticeship at Viking seemed to shatter. To make matters worse, such episodes, reprising as they did her sense of helplessness at the time of the trauma, were not anything she cared to experience in front of other people. She had long taught herself to flee before anyone could observe her like this. But in the present instance, escape was hardly an option. Jackie muttered something to the effect of "Won't they ever stop?" Then, as the publisher looked on, she "visibly collected herself," before posing a few quiet questions about the book. At a later date, Jackie would speak of what had been her own conscious efforts at the time "to separate my lives as a Viking employee and a Kennedy relative." Perhaps, but somehow the phrase has the sound of a therapist's retrospective advice. In any event, Jackie's professional arrangement with Viking afforded her no veto power over which titles the house chose to put on its list, and eventually she accepted that if she wished to go on working there she had little choice but to endure the publication of the Archer novel. But, the question would soon arise, had she thereby countenanced it as well?

When in the fall of 1977 *Shall We Tell the President?* appeared in print, at least one prominent reviewer held Jackie directly responsible for a "bad thriller" that crassly exploited "a terrible fantasy—a continuing American nightmare," the prospect of a third Kennedy killing, in order to boost book sales. "There is a word for such a book," John Leonard wrote in *The New York Times*. "The word is trash. Anybody associated with its publication should be ashamed of herself." The conspicuous pronoun at the end of that wickedly well-crafted last sentence emitted sparks. No feminist gesture, it was widely read as an indictment of Jackie, who of course had been accused of callousness and cold-bloodedness before. Leonard, whose excoriating review drew a good deal of attention, soon publicly confirmed that he had indeed been referring to Jackie. In the past, she had been castigated for her efforts to block the Manchester book. This time, the complaint was that she had failed to obstruct *Shall*

We Tell the President? "She could have stopped its publication if she wanted to," Leonard maintained.

Nor, her employer chimed in, had she even tried. Interviewed by *The Boston Globe*, Guinzburg insisted that she "didn't indicate any distress or anger when I told her we bought the book in England several months ago." Jackie's reply to Guinzburg's published account was to quit her job on October 13, 1977. Guinzburg had witnessed her intense bodily reaction to news of the book; he knew the pain his words had caused her. Now she simply could not abide the fact that he had chosen to tell the world a very different story. "When it was suggested that I had had something to do with acquiring the book and that I was not distressed by its publication, I felt I had to resign," Jackie said in a public statement. But just as her announced reasons for coming to Viking in the first place had been greeted with broad public disbelief, so too were the reasons she offered for her departure. Thereafter, suspicions abounded that she had exaggerated or altogether fabricated her upset about the assassination novel, and that, in truth, she had quit her job solely due to pressure from her first husband's family. To be sure, the Kennedys were far from delighted about the Archer novel, but in view of what Guinzburg later revealed about Jackie's response when he first spoke to her of the book, her explanation rings true. In the wake of her departure from Viking, Guinzburg continued to publicly avow that he had observed no distress on her part: "My own affection for the Kennedy family and the extremely effective and valued contribution that Mrs. Onassis has made to Viking over the past two years would obviously have been an overriding factor in the final decision to publish any particular book which might cause her further anguish. Indeed, it is precisely because of the generous and understanding response of Mrs. Onassis at the time we discussed this book and before the contract was signed which gave me confidence to proceed with the novel's publication." In short, the man who only recently had defended Jackie's genuineness now sought to call it into question.

Three weeks later, at a time of broad public curiosity about her post-Viking plans, Jackie, wearing an Oscar de la Renta sequined skirt and chiffon top, limited to a mere five minutes her visit to the Louis XV–style limestone town house on East Sixty-fourth Street where a private preview of the exhibition *Paris–New York: A Continuing Romance* was in progress at the Wildenstein galleries. Clutching champagne glasses, Givenchy-, Adolfo-, and Halston-clad socialites inspected French and American paintings and drawings at a benefit for the New York Public Library, organized by Brooke Astor, Mary Rockefeller, John Sargent, and others. As it happened, the full-bearded, sturdily built Sargent, president of the mass-market publishing giant Doubleday & Company, had been Jackie's cohost at a small preliminary dinner party earlier that evening, where the guests had included Louis Auchincloss, the *New Yorker* writer Brendan Gill, and the historian Barbara Tuchman, whose book *The Guns of August,* about the First World War, President Kennedy had much admired. Despite the literary tone of the Onassis-Sargent event, Tom Guinzburg, though he too had purchased a ticket to the art gallery preview, had been conspicuously relegated to another hostess's dinner table, leading to talk, apparently not without factual basis, that Jackie wished to avoid him. Her pairing this evening with Sargent, who in addition to being one of the nation's premier publishing executives had the richly earned reputation of a ladies' man and society reveler, spurred the fashion columnist Eugenia Sheppard to wonder in print whether Jackie might already have made some sort of arrangement with Doubleday.

Neither then, nor three months later when Doubleday announced her appointment to the post of associate editor, did the firm known for producing more books per year than any of its rivals seem a likely haven for her. Jackie was meticulous about matters of book design; Doubleday titles tended to be shoddily produced. Jackie had highly cultivated aesthetic tastes; Doubleday's target audience was middlebrow, the firm's objective being, as Edna Ferber once remarked, the placement of "books in the hands of the unbookish." So why did Jackie choose Doubleday rather than one of the small New York firms specializing in art and illustrated books with whom she also had had talks in this period? John Sargent's record in the matter of an earlier assassination-themed book whose publication had threatened to be painful to Jackie was surely no impediment to his efforts to sign her. Doubleday had been scheduled to bring out the American edition of a new book by the British writer J. G. Ballard, *The Atrocity Exhibition*, which featured fantastical riffs on the murder of JFK that the author billed as "pornographic science fiction." Prominent in the work was a section titled "Plan for the Assassination of Jacqueline Kennedy," which when it appeared as a stand-alone piece in the British literary magazine *Ambit* in the late 1960s had prompted Randolph Churchill, who was personally devoted to Jackie, to militate to have the journal's London Arts Grant canceled. Presently, when John Sargent learned that the offending work was on Doubleday's list of upcoming titles—indeed, that finished books were ready to be shipped to stores—he had the entire print run pulped. At so cost-conscious a publisher, the destruction of all those books—a gesture of respect for Sargent's old friend Mrs. Onassis—was a huge deal. Eight years later, when Jackie accepted Sargent's invitation to come to Doubleday, she was choosing a firm whose chief executive had emphatically put her sensitivities first in a way that Tom Guinzburg, for all of his public posturing, had simply failed to do.

Jackie's arrival at Doubleday's Park Avenue headquarters that February of 1978 had a Sisyphean quality. Again, there were the reporters and other curious people who descended en masse to monitor her comings and goings. Again, there was abundant skepticism about her intentions, some of her new coworkers being among the doubters. John Sargent, for his part, detected a certain amount of initial resentment among Doubleday staff members—"a feeling that perhaps Jackie wasn't all that serious . . . [a] perception among the troops that this was just a diversion for her." Jackie had spent the better part of two years proving herself at Viking, yet now it fell to her to demonstrate all over again that she really did mean to build an important career. More than that, she somehow had to make it possible for colleagues to deal with her as though she were any other Doubleday employee, which of course she was not. In effect, Jackie's challenge was identical to the one that had faced her at Viking, and many were the predictions that her new job would end in disappointment and debacle as well. This time, however, she proved the skeptics wrong. At length, Jackie made such a point of wanting to be treated like everyone else, downplaying her glamour, scoffing at her fame, that, to Sargent's sense, her new colleagues "couldn't help but be charmed."

At this most intensely and unabashedly commercial of houses, where she was to spend the rest of her career, Jackie would go on to publish numerous best sellers, the memoirs of Gelsey Kirkland and Michael Jackson, Joseph Campbell's *The Power of Myth*, and Bill Moyers's *Healing and the Mind* notable among them. But what might be best described as her signature titles tended to be smaller, more personal affairs, reflecting as they did a certain late-twentieth-century patrician sensibility—the product of a once all-powerful world that she wistfully acknowledged to be in decline. With their overlay of poetic regret, a good many of the books Jackie produced at Doubleday—stylish volumes about such topics as women in the age of the Sun King, Indian court life from 1590 to 1947, the garden photography of Eugène Atget, and Stanford White's New York—might almost have been created to adorn the window display at the carriage trade Madison Avenue Bookstore (now defunct), where she was herself a customer.

Interestingly, a similar preoccupation with cultural evanescence infused Jackie's work during this period on behalf of the landmarks preservation movement. At various times, she spoke with poignance of Manhattan monuments disappearing, of patches of sky being snatched away, of a cityscape that was dying "by degrees." Pressed to explain why she had become involved in the fight to save the ornate Beaux Arts–style Grand Central Station, whose bankrupt owners hoped to raise money by allowing a fifty-five-story commercial tower to be built above it, Jackie said: "It's a beautiful building that I'm used to seeing. I'd be outraged if it was replaced by steel and glass." The occasion for this remark was a widely publicized April 16, 1978, train trip by some three hundred authors, artists, performers, and other preservationists to Washington, D.C., where the U.S. Supreme Court was to hear the owners' suit to remove Grand Central's previously accorded landmark designation in order that construction on the modernist Marcel Breuer–designed tower might begin. For all the notable names on the passenger list of the Landmark Express, as the train had been named for the day, none elicited greater press interest than that of Jacqueline Kennedy Onassis. Her participation brought the preservationists' cause national publicity that by their own reckoning they could not otherwise have hoped to attain. For once, instead of ducking the melee of cameras and reporters, Jackie seemed eager to speak up: "A big corporation shouldn't be able to destroy a building that has meant so much to so many for so many generations. If Grand Central goes, all of the landmarks in this country will go as well." Still, it was less anything Jackie said or did that was so helpful as it was the very fact of her presence.

After the Supreme Court upheld the railroad station's protected status, Jackie went on to play a prominent part in other Manhattan landmark disputes. She lent her star wattage to avert the razing of Lever House; to halt the construction of a fifty-nine-story office tower above St. Bartholomew's Church; and to force a developer to decrease the size of a new office complex planned for Columbus Circle. The dynamic in all of this was comparable to what had occurred when she managed to secure the release of the princess's sleigh from the Soviet archives; or when, at a later date, she won the assent of heretofore intransigent French authorities to let the photographer Deborah Turbeville into certain spectral back rooms of the palace of the Bourbons for the Doubleday book *Unseen Versailles,* the original creative concept for which had been Jackie's. The exercise of personal power was certainly not a new experience for Jackie. In the past, she had done it on behalf of JFK, RFK, and others. The difference at this point was that she was acting not to advance anyone else's purposes, but rather her own. Her interventions had important private consequences, in addition to the well-known public ones. Quite apart from any books produced or landmarks saved, Jackie's successes contributed to her quiet, ongoing process of healing, as she whose life had been forever transformed by eight and a half seconds of absolute powerlessness asserted again and again that she was anything but helpless.

Similarly conducive to Jackie's health of spirit was her 1978 purchase of some 375 acres of undeveloped land on Martha's Vineyard. Having finally been awarded a $26 million settlement by the Onassis estate, Jackie paid $1.1 million for the land, where she began work on the construction of a secluded New England–style gray shingled saltbox summer house, which, by the time it was completed in 1981, would cost another $2 million. One motive for leaving Hyannis Port was that from the time of her early married days, she had never enjoyed any real privacy there. Another sprung from Jackie's long-standing anxiety about the influence upon her son and daughter of certain of their wilder Kennedy cousins, for whom drugs had lately become a significant problem.

Successful book editor; highly effective "public face" of the landmarks preservation movement; soon-to-be chatelaine of a Martha's Vineyard estate; and exceedingly rich besides—by 1979, Jackie had certainly accomplished much since she moved back to the States full-time after the death of Aristotle Onassis. Yet, one element necessary to any trauma survivor's course of recovery continued to be missing: a feeling of basic safety. How could she feel at all safe when the "continuing American nightmare" about a third Kennedy killing remained so prominent a factor in national life? 1977's *Shall We Tell the President?* had been a work of fiction, but there was nothing make-believe about Teddy Kennedy's decision, two years later, to challenge Jimmy Carter in the 1980 Democratic presidential primaries, precisely as the character in the assassination novel had done.

Though Teddy's formal announcement was still weeks away, most people at the October 20, 1979, dedication of the recently completed John F. Kennedy Library in Dorchester, Massachusetts—including President Carter himself—had at least some idea of what the senator was finally about to do. For many attendees, a mixture of exhilaration and anxiety tinctured the proceedings. Exhilaration, because these were precisely the individuals whom McGeorge Bundy once described as that "circle of people who felt that their happiness and hopes died on the twenty-second of November unless they could be revived by the younger brother." Anxiety, because of the presentiment tersely recorded by Arthur Schlesinger in his diary: "Ted will be shot if he runs."

Jackie, who had been a driving force behind the creation of the library, took a seat beside her children on the blue-carpeted outdoor stage. Red roses adorned either side of a podium at which eighteen-year-old John Junior was scheduled to read Stephen Spender's elegiac poem "I Think of Those Who Were Truly Great"; and where both Jimmy Carter and Teddy Kennedy were set to speak. Twelve years after the christening ceremony for the aircraft carrier *John F. Kennedy,* when the fiercer rivalry of LBJ and RFK had been similarly on display, Jackie remained coolly composed in the presence of many of the identical faces from her White House years that had formerly posed such a threat to her self-possession. Today, the dreaded trigger did not come in the form of one of those familiar visages, but rather from that of a person she hardly knew. Striding onstage to the accompaniment of "Hail to the Chief," the president shook hands with various other Kennedy family members before he reached Jackie. Observers of the scene could not but be struck by what happened next.

When Carter leaned in to kiss her, Jackie, by Schlesinger's account, "seemed to recoil visibly." To the eye of Richard Burke, Teddy's aide, it was as if Jackie had been "bitten by a snake." In the wake of that tense encounter, many were the efforts to parse her bodily response in terms of current presidential and sexual politics. But the moment was also suggestive of the terrors with which, for Jackie, another Kennedy White House bid was inevitably freighted. The picture of her suddenly stiffening, then drawing back, recalls other such occasions, whether with Galella or Guinzburg, when she also had reacted to a sense of looming threat as if she were about to be, or had just been, physically attacked. Interestingly, she persisted in this spirit afterward when she caustically remarked to Schlesinger that Carter had acted as if the presidency carried with it the droit du seigneur—a feudal lord's privilege to take the virginity of his serf's daughters. But it is also telling that in contrast to her behavior at the battleship christening, this time Jackie did not require Bob McNamara or some other cavalier to help extricate her from the ceremony. Today, the flickers of agitation and apprehension vanished almost as abruptly as they had disclosed themselves, and her face became again the "enameled mask" that was its more habitual guise.

Nor at this point would Jackie find it quite impossible, as she had when RFK chased the Democratic presidential nomination in 1968, to publicly participate in the effort to secure a Kennedy restoration. She consented to appear at a limited number of Teddy's campaign and fundraising events. Still, in view of the suggestive fissures in Jackie's demeanor at the library ceremony, it is hard not to hear at least a trace of irony in her insistence that she was "rather thrilled" at the prospect of his insurgent candidacy. What seems clear, at any rate, is that by this time her fears had diminished in intensity and oppressiveness to the degree that she was finally able to confront them.

Jackie appeared alongside eighty-nine-year-old Rose Kennedy (who had been widowed in 1969) when Teddy announced his intentions at Faneuil Hall in Boston on November 7. Thereafter, she cut a sometimes robotic figure on the hustings, greeting voters with what one press account described as "a fixed smile on her face and a right hand frozen open for handshakes." Seated onstage beside Teddy at a Queens, New York, event, she made a point of pushing the microphones in front of her away. Was the gesture simply a reflection of Jackie's ancient distaste for politicking or, under the circumstances, was it something else besides? Was she working very hard to anticipate and modulate the reactions of body and brain to the crowds and cameras, not to mention the sharpshooters and anti-sniper teams that were part of a Secret Service detail said to be larger than the one assigned to President Carter? Ironically, the senator's Uzi-machine-gun-toting protectors had the unfortunate effect of heightening the overall sense of peril. Wherever Jackie accompanied Teddy now, there were always extra press people on hand in addition to the standard pool reporters in case another assassin suddenly sprang out of nowhere. Among themselves, certain of the journalists darkly referred to the task of covering Teddy as a "death watch."

Finally, however, this particular campaign ended not with the bang for which everyone had been so excruciatingly on guard, but with a whimper. Teddy performed disastrously in on-camera interviews, flubbed questions about Chappaquiddick, and failed either to articulate his concept of presidential leadership or to explain why Democrats ought to choose him over Carter. The senator lost a majority of primaries and bowed out early at the Democratic National Convention in New York. Thus ended the struggle to reclaim the crown that had begun seventeen years previously at Andrews Air Force Base when Bobby Kennedy rushed onto the presidential jet to collect Jackie. The historian Garry Wills characterized Teddy's unfortunate campaign as "the end of the entire Kennedy time in our national life." By contrast, for Jackie personally, it had proven to be very much a beginning. Jackie had at last faced down the danger, and, crucially, the instant of horror had failed to recur. Like other survivors of psychological trauma, Jackie would never be able to fully expunge the old terrors. In the course of Teddy's 1980 campaign, she had, however, begun to discover a way to live with them.

Jimmy Carter, of course, went on to be defeated by his Republican challenger, Ronald Reagan. Meanwhile, it had been among the quieter accomplishments of Carter's single term to have named a new Veterans Administration national director, Max Cleland, a disabled Vietnam veteran intensely sympathetic to the problems of others who had been damaged in that unpopular war. Cleland's appointment, coupled with the inclusion of PTSD as an officially sanctioned diagnosis in the 1980 edition of the *Diagnostic and Statistical Manual of Mental Disorders* of the American Psychiatric Association, marked a watershed in the treatment of readjustment issues experienced by veterans of the Vietnam War and subsequent conflicts.

Jackie, whose struggle with PTSD had started long before President Johnson committed U.S. combat forces in 1965, was operating on a different timetable from that of the Vietnam vets. By the time there existed an accepted name for what she had been suffering, her journey of recovery was already well under way. She had had to proceed in the absence of a conceptual framework that might have assuaged her feeling of isolation and helped her begin to make sense of her ordeal rather than suspect, as she had at times, that she was losing her sanity. But she had had significant advantages as well. Obviously, not every survivor of psychological trauma possessed the glittering backstory that had been so vital to the success of Jackie's efforts to regain a sense of control. Not everyone had access to an eminent psychoanalyst or the financial means to undertake the construction of a serene, secure world of one's own on Martha's Vineyard.

Jackie's comments at an October 28, 1980, dinner party in New York City suggest how the woman herself perceived the arc of her life. Her dinner partner that evening, the British poet Stephen Spender, who had last encountered her before JFK became president, asked what she considered her greatest achievement to have been. Notably, it was not her fabled tenure as first lady, not the conquest of Paris or the myriad other triumphs of the White House years, not her demeanor at President Kennedy's funeral and what it had meant to so many Americans, that Jackie spoke of when she replied without hesitation: "I think it is that after going through a rather difficult time, I consider myself comparatively sane. I am proud of that."

Sixteen

B y the time of the book party for Louis Auchincloss's new non-fiction work, *Maverick in Mauve,* which Doubleday was bring-ing out that fall season of 1983, more than thirty years had passed since the champagne-stoked evening when Auchincloss, then aged thirty-four, and Jackie Bouvier, aged twenty-two, had both been in crisis over how they intended to spend the rest of their lives. Auchin-closs, who had wanted to write rather than pursue the traditional law career his parents envisioned for him, had just published a novel, *Sybil,* whose female protagonist reminded Jackie of her own dilemma as the bride-to-be of a nice but bland New York stockbroker named John Hus-ted. "That's it. That's my future. I'll be a Sybil Husted," Jackie had pro-claimed, not long before she decided to return her sapphire-and-diamond engagement ring in favor of chasing a less predictable and therefore more alluring relationship with Jack Kennedy.

In the intervening decades, Auchincloss, who had successfully pursued careers both as an author and an attorney, had published more than thirty works of fiction, history, and biography—including the novel regarded in some quarters as his finest book, *The Rector of Justin*. After Jackie went to Doubleday, she commissioned him to contribute learned pieces to a volume about the privileged French of the waning eighteenth century, and to the Deborah Turbeville book about the "ghosts and memories" that haunted Versailles. At length, Jackie had acquired the publication rights to *Maverick in Mauve*, an edition of the diary of his wife's grandmother, the society figure Florence Adele Sloane, which Auchincloss had supplemented with his own piquant commentary and analysis. Strange to say, yet again he had produced a volume with which Jackie identified passionately and profoundly. By Jackie's own account, it was not the choice details of mauve-decade (1890s) opulence and social intercourse that spoke to her so much as the diarist's status as a survivor whose existence had been transformed by a jolt of sudden tragedy that snatched away well-nigh everything she had possessed but a moment before. Jackie was especially interested in the process that had allowed Adele, as she was known, to survive and thrive afterward. In the course of the book party at the Museum of the City of New York on upper Fifth Avenue where Auchincloss served as president, Jackie detailed her response to Adele's story in conversation with the writer Marie Brenner: "What was so moving to me was the spirit of this woman . . . That her life would seem to be ideal, and then tragedy would strike her . . . but somehow her spirit and her character would carry her through." Jackie might almost have been speaking of herself in the years of trial since Dallas.

Set alongside each other, the particular pair of Louis Auchincloss works with which Jackie identified across a span of three decades points to a crucial difference between her twenty-two- and fifty-four-year-old selves. Jackie Bouvier had scorned predictability, whether in life or in the man whose role it would be to provide her with that life. By contrast, an abiding sense that the earth beneath one's feet could crumble at any moment had led the Jackie Onassis of these later years, like Adele a survivor, to crave and cultivate predictability. After she had dated a number of Manhattan men, the writer Pete Hamill and the filmmaker Peter Davis prominent among them, she had finally entered into a loving and lasting relationship with a partner who was quite unlike any of the potential husbands that would have most appealed to her in her restive post-deb years. Plump, pouchy-eyed, and still officially married to the mother of his three children, Maurice Tempelsman, international diamond trader and financier, was conspicuously devoid of the personal panache that Jackie's two husbands, for all of their dramatic differences, had shared. Also unlike Kennedy and Onassis, Tempelsman was steady, reliable, and absolutely devoted to Jackie.

Born in Belgium in 1929 one month after Jackie, Tempelsman had grown up in an Orthodox Jewish, Yiddish-speaking family that escaped to the United States in 1940 as Hitler was conquering Europe. Living in a Jewish-émigré community on New York's Upper West Side, Tempelsman when he was still a teenager went to work for his father in the diamond trade. Early on, he became associated with the DeBeers diamond cartel in South Africa. Jackie had first encountered Tempelsman in the 1950s when he introduced Jack Kennedy, then a U.S. senator and presidential aspirant, to leading figures in the South African diamond business. During the White House years, Tempelsman, a supporter of Democratic political causes, had been a guest, along with his wife, Lilly, at the 1961 state dinner in honor of President Ayub Khan of Pakistan, at which Jackie had displayed her new personal confidence and clout in the aftermath of Paris and Vienna. Early in her second widowhood, Tempelsman had taken over as her financial adviser upon the death of her previous money manager, the financier André Meyer. As he set to work adroitly multiplying Jackie's settlement from the Onassis estate, he emerged by degrees as a discreet presence in her social life, squiring her at dinner parties and cultural events.

"MT," as Jackie liked to refer to him, had a cast of mind that was similar to hers in important respects. Art and antiquity, ballet, theater, reading, scholarship—these and other shared interests they delighted in speaking of to each other, often in melodious French. That they were so often observed about New York conversing in a language other than English suggests the manner in which, when they were alone together in public, a kind of mist hung about them that excluded anyone else. Above all, Jackie's new companion proved to be wonderfully protective. When, as they loved to do, she and he took long walks in Central Park near her home, he shielded her from photographers and others who threatened her serenity. Jackie once compared life with JFK to "living in a whirlwind." By contrast, with Tempelsman, everything seemed somehow to proceed at a stately pace.

At length, Tempelsman moved to a hotel not far from where Jackie lived, then at last into her Fifth Avenue apartment, where he resided for the rest of her life. Jackie, when she married Jack Kennedy and Aristotle Onassis, had become part of their personal and professional universes, emphatically so. She would have been expected to do the same had she become John Husted's bride. Significantly, Jackie's last love, when he assumed what was to become his regular place at one end of the candlelit, rustic plank pine dining room table at Red Gate Farm, as her Martha's Vineyard estate was known, joined her in a life she had created for herself—a life painstakingly constructed to fit her own needs.

No setting more fully embodied the spirit of that life than the oasis where Jackie spent the better part of every summer, between Memorial Day and Labor Day. At a glance, the decor at Red Gate Farm seemed nothing if not cozy and comfortable. Rough-hewn benches, baskets, and other countrified pieces mingled with inviting, unostentatious chairs and sofas. Flowers in a variety of receptacles were scattered throughout the house. But the prevailing air of casualness and happenstance was deceptive. As in the homes of her friend and preceptress Bunny Mellon, on close inspection every visual element was calculated and perfect—perhaps, to certain tastes at least, a bit too perfect. Jackie's dominion extended to the tiniest details. She wrote out her copious instructions to staff on index cards, such as the one affixed to a kitchen cabinet interior, which specified exactly which flowers were to be placed in which vessels in which areas of the house. Even in such minor matters, she wanted there to be no surprises. Though officially on holiday, Jackie lived by rigid rules. She rose unvaryingly at seven and ate breakfast—a half bowl of bran cereal with skim milk, fruit, and coffee—served on a tray in bed, before the wood fire she insisted be laid no matter the weather. Religiously, she massaged her face with cold cream in anticipation of donning a bathing suit, cap, and rubber fins for a strenuous two-hour swim in Squibnocket Pond, which bordered her property.

What may have been the most sustaining ritual of all took place in the interval between lunch and dinnertime. Of a summer's afternoon, Jackie would sit barefoot on a padded chaise in the brick patio behind the house, laboring in solitude on manuscript pages, which she festooned with penciled corrections and comments. To understand the signal role that editing came to play in her life, it is worth revisiting the scene witnessed by Theodore White a week after President Kennedy's assassination. The *Life* magazine writer, in the course of his interview with Jackie, was confronted with a fascinating dichotomy. First, the widow's exceptionally vivid and visceral memories of Dallas asserted themselves, to the journalist's perception, "as if controlling her." Then, in turn, it was she who seized control, burying his typed pages beneath an avalanche of scribbled revisions. What White seems to have observed that strange stormy night in 1963 were the manifestations of two distinctly different parts of her brain at work. Jackie's spoken evocations of "the blood scene" issued ineluctably from the limbic system, the brain's survival center, where such images and sensations are stored. Her emphatic pencil marks on White's first draft were the product of the cerebral cortex, where rational thinking takes place. The latter appears to have been her instinctive way of regaining control after the absolute loss of mastery in the just-completed episode of remembering and re-experiencing. On a personal level, the editing process seems to have performed a similar function in the course of Jackie's last years. When she worked with single-minded intensity on a manuscript, she was in control and, to whatever extent remained possible, at peace. That peace was hard-won, and tenuous at best.

Thus her son's fury when his girlfriend, Christina Haag, innocently violated the cardinal rule that Jackie's precisely delineated private time at Red Gate Farm must not be intruded upon. "What were you doing there? You never, never go there between lunch and dinner," John angrily challenged Christina, after she mentioned having happened upon Jackie at work in the patio. Even as a tiny tousle-haired boy, John had been unfailingly protective of a mother who, much as she strove to give him and his sister the semblance of a normal life, could hardly conceal the loss of control that intermittently afflicted her. When, in 1965, Jackie sadly referred to how much both children bore upon their shoulders, was she referring to their having to cope not just with the loss of a father, but with her terrifying troubles as well? Once, as little John perused a children's book about JFK, he was heard to exclaim with alarm: "Close your eyes, Mummy!" Whereupon he ripped out a photo illustration of the presidential limousine in Dallas, before offering the volume to Jackie. Long afterward, John's outburst at the girlfriend who had walked in on his mother spoke to his perception of the fragility of the arrangements Jackie had made and the atmosphere of safety and serenity thereby attained.

Whatever control she had managed to retrieve over time could be fractured in an instant. The precipitating event might take the form of an obvious reminder, as when at a 1983 private screening of a new film featuring her friend Rudolf Nureyev, she reacted to images of his fictional character's being shot by suddenly crying out, obscuring her face with both hands and refusing to remove them until the movie was at an end. But it might just as well be any surprise that Jackie interpreted as threateningly intrusive, whether it be a publisher's first mention of the Archer book or a president's violation of her zealously guarded personal space. As it happened, Jackie had not been at all ruffled by the sight of her son's girlfriend in the rear patio at an hour when only Jackie was supposed to be there. On the contrary, the women had proceeded to enjoy a relaxed, friendly conversation. John's overwrought reaction to word of the chance encounter is suggestive of the acute anxiety with which his young life had long been charged, living as he did with an injured parent for whom the process of recovery was necessarily unending, resolution of the trauma never complete.

Might it have been otherwise? Was there some other, more effective arrangement Jackie could have made for herself and her children after the deaths of JFK and RFK? She appears to have contemplated the road not taken when, in 1985, she traveled with Teddy and other Kennedy family members to the village of Talsarnau in North Wales to attend the funeral of David Harlech. Like his adored first wife, Sissie, and his worshipped older brother, Gerard, before him, David had been killed in an automobile accident. The strange coincidence led to talk that the Harlechs, like their great friends the Kennedys, were cursed. Jackie's presence at David's funeral drew a great many press people who would hardly have come otherwise. On February 1, as she entered the twelfth-century parish church at Llanfihangel-y-traethau, she remained silent while Teddy, beside her, spoke to reporters of David's having been like a brother to the Kennedys, of Rose's having long regarded him as another son, and of JFK's opinion of him as the smartest man he had ever known. After the service, attended by some ninety mourners who crowded into the tiny church, and by another hundred outside, David was buried in an adjoining walled graveyard. As Teddy looked on with mounting distress, Jackie's composure began to evaporate. She shut her eyes tightly, her face contorted. Teddy did not pursue her, indeed no one did, when she suddenly rushed off—propelled, it would seem, by the familiar urgent wish to escape. At length, the rest of the party repaired to David's seventeenth-century stone-manor house, which was set on some

4,200 acres of lawns, gardens, waterfalls, farmland, and wild woodland. His second wife was to preside over a family luncheon, attended by people whom Jackie would naturally have associated with the tales she had first heard in 1952 from John White, and two years later from David himself, of the young London set that had embraced Jack and Kick before the war.

Wearing high black boots and a long, fur-lined black wool coat, Jackie wandered alone in the hills. At the top of a ridge loomed a stone lookout tower that gave long views of the ruins of Harlech Castle, the medieval fortification that had withstood the longest siege in British history, during the Wars of the Roses in the fifteenth century. The castle perched on a steep cliff face with a long stairway that had once provided a supply route to the sea. The waters had long since receded, but the stone ruins remained the picture of impregnability against the outside world. Jackie had never seen all this before, not in the years when Sissie was alive, nor afterward when everything Lord Harlech possessed had been on offer if only Jackie accepted his marriage proposal.

By the time Jackie appeared at the house, more than two hours had passed and guests were starting to leave following the meal. Immediately, she gravitated to David's eldest daughter, Jane. "My God," Jackie said with visible emotion, "if only I'd known this place then." Was Jackie reflecting on what might have been had she chosen to become Lady Harlech rather than Mrs. Onassis? Such was the younger woman's sense, at any rate. Still, for all of the security that broad acres and mighty fortifications seemed to provide, David and his family had hardly been insulated from the tempestuous times. His son Julian Ormsby-Gore had committed suicide after a losing battle with drugs; and Alice Ormsby-Gore, who had been Caroline's playmate during the presidency, had become addicted to heroin in the course of a relationship with Eric Clapton, and would herself eventually die of an overdose. Had Jackie sought refuge in Wales, Lord Harlech's estate almost certainly would have succeeded no better than Skorpios had in giving her what she wanted and needed. Under the circumstances, no castles or island kingdoms would have been sufficient. To paraphrase Harold Macmillan in the intuitive 1964 letter that had long meant so much to Jackie, that was something she simply was going to have to find within herself. Intermittent relapses and resurgences of traumatic memories notwithstanding, by the mid-1980s there was ample evidence that, to whatever degree possible, she had found it.

Fog enveloped Hyannis Port shortly before midnight on July 18, 1986, when Jackie, standing in the middle of the huge white tent on the heavily policed Kennedy family property where her daughter's wedding supper was to take place the next day, extended both sinewy arms and exulted: "Isn't it wonderful?" In years past, Jackie, on the principle that safety was to be found only in an absence of feelings, might have fought against allowing herself to experience such delight; but that was very far from her attitude now. Ostensibly, she was referring to the elaborate preparations under way—the numerous tables in the process of being set up for more than four hundred guests, the flower baskets to be filled and overhead Japanese lanterns to be arrayed. But it is not too much to suppose that Jackie's outstretched arms also registered the immense pleasure and pride she took in both of her children: Caroline, now twenty-eight years of age, and John, twenty-five, the latter hovering nearby. In harsher times when, by Jackie's own account, the prospect of death had held no small attraction for her, the children had given her a reason to live. In the beginning, she had struggled to put JFK out of her thoughts expressly for the sake of her daughter and son. She had striven to pull herself together enough to be helpful to them. She had pledged to try to make them the people their father would have wished them to become. She had alternated between worrying that because she had been overly intense as a parent they would grow up to be awful; and hoping that if they turned out well, that would constitute her "vengeance on the world."

On a hazy summer day at the Cape, Caroline was married to forty-one-year-old Edwin Schlossberg in the small white, flower-filled Church of Our Lady of Victory, about six miles from the Kennedy family property. The bride, a Radcliffe graduate and second-year student at Columbia Law School, had met Schlossberg, the holder of a Columbia University doctorate and president of a New York firm that designed museum shows, when she had been employed at the Metropolitan Museum after college. Her brother, a Brown University graduate who was about to begin law studies of his own at New York University that fall, served as Schlossberg's best man. At the wedding supper afterward, John also functioned as his mother's escort-of-record, dancing attendance on Jackie, who wore a pistachio-colored crepe dress and white gloves, and seemed by turns joyful and sad.

In the years that followed, Jackie saw her daughter, and then her son, graduate from law school. She became a grandmother to Rose, Tatiana, and John Schlossberg. She watched JFK Jr. address the 1988 Democratic National Convention in Atlanta, a charming debut that led to wide speculation about whether he intended to assume the role of family standard-bearer. She saw him anointed *People* magazine's Sexiest Man Alive and she watched him struggle manfully with an inability to pass the bar exam until his third attempt. Publicly he shrugged off his failures and the accompanying jeers of the press (which included the *New York Post* headline "The Hunk Flunks"), but in private he wept.

On a November evening many years after President Kennedy's assassination, when Jackie, aged sixty-one, was dining with her son at home in New York during what she still referred to as her difficult time of the year, she said something she had never told him before. She declared that were his father to return to her now, she wondered whether she might not send him away. When, after a moment's hesitation, Jackie, whose eyes were closed at the time, held up her hand, palm facing outward, the gesture, as vehement and expressive as any in a Martha Graham solo, encapsulated one PTSD sufferer's long lonely struggle to shut out the tragic past. For people who have witnessed the violent death of someone they loved, part of the problem later can be the difficulty of letting go. By endlessly reconstructing and replaying the ghastly sequence of events that culminated in trauma, the survivor in some sense keeps the beloved alive, if only in mind. Jackie's soulful conversation with her son suggests that she who had once consciously endeavored to put her murdered husband out of her thoughts for the children's sake was finally prepared to try again, but this time for herself.

Jackie made another significant advance when she was in her early sixties. Interestingly, it was not until these last years that she finally acquired the thick hide that she had heretofore lacked when, in RFK's words at the time of the Manchester controversy, she had been "so upset and really crushed" by the tremendous amount of severe public criticism directed against her. Through the years, she had been painted as selfishly willing to prolong the nation's trauma; as wallowing in self-pity; as faking her pain; as faithless to the legacy of the martyred president; as ready to sell herself to the highest bidder; and even as the cause of her second husband's decline and demise. Much of this had been devastating to her. When Jackie resigned her post at Viking, she had been frantic that anyone could actually believe that she had not been sincerely distressed by the publication of the Archer book. "I just don't understand sometimes why they work so hard at hurting me," she once remarked apropos of her legion of detractors. At a certain point, however, the excruciating solitude of Jackie's ongoing experience of the aftershock of Dallas seemed to liberate her from worrying about how the public saw her. She was one of the most famous women in the world, photographed and written about wherever she went, yet by her lights, few people had even the remotest understanding of what she had long had to endure in what she once called, in another context, "my most secret heart." So what did it really matter what anyone said?

A shared sense of being beleaguered and misperceived had long undergirded Jackie's enduring personal bond with Bob McNamara. In these last years, however, she and McNamara, now retired and a widower, diverged in important respects. By this time, there could be no doubt that Jackie had survived and thrived. McNamara, by contrast, was a disappointed and defeated man. Jackie, after numerous failed attempts, had finally succeeded in fashioning a new life. McNamara, said an associate, was still "crawling around the ruins of a life." Jackie assiduously cultivated an aura of sanity. McNamara, with his tearful outbursts and thousand-yard stare, seemed at times haunted and half mad. When Jackie learned that the beloved friend whom she credited with having helped her in her dark times was himself in despair about an unflattering biography of him that had recently been published, she did what she could to mitigate his pain.

In a February 24, 1993, letter, Jackie offered the seventy-six-year-old McNamara some advice that sounded as if it were based on personal experience and reflection. She suggested that by letting himself get upset, he was just allowing his critics to diminish him. Jackie remained confident that people would eventually learn the truth about McNamara—at least the truth as she and he perceived it—and take the correct measure of his actions. Meanwhile, she paraphrased Eleanor Roosevelt: "No one can humiliate me without my assent." In short, Jackie was advising this man, whose fatal flaw had perhaps been too devout an adherence to the illusion of control, to at least try to master his own emotions.

That same year, Jackie finally overcame her long-standing reluctance to allow herself to, in JFK Jr.'s phrase, "reconnect" with political Washington in an emotional sense. On August 24, Jackie, wearing a red-and-white polka-dot scarf, prepared to greet Bill and Hillary Clinton in Martha's Vineyard. She had invited the Clintons, who were staying at the home of Bob McNamara, to join her and Maurice Tempelsman, along with Teddy Kennedy and other family members, on a four-hour-plus cruise on Maurice's yacht. To the perception of Jackie's son, the January 1993 inauguration of President Clinton, a forty-six-year-old JFK devotee who, on the eve of his own swearing-in, had made the gesture of placing white roses on the graves of both Kennedy brothers in Arlington

National Cemetery, had marked something of a sea change in Jackie's overall attitude toward Washington. In the years since the assassination, Jackie had consented to return to the White House on only one occasion, in 1971 during the Nixon presidency to view the official painted portraits of her and JFK. Otherwise, Jackie had preferred to stay away for fear of the unwelcome recollections that a visit threatened to unseal. Notably, in the Clinton years, Jackie, though she had a standing invitation from Hillary Rodham Clinton, persisted in her avoidance of the many potential triggers that awaited her there. The warm friendship she conducted with both Clintons on her own home ground was another matter, however. According to her son, Jackie "seemed profoundly happy and relieved to allow herself" to connect again with Washington through them. The relationship, John wrote in a 1994 letter to the Clintons, had "helped her in a profound way."

That August of 1993, Jackie for her part was also intent that the Clintons' much-trumpeted vacation visit to Martha's Vineyard also help the sixty-one-year-old Teddy Kennedy, who faced a tough reelection campaign in 1994. After his failed 1980 quest for his party's presidential nomination, he and his wife, Joan, had divorced; whereupon he had embarked on what would amount to a decade-long spree of public carousing and womanizing that was extensively depicted in the press. The Kennedys had come to political prominence through the youthful figures of Jack and Bobby, who, on account of their early deaths, had remained eternally young and handsome in the popular imagination. To many Massachusetts voters, especially newer, younger ones, Teddy Kennedy, heavy and lumbering, was a relic from another era. Factory closings and unemployment had become a significant problem in the state, prompting citizens' questions about what the dissipated, seemingly irrelevant old man planned to do about it.

Meanwhile, two episodes that coincided with Teddy's present term of office had raised important questions about the degree to which his private life had impacted on his political effectiveness. Public knowledge of the senator's dissolute behavior had plainly and severely constricted him during the 1991 airing of Anita Hill's charges of sexual harassment against Clarence Thomas. How could Teddy hold President George H. W. Bush's Supreme Court nominee to standards of conduct that the senator had long and famously failed to meet himself? If Teddy said relatively little at the hearings, was it not because to say anything would seem like hypocrisy? So a good many people, not least the senator himself, appeared to believe. When Teddy did speak up, however briefly, in Anita Hill's defense, his remarks were met by Republicans' snide allusions to Chappaquiddick. That same year, revelations at the time of the William Kennedy Smith rape trial that on the night of the episode in question, Teddy had escorted the nephew who now stood accused (and was subsequently acquitted of all charges) to a Palm Beach bar that had the reputation of a pickup spot for older males in search of female companionship did the senator's reputation no favors. Teddy delivered a mea culpa at the Kennedy School of Government ("I recognize my own shortcomings— the faults in the conduct of my private life. I realize that I alone am responsible for them, and I am the one who must confront them") and he entered into a stable and apparently stabilizing second marriage with lawyer Victoria Reggie. Despite his efforts to this point, however, Teddy's supporters had reason to be concerned that it was not enough for voters, and that after three decades in the Senate he could well be defeated the following year.

Looking ahead to 1994, Jackie, so much of whose life had been about optics and nuances, seized on the opportunity that Bill Clinton's visit presented, if only the choreography were precisely as it must be. In ancient times, it had been the role of old Joe Kennedy to artfully arrange such matters for his politically ambitious sons, but today the task was Jackie's. Upon learning that the young president and his wife were about to come aboard the yacht, she directed Teddy, who was with her on the upper deck, to welcome them. When Teddy pointed out that Maurice was already in place, Jackie flung back that Maurice was not seeking reelection in the state of Massachusetts. Teddy was, and it had better be he who was reported as having greeted President Clinton.

At the end of 1993, when Jackie, as was her twice-yearly custom, went to Virginia to foxhunt, work on manuscripts, and—she said half in gaiety, half in gravity—exist on Lean Cuisine dinners in her rented, toile de Jouy–wallpapered cottage on a rural dirt road near Middleburg, she was sixty-four years old. Jackie expected the trip to be absolutely routine, but it did not turn out that way. While in Virginia, she fell from her horse. She was taken to a hospital, where, in the course of an examination, a doctor detected a swelling in her groin. Convinced that the problem must be a swollen lymph node caused by infection, the physician prescribed a course of antibiotics, which reduced but did not eliminate the swelling. After Christmas, Jackie was sailing with Tempelsman in the Caribbean when a severe cough, combined with abdominal pain and swollen lymph nodes in her neck, prompted her to contact her doctor in New York, who advised her to fly home immediately. A biopsy indicated that she had non-Hodgkin's lymphoma, a form of cancer, and in early January 1994 she began chemotherapy.

"I feel it is a kind of hubris," Jackie told Arthur Schlesinger in an important conversation after her cancer diagnosis. "I have always been proud of keeping so fit. I swim, and I jog, and I do my push-ups, and walk around the reservoir . . . and now this suddenly happens." As she had done so many times in the decades since Dallas, she again grappled with the randomness of the world and the abruptness of tragedy. On the present occasion, however, instead of going over the myriad actions she might have taken to make life turn out otherwise, she did something very different. She enumerated what had been her determined efforts to stay fit and healthy, and she ruefully remarked on the fact that the dreadful diagnosis had come in spite of them. And, crucially, as she spoke of all this she laughed—not just in acknowledgment of the futility of her efforts, but also of the hubris (Jackie specifically used the ancient Greek term for excessive pride) of which she had been guilty in believing that she had more control over her destiny than she actually did.

Meanwhile, a public announcement of the former first lady's condition went out via a spokesperson, who noted that Jackie's prognosis was excellent. In fact, the doctors had informed Jackie that there was only a 50 percent chance that the lymphoma could be stabilized. Jackie, often sporting Band-Aids and bruises from the treatment, continued to appear at the publishing house as though nothing very much were wrong. In mid-March, however, an MRI detected that the lymphoma had migrated to her brain and spinal cord. Doctors inserted a tube in her brain to administer powerful anti-cancer drugs, but at length the lymphoma proved to be unconquerable.

Maurice Tempelsman, who had established a temporary office in Jackie's apartment, remained with her throughout, pressing her hand, stroking her cheek, whispering to her. On Sunday, May 15, he accompanied Jackie on one last visit to Central Park, though she had become exceedingly fragile and could hardly go any distance before she had to be guided back to her residence. The following day Jackie grew disoriented as she lapsed into a fit of shaking chills. Tempelsman brought her to New York Hospital–Cornell Medical Center, where tests found large amounts of the lymphoma in her liver. Jackie, when she learned that the doctors had nothing more to offer, chose to go home to die.

Jackie was in her own bedroom—the same where she had received the news of Bobby Kennedy's shooting—when her life ended on Thursday evening, May 19. Tempelsman and both of her children were with her at the time. The next day, thirty-three-year-old JFK Jr., reverting to a theme that had often preoccupied his mother in her various endeavors, highlighted the degree of control she had at least exerted over the circumstances of her passing. "She did it in her own way and in her own terms," John told reporters gathered in front of the apartment house, "and we all feel lucky for that."

Three days later, crowds watched from behind police barricades along Park Avenue as Jackie's coffin, which was covered with ferns and a cross of white lilies of the valley, was carried into the limestone nineteenth-century St. Ignatius Loyola Church. At the service, which was attended by some one thousand invited guests, JFK Jr. read from the prophet Isaiah, and Caroline and Maurice recited poems by Edna St. Vincent Millay and C. P. Cavafy, respectively. Not a few attendees took note that the eulogy, delivered by Teddy Kennedy, involved an instant rewrite of history, as there was not a single mention of Jackie's controversial second marriage. After the funeral Mass, her body was flown by chartered jet to National Airport in Washington. President Clinton was waiting when the aircraft landed, and he accompanied the family to Arlington National Cemetery, where Jackie was to be buried alongside JFK.

Caroline had asked the eighty-one-year-old Archbishop Philip Hannan, whom her mother had designated to deliver the eulogy for President Kennedy at St. Matthew's in Washington in 1963, to preside over Jackie's burial. At the time of the marriage to Aristotle Onassis, the priest had been severely critical of Jackie's decision to enter into a union that he regarded as one "of convenience," so he was at once surprised and delighted by Caroline's summons. His violet zucchetto and robe, along with the peach-hued lapels of Hillary Rodham Clinton's black suit, provided the sole jolts of color amid the black-attired funeral procession, which accompanied the coffin from the hearse to the hillside burial site overlooking the Potomac River. "O, God," Archbishop Hannan intoned, "you are our promised home. Lead your servant Jacqueline to that home bright with the presence of your everlasting life and love, there to join the other members of the family."

In 1963, this same priest had secretly come to Arlington Cemetery at Jackie's request to reinter the two tiny white coffins that held the remains of Arabella and Patrick. That night, so soon after Dallas, Jackie, who was then still in residence at the White House, had bombarded him with questions about the suddenness and senselessness of her husband's death, but also with her concerns about the unwanted role that had already been thrust upon her by an anguished American populace that, in her view, regarded her less as a woman than as a symbol of its own pain. She had spoken, too, of her uncomfortable sense that henceforward she was destined to have to bear the weight of popular opinion, the public's shifting, not always favorable, feelings about her.

And so, at length, it had occurred. Because of the disparity between Jackie's needs and those of the society in which she lived, she went from being idealized to stigmatized. A dozen years would pass before she began in earnest the long, slow, painful, not always linear and logical process of resolution and recovery. As she sought empowerment through her publishing career and landmarks-preservation advocacy; as she acquired acreage and built a new home; as she faced her fears by participating in the last Kennedy brother's campaign for the 1980 Democratic presidential nomination; as she enjoyed her "vengeance on the world" due to her children's successes; as she managed to connect again with political Washington through the vehicle of the Clintons—Jackie had been healing, however imperfectly and incompletely, before the nation's eyes.

And then suddenly, she was gone.

In the aftermath of JFK's funeral, Jackie had voiced resentment to Archbishop Hannan about the many people who had praised her bearing during the ceremonies. Again, at the time of her own death, many were the tributes, published and spoken, to the manner in which she had comported herself, both in 1963 and in the decades that followed. Edited out were the messy, disquieting, enigmatic parts of the picture—the quintessentially human story of one woman's thirty-one-year struggle with the memory of horrific events that her countrymen had long been impatient to banish from consciousness. In a sense, during this period of national commemoration and remembrance of the life of Jacqueline Kennedy Onassis, they at last found it possible to forget.

When the old priest had finished his prayer, the bells at Washington's

National Cathedral, across the river, tolled sixty-four times, once for each year Jacqueline Kennedy Onassis had lived. Caroline thereupon placed a white flower on her mother's casket, and both she and John kissed the mahogany surface. After Caroline left to join her husband, John lingered to kneel at and touch the graves of his father and the babies.

SOURCE NOTES

One

3 recounted the episode: Jackie to Woodley, n.d., Hantman's Auctioneers.

3 petrified: Ibid.

4 In the aftermath: John H. Davis, *Jacqueline Bouvier: An Intimate Memoir* (New York: Wiley, 1996).

4 "devastatingly witty": Jackie to Woodley, n.d., Hantman's Auctioneers.

4 agony: Ibid.

4 "all physical:" Ibid.

4 She acknowledged: Ibid.

4 said she would love it: Ibid.

4 While Bev's letters: Ibid.

5 prison: Jackie to Bev, n.d., Christie's.

5 "If schooldays . . .": Ibid.

5 Sarah Porter: Nancy Davis and Barbara Donahue, *Miss Porter's School* (Farmington, Conn.: Northeast Graphics, 1992).

5 Harvard-Yale game: Jackie to Woodley, n.d., Hantman's Auctioneers.

7 "the most beautiful . . .": Kathleen Bouvier, *Black Jack Bouvier: The Life and Times of Jackie O's Father* (New York: Pinnacle, 1999).

8 Jackie's first husband would laugh: Betty Coxe Spalding, author interview.

8 "a most devastating . . .": Bill Adler, *The Uncommon Wisdom of Jacqueline Kennedy Onassis: A Portrait in Her Own Words* (Secaucus, N.J.: Citadel, 1994).

8 cartoonish dirty old man: Puffin Gates quoted in Sarah Bradford, *America's Queen: The Life of Jacqueline Kennedy Onassis* (New York: Viking, 2000).

8 she had confessed: Jackie to Woodley, n.d., Hantman's Auctioneers.

9 blazing away: Ibid.

9 It struck her: Ibid.

10 solemnly advised: Ibid.

11 a huge lonely place: Jackie to Bev, n.d., Christie's.

11 "I do love . . .": Ibid.

11 "I do think . . .": Ibid.

12 "I've always . . .": Jackie to Bev, January 20, 1946, Christie's.

13 "that goddamn Vassar": Davis, *Jacqueline Bouvier.*

15 "round out": Mark Pottle, ed., *Daring to Hope: The Diaries and Letters of Violet Bonham Carter, 1946–1969* (London: Orion, 2002).

16 "Not because of . . .": Adler, *Uncommon Wisdom of Jacqueline Kennedy Onassis.*

16 Most were in: Louis Auchincloss, author interview.

16 "I didn't know . . .": Adler, *Uncommon Wisdom of Jacqueline Kennedy Onassis.*

18 "like the maid . . .": Mary Van Rensselaer Thayer, *Jacqueline Bouvier Kennedy* (Garden City, N.J.: Doubleday, 1961).

19 "As to physical . . .": Ibid.

20 "Shall we go . . .": Charles Bartlett, interview, John F. Kennedy Library.

21 "little girls": Frank Waldrop, interview, Massachusetts Historical Society.

21 "hang around": Ibid.

22 "What I hope . . .": Jackie to Bev., n.d., Christie's.

23 seemed to clarify: Louis Auchincloss, author interview.

23 "spunk": Louis Auchincloss, *Sybil* (Boston: Houghton Mifflin, 1951).

23 "the assembled tribe": Ibid.

23 "Oh, you've written . . .": Louis Auchincloss, author interview.

24 "That's it. . . .": Ibid.

Two

25 during Christmas: Frank Waldrop, interview, Massachusetts Historical Society.

25 "Hell, there's . . ." Ibid.

26   John White: Author background interviews with Betty Coxe Spalding, Elizabeth Cavendish, Richard Holderness.

26   *The Front Page*: John White, interview, Massachusetts Historical Society.

26   favorite daughter: Rose Kennedy to Nancy Astor, June 14, 1948, University of Reading.

27   "It is a . . .": Lynne McTaggert, *Kathleen Kennedy: Her Life and Times* (New York: Doubleday, 1983).

27   "came at": John White, interview, Massachusetts Historical Society.

28   "winsome": Ibid.

28   "fadeaway": Ibid.

28   "kooky": William Walton, interview, Massachusetts Historical Society.

28   "insipid": John Husted quoted in Kitty Kelley, *Jackie Oh!* (Secaucus, N.J.: Lyle Stuart, 1978).

28–29   "just a glimpse . . .": William Walton, interview, Massachusetts Historical Society.

29   no one had been closer: Jean Lloyd, author interview.

30   "comfortably close": John White, interview, Massachusetts Historical Society.

30   "the charm that makes . . .": Inga Arvad, unpublished memoir.

30   "I wouldn't trust . . .": John White, interview, Massachusetts Historical Society.

30   Patsy Field assumed: Patsy Field, interview, Massachusetts Historical Society.

31   "drivel . . . It doesn't mean a thing": Quoted in Kelley, *Jackie Oh!*

32   Joseph Alsop: Author background interviews with Deborah Devonshire, Betty Coxe Spalding, Elizabeth Cavendish, Nicholas Henderson.

32   "one of the most enchanting . . .": Joseph Alsop, *I've Seen the Best of It: Memoirs* (New York: Norton, 1992).

32   "ornamental": Ibid.

34   believed she was the one to change him: Jane Suydam, author interview.

36   "pathetic": *Jacqueline Kennedy: Historic Conversations on Life with John F. Kennedy* (New York: Hyperion, 2011).

36   "vulnerable": Ibid.

36   a man could retire: John P. Mallan, "Massachusetts: Liberal and Corrupt," *New Republic*, October 13, 1952.

37   "He has got to . . .": Dorothy Schiff's notes quoted in Jeffrey Potter, *Men, Money & Magic: The Story of Dorothy Schiff* (New York: Coward, McCann, 1976).

38   "won't leave me alone!": Deborah Devonshire, author interview.

38   Janet had begun to worry: Janet Auchincloss, interview, John F. Kennedy Library.

39   Jackie indignantly refused: Ibid.

40   "Very few people . . .": Jacqueline Bouvier to Rose Kennedy, June 29, 1953, in Amanda Smith, ed., *Hostage to Fortune: The Letters of Joseph P. Kennedy* (New York: Viking, 2001).

41   "I am a bit . . .": Joseph P. Kennedy to Torby MacDonald, John F. Kennedy Library.

41   "jittery": Phyllis MacDonald, interview, Massachusetts Historical Society.

41   "You understand": Ibid.

42   "almost homely . . .": Jewel Reed, author interview.

42   expressed astonishment: Betty Coxe Spalding, author interview.

42   "I don't know . . .": Gunilla von Post, *Love, Jack* (New York: Crown, 1997).

42   "would have canceled . . .": Ibid.

43   "social-climbing upstarts": John H. Davis, *Jacqueline Bouvier: An Intimate Memoir* (New York: Wiley, 1996).

44   John White waved: Betty Coxe Spalding, author interview.

Three

45   "How perfect . . ." Jacqueline Kennedy to Ambassador and Mrs. Kennedy, September 1953, Early American History Auctions.

46   "unbelievably heavenly:" Ibid.

47   suggested that Jackie: Jewel Reed, author interview.

47   "What shall I do?": Ibid.

47   "only big enough . . .": Bill Adler: *The Uncommon Wisdom of Jacqueline Kennedy Onassis: A Portrait in Her Own Words* (Secaucus, N.J.: Citadel, 1994).

48   "Were you talking about . . .": *Jacqueline Kennedy: Historic Conversations on Life with John F. Kennedy* (New York: Hyperion, 2011).

48   The ability to laugh at himself: Andrew Devonshire, author interview.

48   he talked to her more: Betty Coxe Spalding, author interview.

48   "the only one": Ibid.

48   "bored": Ibid.

48   "wonderful": Ibid.

48   "a substitute for Kick": Ibid.

48   "to take any guff": Ibid.

48   "a duck with . . ." Veronica Maclean, *Past Forgetting: A Memoir of Heroes, Adventure, and Love* (London: Headline Review, 2002).

49   "They spoke of me . . .": Gore Vidal, *Palimpsest: A Memoir* (New York: Random House, 1995).

51   "heresy": Betty Coxe Spalding, author interview.

51   "favorite of all the children": Rose Kennedy to Nancy Astor, June 14, 1948, University of Reading.

51   "the Big One": Fiona Arran, author interview.

52   "international publicity": Joseph P. Kennedy to Paul Murphy, April 18, 1939, John F. Kennedy Library.

52   he began to speak: Betty Coxe Spalding, author interview.

52   meant to study the electioneering: Maclean, *Past Forgetting*.

53   "Life with him . . .": *Jacqueline Kennedy: Historic Conversations on Life with John F. Kennedy.*

54   some of the most valuable: Jacqueline Kennedy, interview, John Sherman Cooper Oral History Project, University of Kentucky.

55   Dr. Elmer Bartels: Elmer Bartels, interview, Massachusetts Historical Society.

56   "schooled himself": McGeorge Bundy, interview, John F. Kennedy Library.

56   "an actor's control": Charles Spalding quoted in Ralph G. Martin, *A Hero for Our Time* (New York: Fawcett, 1984).

56   considered quitting her job: Evelyn Lincoln, *My Twelve Years with John F. Kennedy* (New York: McKay, 1965).

57   "the depth of Jack's . . .": Lem Billings quoted in Doris Kearns Goodwin, *The Fitzgeralds and the Kennedys: An American Saga* (New York: Simon & Schuster, 1987).

57   "I don't think . . .": Jane Suydam, author interview.

57   "eyes filled with . . .": Ibid.

57   "the humiliation she . . .": Lem Billings quoted in Goodwin, *Fitzgeralds and the Kennedys.*

57   "I expect to be . . .": John F. Kennedy to Gunilla von Post, March 2, 1953, Legendary Auctions.

58   "never alone": *Jacqueline Kennedy: Historic Conversations on Life with John F. Kennedy.*

59   "It now appears . . .": John F. Kennedy to Gunilla von Post, June 28, 1953, Legendary Auctions.

Four

60 "kind of strange": Elmer Bartels, interview, Massachusetts Historical Society.

60 "behind the drapes": Ibid.

61 "good control": Ibid.

61 As late as August: John F. Kennedy to Gunilla von Post, August 16, 1954, Legendary Auctions.

61 By September: John F. Kennedy to Gunilla von Post, September 13, 1954, Legendary Auctions.

62 "a normal life . . ." Bill Adler, *The Uncommon Wisdom of Jacqueline Kennedy Onassis: A Portrait in Her Own Words* (Secaucus, N.J.: Citadel, 1994).

63 "spend weekends with": Ibid.

63 "I don't care. . . .": *Jacqueline Kennedy: Historic Conversations on Life with John F. Kennedy* (New York: Hyperion, 2011).

64 self-dramatizing: Isaiah Berlin, interview, John F. Kennedy Library.

64 "liberated": Frank Waldrop, interview, Massachusetts Historical Society.

64 to take notes: Martin, *A Hero for Our Time.*

64 "American cousin": Anne Tree, author interview.

64 "the brightest man . . .": *Jacqueline Kennedy: Historic Conversations on Life with John F. Kennedy.*

64 "the most wounded": Ibid.

64 virtually as a brother: Andrew Devonshire, author interview.

65 "short straw in life": Ibid.

65 "prime runner": Victoria Lloyd, author interview.

66 "another cousin": Alexander Stockton, author interview.

68 Jackie prayed: Carl Sferrazza Anthony, *As We Remember Her: Jacqueline Kennedy Onassis in the Words of Her Family and Friends* (New York: Harper Perennial, 2003.)

68 ten days: Jacqueline Kennedy to Henry Luce, 1954, Library of Congress.

68 "It will be . . .": Jacqueline Kennedy to Lyndon B. Johnson, November 4, 1954, Lyndon B. Johnson Library.

68 "I was terribly . . .": John F. Kennedy to Gunilla von Post, November 11, 1954, Legendary Auctions.

68 "without fail": Ibid.

69 haunted him: John F. Kennedy to Gunilla von Post, December 18, 1954, Legendary Auctions.

69   to fantasize about: Ibid.

69   "just to keep . . ." *Jacqueline Kennedy, Historic Conversations on Life with John F. Kennedy*.

71   "foreign ideology that . . .": John F. Kennedy, *Profiles in Courage* (New York: Harper & Brothers, 1956).

74   arranging to have a backup: John F. Kennedy to Elsa Fogelstrom, August 22, 1955, Legendary Auctions.

74   "to work and learn . . ." Evelyn Lincoln, *My Twelve Years with John F. Kennedy* (New York: McKay, 1965).

74   telegraphed Gunilla: John F. Kennedy to Gunilla von Post, August 10, 1955, Legendary Auctions.

74   contacted his father: John F. Kennedy to Joseph P. Kennedy, n.d., in Amanda Smith, ed., *Hostage to Fortune: The Letters of Joseph P. Kennedy* (New York: Viking, 2001).

76   reported to Gunilla: John F. Kennedy to Gunilla von Post, August 22, 1955, Legendary Auctions.

77   "It's best if . . .": Janet Travell, *Office Hours Day and Night: The Autobiography of Janet Travell, M.D.* (New York: New American Library, 1968).

77   a one-story house: Janet Auchincloss, interview, John F. Kennedy Library.

77   drawers and shoe shelves: Ibid.

78   "very intrigued": Joseph P. Kennedy to Edward Kennedy, September 3, 1955, John F. Kennedy Library.

78   "surreptitious candidacy": Herbert S. Parmet, *Jack: The Struggles of John F. Kennedy* (New York: Dial, 1980).

80   expected to go with George Smathers: John F. Kennedy to Joseph P. Kennedy, June 29, 1956, John F. Kennedy Library.

80   "redneck": George Smathers, Senate interview.

80   disliked Smathers: *Jacqueline Kennedy: Historic Conversations on Life with John F. Kennedy*.

80   Smathers for his part: George Smathers, author interview.

80   that politician had been George Smathers: Ted Sorensen, *Counselor: A Life at the Edge of History* (New York: Harper, 2008).

81   "Don't feel sorry . . .": Parmet, *Jack: The Struggles of John F. Kennedy*.

81   crying openly: George Smathers, Senate interview.

81   "like Jack in a wig": Deborah Devonshire, author interview.

82   "very disappointed": George Smathers, Senate interview.

82 "Jackie got too excited . . .": Travell, *Office Hours Day and Night.*

82 "I could really be president . . .": George Smathers, Senate interview.

83 "Why don't you . . .": Ibid.

83 "pulled something fishy": Arthur M. Schlesinger Jr., *Robert Kennedy and His Times* (Boston: Houghton Mifflin, 1978).

84 "raging spirit": Charles Spalding, interview, John F. Kennedy Library.

84 "fight his way to the top": Ibid.

84 "Action Man": Jane Ormsby-Gore, author interview.

84 at the urging of George Smathers: George Smathers, author interview.

85 worried that: Lem Billings quoted in Doris Kearns Goodwin, *The Fitzgeralds and the Kennedys: An American Saga* (New York: Simon & Schuster, 1987).

Five

86 "Let's face it. . . .": Laura Bergquist, interview, John F. Kennedy Library.

87 "modeled himself, his gestures . . .": Charles Spalding, interview, John F. Kennedy Library.

87 "picked up a lot . . .": Laura Bergquist, interview, John F. Kennedy Library.

87 "passionate self-effacement": Ibid.

87 "self-abnegation": Joseph Alsop to Theodore Sorensen, November 10, 1960, Library of Congress.

88 "such a crush": *Jacqueline Kennedy: Historic Conversations on Life with John F. Kennedy* (New York: Hyperion, 2011).

88 "a relationship that . . .": McGeorge Bundy, interview, John F. Kennedy Library.

88 "more than fair": Ted Sorensen, *Counselor: A Life at the Edge of History* (New York: Harper, 2008).

88 "sneaky": *Jacqueline Kennedy: Historic Conversations on Life with John F. Kennedy.*

89 "rather heatedly": Laura Bergquist, interview, John F. Kennedy Library.

89 "Well, that's not . . .": Ibid.

90 wheeled in the newborn: Janet Auchincloss, interview, John F. Kennedy Library.

90 "I don't think . . .": Betty Coxe Spalding, author interview.

90 he later told: Deborah Devonshire, author interview.

91   "starter": Joseph Alsop to Jacqueline Kennedy, September 9, 1964, Library of Congress.

91   "a higher handicap": Ibid.

92   "as sizable as . . .": Igor Cassini, *I'd Do It All Over Again* (New York: Putnam, 1977).

92   "objects that are . . .": Joseph Alsop to Jayne Wrightsman, September 30, 1960, Library of Congress.

93   "as a true, independent . . .": Ibid.

93   "sloppy kid": William Walton, interview, Massachusetts Historical Society.

94   "at cross purposes . . .": Jacqueline Kennedy to Joseph Alsop, n.d., Library of Congress.

94   "She got elegant . . .": William Walton, interview, Massachusetts Historical Society.

94   ran out of the room in tears: Betty Coxe Spalding, author interview.

95   "on the Churchill ticket": Harold Macmillan diary, Bodleian Library, Oxford University.

96   Churchill had first met Onassis: Anthony Montague Browne, *Long Sunset: Memoirs of Winston Churchill's Last Private Secretary* (London: Cassell, 1995); and Martin Gilbert, *Never Despair: Winston S. Churchill, 1945–1965* (Boston: Houghton Mifflin, 1988).

96   "the man or . . .": Lord Moran, *Churchill: The Struggle for Survival, 1940–1965: Taken from the Diaries of Lord Moran* (Boston: Houghton Mifflin, 1966).

96   "He is a . . ." Ibid.

97   "so hungry": *Jacqueline Kennedy: Historic Conversations on Life with John F. Kennedy.*

97   "I think he thought . . .": William Douglas-Home, interview, John F. Kennedy Library.

97   "his first . . .": William Walton, interview, Massachusetts Historical Society.

98   "from the ravages . . .": Joseph Alsop, *I've Seen the Best of It: Memoirs* (New York: Norton, 1992).

98   "The Auchinclosses lived . . .": William Walton, interview, Massachusetts Historical Society.

99   "She knew all about . . .": Frank Langella, *Dropped Names* (New York: Harper, 2012).

99   "really worth it": Jacqueline Kennedy to Joseph Alsop, n.d., Library of Congress.

99   "It's the only . . .": Ibid.

100 reported to the decorator: Apple Parish Bartlett and Susan Bartlett Crater,

Sister: The Life of the Legendary American Interior Designer Mrs. Henry Parish II (New York: St. Martin's, 2000).

101   a gift for Jackie: Joseph Alsop to Eunice Shriver, August 4, 1960, Library of Congress.

101   "a ghastly little . . .": Jacqueline Kennedy to Joseph Alsop, n.d., Library of Congress.

101   "adore": Ibid.

101   "plain Mrs. Kennedy . . .": Joseph Alsop to Jacqueline Kennedy, August 4, 1960, Library of Congress.

101   He suggested: Ibid.

101   "unreasonable": Jacqueline Kennedy to Joseph Alsop, n.d., Library of Congress.

102   "I couldn't . . .": *New York Times*, September 15, 1960.

Six

103   "I had worked . . .": Thomas Maier, *The Kennedys: America's Emerald Kings* (New York: Basic Books, 2003).

103   "It took . . .": Billy Baldwin, *Billy Baldwin Remembers* (New York: Harcourt, 1974).

105   a bantering manner: Letitia Baldrige, author interview.

105   "Jack got so . . .": *Jacqueline Kennedy, Historic Conversations on Life with John F. Kennedy* (New York: Hyperion, 2011).

108   boasting of a 72 percent: David Ormsby-Gore to Harold Macmillan, March 1, 1961, Public Record Office, Kew.

109   "shattered": Chester Bowles Notes on Cuban Crisis, April 20, 1961, John F. Kennedy Library.

109   "an acute shock": Ibid.

109   "inept": Hervé Alphand, *L'étonnement d'être, Journal 1939–1973* (Paris: Fayard, 1977).

109   "a soft, not very . . .": Chester Bowles, interview, John F. Kennedy Library.

109   "She was undone . . .": Betty Coxe Spalding, author interview.

110   her first injection: Max Jacobson, unpublished memoir.

110   Max Jacobson: Author background interviews with Patrick O'Neal and Betty Coxe Spalding.

110   he did not like: Betty Coxe Spalding, author interview.

110   In the course of their visit: Max Jacobson, unpublished memoir.

111   "the hit of . . .": Kenneth P. O'Donnell and David F. Powers: *Johnny We Hardly Knew Ye: Memories of John Fitzgerald Kennedy* (New York: Little, Brown, 1970).

114   "It's not that . . .": Larry Newman, author interview.

114   "as a means of . . .": Arthur M. Schlesinger Jr., *A Thousand Days* (Boston: Houghton Mifflin, 1965).

115   enjoyed a tryst: Betty Coxe Spalding, author interview.

116   "He liked her . . .": George Smathers, author interview.

116   "She quit bothering . . .": Ibid.

116   "He loves pleasure . . .": Alphand, *L'étonnement d'être.*

117   "low-key": Mary Taylor, author interview.

117   "She was very . . .": Ibid.

117   "a proper trip": Larry Newman, author interview.

117   "I never saw . . .": Ibid.

118   "Would you not . . .": Concerned Citizens of America press release, August 29, 1962, John F. Kennedy Library.

119   "They had turned . . .": Betty Coxe Spalding, author interview.

120   "never seen anything . . .": Ibid.

121   "good for her": Pamela Turnure and Nancy Tuckerman, interview, John F. Kennedy Library.

121   "a poor impression": Henry Labouisse to Dean Rusk, September 3, 1963, John F. Kennedy Library.

122   angry letter-writers: White House social files, Jacqueline Kennedy Greek trip, 1963, John F. Kennedy Library.

123   "gesture of contrition": *First Lady Jacqueline Kennedy Onassis: Memorial Tributes in the One Hundred Third Congress of the United States* (Washington, D. C.: U.S. Government Printing Office, 1995).

123   "big, hesitant smile": Notes of Mrs. Johnson, June 15, 1964, Lyndon B. Johnson Library.

124   "I think she . . .": Pamela Turnure and Nancy Tuckerman, interview, John F. Kennedy Library.

124   "almost the focus . . .": Charles Roberts, interview, John F. Kennedy Library.

124   "You were great . . .": William Manchester, *The Death of a President* (New York: Harper & Row, 1967).

124   "And, then . . .": Maier, *The Kennedys.*

Seven

126 If only she had been looking to the right: Jacqueline Kennedy, Warren Commission testimony.

127 random backfire: Theodore White, original notes delivered to Mrs. Kennedy, December 19, 1963, John F. Kennedy Library.

127 "My God, they are . . .": Nellie Connally, notes on the assassination, Lyndon B. Johnson Library.

127 First with her right, then with . . . : Zapruder film and film stills; Gerald Posner, *Case Closed: Lee Harvey Oswald and the Assassination of JFK* (New York: Random House, 1993).

128 "I have his brains . . ." Nellie Connally, notes on the assassination, Lyndon B. Johnson Library.

128 feared she was about: Dave Powers, Warren Commission testimony.

128 pushed her: Clint Hill, Warren Commission testimony.

128 to keep the brains: Theodore White, original notes delivered to Mrs. Kennedy, December 19, 1963, John F. Kennedy Library.

128 "He's dead . . .": Ibid.

129 "No, I want . . .": Paul Landis, Secret Service internal report testimony.

129 judged that the president: Posner, *Case Closed*.

129 looking but not seeing: Clint Hill, *Mrs. Kennedy and Me* (New York: Gallery, 2012).

129 pushed her out of the way: Diana Bowman, Warren Commission testimony.

129 dropped to her knees: Dr. Malcolm Perry, Warren Commission testimony.

129 erupted from his skull: Dr. Marion Jenkins, Warren Commission testimony.

130 presented him with a fragment: Posner, *Case Closed*.

130 in four sheets: Doris Nelson, Warren Commission testimony.

130 plastic mattress cover: Ibid.

130 "deathly still": Charles Roberts, interview, John F. Kennedy Library.

130 "a completely glazed . . ." Ibid.

130 In the belief that any delay . . . : Kenneth O'Donnell, Warren Commission testimony.

131 "We arrived . . .": Kenneth O'Donnell, interview, Lyndon B. Johnson Library.

131 Gazing in the bathroom mirror: Theodore White, original notes delivered to Mrs. Kennedy, December 19, 1963, John F. Kennedy Library.

132 "almost saturated . . .": Charles Roberts, interview, John F. Kennedy Library.

132 "were in a . . .": Liz Carpenter, December 1963 notes on assassination, Lyndon B. Johnson Library.

132 sweltering: Charles Roberts, interview, John F. Kennedy Library.

132 "by the elbows": Ibid.

132 "God bless you . . .": Ibid.

132 "streaked with tears": Liz Carpenter, December 1963 notes on assassination, Lyndon B. Johnson Library.

133 "a kind of chemical . . .": Joseph Alsop, interview, John F. Kennedy Library.

133 "It was as though . . .": Ibid.

134 those returning from the battlefield: See Charles W. Hoge, *Once a Warrior, Always a Warrior* (Guilford, Conn.: GPP Life, 2010).

134 spoke of the motorcade: William Manchester, *The Death of a President* (New York: Harper & Row, 1967).

134 bereaved and traumatized: On the distinction, see Lenore Terr, *Too Scared to Cry: Psychic Trauma in Childhood* (New York: Harper & Row, 1990).

134 talkathon: Manchester, *Death of a President*.

134 "She moved in a . . .": Benjamin C. Bradlee, *Conversations with Kennedy* (New York: Norton, 1975).

135 "She was in . . .": Robert McNamara quoted in Manchester, *Death of a President*.

135 "keyed up": Manchester, *Death of a President*.

136 it was quickly discovered: George W. Ball, *The Past Has Another Pattern: Memoirs* (New York: Norton, 1982).

136 "under no circumstances . . .": Merle Miller, *Lyndon: An Oral Biography* (New York: Ballantine, 1981).

136 might target: Ball, *Past Has Another Pattern*.

137 revenge-seeker: Ibid.

137 "They can ride . . .": Hill, *Mrs. Kennedy and Me.*

137 "I shall walk . . .": Dean Rusk, *As I Saw It* (New York: Norton, 1990).

138 "From the tone . . .": Rita Dallas, *The Kennedy Case* (New York: Putnam, 1973).

138 "in total detail": Ibid.

138 "total recall": Theodore White, original notes delivered to Mrs. Kennedy, December 19, 1963, John F. Kennedy Library.

138 "the scene took over . . .": Theodore H. White, *In Search of History: A Personal Adventure* (New York: Harper & Row, 1978).

139   "provoked John Kennedy . . .": Arthur M. Schlesinger Jr., *Robert Kennedy and His Times* (Boston: Houghton Mifflin, 1978).

140   "When this is over . . .": Theodore White, original notes delivered to Mrs. Kennedy, December 19, 1963, John F. Kennedy Library.

140   "I said to myself . . .": Ibid.

140   "blood scene": White, *In Search of History*.

140   "it was all told . . .": Ibid.

141   "There'd been . . .": Theodore White, original notes delivered to Mrs. Kennedy, December 19, 1963, John F. Kennedy Library.

141   "softly": White, *In Search of History*.

141   "These big Texas . . .": Theodore White, original notes delivered to Mrs. Kennedy, December 19, 1963, John F. Kennedy Library.

142   "she lived the . . .": White, *In Search of History*.

142   the brain's limbic system: On the nature of limbic memory, see Hoge, *Once a Warrior*.

143   "floodgates": Jacqueline Kennedy, interview, Lyndon B. Johnson Library.

143   "I want to say . . .": Theodore White, original notes delivered to Mrs. Kennedy, December 19, 1963, John F. Kennedy Library.

143   "lonely sick boy": Ibid.

143   "reverted to the . . .": White, *In Search of History*.

143   "satin-red history": Theodore White's handwritten notes of Camelot interview with Jacqueline Kennedy, November 1963, John F. Kennedy Library.

144   "rough-typed": Theodore White to Jacqueline Kennedy, April 27, 1963, John F. Kennedy Library.

144   "historical material": Ibid.

Eight

146   "I just wanted . . .": Lyndon Johnson conversation with Jacqueline Kennedy, December 2, 1963, Miller Center, University of Virginia.

146   initially hoped: Deborah Devonshire diary.

147   "didn't dare bother": Lyndon Johnson conversation with Jacqueline Kennedy, December 2, 1963, Miller Center, University of Virginia.

147   "You got some . . .": Ibid.

147   "Don't send me . . .": Ibid.

148 "God almighty!": Michael Beschloss, ed., *Reaching for Glory: Lyndon Johnson's Secret White House Tapes, 1964–1965* (New York: Simon & Schuster, 2001).

149 "so that he would . . .": Jim Bishop, *The Day Kennedy Was Shot* (New York: Funk & Wagnalls, 1968).

149 "to reclaim the throne": Lyndon Johnson quoted in Doris Kearns Goodwin, *Lyndon Johnson and the American Dream* (New York: St. Martin's, 1991).

149 "the one person": Deborah Devonshire diary.

149 "Shall we go . . .": Evan Thomas, *Robert Kennedy: His Life* (New York: Simon & Schuster, 2000).

150 "the most shattered . . .": Pierre Salinger quoted in Arthur M. Schlesinger Jr., *Robert Kennedy and His Times* (Boston: Houghton Mifflin, 1978).

150 "to set the stage . . .": Charles Bartlett, interview, John F. Kennedy Library.

151 "bargaining power": Arthur M. Schlesinger Jr., *Journals, 1952–2000* (New York: Penguin, 2007).

151 "be finished forever . . .": Ibid.

151 "Yes, but there . . .": Ibid.

151 "coming up, coming up": Jacqueline Kennedy, interview, Lyndon B. Johnson Library.

152 manageable: William Manchester, *Controversy* (New York: Little, Brown, 1976).

152 "as if her life . . .": Philip M. Hannan, *The Archbishop Wore Combat Boots: Memoir of an Extraordinary Life* (Huntington, Ind.: Our Sunday Visitor, 2010).

152 more appropriate: Ibid.

152 "Eventually, the conversation . . .": Ibid.

152 "She understood that . . .": Ibid.

153 "Jackie's bedroom . . .": Mary Barelli Gallagher, *My Life with Jacqueline Kennedy* (New York: McKay, 1969).

153 recurrent nightmares: Betty Coxe Spalding, author interview.

153 "so bitter": Jacqueline Kennedy to Harold Macmillan, January 31, 1964, Bodleian Library, Oxford University.

153 "then I could have . . ." Jacqueline Kennedy, Warren Commission testimony.

153 red roses: Betty Coxe Spalding, author interview.

154 his bounden duty: Andrew Devonshire, author interview.

154 a wrenching experience: Jean Lloyd, author interview.

154 "company and friend . . .": McGeorge Bundy, interview, John F. Kennedy Library.

154　played with Jackie's daughter: *Jacqueline Kennedy: Historic Conversations on Life with John F. Kennedy* (New York: Hyperion, 2011).

154　reported to a friend: Jean Lloyd, author interview.

154　"How did she . . .": Schlesinger, *Journals*.

155　in which his back was turned: Jacqueline Kennedy to Margaret McNamara, December 11, 1963, Sotheby's.

155　"Good night, Daddy": Ibid.

155　brought to the surface: Ibid.

155　"a good time for . . .": Maud Shaw, *White House Nanny: My Years with Caroline and John Kennedy, Jr.* (New York: New American Library, 1966).

155　showed the decorator: Billy Baldwin, *Billy Baldwin Remembers* (New York: Harcourt, 1974).

156　how much Jack had loved him: Jacqueline Kennedy to Harold Macmillan, January 31, 1964, Bodleian Library, Oxford University.

156　"a new life": Ibid.

156　"I don't like . . .": Hannan, *Archbishop Wore Combat Boots*.

156　she feared that real danger: Betty Coxe Spalding, author interview.

157　alarmed: Baldwin, *Billy Baldwin Remembers*.

157　"my house with . . .": Jacqueline Kennedy to Joseph Alsop, September 8, 1968, Library of Congress.

157　"I was shocked . . .": Baldwin, *Billy Baldwin Remembers*.

158　"could ever have been": Jacqueline Kennedy to Harold Macmillan, June 1, 1964, Bodleian Library, Oxford University.

158　"the rock that I . . .": Ibid.

158　"word for . . .": Jacqueline Kennedy to Harold Macmillan, May 17, 1965, Bodleian Library, Oxford University.

159　"crashing back . . .": Jacqueline Kennedy to Harold Macmillan, January 19, 1968, Bodleian Library, Oxford University.

159　"read & re-read": Harold Macmillan to Jacqueline Kennedy, February 18, 1964, Bodleian Library, Oxford University.

159　"lived through two wars": Ibid.

159　"scarcely a friend . . .": Ibid.

159　"But this . . .": Ibid.

160　"a sort of . . .": Ibid.

160　"You have shown . . .": Ibid.

160　undertook to write back: Jacqueline Kennedy to Harold Macmillan, June 1, 1964, Bodleian Library, Oxford University.

160   when in the morning: Ibid.

160   asked David: Ibid.

160   "a little better": Ibid.

162   with alacrity: Schlesinger, *Journals*.

163   excruciating: *Look* magazine, November 17, 1964.

164   "bound in black . . .": *Look* magazine, April 4, 1967.

164   contrived to deal: Edwin Guthman, author interview.

164   "overwhelming": Charles Spalding, interview, John F. Kennedy Library.

165   "everybody's terrible sense . . .": Ibid.

165   "I remember . . .": Schlesinger, *Robert Kennedy and His Times*.

166   her emotional state: John Corry, *The Manchester Affair* (New York: Putnam, 1967).

166   "I don't know . . .": Thomas Maier, *The Kennedys: America's Emerald Kings* (New York: Basic Books, 2003).

166   "I would have been able . . .": Ibid.

166   "Do you think God . . .": Ibid.

166   "to pray . . .": Ibid.

167   "a cameolike quality . . .": William Manchester, *Goodbye, Darkness: A Memoir of the Pacific War* (New York: Dell, 1982).

167   the hyperawareness that soldiers experience: See Charles W. Hoge, *Once a Warrior, Always a Warrior* (Guilford, Conn.: GPP Life, 2010).

167   "It lay too deep . . .": Manchester, *Goodbye, Darkness*.

167   "a troubled man . . .": Ibid.

168   "It's rather hard . . .": Jacqueline Kennedy, interview, Lyndon B. Johnson Library.

168   daiquiris: Manchester, *Controversy*.

168   "abrupt, often monosyllabic . . .": Ibid.

168   she needed to learn somehow: See Bessel A. van der Kolk, Alexander C. McFarlane, and Onno van der Hart, "A General Approach to Treatment of Posttraumatic Stress Disorder" in Bessel A. van der Kolk, Alexander C. McFarlane, and Lars Weisaeth, eds., *Traumatic Stress: The Effects of Overwhelming Experience on Mind, Body, and Society* (New York: Guilford Press, 1996).

169   "I just talked . . .": Jacqueline Kennedy, interview, Lyndon B. Johnson Library.

169   "was really thinking . . .": Thomas Maier, *The Kennedys: America's Emerald Kings* (New York: Basic Books, 2000).

169   "I was glad . . .": Ibid.

169   "to climb a little . . .": Hannan, *Archbishop Wore Combat Boots*.

171 "Do you want . . .": Jacqueline Kennedy, Warren Commission testimony.

172 the efforts of Vietnam veterans: See Judith Herman, *Trauma and Recovery* (New York: Basic Books, 1997); and Wilbur J. Scott, *Vietnam Veterans Since the War: The Politics of PTSD, Agent Orange, and the National Memorial* (Norman: University of Oklahoma Press, 2004).

172 Symptoms of PTSD include: National Center for PTSD, United States Department of Veterans Affairs.

173 People who have witnessed: See Hoge, *Once a Warrior.*

173 the acknowledgement of humankind's existential vulnerability: See van der Kolk, McFarlane, and van der Hart, "General Approach to Treatment of Post-traumatic Stress Disorder" in Van der Kolk, McFarlane, and Weisaeth, eds., *Traumatic Stress.*

174

174 "I think we gotta . . .": Michael R. Beschloss, ed., *Taking Charge: The Johnson White House Tapes, 1963–1964* (New York: Simon & Schuster, 1997).

174 "the Bobby problem": Jeff Shesol, *Mutual Contempt: Lyndon Johnson, Robert Kennedy, and the Feud that Defined a Decade* (New York: Norton, 1997).

175 "I don't want . . .": Kenneth P. O'Donnell and David F. Powers, *Johnny We Hardly Knew Ye: Memories of John Fitzgerald Kennedy* (New York: Little, Brown, 1970).

175 "I'm so scared . . .": Lyndon Johnson conversation with Jacqueline Kennedy, January 9, 1964, Miller Center, University of Virginia.

176 "a little better": Jacqueline Kennedy to Harold Macmillan, June 1, 1964, Bodleian Library, Oxford University.

176 "I was trying . . .": Jacqueline Kennedy, Warren Commission testimony.

176 to attempt to start a new life: Jacqueline Kennedy to Margaret McNamara, July 21, 1964, Sotheby's.

176 a recluse: Ibid.

177 pitched her unsuccessfully: Stanley Tretick to Jacqueline Kennedy, May 21, 1964, Mugar Memorial Library, Boston University.

177 "My feeling . . .": Stanley Tretick to Jacqueline Kennedy, July 12, 1964, Mugar Memorial Library, Boston University.

178 "When did he . . .": Jean Kennedy Smith quoted in Robert Caro, *The Passage of Power* (New York: Knopf, 2012).

178   "getting Bobby over the hump": Ethel Kennedy to Marie Harriman, August
       1964, Library of Congress.

178   "It seemed to me . . .": Charles Spalding, interview, John F. Kennedy Library.

178   "I am a living . . .": *Look* magazine, November 17, 1964.

179   "He's got the . . .": Beschloss, *Taking Charge*.

179   "There have been . . .": Ibid.

180   "a turning point": Ethel Kennedy to Marie Harriman, August 1964, Library of
       Congress.

181   "I just want . . .": Beschloss, *Taking Charge*.

182   "Mr. President . . .": Johnson conversation with Edward Kennedy, August 13,
       1964, Miller Center, University of Virginia.

182   "I want to . . .": Ibid.

183   ought never to have: Jacqueline Kennedy to Joseph Alsop, August 31, 1964,
       Library of Congress.

183   "opened the floodgates": Ibid.

183   seemed only to proliferate: on the proliferation of traumatic triggers see Ba-
       bette Rothschild, *The Body Remembers: The Psychophysiology of Trauma and
       Trauma Treatment* (New York: Norton, 2000).

184   "just the reverse": Jacqueline Kennedy to Joseph Alsop, August 31, 1964, Library
       of Congress.

184   "miserable self": Ibid.

184   "You have never . . .": Joseph Alsop to Jacqueline Kennedy, September 9, 1964,
       Library of Congress.

184   "to walk around the city . . .": Jacqueline Kennedy to C. Douglas Dillon, Sep-
       tember 11, 1964, John F. Kennedy Library.

185   read nothing: Jacqueline Kennedy to Joseph Alsop, November 24, 1964, Library
       of Congress.

186   "The idea of it . . .": Jacqueline Kennedy to Jim Bishop, September 17, 1964,
       Lyndon B. Johnson Library.

186   "This whole year . . .": Ibid.

186   "would be just . . .": Ibid.

186   "This morning . . .": Jim Bishop to Jacqueline Kennedy, September 28, 1964, Lyn-
       don B. Johnson Library.

187   "I picked them up . . .": Dorothy Schiff's notes quoted in Jeffrey Potter, *Men,
       Money & Magic: The Story of Dorothy Schiff* (New York: Coward, McCann,
       1976).

187   "It was terrible . . .": Ibid.

188   "They're for him . . .": Evan Thomas, *Robert Kennedy: His Life* (New York: Simon & Schuster, 2000).

188   "People tell me . . .": Dorothy Schiff's notes quoted in Potter, *Men, Money & Magic*.

189   "when you get . . .": Alexander Stockton, author interview.

190   "circle of people . . .": McGeorge Bundy, interview, John F. Kennedy Library.

190   "to put . . .": Jacqueline Kennedy to Harold Macmillan, May 17, 1965, Bodleian Library, Oxford University.

190   went to bed with him: Edward Klein, *Just Jackie* (New York: Ballantine, 1998).

191   feared they were overly emotional: Jacqueline Kennedy to Joseph Alsop: November 30, 1964, Library of Congress.

Ten

192   "I just heard . . .": Lyndon Johnson conversation with Jacqueline Kennedy, March 25, 1965, Miller Center, University of Virginia.

193   whom Alsop had recently: Joseph Alsop to Jacqueline Kennedy, February 26, 1965, Library of Congress.

193   "I did not know . . .": Jacqueline Kennedy to Lyndon Johnson, March 28, 1965, Lyndon B. Johnson Library.

194   "snow in May": *Daily Telegraph* (London), May 15, 1965.

194   biased vision: on the PTSD sufferer's biased perception, see Bessel A. van der Kolk and Alexander C. McFarlane, "The Black Hole of Trauma" in Bessel A. van der Kolk, Alexander C. McFarlane, and Lars Weisaeth, eds., *Traumatic Stress: The Effects of Overwhelming Experience on Mind, Body, and Society* (New York: Guilford Press, 1996).

195   "a very low mood:" Stanley Tretick quoted in Kitty Kelley, *Capturing Camelot: Stanley Tretick's Iconic Images of the Kennedys* (New York: Thomas Dunne Books, 2012).

195   "a proper talk": Harold Macmillan to Jacqueline Kennedy, June 6, 1965, Bodleian Library, Oxford University.

195   a new long letter: Jacqueline Kennedy to Harold Macmillan, May 17, 1965, Bodleian Library, Oxford University.

196   "Have you ever . . .": Michael Beschloss, ed., *Reaching for Glory: Lyndon Johnson's Secret White House Tapes, 1964–1965* (New York: Simon & Schuster, 2001).

197   "gave the most . . .": Jacqueline Kennedy to Margaret McNamara, December 11, 1963, Sotheby's.

197 She regarded him: Jacqueline Kennedy to Joseph Alsop, September 8, 1968, Library of Congress.

197 shining knight: Jacqueline Kennedy to Robert McNamara, February 24, 1993, Sotheby's.

197 in her dark times: Jacqueline Kennedy to Robert McNamara, March 7, 1967, Sotheby's.

197 read to Jackie Henrik Ibsen's *The Master Builder*: Jacqueline Kennedy Onassis to Robert McNamara, March 6, 1969, Sotheby's.

198 "I'm planning . . .": Beschloss, *Reaching for Glory*.

199 watercolor: Jacqueline Kennedy to Robert McNamara, Summer 1965, Sotheby's.

199 "I reacted . . .": Robert S. McNamara, *In Retrospect: The Tragedy and Lessons of Vietnam* (New York: Times Books, 1995).

200 well-founded objection: Jacqueline Kennedy, "Comments (to Arthur Schlesinger)," n.d., John F. Kennedy Library.

200 substitute: Theodore Sorensen, *Kennedy* (New York, Harper & Row, 1965).

200 "point after point": *Look* magazine, April 4, 1967.

200 softened: *New York Times*, October 5, 1965.

201 Schlesinger maintained: Arthur Schlesinger to Jacqueline Kennedy, August 10, 1965, John F. Kennedy Library.

201 practically to cut: Arthur Schlesinger to Robert Kennedy, September 4, 1965, John F. Kennedy Library.

201 "mindless existence": Jacqueline Kennedy to Harold Macmillan, September 14, 1965, Bodleian Library, Oxford University.

202 "When winter starts . . .": Ibid.

Eleven

203 "fully emerged from . . .": William Manchester, *Controversy* (Little, Brown, 1976).

204 "It's really mostly . . .": Frank Mankiewicz, interview, John F. Kennedy Library.

204 There had been every reason: Edwin Guthman, author interview.

205 "both possible and . . .": Arthur M. Schlesinger Jr., *Journals, 1952–2000* (New York: Penguin, 2007).

206 "I would appreciate it . . .": John Corry, *The Manchester Affair* (New York: Putnam, 1967).

207 "flickers": William Manchester, *Goodbye, Darkness: A Memoir of the Pacific War* (New York: Dell, 1982).

207 "When I awoke . . .": Corry, *Manchester Affair.*

208 "Do you think . . .": Arthur M. Schlesinger Jr., *Robert Kennedy and His Times* (Boston: Houghton Mifflin, 1978).

208 "He sort of . . .": Corry, *Manchester Affair.*

208 "a little boy who . . .": Ibid.

209 "disaster": Jacqueline Kennedy to Robert McNamara, September 14, 1966, Sotheby's.

209 "peaceful and optimistic": Ibid.

209 "more complex than . . .": Jacqueline Kennedy to Robert McNamara, March 7, 1967, Sotheby's.

209 RFK and Schlesinger found it puzzling: Schlesinger, *Journals.*

210 "television's war": Michael J. Arlen, *Living-Room War* (New York: Viking, 1969).

210 "so overwhelmed . . .": Robert McNamara, *In Retrospect: The Tragedy and Lessons of Vietnam.*

210 "do something to . . ." Ibid.

211 "Whether her emotions . . .": Ibid.

211 echoes the powerlessness: See Alexander C. McFarlane, "Resilience, Vulnerability, and the Course of Posttraumatic Reactions" in Bessel A. van der Kolk, Alexander McFarlane, and Lars Weisaeth, eds., *Traumatic Stress: The Effects of Overwhelming Experience on Mind, Body, and Society* (New York: Guilford Press, 1996); and Babette Rothschild, *Trauma Essentials* (New York: Norton, 2011).

211 hit her across the face: *Beaton in the Sixties: More Unexpurgated Diaries* (London: Weidenfeld & Nicolson, 2003).

212 "The only thing . . .": Manchester, *Controversy.*

213 "Yes, it is a terrible . . .": Frank Mankiewicz, interview, John F. Kennedy Library.

213 "my crazy sister-in-law": Evan Thomas, *Robert Kennedy: His Life* (New York: Simon & Schuster, 2000).

214 "Lady Bird and I . . .": Lyndon Johnson to Jacqueline Kennedy, December 16, 1966, Lyndon B. Johnson Library.

215 advised against it: Lyndon Johnson conversation with Abe Fortas, December 1966, Miller Center, University of Virginia.

215 objected to all that remained: Jacqueline Kennedy to Lyndon Johnson, December 21, 1966, Lyndon B. Johnson Library.

215 "I am sick at . . .": Ibid.

216 "I am so dazed . . .": Ibid.

Twelve

217 "This may be . . .": North American Newspaper Alliance press release, "Playing Queen Too Long?," Lyndon B. Johnson Library.

217 "to prolong the nation's trauma": Vera Glaser, "Uneasy Rests the Crown of JFK's Jackie," *The Cincinnati Enquirer*, December 22, 1966.

218 "a girl who . . .": Arthur M. Schlesinger Jr., *Robert Kennedy and His Times* (Boston: Houghton Mifflin, 1978).

219 9/11 New York City firefighters: on the heroizing and subsequent stigmatizing of the firefighters, see Elizabeth Goren, "Society's Use of the Hero Following a National Trauma" in *The American Journal of Psychoanalysis* 67 (2007).

219 rejection of the sufferer: See Judith Herman, *Trauma and Recovery* (New York: Basic Books, 1997); and Alexander C. McFarlane and Bessel A. van der Kolk, "Trauma and Its Challenge to Society" in Bessel A. van der Kolk, Alexander C. McFarlane, and Lars Weisaeth, eds., in *Traumatic Stress: The Effects of Overwhelming Experience on Mind, Body, and Society* (New York: Guilford Press, 1996).

220 "Mrs. Kennedy 'Irked,' " *New York Times*, December 29, 1966.

221 "tasteless, undignified . . ." Liz Smith, "Jackie Comes off Her Pedestal," *World Journal Tribune*, January 8, 1967.

223 "nothing in her new life . . .": *Look* magazine, April 4, 1967.

223 "She must be seen . . .": *New York Times*, January 23, 1967.

223 "held us all together . . .": *Look* magazine, April 4, 1967.

223 "redemption": Ibid.

224 "So far as . . .": Ibid.

224 "catharsis": Ibid.

224 "ghastly futility": Ibid.

224 "God, it just murders . . .": Jeff Shesol, *Mutual Contempt: Lyndon Johnson, Robert Kennedy, and the Feud that Defined a Decade* (New York: Norton, 1997).

224 "for their own misguided . . .": Jacqueline Kennedy to Robert McNamara, March 7, 1967, Sotheby's.

225 brought Jackie to tears: Ibid.

225   "When has one man ever made . . .": Ibid.

225   "With all the grinding . . .": Ibid.

225   "I know how much . . .": Ibid.

225   "I feel so close . . .": Ibid.

226   "You are the Master Builder": Jacqueline Kennedy Onassis to Robert McNamara, March 6, 1969, Sotheby's.

226   a frenzy of anticipation: Jacqueline Kennedy to Margaret McNamara, June 1, 1967, Sotheby's.

226   "a kind of trance": Ibid.

226   became all the more intense: Ibid.

227   held her breath: Ibid.

227   "I have reached . . .": Rita Dallas, The Kennedy Case (New York: Putnam, 1973).

228   "They were like . . .": Jane Ormsby-Gore, author interview.

229   absence of feelings: On the phenomenon of numbing, see Bessel A. van der Kolk and Alexander C. McFarlane, "The Black Hole of Trauma" in van der Kolk, McFarlane, and Weisaeth, eds., Traumatic Stress; and Herman, Trauma and Recovery.

229   "interested in things . . .": Jacqueline Kennedy to Harold Macmillan, January 19, 1968, Bodleian Library, Oxford University.

230   liken him to Harry Lime: Jacqueline Kennedy to Robert McNamara, October 22, 1967, Sotheby's.

230   flirtatiously lamenting: Jacqueline Kennedy to Robert McNamara, October 27, 1967, Sotheby's.

230   She told McNamara: Ibid.

231   "He's a fine man . . .": Deborah Shapley, Promise and Power: The Life and Times of Robert McNamara (New York: Little, Brown, 1993).

231   "hanging on by . . .": Ibid.

231   Man of La Mancha: Jacqueline Kennedy to Robert McNamara, October 22, 1967, Sotheby's.

231   "anything so brave": Ibid.

231   "with a hell of a blast . . .": Shapely, Promise and Power.

232   "a big blow": Shesol, Mutual Contempt.

232   she said she wondered: Jacqueline Kennedy to Robert McNamara, September 16, 1968, Sotheby's.

232   quarreled over her insistence: Jane Ormsby-Gore, author interview.

233   she told him that: Ibid.

Thirteen

234 watched her nearly jump: *Beaton in the Sixties: More Unexpurgated Diaries* (London: Weidenfeld & Nicolson, 2003).

236 "Do you know . . .": Arthur M. Schlesinger Jr., *Journals, 1952–2000* (New York: Penguin, 2007).

236 "chased on all sides": Lyndon Johnson quoted in Doris Kearns Goodwin, *Lyndon Johnson and the American Dream* (New York: St. Martin's, 1991).

237 "Have four and a half . . .": Michael Arlen, *Living-Room War* (New York: Viking, 1969).

237 "set something loose . . .": Arthur M. Schlesinger Jr., *Robert Kennedy and His Times* (Boston: Houghton Mifflin, 1978).

237 "This would be . . .": Jean Stein, *American Journey: The Times of Robert Kennedy* (New York: Harcourt, 1970).

238 "pulled and pushed": *New York Times*, April 10, 1968.

238 "all the time": Frank Mankiewicz, interview, John F. Kennedy Library.

238 "Of course people feel . . .": Schlesinger, *Journals*.

239 "For him, life . . .": Lee Radziwill, *Happy Times* (New York: Assouline, 2001).

240 "several times": Schlesinger, *Journals*.

240 "If they're going . . .": Evan Thomas, *Robert Kennedy: His Life* (New York: Simon & Schuster, 2000).

240 "Isn't it . . .": *Beaton in the Sixties*.

241 "You don't know . . .": Ibid.

241 "I took her . . .": Charles Spalding, interview, John F. Kennedy Library.

242 more ravaged: Schlesinger, *Journals*.

242 "Well, now . . .": Frank Mankiewicz, interview, John F. Kennedy Library.

242 all too familiar: Schlesinger, *Journals*.

243 "he leaped out . . .": Stein, *American Journey*.

245 "with this terrible look . . .": Jacqueline Kennedy to Robert McNamara, September 8, 1968, Sotheby's.

245 a Celtic ritual: Ibid.

245 she was quick to reject: Schlesinger, *Journals*.

246 White Russians in Paris: Jacqueline Kennedy to Robert McNamara, September 8, 1968, Sotheby's.

247 "stunned" and "perplexed": *Boston Globe*, May 13, 2007.

247 met Onassis that summer: Schlesinger, *Journals*.

248 "I have no . . .": Frank Langella, *Dropped Names* (New York: Harper, 2012).

248 "I wanted to . . .": *First Lady Jacqueline Kennedy Onassis: Memorial Tributes in the One Hundred Third Congress of the United States* (Washington, D.C.: U.S. Government Printing Office, 1995).

249 "the outside world": Jacqueline Kennedy Onassis to James Rowley, December 11, 1968, John F. Kennedy Library.

250 "or rather . . .": Jacqueline Kennedy Onassis to Robert McNamara, September 8, 1968, Sotheby's.

250 "all be annihilated . . .": Ibid.

250 "the terrible . . .": Ibid.

Fourteen

251 "my new life": Jacqueline Kennedy Onassis to Theodore Sorensen, n.d., quoted in Ted Sorensen, *Counselor: A Life at the Edge of History* (New York: Harper, 2008).

251 questioned whether she wanted: Jacqueline Kennedy to Harold Macmillan, January 31, 1964, Bodleian Library, Oxford University.

251 "see and know . . .": Jacqueline Kennedy Onassis to Theodore Sorensen, n.d., quoted in Sorensen, *Counselor*.

251 "what Jack might . . .": Ibid.

254 "Thank God . . .": Billy Baldwin, *Billy Baldwin Remembers* (New York: Harcourt, 1974).

255 "I know I should . . .": Kiki Feroudi Moutsatsos, *The Onassis Women: An Eyewitness Account* (New York: Putnams, 1998).

257 "The children will . . .": Jacqueline Kennedy Onassis to James Rowley, December 11, 1968, John F. Kennedy Library.

258 "serene and happy": Joseph Alsop to Jacqueline Kennedy Onassis, June 1, 1969, Library of Congress.

258 "always": Ibid.

258 who had not abandoned: Jacqueline Kennedy to Joseph Alsop, September 8, 1968, Library of Congress.

258 had loved both Jack and Bobby: Ibid.

259 "like sea or . . .": Ibid.

259 "a good fire": Joseph Alsop to Jacqueline Kennedy Onassis, June 2, 1969, Library of Congress.

259 "It was as if . . .": Moutsatsos, *Onassis Women*.

260 "soft gravel": Lee Radziwill, *Happy Times* (New York: Assouline, 2001).

261 "the bedlam of . . .": Baldwin, *Billy Baldwin Remembers*.

262 Pavlov's dogs: On the Pavlovian metaphor, see Alexander C. McFarlane and Bessel A. van der Kolk, "Trauma and Its Challenge to Society" in Bessel A. van der Kolk, Alexander C. McFarlane, and Lars Weisaeth, eds., *Traumatic Stress: The Effects of Overwhelming Experience on Mind, Body, and Society* (New York: Guilford Press, 1996); and Babette Rothschild, *The Body Remembers: The Psychophysiology of Trauma and Trauma Treatment* (New York: Norton, 2000).

264 "I was frightened . . .": Moutsatsos, *Onassis Women*.

265 terrified: *New York Times*, February 18, 1972.

265 "He lunged . . .": *New York Times*, March 7, 1972.

265 "the best . . .": *New York Times*, March 19, 1972.

266 rendered invisible: on the societal tendency to render the victim invisible, see Judith Herman, *Trauma and Recovery* (New York: Basic Books, 1997).

266 "Does it show . . .": *New York Times*, February 17, 1972.

266 "anguish threshold": *New York Times*, March 15, 1972.

266 James MacGregor Burns: *New York Times*, April 10, 1972.

268 "the center does not . . . : Jacqueline Kennedy Onassis to Harold Macmillan, November 12, 1972, Bodleian Library, Oxford University.

269 she rejoiced: Ibid.

269 suddenly became old: Arthur M. Schlesinger Jr., *Journals, 1952–2000* (New York: Penguin, 2007).

270 feared for the unfortunate man's reason: Anthony Montague Browne, *Long Sunset: Memoirs of Winston Churchill's Last Private Secretary* (London: Cassell, 1995).

270 "Jackie put her . . .": *First Lady Jacqueline Kennedy Onassis: Memorial Tributes in the One Hundred Third Congress of the United States* (Washington, D. C.: U.S. Government Printing Office, 1995).

Fifteen

273 "turned a corner": Andrew Devonshire, author interview.

273 "depressed and lethargic": Letitia Baldrige, author interview.

273 Baldrige proposed: Ibid.

274 a principal objective: See Babette Rothschild, *Trauma Essentials* (New York: Norton, 2011).

274　empowerment: on the role of empowerment in trauma recovery, see Judith Herman, *Trauma and Recovery* (New York: Basic Books, 1997).

275　"more complex than . . .": Jacqueline Kennedy to Robert McNamara, March 7, 1967, Sotheby's.

275　estimated in 1990: Richard A. Kulka, William E. Schlenger, John A. Fairbank, et al., *Trauma and the Vietnam War Generation: Report of Findings from the National Vietnam Veterans Readjustment Study* (New York: Brunner Mazel, 1990).

276　"to work, not to play": Letitia Baldrige, author interview.

276　Dr. Marianne Kris: Marianne Kris to Anna Freud, 1975, Anna Freud Papers, Library of Congress.

277　"remembered": on the metaphor of bodily memory with regard to traumatic experiences, see Babette Rothschild, *The Body Remembers: The Psychophysiology of Trauma and Trauma Treatment* (New York: Norton, 2000).

277　prior connection: Elisabeth Young-Bruehl, *Anna Freud* (New York: Summit, 1988).

277　Kris asked Anna Freud: Marianne Kris to Anna Freud, 1975, Anna Freud Papers, Library of Congress.

279　from whom she sought reassurance: Jean Lloyd, author interview.

279　"to rely on herself . . .": Letitia Baldrige, author interview.

279　"Mrs. Onassis's first major assignment": *New York Times*, November 2, 1976.

280　"bubbling with enthusiasm": Thomas Hoving, *Making the Mummies Dance: Inside the Metropolitan Museum of Art* (New York: Simon & Schuster, 1993).

281　he had spoken: David Harlech, interview, John F. Kennedy Library.

282　"Jackie wouldn't have . . .": *New York Times*, January 14, 1977.

283　intake of breath: Arthur M. Schlesinger Jr., *Journals, 1952–2000* (New York: Penguin, 2007).

283　"It was just . . .": Thomas Guinzburg quoted in Greg Lawrence, *Jackie as Editor: The Literary Life of Jacqueline Kennedy Onassis* (New York: Thomas Dunne Books, 2011).

284　"to separate my lives . . .": *New York Times*, October 15, 1977.

284　"bad thriller": *New York Times*, October 10, 1977.

285　"She could have stopped . . .": *New York Times*, October 15, 1977.

285　"didn't indicate any . . .": Ibid.

286　five minutes: *Palm Beach Daily News*, November 9, 1977.

286　"books in the hands . . .": Edna Ferber quoted in Al Silverman, *The Time of Their Lives: The Golden Age of Great American Publishers, Their Editors and Authors* (New York: St. Martin's, 2008).

287 he had the entire print run pulped: John Baxter, *The Inner Man: The Life of J. G. Ballard* (London: Weidenfeld & Nicolson, 2011).

287 "a feeling that . . .": John Sargent quoted in Lawrence, *Jackie as Editor.*

288 she wistfully acknowledged: Louis Auchincloss, author interview.

290 long-standing anxiety: Betty Coxe Spalding, author interview.

290 "public face": Letitia Baldrige, author interview.

290 a feeling of basic safety: on the importance of the establishment of a sense of safety, see Judith Herman, *Trauma and Recovery* (New York: Basic Books, 1997); and Rothschild, *Body Remembers.*

291 "circle of people . . .": McGeorge Bundy, interview, John F. Kennedy Library.

291 "Ted will be . . .": Schlesinger, *Journals.*

291 "seemed to recoil . . .": Ibid.

291 "bitten by a snake": Richard E. Burke, *The Senator: My Ten Years with Ted Kennedy* (New York: St. Martin's, 1992).

292 droit du seigneur: Schlesinger, *Journals.*

292 "enameled mask": Stephen Spender, *Journals, 1939–1983* (New York: Random House, 1986).

292 "rather thrilled": Schlesinger, *Journals.*

292 "a fixed smile . . .": *New York Times*, February 25, 1980.

293 "death watch": Garry Wills, *The Kennedy Imprisonment: A Meditation on Power* (Boston: Little, Brown, 1982).

293 "the end of the . . .": Ibid.

293 faced down the danger: on the survivor's choice to face danger, see Herman, *Trauma and Recovery.*

295 without hesitation: *First Lady Jacqueline Kennedy Onassis: Memorial Tributes in the One Hundred Third Congress of the United States* (Washington, D. C.: U.S. Government Printing Office, 1995).

295 "I think it . . .": Spender, *Journals.*

Sixteen

297 Jackie identified: Louis Auchincloss, author interview.

297 "What was so . . .": Marie Brenner, *Great Dames: What I Learned from Older Women* (New York: Broadway Books, 2001).

300 "as if controlling her": Theodore H. White, *In Search of History: A Personal Adventure* (New York: Harper & Row, 1978).

300 "the blood scene": Ibid.

301 "What were you . . .": Christina Haag, *Come to the Edge: A Memoir.* (New York: Spiegel & Grau, 2011).

301 how much both children: Jacqueline Kennedy to Harold Macmillan, May 17, 1965, Bodleian Library, Oxford University.

301 "Close your eyes . . .": *Jacqueline Kennedy: Historic Conversations on Life with John F. Kennedy* (New York: Hyperion, 2011).

301 she reacted to images: Diane Solway, *Nureyev: His Life* (New York: Morrow, 1998).

302 cursed: Jean Lloyd, author interview.

303 "My God . . .": Jane Ormsby-Gore, author interview.

304 "Isn't it . . .": Haag, *Come to the Edge.*

304 reason to live: Jacqueline Kennedy to Harold Macmillan, May 17, 1965, Bodleian Library, Oxford University.

304 out of her thoughts: Ibid.

304 pull herself together: Jacqueline Kennedy to Harold Macmillan, September 14, 1965, Bodleian Library, Oxford University.

304 to try to make them: Jacqueline Kennedy to Harold Macmillan, May 17, 1965, Bodleian Library, Oxford University.

304 overly intense: Ibid.

304 "vengeance on the world": Jacqueline Kennedy to Harold Macmillan, September 14, 1965, Bodleian Library, Oxford University.

305 held up her hand: Haag, *Come to the Edge.*

306 "so upset and . . .": Arthur M. Schlesinger Jr., *Robert Kennedy and His Times* (Boston: Houghton Mifflin, 1978).

306 "I just don't . . .": *First Lady Jacqueline Kennedy Onassis: Memorial Tributes in the One Hundred Third Congress of the United States* (Washington, D. C.: U.S. Government Printing Office, 1995).

306 "my most secret heart": Jacqueline Kennedy Onassis to Theodore Sorensen, n.d., quoted in Ted Sorensen, *Counselor: A Life at the Edge of History* (New York: Harper, 2008).

307 "crawling around . . .": Deborah Shapley, *Promise and Power: The Life and Times of Robert McNamara* (New York: Little, Brown, 1993).

307 helped her in her dark times: Jacqueline Kennedy to Robert McNamara, March 7, 1967, Sotheby's.

307 offered . . . some advice: Jacqueline Kennedy Onassis to Robert McNamara, February 24, 1993.

SOURCE NOTES

307 "reconnect": Hillary Rodham Clinton, *Living History* (New York: Simon & Schuster, 2003).

308 "seemed profoundly . . .": Ibid.

310 "I feel it is . . .": *First Lady Jacqueline Kennedy Onassis: Memorial Tributes in the One Hundred Third Congress of the United States.*

312 "of convenience": Archbishop Philip Hannan, *The Archbishop Wore Combat Boots: Memoir of an Extraordinary Life* (Huntington, Ind.: Our Sunday Visitor, 2010).

312 sole jolts of color: *New York Times*, May 24, 1994.

INDEX